Sport Psychology
An Analysis
of Athlete
Behavior

Edited by
William F. Straub, Ph.D

Mouvement Publications
102 Irving Place
Ithaca, New York 14850

Copyright © 1978 by Mouvement Publications
Art work by: Tom Stearns
Typeset by: Syracuse Vari-Typing Service, Syracuse, New York.
Printed in the United States of America
by Wilcox Press, Inc.

ISBN   0-932392-03-2

TABLE OF CONTENTS

CONTRIBUTORS

Michelle M. Agnew, M.S.
University of Scranton
Department of Physical Education
Scranton, Pennsylvania

R. B. Aldermann, Ph.D.
The University of Alberta
Faculty of Physical Education
Edmonton, Alberta
Canada

Leonard Berkowitz, Ph.D.
University of Wisconsin — Madison
Department of Psychology
Madison, Wisconsin

Anne Marie Bird, Ph.D.
California State University —
    Fullerton
Department of HPER
Fullerton, California

Roscoe C. Brown, Jr., Ph.D.
President, Bronx Community
    College of the
    City University of New York
University Avenue
    and West 181 Street
Bronx, New York

Edmund J. Burke, Ph.D.
Ithaca College
School of HPER
Ithaca, New York

Susan Dorcas Butt, Ph.D.
University of British Columbia
Department of Psychology
Vancouver, British Columbia
Canada

Albert V. Carron, Ph.D.
The University of Western Ontario
Faculty of Physical Education
London, Ontario
Canada

Bryant J. Cratty, Ed.D.
University of California —
    Los Angeles
Department of Physical Education
Los Angeles, California

Mary E. Duquin, Ph.D.
University of Pittsburgh
Dept. of Health,
    Physical Education and Recreation
Pittsburgh, Pennsylvania

D. Stanley Eitzen, Ph.D.
Colorado State University
Department of Sociology
Fort Collins, Colorado

Dorothy V. Harris, Ph.D.
The Pennsylvania State University
College of Health,
    Physical Education and Recreation
University Park, Pennsylvania

Wayne Halliwell, Ph.D.
University of Montreal
Department of Physical Education
Montreal, Quebec
Canada

Beth Jelsma, B.A.
University of Rochester
College of Education and
    Human Development
Rochester, New York

John E. Kane, Ph.D.
West London Institute of Higher
    Education
Lancaster House Borough Road
Isleworth Middlesex TW7 5DU
London, England

Douglas Kleiber, Ph.D.
University of Illinois
Children's Research Center
Champaign, Illinois

Walter Kroll, P.E.D.
University of Massachusetts
Sport Sciences
Amherst, Massachusetts

Daniel M. Landers, Ph.D.
The Pennsylvania State University
College of Health,
    Physical Education and Recreation
University Park, Pennsylvania

John D. Lawther, Ph.D.
Professor Emeritus
The Pennsylvania State University
College of Health,
    Physical Education and Recreation
University Park, Pennsylvania

Emma McCloy Layman, Ph.D.
Professor Emeritus
Iowa Wesleyan College
Department of Psychology
Mount Pleasant, Iowa

Guy Lewis, Ph.D.
University of Massachusetts
Department of Sport Studies
Amherst, Massachusetts

Victor H. Mancini, Ed.D.
Ithaca College
School of HPER
Ithaca, New York

William P. Morgan, Ed.D.
The University of Wisconsin –
    Madison
Department of Physical Education
Madison, Wisconsin

Robert Nideffer, Ph.D.
President, Enhanced Performance
    Associates
12468 Bodega Way
San Diego, California 92028

Harry T. Reis, Ph.D.
The University of Rochester
Department of Psychology
Rochester, New York

George H. Sage, Ed.D.
The University of Northern Colorado
Department of Physical Education
Greeley, Colorado

J. P. Scott, Ph.D.
Bowling Green State University
Center for Research on Social
    Behavior
Bowling Green, Ohio

Daryl Siedentop, Ph.D.
The Ohio State University
School of Health,
    Physical Education and Recreation
Columbus, Ohio

Robert N. Singer, Ph.D.
Florida State University
Movement Science Program
Tallahassee, Florida

Michael D. Smith, Ph.D.
York University
Department of
    Physical Education and Athletics
Downsview, Ontario
Canada

William F. Straub, Ph.D.
Ithaca College
School of Health,
    Physical Education and Recreation
Ithaca, New York

Richard M. Suinn, Ph.D.
Colorado State University
Department of Psychology
Fort Collins, Colorado

Jean M. Williams, Ph.D.
The University of Arizona
Department of Physical Education
Tucson, Arizona

Alvin Zander, Ph.D.
The University of Michigan
Research Center for Group Dynamics
Ann Arbor, Michigan

INTRODUCTION

The mind is sport science's last frontier. All other systems have been extensively used to improve athlete performances. The physiology of muscular contraction, for example, has been altered through the use of systematic weight training regimens. Today's players seem to be stronger, faster, and more agile than the athletes of a few years ago. Better nutrition and stress applied at levels above threshold value have changed the anatomy of sport participants. This fact is evident from the results of bone studies in which tensile strength has been increased through the use of overload training methods. Kinesiology, the science of human movement, has been used to make the player's movements more efficient and to produce esthetically pleasing postures found in gymnastics, dance, springboard and platform diving, ice skating and ice dancing. The design of equipment, human engineering, has produced the steel edged ski, fiberglass vaulting poles, air and water suspended helmets, and on-line computers to analyze intricate offensive and defensive systems of play. Even the athlete's blood has been sampled and his/her biorhythms charted. Only the mind seems to have been neglected.

Despite the lack of attention to the integration of mind and body, coaches, even before the immortal Knute Rockne, were interested in the psychological factors which affect their players. Rockne's pep talks in the style of "win one for the Gipper" have been repeated at all levels of competition. Likewise, the late Vince Lombardi's "winning isn't everything; it's the only thing" slogan has become a household word. Yes, interest in psychology of sport has been around for a long time.

Although the approach was often crude by modern day standards, Rockne, Lombardi, and others saw the need to intertwine the soma and psyche to produce superior performance. But, that was in the past and today a new psychology of sport is unfolding — the science of athlete behavior. In layperson's terms, psychology of sport is defined as the application of psychology to athletics.

This book, written by some of the leading sport psychologists in England, Canada, and the United States, is designed to help coaches and students of sport psychology become more aware of the techniques available to change athlete behaviors. The coverage is not all inclusive but selective of the topics usually studied in undergraduate and graduate courses. The important areas of motivation, personality, aggression, team cohesion, leadership, attention and anxiety, meditation, and social and cultural aspects are given careful treatment.

The document is not a textbook but a series of readings to be used in conjunction with a standard text. Instructors will find that it enables them to place into the hands of their students important articles written by past and contemporary authorities. More than half of the articles were written specifically for this text; others are considered to be classics. In each case the coverage is thorough and based whenever possible on carefully conducted research. It is not a book of slogans and half truths. Rather, it is a detailed, up-to-date analysis of past and current practices in the emerging science of sport psychology.

The book is also written for the coach on the job who would like to gain greater knowledge of the application of psychology to sport. The coaching experience often enables coaches to formulate ideas about personality, motivation, team cohesion, etc. These readings will make it possible for coaches to expand their understanding of their important ingredients of individual player and team success.

As mentioned above, the authors are some of the most knowledgeable sport psychologists in the world. They come from diverse backgrounds in psychology and/or physical education. Most all of them are active workers in the field and are currently teaching sport psychology classes and conducting research in college or university settings. Some of the authors, like Dorcas Susan Butt, clinical psychologist at the University of British Columbia, were world-class athletes! Others, for example, Emma McCloy Layman and John D. Lawther, are retired, but as professors emeriti, continue to explore the underlying facets of their field.

The coverage begins with an excellent overview of sport psychology by Robert N. Singer, Florida State University. Dr. Singer, a recent inductee into the Academy of Physical Education, is one of our most prolific writers. His theoretical and practical applications of psychology to sport are well known.

Following Dr. Singer's article, Walter Kroll and Guy Lewis, sport psychologist and sport historian respectively, combined their talents to produce the classic: "America's First Sports Psychologist." Kroll and Lewis systematically trace the historical milestones in the rise of sport psychology in the United States. Their selection of Coleman Griffith as America's first sport psychologist is most appropriate. Dr. Griffith's many and diverse contributions in the 1920's at the University of Illinois were unprecedented.

In the final paper within this section, Richard M. Suinn, team psychologist, U.S. National Nordic Ski and Biathlon Teams, presents a comprehensive overview of the practical application of psychology to sport. Dr. Suinn's coverage of topics such as autogenic training, cognitive strategies, meditation, biofeedback, stress management, and visuo-motor behavior rehearsal will acquaint readers with the broad scope of this fast developing discipline. Suinn's indepth knowledge of psychology, particularly its clinical aspects, and his ability to apply it to sport places him in a unique position within the field.

The production of a book is never a single effort. Many people made this document possible. Most of all, appreciation is extended to the authors who took time from their busy schedules to prepare their papers. Appreciation is also extended to the publishers who gave permission to reproduce articles and to the editors of journal papers. Without their cooperation, this book would not have been written.

Most of all, I would like to thank Edmund J. Burke, publisher of Mouvement Publications, for recognizing the need for a book of readings in sport psychology. Dr. Burke read the articles and made valuable suggestions for editorial changes.

Finally, I hope that you enjoy the text and that you will greatly increase your interest and knowledge of the application of psychology to sport.

William F. Straub
Ithaca, New York

Sports Psychology: An Overview*

Robert N. Singer, Ph.D.
Florida State University

What is sports psychology? We in the United States state that it is a new and exciting field with respect to sport: the science of psychology applied to athletes and athletic situations. Professor A. Pouni of the Soviet Union, recognized founder of sports psychology in that country, claimed at the Sports Science Congress held in Moscow in November, 1974, to have initiated research and practice in this area in 1918. The Congress involved 1,000 delegates from 43 countries. If this is true, we cannot accept credit for inventing everything that the Soviets use and in turn legitimize invention rights.

The truth of the matter is that psychology is and always has been an integral part of sport. The facts would also suggest that in Europe, especially in the Soviet Union and its satellite countries, a high premium has been placed on sports science. Sports psychologists, for instance, work with athletes and athletic teams involved in international competition. They undertake laboratory and practical research in this area. These scientists are held in high regard in their countries. Academicians in the United States have usually scorned sport, to search for scientific recognition and prestige in other areas. Our government has not tended to support research in the sports sciences; nor to promote activity in this area. As important as physical culture and excellence in international athletic competition would be to other societies, we seem to place much less emphasis on them and much more on intellectual and academic accomplishments.

What we in the United States are "just discovering" would appear to have been acknowledged for many years elsewhere in the world. Yes, there have been rare exceptions, such as University of Illinois psychologist Coleman Griffith's books on psychology and athletics in the 1920's and '30's. Although an enthusiastic endorsement of the area of sports psychology in the United States is currently indicated by the wave of new university courses and research on relevant topics, the acceptable professional training of sports psychologists and their direct involvement in athletics has yet to come. Optimistically speaking, there are many indications that this dilemma is currently being resolved.

Yet, there are isolated instances in recent times of professionally trained psychologists and psychiatrists working with talented athletes. Their concern has been to make the better athlete better. Their observations, clinical and general, or in the form of recorded personality data, were intended to

*Address given at the 92nd Anniversary Convention, the American Alliance for Health, Physical Education and Recreation, Seattle, Washington, March, 1977.

assist coaches in player selection, position placement, and psychological training procedures.

Unfortunately, such attempts have fallen far short of expectations. But the expectations were too high and unrealistic and in a number of cases, the approaches used were questionable in terms of hoped-for outcomes. One situation worth illustrating here involved psychiatrist Arnold Mandell. Writing in *Saturday Review* (October 5, 1974); he concludes from his two-year experience with the San Diego Charger professional football team that "the shrinks should stay with the rest of the armchair experts — in front of their television sets." According to him, "psychiatry and pro football... don't mix."

We might raise the question, however, as to whether it was Mandell's particular brand of psychiatry that did not mix properly with football. First of all, he admits to little prior knowledge of and experience with football. It would appear that an ideal blend of a professional background in psychiatry and/or psychology along with familiarization with and sensitivity to athletic situations and athletes is a must if any meaningful contributions are going to be made.

Furthermore, although his observations make for interesting reading — e.g., "the wide receiver...is narcissistic and vain, and basically a loner," that defensive ends "display swagger and showmanship," and that the quarterback possesses extreme self-confidence, super arrogance, and "does not feel bound by the rules governing other men" or may demonstrate a strong religious commitment, — we may ask: so what? How does this information help the coach? The athlete? If all Dr. Mandell was paid to do was to analyze the life-styles of football players and to make observations of their personal behaviors, how could he be of service to the Chargers?

The "usual" way in which psychologists have attempted to assist athlete teams is through the administration of self-response personality inventories. Theoretically, it makes good sense to believe that personality traits, or better yet, personality profiles might in some way contribute to the difference in performance between the better athlete and the lesser athlete. They might explain differences between team sport athletes and individual sport athletes. They might distinguish athletes as to positions or events associated with a particular team or sport.

But there are many weaknesses in personality tests and the data they yield. In addition, an unbelievable number of factors relating to abilities, skills, body dimensions, state of training, emotions, past experiences, and the like, interact and contribute to observed athletic behaviors. Considering this, it would be foolish to expect that a single administration of a personality test (and there are many types and formats) can produce information worthy of plugging into a computer and diagnosing in the form of a one-paragraph print-out. Decision-making in sports should be made on a far more sensitive basis. Personality data can be helpful in suggesting ways to understand or treat individual athletes. But research gathered so far is relatively non-sophisticated to allow any major actions by coaches in regard to athletes on the basis of personality scores.

What is badly needed is a broader understanding of the potential ways psychology and sport can mesh. Limitations and possibilities should be recognized. It is with this thought in mind that the present article has been undertaken.

SPORTS PSYCHOLOGY EXPLAINED

The discipline of psychology is associated with attempts to describe, explain, and predict behavior. As a science, serious attempts are made to evaluate behavior and to specify the antecedent conditions causing the behavior of interest. Observation or clinical diagnosis of individuals provides one form of useful data. Other useful information is experimental, or group centered data. These can be statistically analyzed for inferences about behaviors expected from other people with characteristics similar to those tested when alike conditions are present. Experimental and observational methods, then, form the basis of psychological attempts at furthering our knowledge about behavior.

Laws of behavior are formed when events occur with a great deal of certainty for the average person when specified conditions are present. There are many behavioral processes, functions, and systems common to all. Instances where and why individual variations might occur need to be understood as well. Thus, normative information and variability information, commonalities and individual differences, have to be recognized if there will be an attempt to understand and modify behaviors. Sports psychology is an applied psychology; the science of psychology applied to athletes and athletic situations. In a broader context, the one I would propose, it refers to psychology and the medium of sports, with consideration for individuals of all ages, both sexes, and with varying degrees of skill.

On one hand consideration may be given to the athlete and (1) the identification of psychological attributes, (2) the development of these attributes, and (3) the conditions that will affect this development. On the other hand, psychological consideration may be directed to athletic teams and sports activities. See Figure 1 for the Russian concept of sport psychology.

A number of specialty areas have been identified by the American Psychological Association as branches of psychology. An analysis of athletics suggests that five of these areas hold most relevance in the field of sports psychology. They are presented in Table 1, are self-explanatory, and consequently need no further discussion here. They do indicate, however, that sports psychology can potentially encompass many aspects of sport that are identifiable and concrete rather than mystical and hazy. Obvious as well is the importance of understanding the application and relevance of psychology to any potential or highly skilled athlete as well as to any athletic activity or situation, thereby benefitting coaches, athletes, parents of athletes, and others.

For a number of years, those associated with athletics have searched for and obtained guidance from experts representing various scientific fields. Exercise physiologists, biomechanics specialists, nutritionists, athletic trainers, and medical doctors have been of invaluable assistance. It is now time for the sports psychologist to make his unique contributions as well.

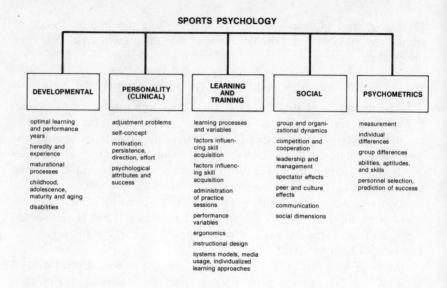

SPORTS PSYCHOLOGY

DEVELOPMENTAL	PERSONALITY (CLINICAL)	LEARNING AND TRAINING	SOCIAL	PSYCHOMETRICS
optimal learning and performance years	adjustment problems	learning processes and variables	group and organizational dynamics	measurement
heredity and experience	self-concept	factors influencing skill acquisition	competition and cooperation	individual differences
maturational processes	motivation: persistence, direction, effort	factors influencing skill acquisition	leadership and management	group differences
childhood, adolescence, maturity and aging	psychological attributes and success	administration of practice sessions	spectator effects	abilities, aptitudes, and skills
disabilities		performance variables	peer and culture effects	personnel selection, prediction of success
		ergonomics	communication	
		instructional design	social dimensions	
		systems models, media usage, individualized learning approaches		

Table 1. *The branches of psychology apparently most related to sports psychology.*

The mind and the heart, in crude terms, may make the difference between winning and losing. Attitudes, emotions, psychological traits, being a "good" competitor, adjustment to cooperation and competition, and adjustment to daily living through sport experiences constitute the fertile arena of psychological study. Even with the absence of a trained sports psychologist, the coach must be a "practical" psychologist. He should be prepared to deal effectively with the psychological aspects of athletic situations.

TYPICAL PSYCHOLOGICAL PROBLEMS CONFRONTING ANY COACH

In spite of the fact that there are always many situation-specific dilemmi, it is quite possible to identify problems in common from sport to sport. The following list is representative of the most recurring in each of the five psychological areas identified previously.

1. *The identification of athletes with ideal psychological attributes who will make the squad and useful contributions to it.* The testing, prediction, and selection of personnel are basic components of psychometrics. The measurement and analysis of personal qualities might also be termed "psychodiagnostics." These data are extremely valuable with athletic teams in which the primary goal is winning in competition. They might suggest those athletes who might benefit most on a probability basis from training; that is, "most trainable" or "most coachable." Pertinent information on capabilities, characteristics, and attributes is also useful in understanding how to train and to treat each athlete.

2. *The understanding and treatment of younger athletes.* The behavioral characteristics and functional potential associated with chronological and maturational ages of youthful athletes suggest methods of communication and treatment. Performance expectations are more realistic with such

information. Contemporary life styles and values of youth are sometimes at odds with the older and more mature coach. These gaps need not be detrimental to coach-athlete relationships if the athletes are handled properly. Developmental psychology suggests optimal years for performance at certain activities. It also describes developments in childhood, adolescence, young adulthood, and the aged, with direct implications for performance expectations and treatment possibilities.

3. *The progression of athletes as quickly as possible from performance potential to performance realization.* The type and speed of improvement of athletes' traits, capabilities, and psychological processes depend on the way practice routines and sessions are designed and administered. The coach manages the practice environment, the physical conditioning and skills training program, the techniques and strategies used, and the avenue of communication between him and the athletes. The psychology of learning offers concepts in reinforcement, knowledge of results, skill sequence, transfer of training, motivation, media usage, and instructional and training design in general.

4. *The motivation of athletes during the pre-season, season, pre-event, and event.* Motivation needs to be viewed dynamically so as to encompass personal (individual) factors, task dimensions, socio-cultural influences, situational demands, and environmental alternatives. Optimal levels of arousal are necessary to achieve different goals. Motivation for selection and persistence at an activity and motivation at the time of competition require different considerations. Athletic performance at any one time is a function of learning and motivation. Attitudes, emotions, and feelings are involved in motivation, and must be in the appropriate direction and at the optimal level for each situation. In the U.S.S.R., motivation and the athlete is described in terms of concern for psychic conditions and states as well as psychoregulative systems.

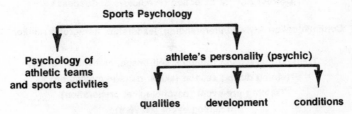

Figure 1. *Overview of sports psychology, the USSR point of view, as presented by Professor Albert Rodionov at the sports psychology meeting held during the International Sports Science Congress, Moscow, November 24 — December 1, 1974.*

5. *The development of team morale, effective competitive and cooperative situations, and understanding of group dynamics and leadership.* Social psychology is extremely relevant to problems and tasks associated with statement number 5. How does the coach maintain a spirit of open competitiveness within a framework of cooperation on a team for selection for available positions or events? What are the best communicative styles between the leadership and the group members? Group cohesion is related

to potentially fruitful team performance. In sports where team members must perform in an interactive process with each other, as in team sports, the situation is especially complicated for the coach. Individual and group productivity, besides reflecting personal skills and abilities, is influenced by the personal-social climate in the team of athletes.

6. *Understanding the psychological problems of individual athletes.* Without a professional clinical psychological background, we cannot expect the coach to identify and remediate all individual athlete personal problems, no matter the degree. But potentially serious problems should be recognized, and family and professional services advised. More minor problems are perceived by the sensitive coach and dealt with accordingly. Personality traits can be evaluated through tests designed to measure such qualities, and this information might be helpful in understanding the behaviors of the athletes. In fact, these behaviors would be expected to some extent, and the coach would be better prepared. Adjustments to competition, success and non-success, new environmental surroundings, new ways of living, and the like, place a heavy burden on individuals. The coping processes operate well for some, disappointing for others.

PSYCHOLOGICAL FACTORS AND ATHLETIC SUCCESS

We have just identified and briefly described six of the major problems common to most sports, as representing dimensions of different psychological sub-fields. From another perspective, Figure 2 demonstrates in

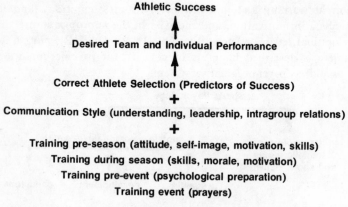

Figure 2. *Factors, with psychological implications, leading to athletic success.*

skeletal form the relationship of factors with psychological connotations as they influence the potential states of individual athletes and the team itself. They help to emphasize, in this format, the tremendous role of sports psychology in the athletic world.

Figure 3 describes athletic success in more general terms but in a more complete picture. Achievements are viewed as dynamically influenced from birth until ready for organized competition, within the particular socio-cultural setting.

8

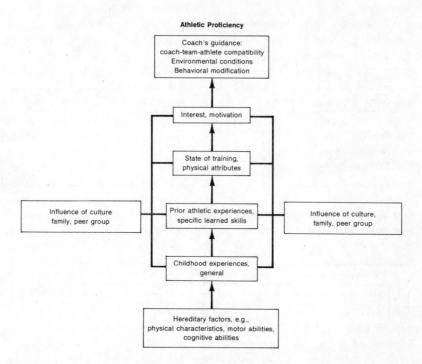

Athletic Proficiency

Coach's guidance:
coach-team-athlete compatibility
Environmental conditions
Behavioral modification

Interest, motivation

State of training,
physical attributes

Influence of culture
family, peer group

Prior athletic experiences,
specific learned skills

Influence of culture,
family, peer group

Childhood experiences,
general

Hereditary factors, e.g.,
physical characteristics, motor abilities,
cognitive abilities

Figure 3. *Foundational blocks toward the achievement of excellence in athletics. (From Singer, Robert N. (ed.)* **The Psychomotor Domain: Movement Behavior,** *Philadelphia: Lea & Febiger, 1972.)*

INDIVIDUAL AND GENERAL BEHAVIORAL CONSIDERATION

In order to influence changes in behavior, one has to understand its properties. Considerations must be given to the underlying systems and functions, how they interrelate, and with respect to similarities in behavioral operations among humans as well as individual difference factors.

There are similar processes that operate within all of us as we attempt to learn skills. Figure 4 illustrates these processes in a systematic manner. These are the processes involved in skill acquisition and performance, and they are identified as interrelated sub-systems, or components, in the human behavioral system. An understanding of these processes would suggest training techniques compatible with the expected limitations of the system at any stage of development. Unfortunately, the information processing capabilities of human systems and response potential to inputs is rarely studied in detail by those associated with the athletic world. Perhaps many training techniques would be changed if this were the case. Going a step further, it is obvious that all human systems do not operate in the same way. Some are better developed to handle certain functions. The variety of factors of previous influence on the system and those creating potential variations in behavior at any time may be placed in four convenient categories. Figure 4 is redrawn as Figure 5 to consider the dynamic interplay

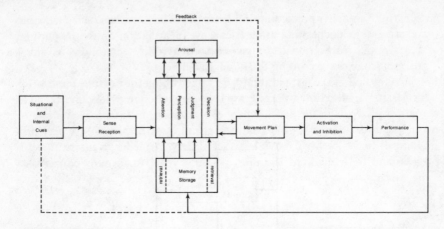

Figure 4. *The human behaving system. (From Singer, Robert N. **Motor Learning and Human Performance,** second edition, New York: Macmillan Co., 1975.)*

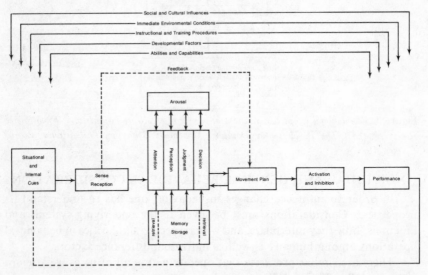

Figure 5. *Variables and other systems potentially influencing the human behaving system. (From Singer, Robert N. **Motor Learning and Human Performance,** second edition, New York: Macmillan, 1975.)*

of these factors with the typical human system, thereby creating a difference in performance potential and performance realized from system to system at any period of time.

The processes and components involved in the learning and the performance of the average athlete need to be examined as they might be affected by developmental factors, abilities and capabilities, training and environmental conditions, and cultural and social factors. The first two categories include individual difference factors, as human systems will possess dissimilar performance potential as a function of them. The latter two categories have to do with effects of environments, training, schedules, and the like. As such, there are fairly predictable influences on behavior when such conditions are present. Coaches and athletes can use information on the psychology of learning, instructional design, and behavioral technology to shape athletic behaviors according to sound guidelines.

At the end of the last paragraph we talked about the possible implication for sport of the contemporary work of educational psychologists. The continued efforts in the development of the science of teaching, of planning and communication approaches incorporating principles of systems procedures, of the creative ways to use a variety of media in interaction for group and individualized learning, are quite relevant to daily concerns of the coach.

INTERNATIONAL DEVELOPMENTS

Before analyzing specific international thrusts in sports psychology, a major point needs to be made here. Ideally, it would be a wonderful situation if voluminous research data, on athletes and athletic situations, would be available to influence theoretical directions and practical decisions. Such is not the case, however. Quite the opposite is true. Then again, if we believe that not every learned activity needs to be investigated uniquely across every conceivable type of situation and with every conceivable type of person as a subject, we can accept theoretical directions in many areas of psychology as a framework for understanding, explaining, and predicting situations in sport.

In other words, the basis of the academic literature in sports psychology need not evolve only from research with athletes or in athletic mediums. Sports psychologists should be conversant with and take advantage of the stage of development of the discipline of psychology and other disciplines relevant to sport. Furthermore, there are concerns in sport about which there would be great difficulty in attempting to collect valid data through quality research efforts. Real-life situations often defy the research control necessary to make "truthful" statements on the factors of concern. Consequently, we look to contrived situations for an understanding of behaviors across many circumstances. This information is especially valuable where confusion reigns, where common sense has not led to a clear solution of a problem.

As to present international developments in sports psychology, it should be pointed out that the field itself was virtually unknown to the western world until ten years ago. Developments can be analyzed according to 1. professional organizations, 2. scholarly activity, 3. elite versus mass sport, 4. direct involvement in sports, and 5. the professional training of a sports psychologist.

1. *professional organizations.* The first publication of the *International Journal of Sport Psychology* in 1970 included the Statutes of the newly-formed International Society of Sports Psychology (ISSP). The Society evolved following the first world congress on sports psychology held in Rome, Italy, in 1965 under the direction of Professor Ferruccio Antonelli of Italy.

Regional and societal organizations sprung up all over the world. The North American Society for the Psychology of Sport and Physical Activity (NASPSPA) was incorporated officially in 1967, and in its first year the organization began publishing the *Sports Psychology Bulletin*. The membership at present consists of approximately 200 individuals, representing serious scholars concerned with sporting behaviors.

Membership in ISSP in 1966 ranged from 648 to 900, depending on which groups were considered as affiliates. If all of them were included there would be approximately 900 members from 38 countries in that year. Antonelli indicated at the second world congress held in Washington, D.C. in 1968, that there were 1500 members from 49 countries. The number of regional sports psychology organizations has continued to grow, as have the memberships through the years.

2. *scholarly activity.* Major thrusts are being made on attempting to describe personality, ability, and other characteristics that might distinguish highest level from average level athletes; various types of sportsmen; and those athletes with the psychological potential to be trained for championship caliber competition. Also, social facilitation theory, in terms of coaction and audience effects on performance, has generated much research in situations involving psychomotor behaviors. Instructional and training strategies are also being examined, but usually with the average person attempting to acquire athletic skills or some movement-oriented behavior.

In some parts of the world, pre-event activities including autogenic training and other relaxation programs, hypnosis, biofeedback techniques, and self-regulation methods are analyzed with athletes as subjects. The identification of, and training for, ideal general and individual arousal states immediately prior to competition, is obviously very worthy of the attention of sports psychologists. Developmental sports psychology is beginning to receive badly needed attention, as younger athletes are studied for performance potential and the effects of training and competition on their overall behaviors. Characteristics unique to female athletes as compared to male athletes are becoming known. Family influence and other social-economic-political-cultural factors are noted with the use of case studies and descriptive data. Many more topical areas could be identified here, but the preceding examples should suffice as an indication of some important directions.

3. *elite versus mass sport.* With what level of athletic proficiency should the sports psychologist be involved? In what types of roles? The more typical and glamorous interpretation of the field of sports psychology is its association with the talented, or elite, athlete.

With this philosophy, it would be highest level athletic competitors in a particular country, national or international, who would be the focus of scholarly study and the beneficiary of special assistance. The sports psychologist would take the already gifted athlete and attempt to contribute to his or her further development.

Another position or philosophy is that sports psychology would be devoted to the study of the masses of people involved in any medium of sporting activity. It is the one I would strongly endorse. Psychological methods of understanding and assisting athletes of both sexes, at all ages, and with varying levels of skill is one major thrust. The psychological effects of sports experience, at all levels of accomplishment, would be another major thrust. The gifted athlete and the beginning athlete are both worthy of help and guidance. The handicapped and the non-handicapped, males and females, sports for all, education through sport, and education for sport, can all be acceptable propositions for the sports psychologist.

4. *direct involvement in sports.* An obvious role of the sports psychologist is in making continuous or intermittent contributions to a team of athletes. This specialist would assist athletes and coaches in developing the optimal social climate and psychological preparation of athletes. Such a procedure is fairly common in East European countries, with regard to the highest skill-level teams. Although, in a practical sense, the primary contributions of psychologists with elite teams have been in clinical-social areas, there is no reason that these contributions cannot be expanded to include many of the possibilities presented earlier in Table 1.

There are other possibilities as well. It might be speculated that the sports psychologist could be involved in:

A. *community athletic programs for children* — helping to establish guidelines and to educate parents and coaches about factors relating sports participation with growth and development;

B. *correctional institutes* — preparing individualized sports recreational programs geared to assist inmates in developing self image, confidence, skills, and physically and emotionally acceptable outlets of expression, which in turn would hopefully prepare them better to adjust to life when they are released from the correctional institutes;

C. *handicapped programs* — dealing with the physically handicapped, the emotionally disturbed, the mentally retarded, and developing especially viable sports recreational programs;

D. *industrial firms* — developing sports recreational program for workers on the job.

5. *the professional training of a sports psychologist.* How should this specialist be adequately prepared for the varied possible types of involvement described throughout this paper? In what direction and to what extent academically? With what research tools? With what kinds of practical experiences in athletic situations?

It would appear that almost everyone (of the small number) involved to some degree in aspects of sports psychology in the United States has been trained as physical educators, with some specialism in psychology. In many European countries, sports psychologists have received degrees in psychology, with their own personal athletic experiences to draw upon. The movement, interestingly enough, has been an emphasis on research and academic issues in the United States, while the emphasis is on the direct working with athletic teams in other countries. Consequently, the interpretation of the role in a given society may suggest alternatives in possible professional preparation. At Florida State University, for example, we have identified a sports psychology emphasis area, along with motor learning and skill acquisition, biomechanics, motor development, and exercise physiology, in the Movement Science Program. It is quite multidisciplinary in nature. Academic content and research tools are emphasized. Other programs might emphasize more practical involvement and less intellectual activity. It would appear that the most desirable program is one that involves both practical work and academics to the greatest extent possible.

At Florida State University, our Movement Science program allows graduate students to emphasize one of five fields of study: motor learning and skill acquisition, exercise physiology, biomechanics, motor development, or sports psychology. We are one of the few universities in the United States to develop the sports psychology specialty. Currently, five doctoral students are undertaking this specialty at Florida State University. This area of study is extremely multidisciplinary, with excellent cooperation from the faculty members in such departments as psychology, sociology, statistics, educational research and measurement, and the like.

A tremendous interest has been shown by faculty and students alike in our Movement Science Program (the only one in the United States) as well as the sports psychology specialty area. With the realization of trained professionals, it is hoped that the sports world, community agencies, and community youth programs will avail themselves of the services of these sports psychologists. The elite and the masses should benefit considerably from their contributions.

CONCLUDING STATEMENTS

The purpose of this material was to provide an overview of the contemporary status of sports psychology, with implications for the future. Possible interpretations of the field of sports psychology were offered, with special relationships drawn from the discipline of science to the world of sport.

Subsequently, typical problems confronting coaches were presented. The role of psychology as a potential means to help solve them was shown. Although practical experience and common sense can and certainly should be applied wherever possible, research and theory derived from the science of psychology may provide more concrete rationales for decisions reached and procedures implemented.

Psychological factors associated with athletic proficiency were presented to provide a dynamic framework of their relationships. Since psychology, as defined, is the study of human behavior, it was shown how behavioral processes are in common and yet how and why individual differences occur. An understanding of general behavioral considerations, differences among people, as well as how to affect changes in people, is necessary for any coach to be consistently effective.

International developments in sports psychology, with respect to professional organizations, scholarly activity, involvement in elite or mass sport, direct involvement in sports, and the professional training of a sports psychologist, were presented briefly to conclude the overview of the contemporary status of sports psychology. For all intents and purposes, the field is refreshingly new, its potential in a variety of sports mediums is exciting to think about, and a promising future awaits it.

It is always exciting when a baby is born. Likewise, continuous excitement accompanies its development as more of its potential is realized. No matter the number of years sports psychology has in fact been in existence, it is still in an infantile stage. But it is developing quickly, with a strong base of support. With maturity comes independence, potential realized, and meaningful contributions of benefit to the world. We look forward with eager anticipation to sports psychology in that stage of fulfillment.

America's First Sport Psychologist*

Walter Kroll, P.E.D.
*Guy Lewis, Ph.D.***
University of
Massachusetts

The first American to engage in formal study of the psychological aspects of sport was Coleman Roberts Griffith, and his accomplishments were of sufficient importance to earn for him the title of "Father of Sports Psychology." Griffith began his investigation at the University of Illinois in 1918 when he conducted a "series of informal observations" on some of the psychological factors involved in basketball and football.[1] Two years later, he began to test football players with a Sanborn reaction-timer.[2]

These studies impressed and excited the imagination of George Huff, Director of Athletics, University of Illinois, and Director of the Department of Physical Welfare, forerunner of the present College of Physical Education. Huff formulated a plan to provide support for a research facility and staff. He proposed to have the Athletic Association assume responsibility for the cost of equipment and the salaries of clerical and professional staff, provided the University would make space available for a laboratory. On September 15, 1925, the Board of Trustees approved the plan, and shortly thereafter Griffith officially became Director of the Athletic Research Laboratory.[3] The facility consisted of two rooms located in the gymnasium: one of 550 square feet was designated the psychological laboratory; the other of 500 square feet, the physiological laboratory. Included was a workshop and a rat colony from Wistar Institute.[4] Griffith was delighted with the set-up. He later wrote: "few other psychological laboratories devoted to a single group of psychological problems are better equipped than this laboratory for research in athletics."[5] In it, according to the commission he received from Huff, Griffith was to study problems in the psychology and physiology of athletic activities, but, in so doing, he was not to ignore making contributions to "pure psychological and physiological science."[6]

Griffith devoted most of his energy to investigating three content areas: psychomotor skills; learning; and, to a lesser extent, personality variables.

*An article published in *Quest*, 13, 1–4, 1970. Reprinted with permission of the publisher.

**The authors wish to express to Professor Larry Locke their appreciation for his numerous contributions to the completion of this biographical sketch. Research on the topic began because he recognized the fact that Griffith deserved recognition in a monograph devoted to the psychology of sport. Professor Locke also supplied much of the source material used in preparation of the manuscript.

To pursue knowledge about these areas, he developed a number of tests and many pieces of special apparatus. These included: (1) apparatus for reaction time to muscular load; (2) test of baseball ingenuity; (3) test of muscular tension and relaxation; (4) tests of four different types of serial reaction times; (5) tests for steadiness, muscular coordination, and learning ability; (6) tests for reaction time to light, sound, and pressure; (7) test for measuring flexibility of coordination; (8) test for measurement of muscular sense; and (9) test of mental alertness developed especially for athletes.[7]

The complexity of the questions the psychologist had to ask about sport were so engrossing and answers so elusive that he used every known means and all available opportunities to gather information. Valuable, but not as important to Griffith as objective data gathered in a scientific setting, were the insights gained from carefully studying both the athletes in competitive situations and the verbal responses received to precisely worded questions during interviews. Griffith, especially curious about the triggering of the automatic skill response, used the result of an interview held with Harold "Red" Grange during the 1924 Michigan-Illinois game to illustrate that successful athletes had the capacity to effectively react to stimuli without assistance from the conscious. Grange scored four touchdown runs before the first 12 minutes of the contest had elapsed, and, before the game ended, he added one more. Yet, when questioned by Griffith, Grange was unable to recall a single detail in any of the feats.[8]

Through correspondence with Knute Rockne, he was able to gather additional subjective evidence relative to his theory of the role of motivation in sport. Rockne agreed with Griffith's point of view and, to illustrate the point, once wrote: "I do not make any effort to key them up, except on rare, exceptional occasions. I keyed them up for the Nebraska game this year, which was a mistake, as we had a reaction the following Saturday against Northwestern. I try to make our boys take the game less seriously than, I presume, some others do..."[9]

Recognizing the need to make known to coaches ways in which knowledge could be applied to teaching sports, Griffith produced a number of articles and two books. He was a frequent contributor to the *Athletic Journal.* In these articles he dealt with a wide range of practical topics such as mental stance and errors in the basketball free throw.[10] In 1926, he published the first of his two classics in sports psychology, *Psychology of Coaching.* He followed this with *Psychology and Athletics* two years later. A book he failed to complete was tentatively titled Psychology of Football. Eighteen chapters of this unpublished work are housed with the Griffith Papers in the Archives of the University of Illinois Library.

At the University of Illinois, he taught a course in sports psychology and assisted graduate students with their research. The first stage in the development of the course came when he offered a special section in introductory psychology to athletes. This section was supplanted in the fall of 1923 by a totally new course called Psychology and Athletics in which Griffith sought to make a serious psychological analysis of all phases of athletic competition.[11] He made available the resources of the laboratory to those graduate students who wished to investigate specific topics. The first theses dealing with the psychological aspects of sport and physical activity were completed during his tenure as director.[12]

Griffith's work as Director of the Athletic Research Laboratory came to an end in 1932. The Athletic Association, faced with declining revenues, decided to economize by withdrawing financial support from the project. Griffith resigned his position and America's first research laboratory in sports psychology closed its doors.[13]

Once his responsibilities as Director of the Athletic Research Laboratory came to an end, Griffith turned his energies primarily to his duties as professor of educational psychology, an appointment that began in 1921, and to service to the University of Illinois. He did, however, conduct an extensive research project for the Chicago National League Ball Club in 1938.[14] The same year the Athletic Research Laboratory closed he was named Director of the Bureau of Institutional Research, and from 1944 to 1953 he was Provost of the University.

An extremely productive researcher and writer, Griffith published more than 40 articles; they appeared in the most prestigious journals in psychology and education. He was especially interested in the effects of rotation upon equilibrium and nystagmus. Among the studies reported were: "Concerning the Effects of Repeated Rotation upon Nystagmus"; "The Decrease of After-Nystagmus During Repeated Rotation"; "Experimental Study of Dizziness"; "The Organic Effects of Repeated Bodily Rotation"; "An Experimental Study of Equilibration in the White Rat"; and "Are Permanent Disturbances of Equilibration Inherited?" In addition to the two books in sports psychology, Griffith was the author of: *General Introduction to Psychology* (1928); *An Introduction to Applied Psychology* (1934); *Introduction to Educational Psychology* (1935); *Psychology Applied to Teaching and Learning* (1939); and *Principles of Systematic Psychology* (1943).

Griffith was born at Guthrie Center, Iowa, May 22, 1893. He received an A.B. degree from Greenville College in 1915 and a Ph.D. from the University of Illinois in 1920. With the exception of the academic year 1915-16, when he served as an instructor in psychology at Greenville College, his professional affiliation was with the University of Illinois. After retiring in 1953, he continued active in professional matters until his death in February 1966. In December, 1964, at the first meeting devoted to an examination of "The Body of Knowledge in Physical Education" by the Western Conference of Physical Education Directors, he presented a paper titled "Sport and the Culture."[15] During his career he received numerous honors and distinctions from professional psychological and educational societies, and, in 1946, Greenville College bestowed upon him the LL.D. degree. Physical education associations, however, have failed to recognize the importance of his contributions.

The reason that such outstanding accomplishments have not been given a prominent place in the annals of the profession is wholly or in part due to the striking void between the period in which Griffith was productive and that of contemporary research in the psychology of sport. Impetus, then, for the recent surge of interest in psychological studies came from a source other than Griffith. In the absence of connective links between the beginning and the present, the designation "Father" suggested on the basis of original contributions to the field of study may not be a fitting one. However, due to the significance of his pioneer work and the obvious failure of physical educators to claim the legacy offered by America's first sports psychologist, Griffith should properly be remembered as a prophet without disciples.

REFERENCES

1. Griffith, Coleman. "A Laboratory for Research in Athletics." *Research Quarterly, 1,* (October, 1930), 35.
2. *Ibid.*
3. Seidler, Armond H. "A History of the Professional Training in Physical Education for Men at the University of Illinois." M.S. thesis, University of Illinois, 1948, pp. 51 and 52.
4. Griffith, *op. cit.,* pp. 36 and 37.
5. *Ibid.,* p. 37.
6. *Ibid.,* p. 37.
7. *Ibid.,* pp. 39 and 40.
8. Tape of an interview of Dr. H. E. Kenney (former student and later colleague of Griffith's) conducted by Dr. Larry Locke on September 25, 1969. In possession of Dr. Locke and housed at the University of New Mexico.
9. Letter from Knute Rockne (signature initialed F. M.) to Coleman Griffith, December 13, 1924, Box 1, General Correspondence, Coleman R. Griffith Papers, University Archives, University of Illinois Library.
10. For example, *Athletic Journal* titles in 1929 were: "Stance," "Mental Stance," "Recent Changes in Basketball Tactics from the Point of View of Psychology."
11. Griffith, *op. cit.,* pp. 35 and 36.
12. Letter from C. O. Jackson to Walter Kroll, November 9, 1968, verified fact that Griffith had directed Jackson's thesis, "The Effect of Fear on Muscular Coordination." King J. McCristal in a letter to Walter Kroll, October 22, 1968, stated that Griffith directed his thesis, "An Experimental Investigation of Foot Rhythms Involved in Gymnastic and Tap Dancing." The studies were reported in the *Research Quarterly* in 1933.
13. Seidler, *op. cit.,* p. 56.
14. "General Reports, Experimental Laboratories, Chicago National League Ball Club, January 1, 1938 - January 1, 1939," Box 13, Coleman R. Griffith Papers, University Archives, University of Illinois Library.
15. Zeigler, Earle F., and McCristal, King J. "A History of the Big Ten Body-of-Knowledge Project in Physical Education." *Quest,* IX (Winter, 1967), 80.

Psychology and Sports Performance: Principles and Applications*

*Richard M. Suinn, Ph.D.*** **
Colorado State University

This paper will offer a way of conceptualizing psychological aspects of competition, and hopefully show the relation between how you analyze an athlete's performance and what you recommend. The focus will be on some current psychological approaches used in the U.S. and abroad, such as autogenic training, cognitive strategies, meditation, biofeedback, stress management training, and visuo-motor behavior rehearsal.

Figure 1 is a basic conceptualization to the effect that athletic performance can be considered a product of aptitude and the strength of an acquired skill. In other words, one's level of performance is influenced by innate ability combined with what one has gained through learning and experience and training. What we are interested in is what influences skill acquisition. As noted, skill may be considered a result of the strength of correct athletic responses, the ability to transfer these from practice to competition conditions, and the ability to either eliminate or at least control incorrect responses.

First taking the topic of correct responses, these may be analyzed as including isolated motor responses, preparatory or arousal responses, adapting responses, linking responses, and cognitive or thought responses. What I am saying is that this package of various types of responses fits together to form the correct motor skill demanded in performance. The isolated motor response would be the physical action learned and shaped through coaching. This might be the technique of the leg drive, the downhill tuck position, the squeeze of the trigger, or the full extension of the arm. Preparatory or arousal responses are traditionally recognized by athletes as important and only now coming under study by psychologists. These are the 'psyching up' preparations. In some cases, this is equivalent to the warming up exercises that are used to prepare the muscles to perform. Arousal levels may be influenced by physical or by psychological steps.

*From a paper presented at the Association for the Advancement of Behavior Therapy, Atlanta, Georgia, 1977.

**Head, Psychology Department; Team Psychologist, U.S. National Nordic Ski Team, U.S. Biathlon Team.

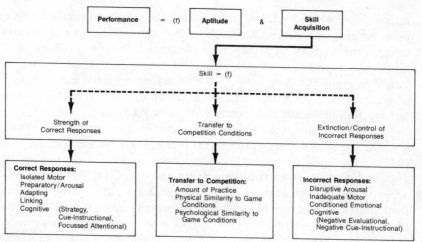

Figure 1. *Factors affecting sports performance.*

Taking a number of runs on a course may stimulate one's competitive drive just prior to the event. The simple action of talking to another competitor about the forthcoming race, meet, or game, can start the adrenalin flowing. In some sports, such as weight lifting, psychological methods may be used as the competitor mentally attempts to dominate the weights. I know of a National Team fencer who successfully whipped himself into extreme anger to sharpen his reflexes. I should quickly point out that preparations may be in either direction, psyching up or psyching down. The crucial step is for the athlete to carefully assess his/her level prior to the performance; if the arousal level is too low for maximum performance then psyching up steps are introduced; if the level is too high, then psyching down is called for. Athletes need to be encouraged to routinely check their levels, and to know themselves well enough to catch the signs associated with optimal arousal. Signs may be general, such as the 'feeling' of being ready. Or the athlete may discover more specific signals, such as reflected in heart rate, or warmth in an extremity, or what thoughts are occurring, or how controllable such thoughts are, or even time of awakening in the morning. Preparatory responses appear to also include what has been called self-efficacy, meaning one's personal expectation of success or confidence. Self-efficacy can vary from competition to competition, especially if the event involves competing against a new opponent, or against different course conditions. On the other hand, it may well be that confidence builds with each success so as to become more and more generalized. Also, success may be defined in terms of goal statements. An athlete may define a subgoal of bettering his/her last times by a fraction, or improving on standings by one place, or even being more fluid or more aggressive or calmer (important goals in themselves but without necessarily being tied down to times or scores). If the athlete sets these subgoals just far enough ahead as to require continuous improvement and effort, but not so unrealistically far ahead as to be unreachable, then the corresponding success will build self-efficacy. Often in slumps, the athlete has unconsciously set the goal of returning within one practice session to 'mid-season' winning form...

after a slump which has taken perhaps weeks or months to develop! Setting more realistic and achievable subgoals that can still be seen as progress towards the winning form may help. Another facet of self-efficacy is not simply the expectation of success in performing, but the sense of being 'ready' to perform. Once again, this may be simply a more specific version of arousal level. We have been experimenting with training athletes in the feeling, both physically and mentally, of being ready.

Adapting motor responses recognize the fact that some sports require a motor action as a *reaction to* another event. Thus the tennis player must emit the appropriate response depending upon the kind of serve by his/her opponent — wide, down the line, topspin, flat, etc. The Alpine skier must adapt to the slalom course as each gate appears rapidly. It is my feeling that the strength of the *Inner Tennis* philosophy appears for these types of responses. Recall that Self 1 is the mind directing the body in an instructional or evaluational way, while Self 2 is the body taking over its own performance. I believe that Self 2 indeed should take over in adapting responses almost along the order of reflexes taking over. Let me talk for a moment about Self 1 and Self 2 and their role in athletics. Self 1 *is* important and should not be discounted. Typically the process of analyzing, thinking about, telling oneself what to do, comes during the acquisition or practice stage. In practice, before an event, it is useful to analyze the course, one's opponent, or technique flaws which need correction. Here is the proper time for the mind to work closely in instructing the body so that later the body can take over. I would agree that once competition begins, that Self 2 takes over and Self 1 becomes an observer. The role of Self 1 in competition itself is generally limited to strategy — "avoid giving him pace on the ball," "look for that fifth gate" — or what we will later call attentional variables. What *Inner Tennis* has revealed is the ambiguity in most training programs. Many instructions have no concrete aspect for the athlete to hold on to. Saying, "You need to improve your timing" or "You're not watching the ball" may sound like concrete instructions, but they do not show the player how to achieve what are real goal-evaluative statements. The goal is improving on timing, the evaluation is that this is good. *Inner Tennis* proposes that the solution is getting rid of evaluation and Self 1 emphasis on instruction of what is right or wrong, and an emphasis instead on Self 2 and what feels proper. But it seems to me also valid to improve on the Self 1 instructions, and to consider Self 1 as appropriately placed in the acquisition or practice sessions or the post-game analyses. One can improve on the ambiguities of Self 1 instructions by directing the athlete to *do* certain things to achieve the goal statement, rather than stating the goal as if it were the instruction. It is one thing, for example, to tell a person to "Relax!" and another thing to train the person in a muscle relaxation exercise usable under stress situations.

I include linking responses to acknowledge that some sports require a flow of movements where the previous move determines or sets the stage for the following one. Figure skating and gymnastics routines fit this category. There is a chain of responses that smoothly lead one to another. In a sense, the rhythm sought by racers in a slalom course is an aspect of linking responses. Sometimes linking responses are introduced into and become important in an event. In work with members of the U.S. Biathlon Team, the problem was presented of how to insure making a correct turn in a relay event. In this event, the competitor skis into a rifle range, fires in the prone position at a target, then skis onto one trail. This trail loops back eventually to the same range, but this time the standing position is used and the athlete then skis onto a different trail. Any hesitation about which trail to ski at the choice point means critical time lost. In training for this event, imagery rehearsal (visuo-motor behavior rehearsal) was used to practice linking responses as follows: "last round fired-up, prone, and to the left trail by the fence..."; this being repeated until the behaviors were firmly linked together. Then, the mental rehearsal shifted to "last round fired standing, -up, and to the right trail by the bridge." These scenes not only had the advantage of practicing linking responses, but also relying upon visual cues to enhance the correct response (e.g., the fence or the bridge). The technique worked so well that one of the participants had dreams all night about "prone to the fence trail... standing to the bridge trail!"

Cognitive or thought processes also form a crucial influence on performance. Cognitive responses include strategy plans, cue-instructional responses, and focussed attentional responses. As indicated earlier, strategy is important in many sports; what line to take in a downhill course, how conservative a gymnastics routine to undertake depending upon your standing, what weakness to exploit in one's tennis opponent. Cognitive factors can also involve what I will call cue-instructional responses. By this I mean the use of a thought or word as a cue to trigger a desired response. For some persons, such cue-instructional thoughts can enhance or maintain performance, e.g., where the words "calm and steady" have been associated through training with reducing competition stress. The cue may actually produce a pattern of actions rather than a single behavior, such as when an Alpine skier thinks "attack the course" and this triggers leaning, tips forward, greater effort, speed retention, and emotional arousal all at the same instant. The key to cue-instructional responses is the amount of practice in associating the desired response with the cue word. Nearly any word can become a trigger if paired enough times with the response, whether the word is "Fire!" paired with the movement of firing through a starting gate or the "7 -" symbol I used once with members of a ski racing team to cue off controlled relaxation (we even had this symbol taped on the back of the protective downhill helmets — the back so that team members riding on the chair lift behind could benefit from seeing the cue).

By focussed attentional responses, I am referring to being able to narrow one's attention and thoughts to the task at hand. Data suggests that successful performance is associated with the experience of being fully aware and tuned into the relevant parts of the event. The audience, distracting conditions, weather, equipment, internal doubts, prior errors, all seem to be outside this focus of attention as though an unpenetrable shield were erected. Where is the attention? It seems to be more on the experience rather than technical details, perhaps the Self 2 rather than the intellect, on the involvement in doing rather than on the how-to-do or what-to-do or how-am-I-doing. In sequencing events requiring linking responses, there is dimension. The rule is that practice makes perfect, if the practice demands are similar to the game demands. Some professional tennis players do not simply practice their serves; instead, they practice serving to Nastase with the imaginal score of '30-40'. If the event is such that the athlete has no control over adverse conditions, then practice should take place under adverse weather or course conditions. Basketball players are never asked in a game to shoot a free throw after a five minute rest; hence they practice free throws *after* a full afternoon of running, and not while fresh and rested.

Finally, skill is influenced by the incorrect responses which interfere with performance. Such incorrect responses may be disruptive arousal, inadequate motor responses, conditioned emotional responses, or various cognitive responses. Disruptive arousal may involve any deviation from the optimal arousal level. A too low level leads to a 'flat' performance, lacking drive, falling short of a full commitment. A too high level involves being hyper-tense. Such a level disrupts coordination, including the timing and display of adaptive and linking responses. Too high a level also leads to greater sense of fatigue and energy consumption.

Inadequate motor responses, of course, represent a basic technique flaw. The athlete has been poorly trained in the technique of the sport. If one views progress towards superior skill as the gradual increase of correct skills with a gradual decrease of deficient actions, then the importance of eliminating inadequate responses becomes clear. Inconsistency in performance is sometimes (but not always) attributable to the recurrence of a deficient motor response. Because of poor earlier instruction, a promising athlete may have acquired many 'bad habits' or technique problems that are as strongly ingrained as his/her good technique. Sometimes this is so strong that the athlete is completely unaware of the flawed action, such as in the ski jumper who did not realize that his arm lifted on one side while in flight. He 'knew' it happened because he saw it in films, but was not actually aware of it at the moment it was occurring. Occasionally this technique of deliberately practicing the incorrect movement is helpful to introduce body awareness. Videotape playback is useful in some ways, but may prove ineffective where the bad habit is overlearned to the point that the athlete has lost awareness. Body awareness training programs are beginning to be experimented with to help sensitize athletes and perhaps increase better body control.

An incorrect response may be a result of conditioned emotionality. We know that a negative emotional reaction can be conditioned in humans; this is how we acquire a reflexive hand withdrawal at a stove when someone shouts, "That's hot!" or how we experience a quick anxiety when hearing, "Look out!" What this entails is the stirring of a negative emotion or an avoidance or self-protective behavior to certain situations, that originally did not create such reactions. An injury may lead to such an association developing whereby the next time the athlete facing the same or similar circumstance, there may be an automatic holding back. Unusual competition conditions may stir unique emotional responses; the Olympic Games hold such a prominent place in our values as to precipitate unusual reactions. In some cases, the stimulus is another competitor. For example, the Franz Klammer of the Austrian team whose very name conjured up anxiety; aided by the stories of the specially made skis which were to give him an even insurmountable added advantage (and which he decided not to use because it wasn't tested). An accumulation of experiences may foster a conditioned adverse response. One of the major problems of slumps is the emotional buildup of tension, depression, loss of confidence, confusion.

Just as cognitive variables may play a useful role, so can they play a disruptive role in performance. Negative thoughts, low self-efficacy, statements of doubt, can interfere with functioning. Such negative evaluation or negatively toned thoughts tend to cue off responses that are incompatible with correct skills. Since thoughts can have an impact on behavior, then negative thoughts will certainly have an impact. There is a real difference between objective evaluational thoughts and negative evaluational ones. An athlete can appraise his/her chances of succeeding and then go out and do the very best. This is more nearly a type of intellectual exercise, devoid of negative influence and maybe even having some positive effects. On the other hand, a negative evaluational thought triggers off negative emotions and disruptive actions that prevent the body from releasing its previously rehearsed skill. For some athletes, the cue-instructional responses may become negative as well. Thus, instead of serving to precipitate desired responses, the cue-instructions prompt disruptive responses. For example, the athlete who continues to say, "Remember, don't make an error!" may inhibit muscle coordination and commit numerous errors. It has been my principle in the use of imagery rehearsal to always practice correcting an error, so that the body *experiences* the correct response, and hence it is not necessary to *remind* oneself about what needs to be done. Instructors are fully aware that it is generally more desirable to emphasize, "Do this" as opposed to "Don't do..."

In the final part of this paper, I would like to tie some of the topics previously discussed to training methods. It should be obvious that a deficiency in the basic motor skill is easily handled by coaching staff, since this falls under the common area of 'technique'. What we might add is the question regarding whether the deficiency is in the isolated motor skill, an adapting motor response, or a linking motor response. As mentioned earlier, if a linking response is weak, then training would emphasize connecting the last response of a chain with the first response of the next chain of responses. Thus, when the athlete does *this,* the immediate next response is *that* (recall the imagery used in preparing the biathlon competitors). If adapting responses are deficient, then the practice would emphasize the external cue which demands a response from the athlete, such as a wide serve. Whereas in linking responses, the athlete emits a response himself/herself which is the signal for going on to the next response; for adapting responses, the athlete must wait for an event to be presented.

Psychological training for arousal is a function of whether a higher level of arousal is sought or a lowering. For the athlete who needs an increase, autogenic training with an emphasis on changing and controlling bodily sensations ('feeling strong and alert') may be appropriate. Biofeedback to increase pulse rate may be applicable for those who are responsive to heart rate. Sometimes, behavioral methods are useful. Such as, exposing oneself to cue conditions that are stimulating (for those who respond to the excitement of the audience, a brief walk among spectators can generate the desire to perform well). Music with a beat may be a helpful procedure. Sometimes, for a cognitively-oriented person, just watching someone else competing increases a sense of readiness. For those athletes who feel that lowering arousal is needed, various relaxation exercises are useful such as deep muscle relaxation with or without muscle or temperature biofeedback equipment. Some relaxation audio cassette tapes are available. For those who are disposed towards mind-quieting methods, meditation and yoga center the attention. And for others, simply relying upon a repeated routine helps to settle (such as awakening at the same hour, dressing in the same way, reading a certain type of material, preparing equipment...everything done exactly in the same order and with a predictable pace). It is interesting to note that just being aware of one's arousal level and knowing of a step to optimize this level may be in itself a major factor in feeling ready.

Self-efficacy is still being studied in terms of methods for improving on this. It may be important to investigate the relative value of using mental rehearsal to practice 'perfection' versus 'coping'. Others have suggested that better performance may be obtained where the rehearsal includes coping with less-than-perfect conditions. For example, we have used visuo-motor behavior rehearsal with Alpine skiers, having them ski a slalom course where 'something unexpected' happens, but 'you are to quickly adjust to it'. The concept of goal-setting mentioned earlier can be a useful means of assuring the continuing buildup of self-efficacy. Slumps may be reversed by a form of goal-setting. Often in slumps, the athlete tries many, many different solutions, randomly moving from one idea to another, becoming more frustrated, and with building frustration becoming even more confused and discouraged. First, the goal of instant recovery must be replaced with the more realistic goal of systematically eliminating steps that do not work, and thereby gradually narrowing down where the problem lies. This attitude suggests that anytime one possible solution does not work this is helpful information rather than a source of frustration, for it helps to narrow the field. One type of attempt at a solution should be tried at least twice before being discarded. Secondly, straightforward signs of progress should be identified ahead of time so as to be noticed when they occur. The sign may be feeling more confortable in the movement, or feeling more fluid, or feeling more like the body is taking over again, or that some accuracy or speed is returning. I have sometimes used pacing techniques where rhythm is a part of the sport, such as in the stride of the cross-country skiing. A pacing technique is simply a rhythmical pacer, such as music to ski to. In many cases, tension control techniques are useful to prevent further motor inhibition, such as relaxation training. In some circumstances, a slump can be broken by introducing responses incompatible with the inhibitory response. For example, a wrestler went into a slump leading to his losing. The more he lost, the more cautious he became, leading to more losses. Soon he felt constricted in his wrestling moves as contrasted with the "free and spontaneous" style of his successful days. My program had him deliberately swing his hands and entire arms in broad, sweeping movements at the starting signal, with rapid and quick taps to his opponent's body. Such gross and wide moves are incompatible with inhibitory, close-to-the-body, 'freezing' movements which were characterizing his slump. As he became looser in movements, this enabled his body to return to its freer style.

Cognitive problems sometimes plague athletes. The thought, "What would happen if...," or "Can I make it to the finish?", or "Don't make that mistake again, you've already lost points (time)" can disrupt even the most competent person. A variety of cognitive approaches have been in use. One method is based upon the principles that two thoughts cannot exist in the same space at the same time. By this approach, one substitutes a different thought that has been prepared ahead of time and practiced. The thought may be one that is relevant, but positive instead of negative, such as, "In a moment I *will* finish and then I can relax." Or the thought may be completely irrelevant and used simply to eliminate the undesired thought, such as those marathon runners who construct houses, do mathematical calculations, or pretend to be trains, as a means of distracting themselves from boredom or pain. Some cognitive strategies involve self-instruction for solutions, for example, "You're trying too hard, relax and get the rhythm." Finally, cognitive restructuring has often been suggested. In restructuring, a different and more positive perspective is placed. Thus, one athlete looks forward to pain since "I know then that I'm putting out to my maximum." A gold medalist marksman brightens up with adverse wind conditions, "It will help me, since I'm ready for it, the others are not." Similarly, one can either react to a fault on the first serve with the thought, "I only have one more serve, I'd better be careful and not double fault" or restructure this into, "My first serve told me something about the range, now I can really count on hitting the next one!"

Where the conditioned emotionality interferes with performance, counter-conditioning or self-control methods can be used. Desensitization is a method combining imagery rehearsal with relaxation. The athlete visualizes the scene involving, for example, the injury but with an emphasis on retaining controlled muscle relaxation. Through this pairing, a new association develops that replaces the previous negative emotion. This method has been useful in reducing 'butterflies' and nervousness in starting gates, and even enabling athletes to confront other competitors without being psyched out. Anxiety management training (AMT) is another method for developing control over stress reactions. By this method, the athlete is trained to recognize early physical-muscular signs of tension buildup, through the use of imagery. Next, the athlete is trained in deep muscle relaxation. Finally, the program increases the athlete's ability to use the relaxation method as an instant means for eliminating tensions wherever or whenever they might occur.

One final mention needs to be made of our use of visuo-motor behavior rehearsal (VMBR), and imagery rehearsal technique. We have some evidence that VMBR is on a continuum of imagery, with 'thinking about' an event on one end, and realistic dream imagery on the other end. VMBR seems nearest to the reality end, with the imagery being so clear and vivid as to reproduce visual, tactual, auditory, motor, and even emotional reactions. Because of this characteristic, VMBR has been a useful method for identifying what happens under game conditions, or for practicing for transfer to game conditions. In the former approach, an athlete uses VMBR to 're-run' a race in order to determine the source of an error. The athlete can then re-do that same race in imagery, but correcting the error. In the latter, VMBR is used as a means of practicing the correct moves for a coming event. Members of an Alpine ski team, for example, use VMBR after course inspection to gain 'experience' in running that course. VMBR was used at the 1976 Winter Olympics to enable skiing the course just minutes prior to the event. This type of mental rehearsal can be used to practice technique, to practice strategy, to practice a general approach (being aggressive), to prepare so well for a difficult part of a course so that the right moves are ingrained, to build confidence, or just to obtain a sense of being familiar with the course by reason of rehearsing it so often.

The major point of this paper is that it is possible to conceptualize sports performance into various component parts, and that such an analysis gives direction for the application of a variety of psychological methods. Training programs then become tailor-made to the specific component needing attention. Further, the conceptualization points out that different athletes may have differing needs, some athletes being more influenced by cognitive factors, others more by arousal levels, others more by emotional factors. Psychological methods, to be useful, must first be appropriate for the person and for the situation. Furthermore, psychological methods require that the athlete carefully assess his/her needs and then be prepared to train enough with the appropriate psychological method as to have good control over its application. Psychological techniques, whether they be biofeedback or VMBR or meditation, demand training in the same way that weight exercises require a commitment to a program. The pay-offs are high, and enable the athlete to finally use an integrated approach to performance, combining physical aptitude with coaching instructions, and fine tuned by physical training and psychological conditioning.

Motivation of the Athlete

Without a doubt, motivation of the individual athlete and team is of great interest to coaches. Although skill is essential to success in sport, without motivation skill is of little value. It is only when skill and motivation are both present that optimum performance results. In sum, performance equals skill plus motivation.

To talk about this important topic, papers are included from nine outstanding sport psychologists. Most all of the dimensions of motivation are included. The coverage begins with Albert V. Carron's article. Dr. Carron, Canadian Sport Psychologist, views motivation as being comprised of four dimensions. They are: (1) dimensions within the athlete, (2) performance consequences dimsnsions, (3) task dimensions, and (4) athletic competition dimensions. Carron concludes his coverage by saying that factors affecting motivation do not operate independently. The four dimensions interact to produce the total level of motivation.

In the second article, Daryl Siedentop, Ohio State University Sport Psychologist, shows the application of contingency management procedure (behavior modification) to change behaviors in sport environments. Dr. Siedentop demonstrates to sport psychologists how to solve behavioral problems in the sports of basketball and football. Although some sport psychologists avoid behavior modification because they believe that is is manipulative and coercive, Siedentop says that it can be used to humanize the athletic setting.

"Strategies for Motivating Young Athletes" by R. B. Alderman, well-known University of Alberta Sport Psychologist, is an important article for those coaches who work with young players. In his paper, Dr. Alderman emphasizes the unique make-up of each individual and the need for coaches to know each player well. Detecting what is important to each player is absolutely essential if the coach is to motivate each individual. Although Alderman indicated that behavior modification, in the form of environmental control, may be effective in motivating the player, he believes that the major thrust should be empathy for the athlete.

Mary Duquin, University of Pittsburgh Sport Psychologist, covers the dynamics of athletic persistence, a neglected topic in athletic motivation. The quality of persistence, Dr. Duquin suggests, influences championship development. Although persistence may be studied as a personality trait, Duquin explains the concept from a social psychological perspective. Based upon group dynamics and attribution theory, she provides six propositions for the development of persistence.

The role of arousal and attentional factors are presented by Daniel Landers, Penn. State University Sport Psychologist. Dr. Landers ties the arousal and attentional components to motivation and performance in sport. He discusses such important constructs as the inverted − U hypothesis, Oxedine's reconceptualization of the Yerkes − Dodson Law, and the effect of arousal on the visual field. High arousal, Landers suggests, often results in a narrowing of the visual field. This behavior may be inappropriate, as Nideffer also indicates, for optimum performance in some sport events.

Back in the 1950's when I began coaching I obtained a copy of John D. Lawther's book *Psychology of Coaching*. It was the first text to appear on the subject since Coleman Griffith's books back in the 1920's. The contents of Dr. Lawther's document helped me obtain greater insight into the psychological factors which affect performance. Now, twenty-eight years later, John Lawther, Professional Emeritus, Pennsylvania State University, makes an important contribution to this book. Lawther's "developmental aspects of motivation" should be read by all persons who work with young children. He not only raises important philosophical questions, but he answers them as well. While giving attention to the important motor-learning aspects of skill acquisition, Dr. Lawther concludes by saying that the coach should be skilled, prepared, energetic, forceful and highly interested in his/her learners.

Professional Alvin Zander, University of Michigan Social Psychologist, begins his paper by saying that, since the beginning of history, people in authority have valued coordinated effort in sport groups. He then presents three approaches to individual motivation. They are: (1) the supportive approach, (2) the reinforcement approach, and (3) the pride-in-performance approach. Dr. Zander covers group motivation, stressing two important motives. They are: (1) the desire for group success, and (2) the desire to avoid group failure. He qualified his approach by saying that it is not a panacea, but it can be useful as a means of understanding, predicting, and furthering the attainment of excellence.

In a paper that was presented at a Symposium on Psychological Assessment in Sport at Wingate, Israel, Dorothy V. Harris stresses that motivation is the key to accomplishment, whether it be in sport, in teaching, in research, or some other challenging pursuit. Stressing the achievement motive, Dr. Harris traces the history of the concept and then talks abut its assessment. The coverage is accurate, carefully documented and systematic.

In the final paper, Wayne Halliwell, University of Montreal Sport Psychologist, makes an important contribution to the intrinsic motivation literature. Based upon Edward Deci's cognitive evaluation theory, Dr. Halliwell talks about how coaches and teachers of physical education may undermine the intrinsic motivation of their players or students. His example of the over-zealous father paying his goaltender son for each shutout is typical of this approach. The son dropped-out of hockey at fourteen years of age. Halliwell concludes by saying that coaches should not only prevent athletes from losing intrinsic motivation, but they should also be capable of formulating strategies to enhance it.

In summary, coaches view motivation as the single most important area of sport psychology. Many sport psychologists share this view. It is too bad that coaches and sport psychologists do not work together more often to solve motivational problems in sport and/or physical education. I am hopeful that the extensive coverage given to motivation by our authors will stimulate greater interest in doing so.

Motivating the Athlete*

Albert V. Carron, Ph.D.
The University of
Western Ontario

ABSTRACT

Motivation is viewed as a necessary, but not sufficient condition for performance. The total level of motivation of the performer is seen as a combination of factors grouped under the broad categories: the athlete, the athletic competition, the task, and the performance consequences. Selected factors within each category are discussed; emphasis is on the application of information to teaching and coaching.

MOTIVATING THE ATHLETE

Factors which contribute to effective individual and/or team performance include: physical stature, degree of conditioning, personality, level of ability, and motivation. All have a direct impact upon the effectiveness of the athlete's performance; however, if one factor were to be selected as most important it would more than likely be motivation. Despite the research emphasis given the area in psychology and education motivation is still poorly understood, particularly as it relates to teaching and coaching of physical education.

Singer (1975) emphasized the importance of motivation in a simplified, but essentially accurate, equation:

PERFORMANCE   =   LEARNING   +   MOTIVATION
(behavior in   (past
a situation)   experience)

It should be apparent from this equation that motivation is a necessary but not sufficient condition for performance. Motivation in the absence of learning would result in purposeless activity, while learning in the absence of motivation would result in no activity. Without sufficient motivation an athlete will not perform well in competition or train effectively in practice.

Effective application of motivational techniques by the teacher or coach depends upon knowledge of the individual and environmental factors affecting motivation, familiarity with many methods and techniques for motivating individuals, and comprehension of the relative effectiveness of each. Clearly, these aspects are interrelated, since knowledge of individual

*An article published in *Motor Skills: Theory Into Practice,* 1:23-34.1977. Reprinted with permission of the publisher.

and environmental factors affecting motivation can provide a rich source of methods and techniques and can provide insight into the effectiveness of various methods. This paper will focus upon the individual and environmental factors affecting motivation, with emphasis upon application to teaching and coaching.

FACTORS CONTRIBUTING TO LEVEL OF MOTIVATION

Motivation serves to energize, select and direct performance. Although this would seem to be straightforward, the sources of potential motivation for the athlete are numerous and extremely diverse. Unfortunately, the coach or teacher has impact upon only a few of these sources. The task of the teacher or coach is to first be aware of the potential sources of motivation, especially those over which influence may be exerted. Secondly, the coach or teacher must be knowledgeable about the relative effectiveness of each. Finally, decisions must be made regarding where and when each specific technique might be put to best use.

The numerous and diverse sources contributing to the total level of motivation can be subdivided and categorized into four dimensions or classes. These are identified in Figure 1 as: dimensions within the athlete; performance consequences dimension; athletic competition dimension; and task dimensions.

The *dimensions within the athlete* are factors specific to the athlete which contribute to the total level of motivation. These factors include the athlete's personality, aspiration level, and intrinsic interest, among others. This is a source of motivation which is largely independent of the actions of the coach.

The results or *consequences of performance dimension* also affects total level of motivation. For example, the outcome of performance usually includes some rewards or punishment and the possibility of that reward or punishment serves as a potential source of motivation for the athlete. The coach or teacher has some influence over this source of motivation.

The *athletic competition dimension* reflects the dynamics of the athletic situation. Variables such as the relative importance of the event, the absence versus the presence of an audience, the composition of that audience, and the ability of the competition are potential sources of motivation. This source of motivation is generally available and relatively independent of the actions of the coach.

Finally, the task itself contains the potential to be motivating *(task characteristic dimension)*. Two aspects are the information feedback available and the amount of change or special attention in the task, commonly known as the Hawthorne Effect. The coach or teacher can exert considerable influence over these aspects, which are particularly crucial in the practice phase.

Although these dimensions are interrelated, as indicated in Figure 1, they have been examined independently by researchers and, for the remainder of this article, each will be considered in turn.

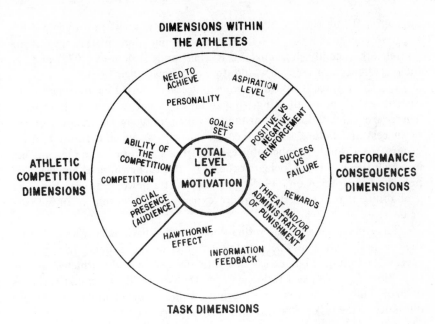

DIMENSIONS WITHIN
THE ATHLETES

NEED TO ACHIEVE
ASPIRATION LEVEL
PERSONALITY
GOALS SET
POSITIVE VS NEGATIVE REINFORCEMENT
ABILITY OF THE COMPETITION
COMPETITION
TOTAL LEVEL OF MOTIVATION
SUCCESS VS FAILURE
SOCIAL PRESENCE (AUDIENCE)
THREAT AND/OR ADMINISTRATION OF PUNISHMENT
REWARDS
HAWTHORNE EFFECT
INFORMATION FEEDBACK

ATHLETIC
COMPETITION
DIMENSIONS

PERFORMANCE
CONSEQUENCES
DIMENSIONS

TASK DIMENSIONS

Figure 1. *The dimensions of motivation which offset the total level of motivation within the athlete.*

Dimensions within the athlete

Level of aspiration/goal setting. The level of aspiration is the "level of future performance in a task as specified by the individual" (Robb, 1972, p. 79). Research evidence has provided strong support that behavior is controlled by its consequences (Bandura, 1973); thus, success and failure have a tremendous influence upon subsequent goal setting and level of aspiration.

The relationship would appear to be cyclical: previous successes/failures influence present aspiration; present aspiration influences successes/failures. Consider a child who has experienced nothing but failure in every sport attempted. The child will undoubtedly have a low aspiration when faced with yet another new sport. However, the cycle of failure-low aspiration-failure may be broken. The teacher or coach must help the individual to set realistic, progressive goals which lead to small but repetitive successes so that success can beget success. This involves setting intermediate, achievable, realistic goals between the athlete's initial performance and final objective. The success experiences will lead to raised aspirations which will contribute to more effective future performances.

As an example, animals which were formerly noncombative have been trained to become more and more vicious in aggressiveness as a result of positive reinforcement (i.e., repeated victories) in battles with progressively stronger opponents. Similarly, severe repetitive defeats can result in enduring submissiveness even against harmless opponents (Kahn, 1951; Scott and Marston, 1953).

The shaping of behavior through manipulation of the consequences (success and failure) of behavior can be a powerful positive tool when used appropriately by the teacher or coach. Unfortunately, improper use has negative consequences. The theories and applications of this type of approach are cogently presented by Rushall and Siedentop (1972) and the interested coach or teacher would do well to read their book.

On the surface it appears simple, success → raised aspirations → success; however, as in all things, the situation is not as clear as it appears. There are extenuating circumstances which mitigate the relative effects of success and failure. These include: the age at which the initial failure occurs, the absolute number of previous defeats/victories, and the sequence in which these victories/defeats occurred. The theory of need achievement presented by Atkinson (1965) provides a framework to examine the probability that a success or failure experience will result in an increase or decrease in motivation.

This theory reflects the influence of both situational variables, under the coaches' control, and personality variables on the tendency to approach success or failure. The coach has little control over the athletes' motive to achieve but can exert influence over the perceived situational variables of probability for success and incentive value. For example, the relative difficulty of the task influences the athletes' perceived probability of success. Thus, the athlete will have little motivation if the task is perceived as too easy or too difficult. Similarly, the importance of the situation influences incentive level. Little motivation results if there is no incentive value in the task. This has implications for both coaches and teachers with regard to communication with students and types of drills used. Often, teachers use approaches which might seem irrelevant to the student. There is little incentive to achieve the objective by effectively carrying out the drill. The teacher should outline reasons for the drill, thereby increasing the incentive to achieve. If the drill itself is too easy or extremely inappropriate little benefit will accrue because of the low incentive value inherent in the drill.

Anxiety. Need to achieve, just discussed, is one personality variable contributing to the total level of motivation. A second personality variable which has been shown to relate to the general drive level of the individual is *anxiety.* Individuals differentiated into classes of high-anxious and low-anxious on the basis of a paper and pencil personality questionnaire were found to differ on a variety of motor performance tasks. The differences in performance were consistent with what would have been predicted on the basis of differences in drive level/motivation. (Carron, 1968; Castaneda, et al., 1956; Duthie and Roberts, 1968; Farber and Spence, 1953.)

Since anxiety level apparently contributes to general drive level, high anxious individuals inherently have greater initial "motivation" than do low-anxious, on the basis of a paper and pencil personality questionnaire, were found to differ on a variety of motor performance tasks. The differences for a low anxious athlete. In fact, if the task were either extremely difficult, or little learning had occurred, or the athlete was of low ability, the high anxious individual might be too highly motivated initially and the coach or teacher would then need to reduce the athlete's anxiety level in order to obtain optimum performance.

Ability and level of learning. The ability and level of learning of the performer should be considered in determining the optimal level of motivation for a particular task. For example, lower levels of motivation are preferable early in learning when the task is more difficult. Later in learning, higher levels of motivation may be beneficial, depending, of course, on the nature of the task. Ability level is somewhat related to level of learning in that certain individuals find some tasks relatively easy and may begin at a more advanced level. In addition, their initial anxiety may be lower in certain situations than individuials of lesser ability.

Performance consequences dimension

Positive and negative reinforcement/rewards. The characteristics of a reinforcer are that a) it is usually contingent upon a specific preceding behavior and b) it affects the likelihood or probability that a particular behavior will reoccur in a similar situation. While reward is similar to reinforcement, reward has the connotation of being positive, whereas reinforcement may be positive or negative. For example, a hockey coach may temporarily bench a player for going out of position, thus negatively reinforcing the athlete's response. Conversely, the coach might commend a basketball player's attempt to drive inside, positively reinforcing that specific behavior.

What is the relative effectiveness of positive versus negative reinforcement? Singer (1975) observed that both can be effective in specific instances. He also pointed out, however, that the more efficacious of the two would appear to be positive reinforcement. Positive reinforcers inform one when he is doing something right and encourage the continuation of the activity in a specific direction, while negative reinforcement is of little value because it merely indicates that the behavior is incorrect without providing information with respect to the correct response or behavior. Information feedback, because of its greater specificity, may be ultimately more useful in most instances. (Information feedback will be considered under Task Dimensions.)

Rewards (which can be considered analogous to positive reinforcement) can take many forms. Oxendine (1968) suggests that there are three classes of rewards: 1) *symbolic,* including praise, decals on helmets, school grades, team crests, etc.; 2) *material,* including money, promise of team jackets for success, trophies, etc.; or 3) *psychological,* including the sense of belonging, the sense of accomplishment, knowledge of improvement, etc. He notes that psychological rewards are the most desirable.

One of the simplest, most natural, and therefore most frequently used forms of reward, particularly by inexperienced coaches and teachers, is praise. There are some disadvantages which could result from overuse of praise:

The most important disadvantage is the individual's tendency to develop a dependence upon extrinsic rather than intrinsic motivation and therefore, develop false values (interest in the reward rather than the activity itself). Another disadvantage...is that the same few children seem to excel most of the time. It appears that the winners of external rewards are usually the children who need them least for subsequent enthusiasm. (Oxendine, 1968, p. 192.)

In our materialistic society children are taught to expect rewards for achievement. Clearly, the teacher and coach are fighting an uphill battle in attempting to re-educate children to rely upon intrinsic rather than extrinsic types of reward. It is one which must be waged nevertheless and which should stress realistic goal setting behavior and evaluation in terms of one's own performance.

Punishment and/or threat of punishment. If reward is conceived of as one end of a continuum, punishment and/or the threat of punishment is the other. Although positive reinforcement is preferable to punishment as a consequence of performance, punishment, when properly employed, can be effective for *some* athletes in *some* instances. It would appear, however, that the disadvantages and strict methods for application of punishment far outweigh benefits derived from its use. Both Oxendine (1968) and Rushall and Siedentop (1972) stress that to be effective, punishment must: a) be used infrequently; b) be severe when employed; c) have minimal emotionality attached; d) be specific rather than general; and e) be applied consistently.

Success and failure. Success or failure would appear to be a consequence of most competitive athletic performances. Either outcome can have an effect upon subsequent motivation, although complete success and complete failure are rare. Care is taken in setting multiple goals, since both success and failure are relative to the goals that the athlete has set and his/her aspirations for that situation.

Coaches, spectators or parents might make judgments regarding the success or failure of the athlete in a race, e.g. "the athlete came first and that equals success" or "the athlete came last and that equals failure." The problem here is that an *absolute* standard is used which does not take into account the athlete's expectations, aspirations and goals. It is possible that an athlete might consistently run a specific race in 13 seconds. In a competitive situation, however, the athlete might run that race in 12 seconds. If she finishes last this performance might be rated a failure on the absolute scale, in spite of the fact that it is a success relative to past performances.

Clearly, the coach or teacher can manipulate performance consequences through establishing of criteria, choice of opponents, choice of task, assistance in goal setting, and evaluation of performance. Consistent success and consistent failure rarely serve to motivate behavior. High probability of failure, about 0.8, and low probability of success, about 0.2, seem to increase motivation. When either probability of failure or probability of success reaches a chance value (0.5), motivation begins to decrease steadily; it reaches a low when success or failure is assured. Singer (1975) has suggested that the chance level of probability, about 0.5, is the time to increase the difficulty of the task, to choose more difficult opponents, to increase the goals or to establish more stringent criterion. If, for example, a student can achieve a foul shooting score of 5 out of 10, a criterion set by teacher and student jointly, more than half of the time, perhaps it is time to raise the criterion to 6 or 7 out of 10. In terms of evaluation of performance the coach or teacher should become more exacting in their demands or encourage the student to be more exacting in self-imposed demands.

Athletic competition dimension/environment

Social Presence. Organized sport and physical activity is carried out, almost without exception, in the presence of others. These others may be an audience of spectators, fellow competitors, coaches, teachers, teammates or officials. It has been demonstrated repeatedly that the presence of others has an influence upon performance. This performance effect is attributed mainly to increased arousal, activation, and drive/motivation (Zajonc, 1965; Cottrell, 1968).

There are a number of factors which influence the degree to which the social presence of others is motivational. The size and the audience characteristics are two such factors. Audience characteristics is a catch-all for variables such as: age; sex; relationship to player (i.e., fellow teammates, girlfriend, boyfriend, parents); and ability.

Another important factor is the function of the audience. Recent research suggests that it is not the mere presence of an audience that results in increased motivation (Cottrell, et al., 1968; Martens and Landers, 1972), but it is the sense of evaluative apprehension on the part of the competitor. Martens (1975) has suggested that evaluative situations are generally motivating because we learn to expect positive or negative outcomes as a consequence of evaluation.

Teachers especially should be aware that social presence has a different effect upon learning than upon performance. In the sense it is used here performance is behavior occurring after substantial learning has taken place; while learning is the process of changing the most probable response from an incorrect to a correct one (Martens, 1975). Individuals under stress will usually emit the most probable response. Since social presence increases motivation and can be considered a form of stress, it follows that individuals who are in the process of learning might be adversely affected by the presence of others, particularly if they view those others as evaluators. For this reason, learners probably require considerable practice time away from, what they perceive as, the evaluative eye of the teacher.

Competition. The nature of sport is such that it is inherently competitive. The athlete competes against one or more other athletes, against self-imposed standards, or against fixed norms. Since these targets, goals or standards are always available in athletic competition, the situation is generally motivating, although the degree to which it is motivating is highly variable. Athletes differ in competitiveness due to individual variation in motives which contribute to competitiveness. These include: fear of failure, need to achieve, anxiety level, and desire for dominance, among others. Some of these have been considered in a previous section *(Dimensions Within the Athlete).*

A factor which contributes to the athlete's level of motivation that is clearly a part of the environment is the level of ability of the opposing team as perceived by the athlete. The more similar in ability the two competitors (individuals or teams) view themselves, with respect to relative ability level, the greater the probability that competitive behavior will occur.

If one athlete does not see any possibility for success there is very little likelihood of competition (Cratty, 1967). In these instances the competition may revert to an attempt to improve the weaker opponent's skill through some form of cooperative performance. For example, if two tennis players or golfers have great disparity in ability, the "game" often reverts to the better player helping the other with tips, coaching instructions, designed to improve the weaker player's game.

If the team or individual appears outclassed, the behavior of the coach must change to fit the situation. It should be obvious that pointing out that "they put their uniforms on one leg at a time, just like us!" is hardly reassuring to an athlete who views the chances for success as nil. Pep talks and other incentives would also be of little benefit in this context. What is needed is for the coach to point out the relative weaknesses of the opponents in contrast to the relative strengths of the athlete or team and indicate how these might best be exploited for potential success. The issue here is that the athlete must perceive some opportunity for success, otherwise little or no competitiveness will be present.

Task characteristic dimension

Information feedback. Information feedback refers to error information which indicates the discrepancy between the completed response and the goal or target, or between the movement as planned and the movement as executed. For example, a teacher or coach may indicate to an archer that the arrow just shot landed two inches to the right of the exact center of the target. In another instance a teacher may inform the learner that the head of the golf club was dropped at the top of the backswing. These two types of information are commonly referred to as knowledge of results and knowledge of performance respectively.[2] As a rule, knowledge of results is available for the performer and so its provision by the coach or teacher is often redundant. On the other hand, knowledge of performance, by definition, is usually unavailable to the learner. (Except, of course, in the instance of kinesthetic feedback which provides knowledge of "how I moved," and is always available to the performer.)

The important issue for the coach to bear in mind is that the most common effect of information feedback is to increase motivation (Ammons, 1956). Athletes receiving feedback tend to pursue the task with greater application and diligence. This may be partly due to the attention given the athlete but it is also due to the fact that the feedback gives the athlete a yardstick by which progress, or lack of it, may be measured. It has also been demonstrated that the effectiveness of the yardstick, particularly for performers with some degree of skill, is directly related to its preciseness. For example, a golfer shooting "blind" to the green can profit from the information that his golf shot was hit over the green. However, for the information to be most effective, the specific distance should be given.

Clearly, the provision for feedback should be one of the major concerns of the coach or teacher, for feedback, properly used, is a crucial factor influencing the learning and/or performance of the individual. Care should be taken to avoid providing information which is readily available so that attention can be given to information the athlete cannot acquire independently. Another function of the coach or teacher concerns the use of feedback. Knowledge of results indicates the effect that a response has upon the environment. The player must learn to use the information to revise the response. For example, a tennis player who serves a ball into the net must consider the possible errors before taking the next serve and adjust it accordingly. Individuals who are encouraged to analyze their behavior in this manner will undoubtedly have an advantage in competition and practice.

Hawthorne Effect. Coaches frequently draw on the principles of the Hawthorne Effect in setting up their practice schedules. The effect is named after a classic series of studies carried out at the Western Electric Company's Hawthorne Plant in Chicago, Illinois (Roethlisberger and Dickson, 1939). The purpose of the experiments was to examine the effect of amount of plant illumination on work output. It was noted that the *productivity of the workers increased whether the level of illumination was increased or decreased. Thus, it was concluded that the level of illumination was not the variable of importance but, rather, the change and special attention given the workers. This phenomenon of an improvement in performance as a result of increased motivation resulting from change(s) in the performance environment has come to be called the Hawthorne Effect.*

Many coaches are sensitive to the need for occasional change in the practice environment, particularly late in a season when individual or team motivation might be low. Thus, football coaches might switch their linemen to the backfield (and vice versa) or have the team play soccer rather than football during the practice. Although the task has been changed and therefore the payoff in football skill acquisition would be negligible, the increased motivational benefits might far outweigh the negative aspects.

While the above examples are among the most extreme illustrations of a coach capitalizing on the well verified Hawthorne Effect, other more subtle examples are available. An example of where the Hawthorne Effect may be applied, but often is not, is in the selection of practice drills. Most coaches who have been involved with a sport for an extended period of time are rather restricted in the number and variety of drills they use. The process is gradual. Through experience in coaching, efficient, effective drills may be added and modified and less utilitarian drills eliminated. The result is that many experienced coaches have a fixed, minimal repertoire of drills which are used repetitively. On occasion, the coach must consider a trade-off. That is, a less effective drill (in terms of teaching potential) might be better in some instances because it is a *change* and therefore is potentially more motivating via the *Hawthorne Effect.*

SUMMARY
At the outset it was stressed that the *factors affecting motivation do not operate independently but, rather, as was illustrated in Figure 1, interact to produce a total level of motivation.* It is important, therefore, that the teacher or coach have information about each of the classes of factors considered: dimensions within the athlete; performance consequences dimension; and task characteristic dimension. Clearly, the teacher or coach cannot hope to

encourage optimal motivation unless the four dimensions are taken into account. For example:

—The coach or teacher who applies similar motivational techniques to all performers is in danger of undermotivating some and over-motivating others depending upon their "normal" anxiety levels and upon their particular likes and dislikes.

—Not only should motivational techniques be varied for different athletes but the particular task should dictate the levels to be produced; simpler tasks require higher levels of motivation than more complex tasks.

—The Hawthorne Effect applies to motivational techniques as well as to task characteristics. Therefore, techniques should be widely varied to maintain effectiveness.

—Need achievement theory suggest that coaches and teachers inform students of the rationale behind various drills, keep the task challenging and appropriate to maintain incentive, and help students set multiple goals so that some success will be guaranteed.

—The effect of audience on the performer depends upon the performer's ability. During early learning the effects are generally detrimental; in the intermediate stages the specific effects may depend upon the characteristics of the audience; and, at high levels the effects are generally positive.

It is hoped that these examples, in addition to those in the article, will enable the teacher or coach to generate other examples more specifically matched to their situation and their performers.

REFERENCE NOTES

1. DUTHIE, J. H. and ROBERTS, G. C. Effect of manifest anxiety on learning and performance of a complex motor task. Paper presented at Second International Congress of Sport Psychology, Washington, 1968.

REFERENCES

AMMONS, R. B. Effects of knowledge of performance: a survey and tentative theoretical formulation. *Journal of General Psychology,* 1956, *54,* 279-299.

ATKINSON, J. W. The mainspring of achievement-oriented activity. In J. D. Krumboltz (ed.). *Learning and the educational process.* Chicago: Rand and McNally & Co., 1965.

BANDURA, A. *Aggression: a social learning analysis.* Englewood Cliffs: Prentice-Hall, 1973.

CARRON, A. V. Motor performance under stress. *Research Quarterly,* 1968, *39,* 463-468.

CASTANEDA, A., PALERMO, D. S. and McCANDLESS, B. R. Complex learning and performance as a function of anxiety in children and task difficulty. *Child Development,* 1956, *27,* 327-332.

COTTRELL, N. B. Performance in the presence of other human beings: mere presence, audience and affiliation effects. In E. C. Simmel, R. A. Hoppe and G. A. Milton (eds.), *Social Facilitation and Imitative Behavior.* Boston: Allyn & Bacon, 1968.

COTTRELL, N. B., WACK, D. L., SEKERAK, G. J. and RITTLE, R. H. Social facilitation of dominant responses by the presence of an audience and the mere presence of others. *Journal of Personality and Social Psychology,* 1968, *9,* 245-250.

CRATTY, B. J. *Social Dimensions of Physical Activity.* Englewood Cliffs: Prentice-Hall, 1967.

FARBER, I. E. and SPENCE, K. W. Complex learning and conditioning as a function of anxiety. *Journal of Experimental Psychology,* 1953, *45,* 120-125.

KAHN, M. W. The effect of severe defeat at various age levels on the aggressive behavior of mice. *Journal of Genetic Psychology,* 1951, *79,* 117-130.

MARTENS, R. *Social psychology and physical activity.* New York: Harper & Row, 1975.

MARTENS, R. and LANDERS, D. M. Evaluation potential as a determinant of coaction effects. *Journal of Experimental Social Psychology,* $972, *8,* 347-359.

OXENDINE, J. B. *Psychology of motor learning.* New York: Appleton-Century-Crofts, 1968.

ROBB, M. D. *The dynamics of motor-skill acquisition.* Englewood Cliffs: Prentice-Hall, 1972.

ROETHLISBERGER, F. J. & DICKSON, W. J. *Management and the worker.* Cambridge: Harvard University Press, 1939.

RUSHALL, B. and SIEDENTOP, D. *The development and control of behavior in sport and physical education.* Philadelphia: Lea & Febiger, 1972.

SCOTT, J. P. and MARSTON, M. V. Nonadaptive behavior resulting from a series of defeats in fighting mice. *Journal of Abnormal and Social Psychology,* 1953, *48,* 417-428.

SINGER, R. N. *Motor learning and human performance, 2nd Ed.* New York: Macmillan & Company, 1975.

ZAJONC, R. Social facilitation. *Science,* 1965, *149,* 269-274.

The Management of Practice Behavior

Daryl Siedentop, Ph.D.
The Ohio State University

Most coaches believe that game performance is directly related to practice preparation. Athletes aren't always motivated to perform maximally during practice sessions. They sometimes limp through drills half-heartedly. Their enthusiasm wanes as the season progresses. The togetherness with which a season began sometimes disappears. Preparation for upcoming competitions becomes increasingly difficult as players are less attentive. Coaches resort to chiding and hassling stragglers. Things sometimes get a little tense. It doesn't have to be that way!

During the past twenty years we have learned a great deal about behavior management programs. The technology of behavior management was perfected in controlled settings such as laboratories, mental hospitals, and prisons, but more recently has been extended to schools, universities, businesses, community centers, national parks, homes, and a variety of other settings.

Do not misunderstand! Behavior management has always been practiced — everywhere. But its application has been mostly unsystematic and almost totally coercive. The technology of behavior management I am describing to you is systematic and based on incentives rather than threats — on rewards rather than punishments.

An understandable, usable behavior technology exists — here and now! It is available for teachers and coaches. It is practical and inexpensive. And, there is growing evidence that in sport settings it will prove to be every bit as powerful as it has in the many other settings to which it has been applied. By powerful, I mean that it will increase performance while at the same time increasing player and coach satisfaction.

The techniques of behavior management were explained in detail by Rushall and Siedentop (1972). Less technical explanations, oriented particularly toward teaching settings, are available in abundance (Sulzer and Mayer, 1977; Williams and Anandam, 1973; Givner and Graubard, 1974; Stephens, 1975). The point is that a literature currently exists which explains behavior management techniques and systems in everyday, non-technical language.

Contingency management.

The primary system for managing the behavior of athletes in practice settings is called contingency management. A *contingency* is the relationship between a behavior and a consequence. It is the management of these relationships that is important for improving athlete productivity in practice settings. Coaches, or coaches and athletes working together, decide on what has to happen during practices. Athletics is full of potential rewards that can be used as incentives. The trade off between practice performances and the earning of rewards is then established and a system to monitor practice performance is perfected. Those athletes that meet the contingencies earn the rewards. Those that don't perform in practice go unrewarded.

That is the basic format of contingency management. Being a good contingency manager requires practice. The first system you try will be a bit clumsy. Behaviors may not be specified with sufficient clarity. The monitoring system might break down. You arrange too small a reward for too much behavior (or vice versa). But regardless of how crude your first effort might be it will get some results and those results will be a reward for you — and you will try it again, improving the system and therefore improving even further the results it generates.

Some examples.

Examples of the management of athlete behavior in practice settings are growing. Rushall and Pettinger (1969) were among the first to publish research which showed significant improvement in practice performance as a result of behavior management systems. They compared the effects of some simple material reinforcers (candy) with other rewards such as coach encouragement on work output in age group swimming. The material rewards were easily the most powerful.

McKenzie and Rushall (1974) did a series of behavioral management studies with age group swimmers. They increased attendance and reduced tardiness and leaving early simply by having swimmers sign in and out with a publicly displayed attendance board. The same concept was used to increase work output in practice. A program board was developed on which swimmers could check off each lap of a programmed workout. The group increased their performance output by 27.1%, which is equivalent to an additional 619 yards for each individual during the practice session!

McKenzie (1972) also tackled the often difficult problem of inappropriate practice behavior. He developed a simple "behavior game" where squads competed in practice to see which could behave best — in this case the behaviors were directly related to improved performance, things like changing strokes, not swimming in to touch, and stopping during a lap. The techniques of "good behavior games" have been outlined by Siedentop (1976) and by Siedentop and Rife (1975). The difference between this kind of contingency management system and others discussed here is that the target behaviors are those social/performance behaviors which are prerequisite to successful practices; i.e., athletes have to be on time, they have to pay attention, they have to avoid "fooling around."

Contingency systems can also be developed to specifically improve execution of athletic assignments. Komaki and Barnett (1977) broke down three important football plays into their sequential parts. An assistant coach rated each part each time it was performed. Simple coach praise and recognition was used when each part of the play was executed properly. Execution of the option play increased from 62% before implementation to 82% after implementation of the system. The power sweep increased from 54% execution to 82%, and the off-tackle counter went from 66% to 80% execution. This was the result of systematic recording and coach recognition of performance. I'm sure that with more powerful incentives execution of assignments in practice scrimmage situations could approach 100%.

Social behavior can also be changed dramatically. All coaches like to see their players be supportive of one another rather than criticize each other. There is no doubt that the players like to hear some words of encouragement from teammates also. Rolider (1978) recently showed that, even in an instructional basketball class, a contingency system could increase the amount of player to player encouragement by 128% over non-system practice sessions. He also showed that if the coach is a high encourager, players will imitate this (a modeling effect) but that the increase is not as great as when incentives are used.

It appears, therefore, that contingency systems can be effective in managing inappropriate behavior in practices, increasing player to player supportive behavior, increasing execution, and improving work output. Separate contingency systems might be developed for each of those important practice concerns or an overall program might be developed. Let me share with you two such systems with which I've recently been associated.

The 100%'ers.

Craig Phillips coaches the Jonathan Alder High School football team in Plain City, Ohio. Craig's athletes are well-motivated but he nonetheless saw the benefit of a total football practice management system. He had several direct concerns. First, his team had been hurt in the previous season by too many penalties, a habit that he was convinced developed in practice sessions. Second, he wanted his team to take early season learning sessions more seriously. Third, like all coaches, he was interested in promoting hustle in practice. And, fourth, he felt a responsibility for several other kinds of school-related and team-related behavior patterns.

In discussing possible rewards to use in a practice management system, it became clear that "starting" in the weekly Friday night game was the strongest incentive. We also decided that players who performed well in games got plenty of recognition. They got praise from fans and peers, their names in school and local papers, and all of the other satisfactions that come from good performances. Helmet decals, now so widely used as rewards for game performance, had been used by Craig, but we decided that we would use them instead as practice rewards. This accomplished two things. It gave us another strong incentive system and it really meant a lot to the players who seldom played. By the middle of the season these players were easily distinguishable to fans when they ran out on the field because they had no decals on their helmets!

After many discussions about what kinds of behaviors to include in the system, we decided on ten categories.

1. School behavior: no unexcused absences, no tardiness, and no class infractions. (Coach Phillips to get a weekly report from teachers.)

2. Player appearance: practice gear worn neatly, locker clean.
3. Player promptness: on time to practice.
4. Help with equipment: players help to get equipment to and from practice field.
5. Quizzes: players to score at least 90% on skull session quizzes.
6. Hustle (conditioning and drills): players move through drills speedily and with enthusiasm.
7. Hustle (scrimmage): players move quickly before and after play is run and provide appropriate effort during play.
8. Penalties: players incur no more than one penalty per scrimmage (penalties are monitored by the scrimmage referee and recorded by a manger).
9. Team relationships: players refrain from criticizing one another and instead encourage each other.
10. Academics: players are rated as having performed adequately in weekly classroom report.

Some of these behavior categories are more difficult to judge than others. The promptness category is easy. The team relationships category takes an able manager to record instances of criticism and encouragement during practice. Helping with equipment is easy to define so that it can be observed reliably. Hustle is much more illusive. But, in our first discussion we had started out with categories such as pride and leadership. Those proved to be too illusive and they were discarded.

The system developed as follows. There are ten categories. A player earns ten points for appropriate performance in each category. On Wednesdays after practice, the coaches collect all the information from the previous week. This includes school reports, classroom reports, and the data collected by managers. The coaches have rated the players in the hustle and appearance categories (placing peer managers in this kind of judgmental role is difficult). All players who have won ten points in each of the ten categories are in the 100%'ers group for that week.

Being in the 100%'ers means three things. First, each 100%'er for the week gets a helmet decal. Second, each 100%'er is in the pool of players from which coaches choose a starting line-up for the week's game. Third, a non-starting player from the 100%'ers is chosen as bench captain for the week's game.

The same procedure is followed each week. If you are not a 100%'er you do not start! That does not mean that you don't play! It simply means that you do not get to be announced and run on the field as a member of the starting line-up.

All of the players who are in the 100%'ers for each week of the season earn a special award at the award's banquet (T-shirt, decal, certificate or some similar award). Coaches select one player from the seasonal 100%'ers to win the "100% trophy" which is emblematic of the player who gives the most for the team.

Eagle effort.
Jim Dawson coaches the Clinton Junior High School basketball team

in Columbus. He has good talent and has had good success. But, he felt that he still wasn't getting from his players the kind of practice effort he thought necessary for them to realize their full potential.

Jim was particularly concerned about the skill drills he used to open each practice, which included a series of lay-up drills and jump shooting drills. He also expressed concern about the team's free throw shooting during practice. Another factor which he wanted to improve was the degree of support and encouragement among teammates in the practice setting. The system we developed was to meet these specific needs.

Since Jim was playing several games a week, it was decided that the weekly "starting line-up" contingency used with the 100%'ers was not applicable. Instead, we decided on a point system and public recording on those points. As mentioned previously, simple public recording of behavior often creates a situation where an individual not only competes with a standard or his/her own previous performance, but also produces some peer competition.

Points were awarded for daily practice performance in lay-up drills, jump shooting drills, and free throw drills. Also, the coach awarded points for being a "team player" which meant that you encouraged your teammates during play and practice. In this system, points could be deducted from your total if the coach saw an instance of lack of hustle or an instance of a "bad attitude." Coach Dawson explained to his players what kinds of things might lose points in those categories, so that the players were well aware of what he considered to be lack of hustle or evidence of a bad attitude.

An "Eagle effort board" was posted in a conspicuous place in the main hall leading to the gymnasium. Students who earned a sufficient number of points were rewarded with an "Eagle effort" award at the post-season banquet.

The results thoroughly satisfied Jim Dawson. In practices before the system was implemented, Jim's players had been making 68% of their driving lay-ups in drills. After the system was implemented they made 80%. In jump-shooting, their performance improved from 37% to 51%. In free throw shooting, they improved from 59% to 67%. And, after implementation of the system, there were very few instances of lack of hustle or bad attitudes cited by the Coach.

But, the most dramatic improvement was in the "team player" category. Before implementation, four to six instances of criticism were detected during each practice session. Approximately ten to twelve instances of peer encouragement were detected. The management system "required" that players encourage one another in order to win their points. During the first practice session after implementation the managers recorded over eighty statements of encouragement among teammates and also reported that they probably didn't record more than one-third of what actually happened. There were simply too many supporting comments to monitor them all. Coach Dawson reports that for several days the supporting comments were "pretty phony." There was much laughter following comments and it all seemed pretty much "put on." But then a funny thing happened. The laughter slowly subsided. The boys got more comfortable saying nice things to one another. The comments got more genuine. At that point, according to Coach Dawson, the mood of his practices changed dramatically. He calls it the most amazing transformation he has seen in his coaching career. By the end of the season, says Jim, "we were more together than I ever could have imagined." Teachers would stop Jim and ask him, "What in the world is going on in your practices?" He could reply in all honesty, "We have started to really help each other."

Guidelines.

The examples of contingency management systems for athletic practices described herein barely scratch the surface of what can be done to improve the productivity of practices and also make them more enjoyable for coaches and athletes alike. The best contingency management systems are always the ones that are made up to fit the specific needs of a situation. You might get a general idea from one of the systems described here, but it will be better when you adapt it to fit your own needs. What follows are guidelines for developing your own practice management system (Rushall and Siedentop, 1972).

1. *Target behaviors must be defined in observable terms.* We have found no problem with things like lay-ups made, laps completed, or even supportive comments made to teammates. We have a great deal more problem when we try to work with a concept such as "hustle." Inevitably we arrive at a definition of hustle by listing all of the behaviors that contribute to it. Thus, more nebulous concepts such as hustle require lists of examples so that athletes know what they are supposed to do and observers can record whether it is being done.

2. *Target behaviors must be specified clearly.* It is crucial that you make clear to athletes exactly what is to be done; that is, it is not enough to say "I want you to hustle." You must specify how often or how much hustle you want. You can't say "work harder" but instead must specify what that means in terms of laps completed, miles run, or number of tackles made.

3. *Practice behavior must be monitored consistently.* Don't set up a system and then neglect the measurement. Your athletes will want to know how they are doing. So will you. Observers must be trained and they must practice. The more you have to observe the more observers you will need. We have had success training student managers to collect these kinds of data.

4. *State the contingency clearly.* You will know immediately when you violate this guideline — your athletes will tell you. If being eligible to start the next game is the reward, then athletes must know exactly what they have to do to earn that reward.

5. *Use the least intrusive reward system.* If your athletes are fairly well motivated already, what they need mostly is a systematic program to direct that motivation. If you coach these athletes, you won't need lots of external rewards. The less motivated your athletes are, the greater is the need for strong external rewards (such as T-shirts patches, trophies, etc.). Manage your rewards carefully. Don't use more than you need to get the job done.

6. *Think small.* When first trying to develop a practice management system, try a small system with limited target behaviors. You will learn

a lot. As your skills as a contingency manager grow, you will want to add to your system, but always in small increments so that you maintain proper control.

7. *Be consistent.* There is nothing that destroys a system more quickly than inconsistent application by the coach. If an athlete has to perform to a certain standard to earn a practice reward and you let him/her earn it because he/she got "close" to the standard, you undermine the system and do a disservice to the athlete. Don't think that you are helping an athlete by rewarding them for less than the standard calls for. If the system needs to be renegotiated because performance and/or behavioral standards are too high, then so be it. But once a system is in place, apply it consistently.

A final word.

Coaches spend too much time directing traffic at practice and keeping athletes on-task. Their usual way of keeping athletes on-task is to hassle them when they are off-task. When this happens often, and our data indicate clearly that it is the rule rather than the exception, the "climate" of practice becomes hostile and negative. That is no fun for anybody, coaches included. A primary benefit of a practice management system is that it produces a high on-task, positive climate. It is a framework within which relationships gradually change to supportive rather than coercive. One might even say that it humanizes the athletic setting! Try it, you'll like it!

REFERENCES

GIVNER, A., and GRAUBARD, P., A handbook of behavior modification for the classroom, New York: Holt, Rinehart and Winston, 1974.

KOMAKI, J. and BARNETT, F., A behavioral approach to coaching football: improving the play execution of the offensive backfield on a youth football team, Journal of Applied Behavior Analysis, 10, 1977, 657-664.

MC KENZIE, T., Effect of various reinforcing contingencies on behavior in a competitive swimming environment, unpublished Master's thesis, Dalhousie University, Halifax, Canada, 1972.

MC KENZIE, T. and RUSHALL, B., Effects of self-recording on attendance and performance in a competitive swimming training environment, Journal of Applied Behavior Analysis, 1974, 7, 199-206.

RUSHALL, B. and PETTINGER, J., An evaluation of the effect of various reinforcers used as motivators in swimming, Research Quarterly, 40, 1969, 540-545.

RUSHALL, B. and SIEDENTOP, D., The development and control of behavior in sport and physical education, Philadelphia: Lea & Febiger, 1972.

ROLIDER, A., Effects of modeling, instructions and incentives on peer encouragement in a competitive basketball setting, paper presented at Midwest Applied Behavior Analysis Convention, Chicago, May, 1978.

SIEDENTOP, D., Developing teaching skills in physical education, Boston: Houghton-Mifflin, 1976.

SIEDENTOP, D. and RIFE, F., Behavior management skills for physical education teachers, Proceedings, NCPEAM, 1977.

STEPHENS, T., Implementing behavioral approaches in elementary and secondary schools, Columbus: Chas. E. Merrill, 1975.

SULZER, B. and MAYER, R., Behavior modification procedures for school personnel, Boston: Houghton-Mifflin, 1977.

WILLIAMS, R. and ANANDAM, K., Cooperative classroom management, Columbus: Chas. E. Merrill, 1973.

Strategies for Motivating Young Athletes

Richard B. Alderman, Ph.D.
The University of Alberta

Motivating the young athlete involves far more than just yelling at him or patting him on the back; far more than just encouraging him with praise or punishing him with extra laps after practice. And with the young, amateur athlete, far more than just using *fear* as is done almost exclusively with professional athletes. It requires knowing what are the most important *factors* influencing the motivational levels in young people and it requires knowing *how* to put this knowledge to its best use.

Good coaches know, or sense, what is important in motivating young athletes and they know what are the most important techniques for doing it. Though such knowledge comes mainly from experience, invariably, upon examination, the things they do are also theoretically sound and consistent with the results from scientific research. It is our contention, in fact, that the gap between what the scientific or theoretical literature tells us and what *good* coaches do in practice is virtually non existent. The purpose of this section, therefore, is to examine some of the major factors operating in athletic motivation and to describe some of the important techniques or strategies that coaches can use in utilizing this information.

MAJOR RELEVANT PRINCIPLES: WHAT A COACH MUST KNOW

Motivation As An Interactional Process

Current thinking in the general psychological literature is now focused on viewing behavior as the result of an interaction between the *person* and the *situation* he finds himself in. Traditionally, the major view of why people behave the way they do rested upon the individual *per se:* namely, his personality, his needs, interests, motives, etc. were what determined his behavior, *regardless* of the situation. Considerable effort, over the years, went into establishing this view of personality as the prime determinant of behavior or that any kind of behavior (including motivated behavior) could be attributed solely to factors *within* the person. Such research, however, has tended to be equivocal (i.e., people behave differently in different situations) and has come under considerable criticism in recent years (e.g., Endler, 1973). Most of this criticism has come from adherents of the *situationist* viewpoint on behavior. Here the position taken is that situational factors or stimuli in the situation itself are the main determinants of behavior and that to understand why someone behaves the way they do simply requires a knowledge of the major properties of the situation itself (e.g., Bandura, 1971; Skinner, 1960 and Mischel, 1973). However, neither of these extreme viewpoints has been totally satisfactory, either from an intuitive standpoint or in terms of factual research data. This has led to a general acceptance of the *interactionism* stance which says that behavior is the result of an indispensable, continuous interaction between the person and the situations he encounters. And that an individual's behavior is not only strongly influenced by significant features of his situation, but also that he *chooses* the situations in which he performs and *selects* significant situational aspects which then serve as cues for his activities in these situations (Endler and Magnusson, 1976).

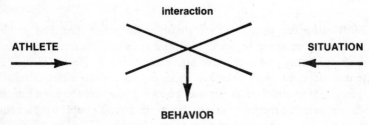

Diagram 1. *Interactional model.*

Without pursuing this more deeply, several pieces of information should be immediately evident to the coach:
1. Athletes are motivated by the situation itself as well as by what lies within them.
2. Athletes bring with them different, partially unique personalities to sports situation and these differentially interact with various features of the situation to produce different kinds of behavior.
3. Each sports situation will have different kinds of strong psychological stimuli operating and these will have a direct influence on how motivated the athlete is.
4. The coach is a part of the situation and as such interacts with the athlete's personality to influence the kinds of behaviors he engages in.
5. Competitive sport is an extremely powerful psychological situation and because of this, will be very influential in *determining* how an athlete behaves.

Therefore, when it comes to "motivating an athlete," coaches must realize, at the outset, that their efforts will always be partially dependent on exactly who the athlete is, what precise kind of situation in which the "motivating" takes place, and on what sort of interaction is operating between the person and the situation. For example, some athletes may be more motivated in competition than in training or practice (or vice versa) and this is probably due in the main to the different manner in which each athlete interacts with the different situations. It is no longer sufficient to just "know" your athletes or to just "know" your sport, you must also "know" how they interact with each other.

Situational Dimensions of Motivation

From the literature, both old and new, we know that situations can be described in two distinctly different ways: in *objective* terms covering the real or actual physical and social features of the environment or in *subjective* terms which focuses on how the individual perceives the significance of the situation. Martens (1975), for example, has done this in his analysis of competition as "a social process" (p. 68) and it is our contention that the same approach can and will be applied to situations involving motivated behavior. Though little actual research has yet been done on the dimensional analysis of sports situations, we do have several pieces of indirect information to help us in understanding the phenomena.

Purely objective stimuli in an actual situation can serve to motivate athletes. Physical stimuli such as the site or the facilities themselves act on an athlete, e.g. the shot and the circle to a shotputter or a swimming pool to a swimmer or a football stadium to a football player. Social stimuli such as the presence of spectators, other athletes, opponents, officials, etc. are objective, actual stimuli that contribute to increased arousal. On the task itself (and all the feedback an athlete receives from his performances) has the potential to motivate an athlete simply because it is a natural requirement in the situation. If you add to this a *subjective perception* of some of the powerful psychological stimuli existing in the situation, one can sense that some situations can heavily influence the motivational level of athletic individuals. Mischel (1973), for example, takes the position that individual differences in behavior are attributable to *specific response potentials* which are activated in specific situations. These response potentials activate into actual behavior because of the *opportunities* and *necessities* for that behavior in that situation. Nowhere is this more evident than in sports situations where we can sense that some athletes are more motivated than others because:

1. They differ in what they *know* they can do in the situation (e.g. veteran athletes may differ from novice athletes because their past experiences influence their perception of the situation).
2. They differ in how they perceive themselves and how they "label" the situation they're in.
3. They differ in their expectancies associated with specific stimuli in the situation and what response potential they have within themselves.
4. They differ in how they attach incentive value to the possible outcomes of the situation (e.g. some athletes are more motivated by a particular situation because they are attaching more incentive value to it than others).

Carron (1975) takes this one step further by observing that some sports situations are *so* powerful in their psychological effect that they can cause relatively the same kinds of behaviors in an athletic group. For example, he says that individual differences in competitiveness are reduced and heightened competitiveness is universally demonstrated when football players are put into one-on-one encounters during a practice. Thus, when a stimulus event is strong enough (either objectively and/or as the athlete perceives it), a direct influence on behavior results.

Coaches, therefore, must be aware that features of the practice, training, or competition environments themselves can strongly affect the athlete's level of motivation. In assessing why one athlete is motivated or not, he must also look to his understanding of situational factors for his answer.

Incentive Motivation In Young Athletes

Almost directly related to the situational dimensions of motivation is the stance taken by Alderman (1976) on *incentive motivation* in sport. Here the focus is on discovering what it is about the sport itself (particularly its nature and demands) that motivates a young athlete to persist in his participation. Incentive motivation simply refers to the incentive value a young athlete attaches to the possible outcomes or experiences he perceives as being available to him in a particular sport. If a boy or girl perceives that particular kinds of experiences are available to them in a sport, and they feel these will be pleasant, enjoyable, or satisfying to them, then they will elect to participate in that sport rather than another. If, in addition, their expectancies are confirmed from actual experiences, then they will persist in that sport and their level of motivation will remain high. If, on the other hand, their expectancies are not confirmed, or the experiences are negative, they will quit or choose another sport. It is a simple stance: namely, if young athletes get what they are seeking in a sport, then they'll be motivated to continue in that sport.

The major research thrust in this area has, therefore, been directed toward identifying the major kinds of experiences or goals that sport provides young participants and toward assessing their relative strength to each other. Initially, the theoretical model used was one by Birch and Veroff (1966) where seven major motive-incentive systems were outlined as being the main, recurrent types of goal directed behavior in human beings. These were identified as sensory, curiosity, achievement, aggression, affiliation, power, and independence type behaviors. Subsequently, this model was modified specific to sport and resulted in again seven but slightly different motive-incentive systems: namely, affiliation, success, excellence, aggression, stress, power, and independence. Initial pilot research on young athletes, ages 11-18, in the main, has indicated some amazingly consistent trends.

Each motive-incentive system (Diagram 2) is characterized by the major kinds of experiences the athlete sees as being available and important to him or her. *Affiliation* incentives are seen as revolving around opportunities for social intercourse, or being socially reassured that one is acceptable or worthwhile by the making of friends or the maintenance of already existing friendships; *power* incentives are characterized by opportunities to influence and control other people, particularly their attitudes, interests, and opinions; *independence* incentives revolve around opportunities to do things on one's own without the help of other people; *stress* incentives focus on the excitement, tension, pressure, and pure action sport can provide; *excellence* incentives are characterized by opportunities to do something very well for its own sake or do it better than anyone else; *success* incentives, on the other hand, are seen as being attached to the extrinsic rewards sport can provide, e.g. social approval, recognition, status, prestige, etc.; *aggression* incentives are seen as opportunities to subdue, intimidate, dominate, or even injure other people. It is hypothesized that these are the major goals which athletes seek in sport and that they are not necessarily independent of each other, but probably amalgamate in various mixtures.

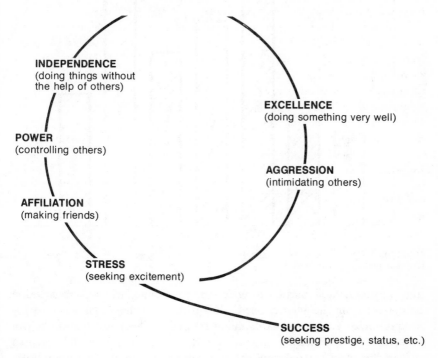

Diagram 2. *Major incentive systems in sport. From: Alderman and Wood, 1976.*

To date, enough data has been gathered on this viewpoint (i.e. using an inventory on several thousand athletes) to give two or three strong indications which might be valuable for coaches:

1. The two strongest and most consistent incentive conditions for young athletes are affiliation and excellence (see Diagram 3).
2. Stress incentives run a consistent third.
3. Aggression and independence incentives consistently lack any strength, even in the individual and physical contact sports.
4. Children are basically motivated by the same incentives *regardless* of their age, sport, sex, or culture.

The data, then, show strong implications for coaches in that a sports situation must be kept very social in nature and that each athlete have not only the opportunity to become excellent, but also that he or she be constantly encouraged for their own personal level of competence. It also shows (over the limited range studied) that incentive motivation stays basically the same from year to year and from sport to sport.

Extrinsic and Intrinsic Motivation

An athlete can be said to be *intrinsically motivated* when, for all intents

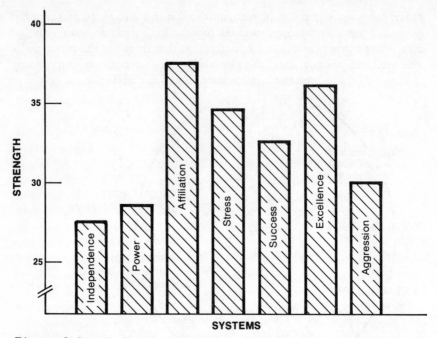

Diagram 3. *Strength of incentive systems for young hockey players (N = 425). From: Alderman and Wood, 1976.*

and purposes, he is participating for the pure enjoyment and satisfaction he derives from the activity itself. If, on the other hand, he is competing because *other* goals or rewards might result from his performance, he can be said to be *extrinsically* motivated. It is, therefore, generally accepted that in real life a person's motivation is a function or combination of both. It is reasonable, in fact, to make the assumption that when the child makes the transition from the "pure" play of childhood to the more formal, rigid, and institutionalized milieu of organized sport, he or she comes under the control of extrinsic reinforcers, i.e., it is almost impossible for them *not* to become extrinsically motivated. That is, the scope of extrinsic rewards is so extensive (ranging from materialistic forms such as trophies, jackets, crests, and prizes to such social forms as approval, recognition, prestige, and status) that is almost *natural* for a child in western society to become motivated by them. In the minds of some people (e.g. Harris 1977, Sage 1977) this is a serious problem; that we are replacing intrinsic motivation with extrinsic motivation and sooner or later children are forced to quit sport when the rewards are no longer forthcoming. For other people (e.g. Ross 1976, Siedentop and Ramey 1977), however, the problem is not only confused by biased interpretations of data, but also that there is some reason to believe that intrinsic motivation can actually be enhanced by extrinsic rewards which are made contingent upon the *quality* of one's performance.

Regardless, however, of the theoretical niceties of this controversy, there are pieces of information coming out of this issue which have direct, practical relevance for the coach:

1. If an athlete feels he is intrinsicallly motivated, then he is probably

perceiving himself as being in control of or as the cause of his own behavior or destiny. His satisfaction is derived from the activity itself because he has a "need" to feel a sense of personal control over his actions. Coaches must encourage their athletes to have this feeling because when they train or practice by themselves (or when external rewards are not forthcoming), they will persist in their endeavors without the help or encouragement of others (adapted from deCharms 1968).

2. One would think that intrinsic and extrinsic motivation would combine additively to increase total motivation. That is, if an athlete is already intrinsically motivated (i.e. he is participating for the pure enjoyment), then additional extrinsic rewards would make him *even more* motivated. This is probably not the case. Rather what happens is that they interact, i.e., the introduction of extrinsic rewards may decrease motivation because they decrease the *perception* of intrinsic motivation or, conversely, motivation may be increased when a reward is withheld (Calder and Staw 1975). Coaches must be careful when they introduce extrinsic rewards for athletic performance because they may cause the athlete to think he is performing primarily to obtain those rewards.

3. A major characteristic of intrinsically motivated behavior (Deci 1975) is the sense of personal control an athlete seeks over his athletic environment. This is said to occur when the athlete intends for something to happen, whether caused directly by himself or by the environment. Coaches must realize that, for many young athletes, sport provides them with opportunities to test themselves and that when such experiences are worthy challenges to their personal abilities, positive outcomes occur. The pursuit of personal excellence should therefore become the major goal-directed activity of young athletes and strongly encouraged by their coaches.

4. If extrinsic rewards are made contingent upon *personal improvement* and not merely on participation, then intrinsic motivation may be enhanced. This, it is hoped (Gerson 1977), will motivate the youngster into continuing his participation in sport because it enhances his own self-concept and provides him with important information about his own level of ability. In this sense then, extrinsic rewards can be used to enhance intrinsic motivation.

Motivation and Positive Reinforcement

In partial contrast to the preceding emphasis on the importance of developing and encouraging intrinsic motivation in young athletes is the position taken by most operant psychologists on the relationship between reinforcement and motivation in sport. It is their basic contention (e.g. Rushall and Siedentop 1972) that motivation in sport is nothing more than the mere "...act of working for reinforcement" and has virtually nothing to do with such things as needs, drives, or instincts. They maintain that motivated behavior is the relationship between behavior and the reinforcing properties of the consequences of that behavior. In simple terms this means that an athlete is motivated or not motivated by what sort of effect occurs following a behavior or a performance he engages in. If the effect is positive, the behavior which caused it will likely occur again; if the effect is negative, then the behavior will be less likely to occur on subsequent occasions. The coach thus becomes a "mediator" of the outcomes of his athlete's behaviors in that he must attempt to control the reinforcing aspects of the sports situation (called reinforcement contingencies) so that desirable/productive behaviors are repeated and undesirable/non-productive behaviors disappear.

The athlete is thus seen as constantly working for or toward some sort of positive reinforcement. This reinforcement occurs when a positive reinforcer appears (or is inserted) when a good behavior occurs. Though there are intrinsic motivation connotations here (i.e. a good feeling following a successful performance is seen as a positive reinforcer), most of the behavior modification approach leans heavily on extrinsic motivators, particularly social reinforcers such as praise, encouragement, approval, and recognition.

We *reward* athletes, but *reinforce* their behavior (Dickinson, 1977). When we give an outstanding athlete a trophy or a medal, we are rewarding him for some season-long or game-long, general demonstration of performance. When we praise him or pat him on the back, however, we are attempting to reinforce some specific behavior he's just engaged in. This is an important distinction for actual coaching. Whenever an athlete does something correct, desirable, or productive, his or her coach must be "Johnny-on-the-spot" with some sort of positive reinforcement. Why? Because the athlete must "make the connection" with what he did to get that reinforcement. He must, either consciously or subconsciously, link up the good behavior (or performance) with the presentation of the positive reinforcement. If he does, then on subsequent occasions he will remember that "good" things happen if he does "such and such" and he will automatically do them. When this starts to occur frequently, we say the athlete has become "conditioned" or in a more general sense, we have *modified* his behavior.

Coaches, therefore, must realize the following if they are to effectively modify the behavior of their athletes:

1. Reinforcement must be made *contiguous* to the behavior it's being used for. It is relatively useless to reinforce a "game" behavior in practice the following week. The coach must reinforce a good behavior the instant it occurs and in the exact environment in which it occurs. You pat him on the back when he comes off the floor, field, or ice.

2. Reinforcement must be *clear* and *specific*. The athlete must know *exactly* which of his previous behaviors is being reinforced and why. For example, you don't say ". . .that was good rebounding"; you say ". . . very good! that's exactly how we want you to block out your check!"

3. Reinforcement must be *continuous* when the youngster is *learning* a behavior or a skill, but *intermittent* once he has acquired it. You don't pat a football player on the back everytime he makes a good tackle or a block; you do it only every once in awhile. If you do it all the time, you will gradually extinguish the strength of the reinforcement.

4. Positive reinforcement of *undesirable* or *non-productive* behaviors must be reduced or eliminated. Consistent "bad" behaviors exist only because, somehow or somewhere, the individual is receiving positive reinforcement for them. The coach must seek out these sources and eliminate them, e.g. "clowning" occurs consistently in an athlete because his teammates laugh at him every time he performs.

5. *Punishment* (sometimes called "negative reinforcement") should be avoided if possible because it tends only to temporarily suppress bad behavior, not eliminate it. Why? Well, in order to be effective, punishment usually has to be: A) severe enough to affect a behavior, and B) always presented when the bad behavior occurs. If punishment is the only alternative available to a coach, then he should:

    A. Punish only relatively unimportant or "new" behaviors.

    B. Always present the alternative good behavior to the athlete when he is punished, i.e., "don't do that, do this!"

This, then, is some of what we know about motivation in young athletes. Though it is not all we know, it does, however, provide us with enough information to suggest *how* we can better motivate our athletes.

MOTIVATIONAL STRATEGIES: *HOW* A COACH CAN MOTIVATE THE YOUNG ATHLETE

Know Your Athletes

Each youngster brings a different background of experiences to the situation with him or her. He or she will be coming from a family that is particularly unique to them and because of this, each of them will have partially different attitudes and opinions toward events and people in the sports environment and each will have different interests and desires in what is happening to them. The coach must face this incredible problem of differences between individuals and interact with them on a purely personal basis. In simple terms: what motivates one boy or girl, does not necessarily motivate another. In order to effectively coach each individual therefore requires a reasonably good understanding of each person's psychological structure or personality.

Though psychological evaluation via personality inventory assessment can aid the coach in handling this problem, by far the best method is in his indirect and direct interactions with the athlete. By closely watching his behavior over a period of time and by asking him how he feels about things or what opinions, attitudes, and interests he has, a coach can easily gain considerably invaluable information about a boy or girl. All a coach has to do to elicit such personal information from a youngster is: (Truax and Carkhuff 1967)

1. Be authentic, non-defensive, and genuine in your interactions with the athlete.
2. Give personal regard without attaching any conditions to it.
3. Be non-possessive in your warmth.
4. Show you have some idea as to how the youngster feels (i.e. accurate empathy).

Knowing one's athletes through good personal communications with them, permits a coach to "individualize" his handling of each athlete. It enables him to:

1. Discover what it is about the sport itself that *attracts* the youngster, i.e. what major incentives are salient for the child, and then make sure they are available to him or her.
2. Discover what it is about the sport itself that *repels* the youngster, i.e.

pain, fear of injury, boredom, lack of success, etc., and then ensure these things are minimized.

Control the Sports Environment

Three major kinds of experiences are important for most, if not all, athletes. The opportunity to pursue *excellence,* the opportunity to belong to and be accepted by a relevant social group (i.e. *affiliation),* and the opportunity for excitement, action, and *stress.* This tells us three important things about how a sports environment should be structured.

First, is the importance of each athlete having the opportunity to improve his or her own personal skill level. From our research on several thousand young athletes (e.g. Alderman 1976), it is obvious that young athletes place far more importance on *being really good* at something than on winning or the status and prestige that goes along with it. Many coaches mistakenly think that youngsters are totally wrapped up in winning but they're not. They are, however, strongly concerned with getting better in their sport and if the extrinsic rewards of success accompany this excellence, it's alright but not crucial. The sports milieu is a highly *task-oriented* one and because of this, the youngsters who persist within it are highly focused on the excellence of their task execution. Every attempt to reinforce or encourage attempts to acquire further skill should be made by the coach and constant flow of information and expertise to the athlete should exist. Structuring the environment, especially the practice and training situations, so that *every* athlete on the team significantly improves in skill will substantially contribute to their levels of motivation.

Second is the importance of creating a friendly, warm, social atmosphere around the team. Young athletes in particular are constantly seeking assurance of their own worthwhileness and because this can be achieved by the acceptance of them from their teammates and coach, the environment must be one that makes this possible. Athletes, like other people, basically fear *social isolation* and/or *social rejection* and they perceive membership in a visible social group, such as an athletic team, as being a justification of their own personal self worth. Affiliation incentives, as they apply to sports involvement, in fact, are as important as excellence incentives and if efficiently managed by the coach, can contribute not only to better individual motivation, but team spirit and pride as well.

Third is the salience of *stress* and/or *arousal* incentives in the sports environment. Athletes, particularly young ones, do not participate in sport because it's humdrum, boring, or monotonous. They want to be stimulated, both physically and mentally. Variety, novelty, uncertainty, and complexity in the environmental stimuli thus become imperative to keep the arousal of athletes at a high level. Practice, training, and competition situations must be carefully managed by the coach to provide lots of action, interest, and excitement. The normal life patterns of young athletes are fairly rigid, stable, and predictable and one of their major drives in sport thus becomes an attempt to avoid such outcomes. They are, in a sense, "stress seekers" and coaches can easily make available such opportunities.

In this connection, we also know that athletes become more motivated when the sports environment is cleanly and neatly organized. When *all* their time is spent in productive activity, with clearly defined and attainable goals, they don't have the opportunity to become disinterested or lazy. Most coaches know this and pre-organize their practices down to the last second.

Consensus and Commitment

Probably the single, most exciting technique for motivating athletes in recent years is that of *shared responsibility* and/or *collaborative goal setting*. Though quite simple and straightforward as a motivational "technique", the rationale underlying this approach breaks with tradition too much to be overly popular with old time style coaches. The basic rationale is simply that by sitting down and thoroughly discussing goals and objectives with the team and by coming to some group consensus or agreement on who is going to share the responsibility for the group decisions which will be made during the season, one cannot only increase individual *awareness* of the goals, but also substantially increase individual *commitment* to them (Botterill 1976). The main assumption is that when an individual is involved, or directly participates, in a group decision making process, there is a direct increase in his sensed commitment to the decisions. Increased commitment leads to better motivation on the part of the athlete.

People do not always do what they say they will do. Usually the difference between such intentions and actual behavior is dependent upon how committed the person is to those intentions. How then can we increase a person's commitment? Well, basically we can achieve this by:

1. Having the person state his intentions in public or in full view of his teammates and coach.
2. Shaping the situation in such a way that his intentions are made freely.
3. Having him state his goals in specific and explicit terms.
4. Remitting group discussion and group consensus on the important goals for each member of the team, i.e. group collaboration.
5. Increasing the individual's self responsibility for the decisions he makes.

Botterill (1976) suggests a simple strategy whereby a coach can directly involve his athletes in collaborative goal setting and thereby influence them into a kind of ". . . psychological contracting" with themselves. This process follows a simple progression:

1. Team meetings before the season starts to identify, define, and state all the various goals and intentions which the team deems important.
2. A subtle direction or guiding by the coach so that all major goal areas are covered.
3. Time for the athletes to think about the process.
4. A statement of goals or objectives in specific, measurable, and actual behavioral terms.
5. Group discussion followed by agreement or consensus by the team on all the goals.
6. Recording of the intentions so that people can be reminded later on their stated intentions.
7. Use of a democratic but task-oriented style of leadership on the part of the coach.

Team members must:

(a) feel free to contribute to the discussion.

(b) recognize the rights of the majority.

(c) be aware of how much commitment is necessary to attain their goals.

And the coach must:

(a) express (and feel) confidence in the group.

(b) direct people to state realistic, attainable goals.

(c) express his dedication to the agreed upon goals.

8. Discussion of and agreement of the controls which will be used to make goal attainment possible.

SUMMARY

To motivate the young athlete coaches must keep in mind two major principles: 1) their motivational structures are partially unique to them as individuals, and 2) the sports environment has within it the potential to either motivate them or turn them off. This means each coach must *know* his athletes very well (i.e. their interests, desires, attitudes, and opinions, etc.) and be able to detect what it is about the environment itself that is important for the individual and control it so that good things happen. When the *interaction* between the athlete and his environment (which includes the coach) is harmonious, good behavior and superlative performance results. When the interaction is discordant, the reverse occurs.

Various strategies for motivating the individual and controlling his environment are available to the coach in not only the psychological literature, but from his common sense as well. However, the major thrust is and always has been an appreciation or empathy for the athlete in what he or she is trying to accomplish. When the coach can fit his own desires to those of his athletes, success for both will be the result.

REFERENCES

ALDERMAN, R. B. Incentive Motivation in Sport: An Interpretive Speculation of Research Opportunities. In *Psychology of Sport*. Fisher, C. (ed.) Palo Alto: Mayfield Pub. Co. 1976.

ALDERMAN, R.B. and WOOD, N. L. "An analysis of incentive motivation in young Canadian athletes" *Canadian Journal of Applied Sports Sciences,* June 1976, 1, 2, 169-176.

BANDURA, A. *Social Learning Theory.* New York: General Learning Press. 1971.

BIRCH, D. and VEROFF, J. *Motivation: A Study of Action.* Belmont, Calif.: Brooks/Cole. 1966.

BOTTERILL, C. "How to improve commitment: A theory of motivation", *Coaching Association of Canada Bulletin 15,* 1976, 6-8.

CALDER, B. J. and STAW, B. M. "Self-perception of intrinsic and extrinsic motivation", *Journal of Personality and Social Psychology,* 1975, 31, 4, 599-605.

CARRON, A. V. "Personality and athletics: A review". In *Status of Psychomotor Learning and Sport Psychology Research,* Rushall, B. S. (ed.) Nova Scotia: Sports Sciences Associates, 1975.

DE CHARMS, R. *Personal Causation: The Internal Affective Determinants of Behavior.* New York: Academic Press. 1968.

DECI, E. L. *Intrinsic Motivation.* New York: Plenum Press. 1975.

DICKINSON, J. *A Behavioural Analysis of Sport.* Princeton, N. J.: Princeton Book Co. 1977.

ENDLER, N. S. "The person versus the situation — a pseudo issue" *Journal of Personality,* 1973, 41, 287-303.

ENDLER, N. S. and MAGNUSSON, D. (eds.) *Interactional Psychology and Personality*. New York: Hemisphere Pub. Corp. 1976.

GERSON, R. "Redesigning athletic competition for children", *Motor Skills: Theory Into Practice*, 1977, 2, 1, 3-14.

HARRIS, D. *Intrinsic Motivation With Implications for Sport*. Paper presented at the NCPEAM-NAPECW Convention, Orlando, Florida, January 1977.

MARTENS, R. *Social Psychology and Physical Activity*. New York: Harper and Row. 1975.

MISCHEL, W. "Toward a cognitive social learning reconceptualization of personality", *Psychological Review*, 1973, 80, 252-283.

ROSS, M. "The self-perception of intrinsic motivation", In Ickes, H. and Kidd, R. (eds.) *New Directions in Attribution Research*. (Vol. 1) Hillsdale, N. J.: LEA Publishers. 1976.

SAGE, G. *Introduction to Motor Behavior: A Neuropsychological Approach*. 2nd ed. Reading: Addison-Wesley. 1977.

SIEDENTOP, D. and RAMEY, G. "Extrinsic rewards and intrinsic motivation", *Motor Skills: Theory Into Practice*, 1977, 2, 1, 49-62.

SKINNER, B. F. "Pigeons in a pelican", *American Psychologist*, 1960, 15, 28-37.

TRUAX, C. B. and CARKHUFF, R. R. *Toward Effective Counselling and Psychotherapy*. Chicago: Aldine Pub. Co. 1967.

The Dynamics of Athletic Persistence

Mary E. Duquin, Ph.D.
University of Pittsburgh

Successful coaches, like successful athletes, often play the role of naive psychologist employing creative applications of psychological theories of which they may not be consciously aware. Indeed, although some theories are deduced from first principles, many are induced from empirical observations of what works or is successful in the field. As the interactions between the sport professional and the researcher in psychology increase, both the practitioner and the theoretician gain from the expertise of the other. While the researcher may be enlightened as to how theories tested in the lab actually operate in real world settings, the sport practitioner becomes better able to label, organize and implement the psychological principles which influence successful athletic performance.

One factor which both coaches and athletes are aware influence championship development is the quality of persistence. Athletes with this quality are variously described as possessing a kind of stick-to-itiveness; of being tenacious, enduring, perservering. Persistence, then, can be viewed from the perspective of a personality characteristic inherent in the successful athlete. Social psychology has, however, over the years, made a theoretical shift from an emphasis on static personality characteristics to an increased emphasis on the importance of the interaction between cognitive processes and situational factors in influencing behavior. This shift in research perspective has produced a wealth of information which can aid the sport practitioner in facilitating desirable behaviors heretofore thought to be constrained by an individual's personality traits.

Drawing mainly from social psychology research in the areas of group dynamics and attribution theory, the following six propositions on persistence are advanced:

Proposition #1:   *Persistence in sport is promoted when the athlete is process oriented.*

Process motivation is more likely to lead to consistent behavior than product motivation because the continued participation of the athlete is not unduly dependent upon an objectively successful outcome. That is, the athlete so enjoys the process of participation that the absence of extrinsic rewards such as trophies, ribbons, or medals does not overly affect his/her motivation to participate in the athletic endeavor. Persistence, then, can be seen to be a function of process motivation. Coaches can, however, nurture this important process orientation in their athletes. One way of fostering a process motivation is to increase the athlete's awareness of the athletic process itself and to allow for the fulfillment of athlete's personal motives. An athlete aware of the functions and effects of the athletic process (e.g. training, diet) is more likely to find within that process factors which are personally rewarding. The athletic process, when conducted by a knowledgeable coach, can allow for the fulfillment of such personal motives as: tension release, the maintenance of health-fitness, the desire for thrill and risk, the chance for competition, aesthetic and asetic experiences, and the opportunity to develop physical efficacy. [4, 14] The strength of any one motive as well as the number of motives propelling the athlete's involvement are likely to have a positive effect on the athlete's persistence.

Proposition #2:   *Persistence in sport is promoted if the group atmosphere in which the activity takes place is perceived by the athlete to be socially supportive.*

The group atmosphere or perceived climate of an environment is related to the athlete's self esteem, satisfaction, and personal growth. [17, 18] Both work effectiveness and job retention are correlated with the extent to which individuals perceive their work environments to be supportive. [9] Thus, persistence in an activity is partially a function of the quality of the environment in which the athlete functions. [3] There are three important dimensions to consider when assessing the group environment. First, the relationship dimension concerns the nature and intensity of the group's interactions and the extent to which members help and support each other.

Within this dimension an athlete's persistence will be related to such factors as the athlete's degree of involvement in the group, institutional spirit, group cohesiveness and the quality of the coach-athlete relationship. [2, 15]

1. **Relationship dimension**
   a. Involvement
   b. Staff support/managerial support
   c. Peer cohesion
   d. Affiliation
   e. Institutional esprit
   f. Expressivity/Spontaneity

2. **Personal development dimension**
   a. Autonomy/independence/responsibility
   b. Personal status
   c. Practical orientation/task orientation
   d. Competition/challenge
   e. Self-expression/self-discovery
   f. Performance self/group

3. **System maintenance and system change dimension**
   a. Order/organization/structure
   b. Control
   c. Clarity of goals and methodology
   d. Physical comfort
   e. Work pressure
   f. Innovation-athlete influence

Table 1. *Dimensions of organizational climate in sports groups (adapted from Insel and Moos, 1974).*

The personal development dimension concerns the athletes' opportunity for personal growth and development of self-esteem. Examples of factors important to assess in this dimension include the degree to which the environment offers the athlete an opportunity for status, challenge, responsibility, self discovery and evaluation. Finally the dimension of system maintenance and system change concerns the extent to which the athletic environment is clear in its expectations, maintains control and is responsive to change. Within this dimension the coach must consider such factors as the degree to which the order and structure of the organization supports the group's goals, the ability of the organization to cumulate input from its members, and the success of the organization in implementing changes in its system.[12] Although the ideal athletic environment may vary depending upon the age and competitive level of the athletes, certain broad statements can be made about supportive environments. Generally an optimum environment would be characterized as "seeking continuity, variety, orderly and purposeful growth" as opposed to an environment that "magnifies authoritarian power and minimizes or destroys human initiative, self-direction, and self-government (19p-221)."

Proposition #3:   *Persistence in sport will be likely if the product of the athlete's activity is, in the majority of cases, successful.*

Success breeds continued participation. The importance of success is especially crucial to the young athlete who has yet to build a strong self confidence and stable history of positive reinforcement for athletic endeavors. Continued failure then is more likely to negatively affect the younger athlete's persistence. Athletic persistence can be promoted if the coach monitors both the progression of skill training and the caliber of the competition against which the athletes are matched.[7] As skill level increases the level of competitiveness is found to be highest when the probability of success approximates 50%.

Proposition #4:   *Persistence in sport will be likely if success in that activity is attributed by the athlete to internal factors.*

Although it may be ego building to hear that an athlete "owes it all to the coach", successful coaches realize the importance of athletes taking responsibility for their own success.[21] Attribution theory states that greater pride is felt when we attribute success to ourselves (via our effort or ability) than if we attribute our success to external factors such as luck, our opponents poor ability, or our coach. Athletes are more likely to persist in an activity in which they feel pride and responsibility for their successful outcomes. Of the two internal attributes, ability and effort, the use of the stable ability attribute is more likely to lead the athlete to predict future success. Athletes, however, often make more use of the unstable effort attribute.[10, 13, 20] The frequent use of the effort attribute may be explained by the fact that although unstable, it is categorized as an "intentional" attribute (i.e. "I am responsible for exerting effort in each competition in order to achieve success"). The ability attribute, on the other hand, (like IQ in an academic setting) is categorized as an "unintentional" attribute for which the athlete is not really responsible. The fact that society tends to reward more for achieved (intentional) status than ascribed (unintentional) status may encourage the more public use of the effort attribute. However, persistence is more likely with athletes who have a strong personal belief in their own ability, for without that belief, persistence may be viewed as a "waste of effort." The coach's role in guiding attributions is most important. In young athletes especially, the coach's confidence in the natural ability or potential of the athlete often precedes and stimulates the athlete's own private self-confidence.[6]

Proposition #5:   *Persistence in sport will be likely if the unsuccessful product of the athlete's activity is defined, in the majority of cases, as subjectively profitable.*

An unsuccessful athletic encounter whether defined objectively as a loss to an opponent or subjectively as a poor performance regardless of objective outcome, is an inevitable experience in athletic participation. Athletic persistence can be jeopardized if steps are not taken to interpret unsuccessful outcomes in a positive manner.

If the probability of success of an athletic performance is extremely low, athletes and coaches should set their own challenging but achievable goals to accomplish within the athletic encounter. After the competition, unsuccessful athletic encounters may be made subjectively profitable in the following ways:

1. If, before the event, the probability of success was low and the outcome was unsuccessful, assessments can be made as to what characteristics or attributes, other than ability, were influential in contributing to the opponents success (e.g. training or coaching techniques).
2. If, before the event, the probability of success was high and the outcome was unsuccessful, athletes and coaches should assess what new information the results of the competition supplied as to the ability level and related characteristics of the successful opponent. An analysis of one's own effort and play in the competition should also be conducted.
3. If before the event, the probability of failure and the probability of success were approximately equal and the outcome was unsuccessful, athletes and coaches should gain information by analyzing what process variables resulted in the failure. Given the match on ability, what unstable factors were responsible for the loss?

Proposition #6:   *Persistence in sport will be likely if failure is attributed by the athlete to unstable factors.*

The use of attribution theory offers predictions as to what kinds of attributions are likely to lead to athletic persistence. [11, 23] After a failure, expectations for future success are likely to be low if the cause of the failure is attributed to such stable factors as lack of ability or task difficulty.[16] With low expectations for future success, the prediction for persistence in activity is also low. But, if failure is attributed to an unstable factor such as bad luck, lack of effort, or injuries, then expectations for the future are likely to be more optimistic, for luck changes, effort can be increased and injuries heal.[22]   Often the most ego enhancing attributional pattern to employ is one in which individuals take credit for their successes while attributing failure to some external factors for which they are not responsible. However, achievement oriented individuals have been found to make internal attributions for both success and failure, that is, they attribute success to their ability and effort and attribute failure to their own lack of effort. [1, 24, 25] This attributional pattern for failure, although generally producing a greater sense of shame as a result of taking responsibility for the failure, is likely to lead to preparations for an increased level of effort in the next encounter.[26] Thus, athletes with a strong belief in the efficacy of their behaviors in influencing their athletic success and failure are likely to exhibit persistence in athletes.

CONCLUSIONS

Athletic persistence is a result of the athlete's attitude toward the consequences of persistent behavior and the normative beliefs regarding the value of persistent behavior in sport.[8] Factors which may determine whether an athlete has a positive attitude toward persistence in sport include the probability that the consequences of persistent behavior will result in athletic success, social support, personal pride and the fulfillment of personal motives. The probability of each of these consequences of persistence and the degree to which the athlete values each of these outcomes determines the athlete's personal attitude toward persistence. Along with the athlete's own attitude, persistence is affected by normative beliefs regarding the value of persistence in sports and the strength of the athlete's motive to comply with these normative beliefs.[5]

In order to facilitate persistence in sport, coaches should be aware of those factors influencing the dynamics of athletic persistence. These factors include: the athlete's level of process orientation, the social support of the athletic environment, the athlete's ability to profit from unsuccessful outcomes, and the kinds of attributions made by the athlete and coach for failure and success in sports.

REFERENCES

1. Bar-Tal, D., & Frieze, I. H. Achievement motivation for males and females as a determinant of attributions for success and failure. *Sex Roles,* in press.
2. Coakley, J. J. *Sport in society.* Saint Louis: The C. V. Mosby Company, 1978.
3. Duquin, M. Institutional sanction for girl's sport program. *Psychology of Sport and Motor Behavior II.* D. Landers (Ed.). Penn State HPER Series No. 10, 1975.
4. Duquin, M. Sport participation: In pursuit of psychological androgyny. *Mouvement: Actes du 7 Symposium Canadien en Apprentissage Psychologie du Sport.* J. Salmela (Ed.). L'Association des Professionels de l'Activite Physique du Quebec. 1975.
5. Duquin, M. Differential sex role socialization toward amplitude appropriation. *Research Quarterly,* 1977.
6. Duquin, M. Attributions Made by Children in Coeducation Sports Settings. *Psychology of Motor Behavior and Sports.* Human Kinetics Publishers. 1978.
7. Feather, N. T. Effects of prior success and failure on expectations of success and subsequent performance. *Journal of Personality and Social Psychology,* 1966, *3,* 287-298.
8. Fishbein, M. & Ajzen, I. *Belief, attitude, intention and behavior.* Addison-Wesley Publishing, Reading, Massachusetts, 1975.

9. Friedlander, F. & Greenberg, S. Effects of job attitudes, training, and organization climate on performance of the hard-core unemployed. *Journal of Applied Psychology*, 1971, 55, 287-295.

10. Frieze, I.H., McHugh, & Duquin, M. *Causal attributions for women and men and sports participation.* Paper presented at the annual meeting of the American Psychological Association, Washington, D.C., 1976.

11. Frieze, I., & Weiner, B. Cue utilization and attribution judgments for success and failure. *Journal of Personality*, 1971, *39*, 591-606.

12. Insel, P. M. & Moos, R. H. Psychological environments. *American Psychologist*, 1974, 179-188.

13. Iso-Ahola, S. A test of the attribution theory of success and failure with Little League Baseball players. *Mouvement. Actes du 7 symposium en apprentissage psych-moteur et psychologie du sport.* de l'Association des professionnels de l'activite physique du Quebec. Octobre, 1975.

14. Kenyon, G. S. Attitude toward sport and physical activity among adolescents from four English speaking countries: In G. Luschen (Ed.) *The Cross-cultured analysis of sport and games.* Champaign, Illinois: Stiples Publishing Company, 1970, pp. 138-155.

15. Loy, J. W., McPherson, B. D., & Kenyon, G. *Sport and social systems.* Reading, Massachusetts: Addison-Wesley Publishing Company, 1978.

16. McMahan, S. D. Relationships between causal attributions and expectancy of success. *Journal of Personality and Social Psychology*, 1973, *28*, 108-114.

17. Moos, R., & Humphrey, B. *Group Environment Scale technical report.* Palo Alto, Calif.: Social Ecology Laboratory, Department of Psychiatry, Stanford University, 1973.

18. Moos, R., & Insel, P. (Eds.) *Issues in social ecology: Human milieus.* Palo Alto, Calif.: National Press, 1974.

19. Mumford, L. *The urban prospect.* New York: Harcourt Brace Jovanovich, 1968.

20. Roberts, G. Win-loss casual attributions of Little League Players. *Mouvement. Actes du 7 symposium en apprentissage psycho-moteur et psychologie du sport.* de l'Association des professionnels de l'activite physique du Quebec. Octobre, 1975.

21. Rotter, J. P.: Generalized expectancies for internal versus external control of reinforcement. *Psychological Monographs*, 80, 1. 1966.

22. Valle, V. A., & Frieze, I. H. The stability of causal attributions as a mediator in changing expectations for success. *Journal of Personality and Social Psychology*, 1976, 33, 579-587.

23. Weiner, B., I. Frieze, A. Kukla, L. Reed, S. Rest and R. M. Rosenbaum: *Perceiving the Causes of Success and Failure.* New York, General Learning Press, 1971.

24. Weiner, B., H. Heckhausen, W. Meyer and R. E. Cook: Causal ascriptions and achievement behavior: Conceptual analysis of effort and reanalysis of locus of control. *J. Personality and Social Psychol.*, 21, 239, 1972.

25. Weiner, B. and A. Kukla: An attributional analysis of achievement motivation. *J. Personality and Social Psychol.*, 15, 1, 1970.

26. Zander, A., Fuller, R., & Armstrong, W. Attributed pride and shame in group and self. *Journal of Personality and Social Psychology.* 1972. 23, 346-352.

Intrinsic Motivation in Sport

Wayne Halliwell, Ph.D.
University of Montreal

In recent years, psychologists have provided substantial evidence which indicates that a person's intrinsic interest in an activity may be decreased by inducing him to engage in that activity as an explicit means to obtain some extrinsic goal. Since sports activities are intrinsically interesting in and of themselves, coaches have been warned that they may be undermining the intrinsic motivation of sports participants by offering too many trophies, jackets, trips and other extrinsic inducements. However, very little has been written about the steps which can be taken to maintain or increase intrinsic motivation in sports.

In this paper, we will examine both sides of the intrinsic motivation issue. First, certain conditions under which athletes may lose intrinsic motivation will be identified and discussed within the framework of cognitive evaluation theory. Following this discussion, strategies will be offered for enhancing an athlete's intrinsic motivation. However, before this can be done, it is necessary to get a handle on what is meant by the term "intrinsic motivation".

The most common definition of intrinsic motivation states that people are intrinsically motivated if they participate in an activity without receiving any apparent external reward. However, this definition has a weaknesss in that it merely describes what intrinsically motivated behavior looks like, but it fails to explain why the behavior occurred.

A more meaningful definition of intrinsic motivation has recently been offered by Edward Deci (1975) as he refers to the psychological processes which underlie a person's actions. According to Deci (1975), *intrinsically motivated behavior is behavior which is motivated by a person's innate need to feel competent and self-determining in dealing with his or her environment.* Therefore, the more that people feel that their actions are self-determined and provide a sense of personal competence, the higher will be their level of intrinsic motivation. On the other hand, if people feel that they are being pushed around by others or if their performance results in constant failure and negative feedback, they will be less intrinsically motivated to participate in that activity.

Since the emphasis in Deci's definition is on a person's feelings and perceptions, it becomes obvious that only the person in question can truly determine whether or not he is intrinsically motivated. Other people can only make inferences about the person's motives by observing the intensity and persistence of his behavior when external rewards are not present. Nevertheless, with a knowledge of the psychological processes which theoretically underlie intrinsically motivated behavior, we can explain why excessive use of intrinsic rewards may cause a decrease in an athlete's intrinsic motivation.

UNDERMINING INTRINSIC MOTIVATION

According to Deci's cognitive evaluation theory, the receipt of extrinsic rewards affects a person's intrinsic motivation by one of two processes. One process by which intrinsic motivation can be affected is a change in perceived locus of causality from internal to external. Since people make choices about their behavior on the basis of their perceptions, this perceptual shift will cause a decrease in intrinsic motivation. It will occur, under certain circumstances, when people receive extrinsic rewards for engaging in activities which they find to be intrinsically interesting.

The following story aptly illustrates how extrinsic rewards can cause a shift in the perceived locus of causation of behavior and result in a decrease in intrinsic motivation.

(An) old man lived alone on a street where boys played noisily every afternoon. One day the din became too much, and he called the boys into his house. He told them he liked to listen to them play, but his hearing was failing and he could no longer hear their games. He asked them to come around each day and play noisily in front of his house. If they did, he would give them each a quarter. The youngsters raced back the following day, and made a tremendous racket in front of the house. The old man paid them, and asked them to return the next day. Again they made noise, and again the old man paid them for it. But this time he gave each boy only 20 cents, explaining that he was running out of money. On the following day, they got only 15 cents each. Furthermore, the old man told them, he would have to reduce the fee to five cents on the 4th day. The boys became angry, and told the old man they would not be back. It was not worth the effort, they said, to make noise for only five cents a day. (Casady, 1974)

Besides causing people to perceive a change in the locus of causality of their behavior, extrinsic rewards may also affect intrinsic motivation by a second process. That is, the receipt of rewards may cause a change in one's feelings of competence and self-determination. Thus, intrinsic motivation will increase if rewards heighten a person's feelings of competence and self-determination, but they will decrease intrinsic motivation if they diminish one's feelings of competence and self-determination.

To determine whether rewards will affect intrinsic motivation by the change in locus of causality process or by the change in feelings of competence and self-determination process, it is necessary to look at the reward recipient's perception of the reward and the reward donor. If people perceive that someone is "controlling" their behavior by offering rewards, the locus of causality process will be initiated. This is what happened when the young boys in the story realized that the old man was controlling their behavior by giving them monetary rewards.

On the other hand, if the informational aspect of a reward is more salient than the controlling aspect, then the feelings of competence and self-determination process will be operative rather than the locus of causality process. In summary, rewards can either increase or decrease a person's intrinsic motivation. If what Deci calls the controlling aspect is more salient, the rewards will decrease intrinsic motivation. But, if the informational aspect is more salient and provides positive information about one's competence and self-determination, intrinsic motivation will be enhanced.

Since most rewards in sport situations are contingent upon superior performance, common sense reasoning would tell us that receiving trophies should increase an athlete's intrinsic motivation because they provide him with information about his competence as an athlete. Unfortunately, such is not always the case. That is, even though the informational aspect of the trophies may provide the athlete with a sense of personal competence, the controlling aspect of these rewards may be more salient than the informational dimension if the reward recipient perceives that his sports involvement is controlled by the pursuit of trophies and other tangible rewards. Thus, instead of increasing the athlete's intrinsic motivation, the extrinsic rewards might undermine his interest in sports by causing him to perceive his participation as a means to an end with the locus of causation of his behavior outside of himself.

This could very easily happen when young athletes feel that they must excel in order to satisfy their parents. Since many parents derive vicarious satisfaction from their sons' and daughters' athletic accomplishments, they frequently exert pressure on their children to win at all costs. In this event, the controlling aspect of athletic awards would be more salient than the informational aspect as the young athletes would perceive that their behavior was controlled by the need to win trophies and satisfy their parents' vicarious needs.

In Canada, a case was recently reported in which an over-zealous father was paying his goaltender son for each shutout which he recorded while playing for a local minor hockey team. Two years later, at the age of 14, the boy dropped out of competitive hockey as he found it no longer to be any fun. In this situation, the monetary rewards were contingent upon the boy's performance and thereby conveyed positive information. However, the controlling aspect of the reward was obviously more prominent than the informational dimension and as a result the boy's intrinsic motivation diminished when he perceived that his behavior was being externally controlled. It may well be that in a similar manner many parents and coaches are unknowingly undermining the intrinsic motivation of young athletes by offering them external rewards for individual accomplishments in age-group athletics.

Although the discussion of the negative effects of external rewards on intrinsic motivation has painted a rather bleak picture for the use of extrinsic incentives in sports settings, it is not intended as a total condemnation of the allocation of rewards to athletes. Instead, it specifies "certain conditions" under which the improper allocation of rewards may undermine a person's interest in sports activities. Furthermore, this discussion serves as a cautionary warning to coaches and parents who may indiscriminately offer extrinsic rewards without considering the potential negative consequences.

In the next section of this paper we will discuss the proper use of extrinsic rewards; however, before doing that, the effect of competition on intrinsic motivation should be examined as it has recently been suggested that it too can cause a decrease in intrinsic motivation. Deci (1978) views the idea of competing to be similar in many ways to working for a reward. According to this view, sport competition has both controlling and informational properties and an athlete may lose intrinsic motivation in two ways.

In one sense, an athlete's behavior may become controlled by an intense need to win or beat an opponent rather than an attempt to better himself. If this is the case, the athlete may derive less satisfaction from his sport experience as he will perceive that the locus of causation for his behavior is external rather than internal. On the other hand, competing in sports provides a source of direct feedback from the environment. If an athlete experiences constant failure his feelings of personal competence will diminish and he will lose interest in sport. Moreover, if his lack of success is accompanied by negative feedback in the form of criticism from his coach, parents, or teammates, an athlete's sense of personal competence will decrease even further and cause a greater loss in intrinsic motivation. Therefore, in addition to extrinsic rewards, an obsession with winning or various forms of negative feedback can also cause an athlete to lose intrinsic motivation.

ENHANCING INTRINSIC MOTIVATION

From Deci's definition of intrinsic motivation, it will be recalled that an increase in feelings of competence and self-determination causes an increase in intrinsic motivation. Hence, any efforts to increase a person's intrinsic motivation must attempt to provide the individual with a perception of control over his own behavior and a feeling of personal accomplishment. This approach has been successfully used by Richard deCharms (1976) in an educational setting.

Noting that the behavior of students is traditionally controlled by teachers, deCharms tried to change this situation by creating a learning environment in which students perceived themselves to be the locus of causality of their own behavior. That is, instead of being "pawns" to the dictates of teachers, students were encouraged to be "origins", or the originators of their own actions. Teachers attended a motivation training workshop where the Origin-Pawn concept (deCharms, 1968) was explained and techniques were developed to increase intrinsic motivation by heightening students' perceptions of control of and responsibility for their behavior. In the classroom, these trained teachers served as models, acting like Origins and treating the children as Origins. In this regard, teachers encouraged students to establish their own realistic, attainable goals and they made every effort to focus the children on their own self. By doing this, the students became more personally responsible and accountable for their actions.

The results of this four year project were very encouraging as students not only displayed more enthusiasm for schoolwork, but their grades improved remarkably and continued to do so following the termination of the project. Therefore, by altering the characteristics of the students' school activities, the project directors were able to increase both intrinsic motivation and academic performance. These findings have obvious implications for enhancing motivation in sport settings as many characteristics of sport activities can also be changed to increase an athlete's perception of control over his behavior.

To this end, it is suggested that athletes should be treated as Origins with an opportunity to have input in the decisions which affect their sport experience. That is, an attempt should be made to increase their feelings of self-determination and personal responsibility for their own actions. Players might be consulted for suggestions concerning the establishment of a code of behavior for their team both on and off the sports field. For example, the importance of respecting game officials might be discussed at a team meeting and the players could be asked to establish team rules which govern each player's conduct on the field. Likewise, input from players could be sought for matters such as a proper dress code or an agreed upon time of arrival in the dressing room before games.

In practice sessions, an Origin atmosphere could be established by asking players to lead certain segments of the practice. For very young athletes this involvement might entail choosing and demonstrating stretching exercises in the warmup session, while older athletes could be encouraged to develop new innovative drills and direct entire practice sessions. At the university level the idea of giving the members of a team the responsibility for comin up with one new drill per week can serve as an effective means of generating interest.

Experienced players should also be encouraged to have input in the development of game plans for team sports. Due to their playing experience, many players will be able to offer insightful suggestions and no doubt this added involvement will leave them with a greater feeling of responsibility for the outcome of a game. As a result, they will place a higher value on the intrinsic rewards associated with both individual and team accomplishments.

In a similar manner, increasing the perceived significance of an athlete's contribution to a team will increase intrinsic motivation by heightening his sense of personal competence and self-worth. Each player's role on the team should be clearly defined and the importance of his contribution should be emphasized at all times. Recognition in the form of praise and task-specific awards such as "unsung hero" trophies both serve as an informative structure for providing feedback and enhancing intrinsic motivation.

Since people have an intrinsic need for exploration and cognitive stimulation (Hunt, 1971), an athlete's enthusiasm during practice sessions can be maintained by varying both the content and sequence of drills. In this regard, not only should a variety of different drills be used, but the order in which they are presented should be varied. These changes will serve not only to enhance intrinsic motivation, but they will also safeguard against loafing which may occur prior to certain conditioning drills which are known to be physically demanding. In other words, it is best to keep players "guessing" to a certain extent and this seems to be a common practice of innovative, successful coaches.

The boredom of practice sessions can also be reduced by giving players a chance to play different positions. This innovation will not only increase the fun aspect of practices but it will also provide players with a greater awareness and appreciation of the task demands of various positions on a team. Thus, players will understand the tactical facet of the game more fully. It is encouraging to see that administrators of minor league baseball programs have successfully used this concept in game situations by instituting a rotation rule which allows players to rotate positions after each inning.

One final remark on enhancing intrinsic motivation deals with the athlete's perception of the probability of success in a given sports activity. This factor is especially important for participants in age-group athletic programs as an early history of failure can cause a youngster to lose interest in sports. To maintain and increase intrinsic motivation in young athletes it is best to provide them with a large number of successful sport experiences. This can be accomplished by matching the environmental demands of a sport activity to the athlete's ability and level of perceptual-motor development. A good example of such matching occurs in T-ball games where the baseball is placed on a tee to compensate for the difficulty which very young athletes experience in visually tracking a moving object. In other sports, similar steps can also be taken to minimize the task demands of given sport activities to provide youngsters with successful athletic experiences which convey positive information about their personal competence.

In summary, with an understanding of the psychological processes which underly intrinsically motivated behavior, coaches should be able to not only prevent athletes from losing intrinsic motivation, but they should also be capable of formulating strategies to enhance motivation without relying solely on the use of extrinsic incentives. It is hoped that the theoretical and practical aspects of intrinsic motivation discussed in this paper have provided the reader with the necessary knowledge to attain these objectives.

REFERENCES

CASADY, M. The tricky business of giving rewards. *Psychology Today,* 1974, *8* (4), 52.

DE CHARMS, R. *Personal causation.* New York: Academic Press, 1968.

DE CHARMS, R. *Enhancing motivation: change in the classroom.* New York: Halsted, 1976.

DECI, E. L. *Intrinsic motivation,* New York: Plenum, 1975.

DECI, E. L. Intrinsic motivation: theory and application, in D. M. Landers & R. W. Christina (Eds.) *Psychology of motor behavior and sport,* Champaign: Human Kinetics, 1978.

HUNT, J. MC V. Intrinsic Motivation: Information and Circumstances. In: H. M. Schroder & P. Suedfeld (Eds.) *Personality theory and information processing.* New York: Ronald, 1971, p. 85-117.

Motivation and Performance: The Role of Arousal and Attentional Factors*

Daniel M. Landers, Ph.D.
The Pennsylvania
State University

Teachers and coaches often wonder why a competent performer sometimes does better or worse than his typical performance level, or why people select the activities they do. Scientific inquiry into questions concerning the "why" underlying behavior occurs in the field known as the psychology of motivation. This field examines factors within the individual that initiate activity and determine the long- or short-range goals to which the activity is directed. Motivation, therefore, is defined as "an internal factor that arouses, directs and integrates a person's behavior".[1] *Motivation like other psychological constructs is not observed directly, but, rather, is inferred from goal-directed behavior.* Motivational constructs, whether they are called drives, needs, or motives, are implicitly assumed to underlie the performance of motor skills.

Within the area of motivation, there are numerous theories and hypotheses that can be used to explain behavioral perseverance and activity selection. These explanations differ in their degree of generality, the degree to which their constructs can be operationally defined and tested empirically, their ability to predict motor behavior, and the degree of research support they have received. *One commonality that these contemporary motivational theories and hypotheses have is that they conceptualize behavior as varying along two basic dimensions, direction and intensity.* The former specifies *the qualitative, the latter the quantitative aspect of behavior.* Whereas psychology was once concerned only with the directional, qualitative component of behavior, the relatively recent methodological developments in electrophysiological measuring techniques allows various actions and performances of the organism to be contrasted to a physiological correlate. This correlate is claimed by the arousal-activation theorists to reflect the general intensity level of our physiological processes. This intensity level, termed arousal, is frequently used interchangeably with other intensity-related terms such as stress, tension and activation. *Arousal refers to the*

*An article published in the Proceedings of the National College Physical Education Association for Men Annual Meeting, Orlando, Florida, January, 1977. Reprinted with permission of the publisher.

degree of energy release of the organism which varies on a continuum from deep sleep to high excitement.[2] This energy can be measured centrally by means of an electroencephalogram, but is more commonly inferred from a combination of peripheral, autonomic measures of arousal such as heart rate and muscle tension.

Within the time allotted me, I will present some of the research on the effects of arousal on motor behavior. Two aspects of these effects will be examined. The first of these, *the inverted-U hypothesis, is a universal prediction concerning arousal and performance while the second, perceptual narrowing or "tunnel vision," involves our ability to selectively allocate attention.* Rather than focusing on many of the theoretical issues discussed by contemporary investigators, I will focus instead on the empirical basis for these arousal effects and how they might conceivably account for performance on different types of sport tasks.

THE INVERTED-U HYPOTHESIS

One of the most commonly observed effects of arousal is its non-monotonic relationship with quality of performance. According to the inverted-U notion, as the subject's arousal level increases from drowsiness to alertness, there is a progressive increase in performance efficiency. But, once arousal increases beyond, for example, alertness toward a state of high excitement, there is a progressive decrease in task performance. Thus, this hypothesis suggests that behavior is aroused and directed toward some kind of "balanced" or optimal state.

Since 1908 when Yerkes and Dodson[3] first examined the relationship between arousal and performance of laboratory animals, the inverted-U hypothesis has received considerable research attention. As in tests of most psychological hypotheses there is both evidence for and against. Before considering this evidence, it is imperative to determine criteria that would define the conditions under which an adequate test of this hypothesis can be made. In this way only those studies meeting these criteria will be considered., thus avoiding the inescapable confusion that is often evident in reviews of this area. Therefore to test the inverted-U hypothesis there must be at least three or more levels of a situational stressor applied, and there must be corroborative evidence that an experimental exposure is, in fact, stressful. Berkun[4] suggests the following three criteria for providing corroborative evidence for stress: (1) the performance of subjects assumed to be stressed must differ from a nonstressed-control group; (2) the participants must subjectively report feeling distress in the situation of interest; and (3) there must be an indication of disruption of normal physiological processes.

The performance effects from studies meeting these criteria are remarkably similar, regardless of the type of stressor employed. An example of the effects commonly observed under carefully controlled laboratory conditions is shown in Figure 1. The subjects in this experiment by Martens and Landers[5] displayed maximum performance on a motor-steadiness task at intermediate levels of the physiological measure. These palmar sweating decreases from the subjects' own preexperimental (basal) measures were associated with increasing psychological stress. For the high-stress group they are also related to heart rate increases and subjective self-reports of high arousal. Martens and I induced arousal in this study by instructing subjects that they had a high, moderate, or "zero" probability of receiving an electric shock. We actually gave no shocks at all, but these preadolescent boys assumed otherwise. Other investigators report very similar findings. Wood and Hokanson[6] have observed a similar patterning of performance when arousal has been experimentally produced by varying muscle tension. Fenz and Epstein[7] report a similar relationship between physiological measures, self-report measures, and jumping efficiency of sport parachutists. Babin[8] and Levitt[9, 10] have also found reaction-time performance curves resembling an inverted-U that were produced during total-body exercise on a treadmill or bicycle ergometer of varying workload intensities or durations. There are, of course, some experiments that do not show inverted-U curves,[11, 12] but the weight of the evidence seems to support the inverted-U hypothesis. Overall, the findings suggest two general conclusions. First, the inverted-U hypothesis seems to generalize across field and experimental situations. Second, the same performance patterning generally exists for arousal induced psychologically or physically through drugs, exercise or muscle tension.

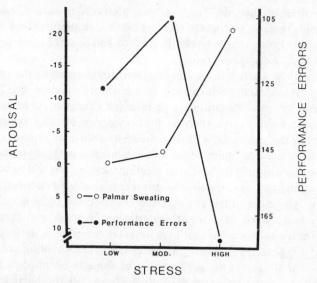

Figure 1. *Relationship between palmar sweating, task performance and stress induced by threat of electric shock. (From Martens and Landers, 1970.)*

Mediating Factors

The arousal-performance relationship is more complex than the general pattern that has been presented thus far. Individual differences in susceptability to arousal have been frequently observed. The Martens and Landers study,[13] for example, also showed an inverted-U performance relationship for subjects varying in levels of trait anxiety. Furthermore, research reported by Fenz and Epstein[14] and Mahoney and Avener[15] demonstrate differences between more competent performers and those who are less competent. The "athletes" were experienced and novice sky divers in one study, and in the other study they were gymnastic qualifiers and nonqualifiers for the 1976 Olympic Games. In both studies, the more successful athletes reduced their arousal levels in the crucial moments just prior to competition while the less successful failed to do so. Subjective self reports from the less successful athletes seem to suggest that they aroused themselves to a state of high excitement by conjuring up images which generated self doubts and impending tragedies. These results suggest that absolute levels of arousal may be less important than patterns of arousal change and the methods used by athletes to cope with precompetitive anxiety.[16] If this is true, absolute levels of arousal may not necessarily be a determinant of performance. Instead it may merely serve as a convenient indicator of the state of those processes that are actually of great significance for performance, such as the appropriateness of the arousal pattern for the particular task.

An additional factor mediating the relationship between arousal and performance is the difficulty or complexity of the task. There is much conjecture concerning the mediating effects of task difficulty,[17, 18, 19] but few studies conducted on its effects. The limited available evidence suggests that the optimal level of arousal is lower for more difficult tasks than for easy tasks. The most direct evidence for this comes from research done on animals.[20, 21] There is, however, some indirect evidence from research using humans as subjects. Carron[22] reported that initially high-anxious subjects perform more poorly than low-anxious subjects when they receive an electric shock for slow responses. However, as subjects continue to practice so that the balancing task becomes easier, high-anxious subjects are shown to be superior to low-anxious subjects. These results are suggestive of the mediating effects of task difficulty, but are inconclusive since only two levels of stress were employed and corroborative evidence for the existence of stress is lacking. This indirect evidence together with the more substantive tests conducted with animals supports the Yerkes-Dodson Law[23] that motivation decreases with increasing task difficulty.

Other task effects have been suggested. Both Gutin[24] and Oxendine[25] see evidence for steadiness and balancing tasks being a special case for not demonstrating an inverted-U curve. This evidence, however, conflicts with the Martens and Landers[26] study where the inverted-U pattern was found for a tracing task involving arm steadiness. The linear decrements that are observed in some of these studies may be an artifact due to stress levels being insufficient in number or inadequately spread (from very low to very high) to observe an inverted-U relationship. A more convincing exception to the inverted-U curve is evident with measures of movement time. Movement time becomes progressively faster as levels of exercise-induced stress become higher.[27, 28] The importance of this finding for sport performance depends on the relative contribution of the reaction time and movement time components to the overall goal response (i.e., response time). The movement-time increments associated with high arousal are only of value, in terms of the goal response, if they offset the reaction-time decrements experienced under these same conditions. Considerable field experimentation is needed to determine the relative advantage of high arousal states on the few sport activities where movement time and reaction time are the sole task or response determinants.

Oxendine's Re-analysis

Oxendine[29] astutely observes that the inverted-U hypothesis falls short of providing teachers and coaches with a set of guidelines for the conduct of his or her activities. As Oxendine sees it, the problem with the inverted-U hypothesis lies with the coach or teacher knowing whether a task is complex or simple, or whether an individual's arousal level is low or high. To resolve some of these ambiguities, Oxendine formulated his own set of guidelines for teachers and coaches. Based upon much of the research evidence presented thus far, Oxendine offered the following generalizations on the arousal-performance relationship:

1. "A high level of arousal is essential for optimal performance in gross motor activities involving strength, endurance and speed.
2. A high level of arousal interferes with performances involving complex skills, fine muscle movements, coordination, steadiness, and general concentration.
3. A slightly above-average level of arousal is preferable to a normal or subnormal arousal state for all motor tasks."

Although Oxendine's generalizations serve the practical purpose for which they were intended, their correctness can be criticized on several grounds. I have particular difficulty with the compatability of the first and third generalizations with the empirical support that is presently available. Outside the laboratory situation there are probably few situations in sport where a slightly above average or a high level of arousal is best for optimal performance. The studies upon which Oxendine based these general statements were either uncontrolled field studies or laboratory studies on reaction time with few distracting elements present, and arousal varied in most cases with only two levels. In other studies,[30, 31, 32, 33] fastest reaction times[34] are associated with intermediate (not high) levels of physiological arousal. Competitive swimmers performing a task seemingly involving only speed,[35] also experience a deterioration in their performance under conditions of high physiological arousal.[36] In sport situations involving speed, strength, or endurance, the athlete must be able to focus attention on the important factors relevant to the task. High arousal causes attention to shift, often causing increases in error rate.[37] The swimmer, for instance, may incorrectly coordinate the timing of his dive or turn, or he may be concentrating his attention on the coach, the officials, or his girlfriend rather than the task he is performing. These behaviors are also characteristic of high arousal and should be avoided. What is missing from Oxendine's analysis is the role that attention plays in most skills, including those involving speed, endurance and strength. Attention can be directed to a variety of environmental cues, particularly cues detected by the auditory and visual senses. The attentional processes to be discussed function the same for auditory[38] and visual cues. However, the visual sense is perhaps of primary importance in most sport situations, and therefore the voluminous research literature on visual detection of cues will be examined next.

ATTENTIONAL PROCESSES AND VISUAL FIELD NARROWING

One of the commonly reported effects of arousal is its effect on the narrowing of the visual field. Recent studies have shown that the subject maintaining performance on a visually central or primarily important task is less able to respond to peripheral or secondary stimuli when under stress. The generalization that emerges from these studies is that peripheral stimuli have lower priority when central (foveal)-demanding stimuli and peripherally presented stimuli vie for attention.[39] For motor performance, the significance of the peripheral visual field lies in the fact that it occupies more than 98% of the light sensitive region of the retina, and the loss of peripheral sensitivity (as would occur under high arousal) would interfere with the capacity of the visual system to process information. The importance of this "tunneling vision" has obvious implications for sport performance. Lets consider for a moment the football quarterback under low-, moderate-, and high-arousal states. As illustrated in Figure 2, the quarterback having low arousal has a broad perceptual range and therefore, either through lack of effort or low selectivity, irrelevant cues are accepted uncritically. Performance in this case is understandably low. When arousal increases up to a moderate, or optimal level, perceptual selectivity increases correspondingly, and the quarterback's performance improves, presumably because he tries harder or is more likely to eliminate task-irrelevant cues. Arousal increases beyond this optimal point permit further perceptual narrowing and performance deteriorates again, in accord with the inverted-U hypothesis. In other words, the quarterback under high arousal may be focused too narrowly to detect receivers open in the periphery. There is controversy concerning what is actually happening to the performer's attention under high arousal. Easterbrook[40] argues that the range of usable cues is further restricted to the point of eliminating relevant-task cues. High arousal, however, is also

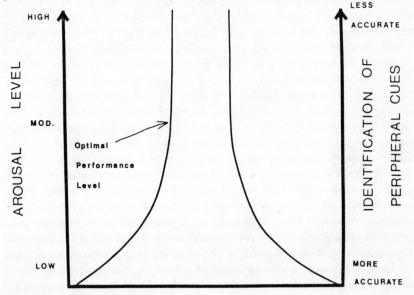

Figure 2. *Arousal level and breadth of attention to relevant task cues.*

associated with distractability, which as Wachtel[41] has correctly pointed out, forces investigators to not only distinguish between the breadth of cues we attend to, but also the amount that we scan the visual field.

The relationships in this figure are not intended to indicate that visual narrowing causes the inverted-U arousal-performance relationship. Other mechanisms have been suggested,[42] but the tunneling vision that occurs with increasing arousal remains as a "leading suspect" in producing all or part of the performance effects observed. There always remains a possibility, however remote, that some other variable causes both peripheral vision and performance to change as arousal increases. Whatever the cause, the relationships indicated in Figure 2 are empirically supported and can be used to the advantage of the enlightened teacher or coach.

Research Evidence

The number and variety of studies supporting the perceptual narrowing accompanying arousal is impressive. The common denominator in these studies is that the central task is more demanding of the subject's attention than the peripheral task. In many of these laboratory experiments, the manipulation of arousal has been controlled. For instance, Callaway and Thompson[43] used the drug atropine, which decreases arousal, and amphetamines to increase arousal. Atropine improved subjects detection of peripheral cues and amphetamines had the opposite effect. Similar effects have been found with other stressors such as heat and humidity,[44] electric shock,[45] sleep deprivation,[46] incentives,[47] and hypoxia.[48] The effects are also evident in automobile drivers[49, 50] and flyers[51] who reduce peripheral cues with an increase in motion. Berkun[52] also reported peripheral narrowing when subjects were led to believe that there was an immediate possibility of personal injury or liability of another's injury.

In making application to sport it is important to determine whether the perceptual narrowing effects I have described thus far can generalize to sport settings. There is not a great deal of field work on this topic, but what little is available does indicate that the findings are generalizable. Fenz and Epstein,[53] for example, observe that arousal in sport parachutists "serves a useful function by focusing the individual's attention on the danger area." Similar conclusions are reached by Weltman and Engstrom[54] in their study of novice scuba divers. In this study the divers responded to a peripheral light while at the same time performing a central task. Response times were examined in the following testing environments ordered in terms of perceived stress: (1) on the surface in test cubicles, (2) in an enclosed 15-ft. diving tank, and (3) in the open ocean at a depth of 20-25 ft. These investigators found that response times progressively lengthened as subjects moved from the surface to a diving tank and to the open ocean, whereas central-task performance was not changed. A subsequent laboratory experiment by the same investigators[55] replicates these results and discounts the possibility that their field results could have been due to other visual changes accompanying cold-water submergence. Weltman and Engstrom[56] also detected marked individual differences between divers in the ocean environment. They reclassified the divers into a group that was steady across the three environments and another that showed a marked response latency in the ocean. Although the response latencies of the "steady" and "unsteady" subgroups were about the same on the surface, they differed dramatically underwater with reactions to the peripheral light increasing over surface scores as much as 226% in the tank and 310% in the ocean. Such profound individual differences are not surprising since it is well known that individual's arousal levels are dependent on their prior experience with like stressors and their perception and interpretation of the stressful situation.

Nideffer has examined the relationship between arousal and attention in male intercollegiate swimmers. If arousal becomes too high, swimmers may narrow their visual field and make what Nideffer call errors of under-inclusion. Nideffer[57] has developed an objective, self-report Test of Attentional and Interpersonal Style (TAIS) and compared the coach's performance ratings of competitive male swimmers to the swimmers' attentional scale scores. Swimmers scoring high on one of the TAIS scales measuring "underinclusion" (focus is too narrow when it should be broad) were described by their coach as: choking under pressure, "falling apart" after making early performance errors, and "becoming worried about one particular thing and being unable to think about anything else." Swimmers who were inconsistent in their performances also tended to be overloaded with external and internal stimuli and unable to effectively narrow attention.

Mediating Factors

Vision in the peripheral field is quite variable among different people and can even vary over time within the same individual. For as yet unknown reasons, women have better peripheral vision than men.[58] It appears, however, that women are also more susceptible to stress[59] and evidence greater visual narrowing[60] in sport situations involving high risk. In addition to these sex differences, Burg[61] observed that peripheral vision improves up to about age 40 and then declines progressively. These differences, however, may not be as permanent as many investigators had previously believed. Abernathy and Leibowitz[62] demonstrate convincingly that subjects can improve their discrimination of peripherally presented lights with practice. When subjects were given knowledge of results after each trial, they increased their discrimination of the light threshold from the beginning to the end of the experiment considerably, in some cases as much as a hundred times the final threshold. This learning data suggests that peripheral discrimination is highly modifiable through the prior experiences and ability of the athlete.

The decrement normally found for peripheral vision disappears when the rules for allocation of attention and effort are changed. If, for instance, the peripheral task is emphasized, no decrement in peripheral vision is observed under high arousal.[63] Also, when the perceptual load is reduced and the task is made simpler by eliminating competition between peripheral and central tasks, peripheral vision is unimpaired.[64] Results showing variation in peripheral vision as a function of the complexity of dual-task competition has led Easterbrook[65] to suggest that the task difficulty differences are related to the Yerkes-Dodson Law. He assumed that the range of essential task cues is narrower for simple than for complex tasks. This relationship is illustrated in Figure 3. This figure indicates that the optimal level of arousal is higher for simple tasks. It also implies what Carron[66] has shown empirically; that is, chronically over-aroused individuals perform more poorly on complex tasks and relatively better on simple tasks.

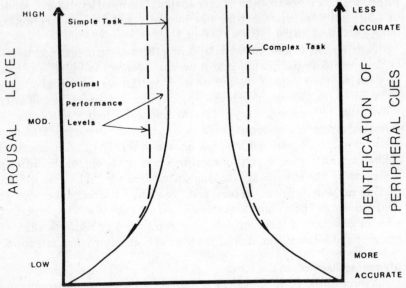

Figure 3. *Arousal level and breadth of attention to relevant task cues as a function of task difficulty.*
NOTE: *The point of optimal performance is higher on the arousal continuum for simple tasks than for complex tasks.*

By considering the combined effects of arousal on attention and optimal performance levels it becomes readily apparent that it is important for the coach to know in advance the demands his particular sport makes on the participant with respect to attentional variables. Unfortunately, there are no simple generalizations that can be offered since attentional demands not only differ across sports, but differ from position to position within a given sport. As a rough guide, Nideffer[67] suggests that a broad focus is useful in "open skills" that require "the individual to be aware of and able to respond to a complex rapidly changing environment." This would be characteristic of the quarterback and linebacker responsibilities in football, a three on two fast break situation in basketball and soccer, and a double play in baseball. By contrast, a narrower focus is useful in intricate, complex "closed skills", such as bowling, hitting and pitching in baseball, golfing, archery, and horseshoe pitching, where only one stimulus (e.g., a ball or pins) is relevant. A relatively narrow focus is also needed in all-out endurance, strength, or speed activities where accuracy is not of prime concern. The sports demanding narrower attentional focus can tolerate higher levels of arousal since there are fewer task cues and therefore less chance of task-relevant cues being eliminated through the perceptual narrowing process.

The task of identifying individuals with high precompetitive anxiety and an attention focus that is inappropriate for the prescribed task has now been simplified by the recent creation of objective self-report instruments. One of these is Martens' Sport Competition Anxiety Test[68] and the other is Nideffer's Test of Attentional and Interpersonal Style.[69] These instruments have high test-retest reliability and some degrees of validity. Once identified, we can offer specific suggestions and exercises to help athletes gain control over their attentional processes. Attentional focus can be broadened or narrowed by adjusting the individual's arousal level in the sport situation. Some athletes may need their attention narrowed by an increase in arousal. A knowledgeable teacher or coach might use "pep talks", reproof, rewards, or other stress-creating devices to assist this individual. On the other hand, the aspiring young quarterback may need his focus broadened to play more effectively. This, of course, is not achieved by the coach angrily chastizing him for not finding a secondary receiver "open" in his peripheral-visual field. A much better approach is to attempt to relax this individual by telling him "it's o.k." and emphasizing the positive aspects of his game. If this doesn't work, there are always desensitization techniques that can be used to "psych down" the athlete and thereby reduce the effects of a heightened arousal state. Many of the relaxation, hypnosis, meditation and biofeedback techniques described by Fisher[70] can be used under the supervision of a qualified professional to lower arousal and broaden attention. Furthermore, an extended training period or scheduling opponents of lesser ability early in the season might create a greater sense of accomplishment and confidence which can assist athletes in coping with precompetitive anxieties. If the individual is performing at low or moderate levels of stress (as may often occur during practice sessions), sensitization to peripheral cues can conceivably be increased through training with feedback given immediately after each error is made. It is not known at this time whether this perceptual broadening can occur at higher levels of arousal. Many techniques are now at the sport psychologist's disposal to lend assistance to the athlete with emotional problems that tend to detract from his potential performance. In spite of these recent advances, Oxendine's[71] closing comment is still as appropriate today as it was in 1970; that is, we need much more field research in sport settings "before refinement can be made in the use of these or other techniques for promoting the desired arousal level of athletic participants."

REFERENCE NOTES

1. Edward J. Murray, Motivation and Emotion, (Englewood Cliffs, New Jersey: Prentice-Hall, 1964), p. 7.
2. Elizabeth Duffy, "The Psychological Significance of the Concept of "Arousal" or "Activation." *Psychological Review*, LXIV (5, 1957) 265.
3. Robert M. Yerkes and John D. Dodson, "The Relation of Strength of Stimulus to Rapidity of Habit-Formation." *Journal of Comparative Neurology of Psychology*, XVIII (4, 1908) 459.
4. Mitchell M. Berkun, "Performance Decrement Under Psychological Stress." *Human Factors*, VI (Feb., 1964) 21.
5. Rainer Martens and Daniel M. Landers, "Motor Performance Under Stress: A Test of the Inverted-U Hypothesis." *Journal of Personality and Social Psychology*, XVI (1, 1970) 29.

6. Charles G. Wood and Jack E. Hokanson, "Effects of Induced Muscular Tension on Performance and the Inverted U Function." *Journal of Personality and Social Psychology,* I (5, 1965) 506.

7. Walter D. Fenz and Seymour Epstein, "Stress in the Air." *Psychology Today,* III (Sept., 1969) 27.

8. W. Babin, "The Effect of Various Work Loads on Simple Reaction Latency as Related to Selected Physical Parameters." Doctoral Dissertation, University of Southern Mississippi, 1966.

9. Stuart Levitt and Bernard Gutin, "Multiple Choice Reaction Time and Movement Time During Physical Exertion." *Research Quarterly* XLII (Dec., 1971) 405.

10. Stuart Levitt, "The Effects of Exercise-Induced Activation upon Simple, Two-Choice and Five-Choice Reaction Time and Movement Time." Doctoral Dissertation, Teachers College, Columbia University, 1972.

11. L. E. Murphy, "Muscular Effort, Activation Level, and Reaction Time." *Proceedings of the 74th Annual Convention of the American Psychological Association* (1966) 1.

12. Lawrence R. Pinneo, "The Effects of Induced Muscle Tension During Tracking on Level of Activation and on Performance." *Journal of Experimental Psychology,* LXII (5, 1961) 523.

13. Martens and Landers, *op. cit.*

14. Fenz and Epstein, *op. cit.*

15. Michael J. Mahoney and Marshall Avener, "Psychology of the Elite Athlete: An Exploratory Study." Unpublished paper, Department of Psychology, The Pennsylvania State University.

16. *Ibid.*

17. Donald W. Fiske and Salvatore R. Maddi (Eds.), Functions of Varied Experience, (Homewood, Illinois: Dorsey, 1961).

18. Rainer Martens, "Arousal and Motor Performance." In Jack H. Wilmore (Ed.), *Exercise and Sport Science Reviews,* (2, 1974) 155.

19. Joseph B. Oxendine, "Emotional Arousal and Motor Performance." *Quest,* XIII (Jan., 1970) 23.

20. Peter L. Broadhurst, "Emotionality and the Yerkes-Dodson Law." *Journal of Experimental Psychology,* LIV (5, 1957) 345.

21. Yerkes and Dodson, *op. cit.*

22. Albert Y. Carron, "Complex Motor Skill Performance Under Conditions of Externally Induced Stress." Master's Thesis, University of Alberta, 1965.

23. Yerkes and Dodson, *op. cit.*

24. Bernard Gutin, "Exercise-Induced Activation and Human Performance: A Review." *Research Quarterly,* XLIV (3, 1973) 256.

25. Oxendine, *op. cit.*

26. Martens and Landers, *op. cit.*

27. Levitt and Gutin, *op. cit.*

28. Levitt, *op. cit.*

29. Oxendine, *op. cit.*

30. Babin, *op. cit.*

31. G. L. Freeman, "The Relationship Between Performance Level and Bodily Activity Level." *Journal of Experimental Psychology* XXVI (5, 1940) 602.

32. Levitt and Gutin, *op. cit.*

33. Levitt, *op. cit.*

34. Note that simple movement time is hastened at higher levels of arousal. Unlike most sport situations, the movement time studies contain few, if any, environmental stimuli that may act to distract the subject.

35. Oxendine, *op. cit.*

36. Robert M. Nideffer and Thomas J. Yock, "The Relationship Between a Measure of Palmar Sweat and Swimming Performance." *Journal of Applied Psychology,* LXI (3, 1976) 376.

37. Michael I. Posner, Raymond M. Klein, Jeffrey Summers and Stephen Buggie, "On Selection of Signals." *Memory and Cognition* I (1, 1973) 2.

38. Stephen J. Bacon, "Arousal and the Range of Cue Utilization." *Journal of Experimental Psychology,* CII (1, 1974) 81.

39. Herschel W. Leibowitz, "Detection of Peripheral Stimuli Under Psychological and Physiological Stress." In *Visual Search* (National Academy of Science-National Research Council, Washington, D.C., 1973) 64.

40. J. A. Easterbrook, "The Effect of Emotion on Cue Utilization and the Organization of Behavior." *Psychological Review*, LXVI (3, 1959) 183.

41. Paul Wachtel, "Conceptions of Broad and Narrow Attention." *Psychological Bulletin*, LXVIII (6, 1967) 417.

42. A. T. Welford, "Stress and Performance." *Ergonomics*, XVI (5, 1975) 567.

43. Enoch Callaway III and Samuel V. Thompson, "Sympathetic Activity and Perception: An Approach to the Relationships Between Autonomic Activity and Personality." *Psychosomatic Medicine*, XV (5, 1953) 443.

44. A. E. Bursill, "Restriction of Peripheral Vision During Exposure to Hot and Humid Conditions." *Quarterly Journal of Experimental Psychology*, X (3, 1958) 113.

45. Paul L. Wachtel, "Anxiety, Attention, and Coping with Threat." *Journal of Abnormal Psychology*, LXXIII (2, 1968) 137.

46. W. H. Teichner, "Compensation and Concentration Concepts for Research and Evaluation of Human Performance." Paper presented at Human Factors Society tenth annual meeting, Anaheim, November, 1966.

47. Harry P. Bahrick, Paul M. Fitts and Robert E. Rankin, "Effect of Incentives Upon Reactions to Peripheral Stimuli." *Journal of Experimental Psychology*, XLIV (6, 1952) 400.

48. John L. Kobrick and E. Ralph Dujek, "Effects of Hypoxia on Voluntary Response Time to Peripherally Located Stimuli." *Journal of Applied Physiology*, IXXX (Oct., 1970) 444.

49. I. D. Brown, "Studies of Component Movements, Consistency, and Spare Capacity of Car Drivers." *Annals of Occupational Hygiene*, V (5, 1962) 131.

50. D. B. Vinson, "Monitoring Race Car and Non-Competitive Drivers." Presented at the International Telemetering Conference, Los Angeles, October, 1966.

51. Don E. Flinn, "Functional Stress of Altered Awareness During Flight." *Aerospace Medicine*, XXXVI (June, 1965) 537.

52. Berkun, *op. cit.*

53. Fenz and Epstein, *op. cit.*

54. Gershon Weltman and Glen H. Egstrom, "Perceptual Narrowing in Novice Divers." *Human Factors*, VIII (Dec., 1966) 499.

55. Gershon Weltman, Janice E. Smith and Glen H. Egstrom, "Perceptual Narrowing During Simulated Pressure-Chamber Exposure." *Human Factors*, XIII (2, 1971) 99.

56. Weltman and Engstrom, *op. cit.*

57. Robert M. Nideffer, "Test of Attentional and Interpersonal Style." *Journal of Personality and Social Psychology*, XXXIV (3, 1976) 394.

58. Albert Burg, "Lateral Visual Field as Related to Age and Sex." *Journal of Applied Psychology*, LII (1, 1968) 10.

59. R. Gary Ness, "Stress Perception Among Novice Divers: A Comparison by Age, Sex and Height of Dive Attempt." In Daniel M. Landers (Ed.), Psychology of Motor Behavior and Sport — 1976 (Vol. 2), (Champaign, Ill.: Human Kinetics Publ., 1977).

60. Weltman and Engstrom, *op. cit.*

61. Berg, *op. cit.*

62. Charles N. Abernathy and Herschel W. Leibowitz, "The Effect of Feedback on Luminance Thresholds for Peripherally Presented Stimuli." *Perception and Psychophysics*, X (1, 1968) 172.

63. Bursill, *op. cit.*

64. Donna J. Cornsweet, "Use of Cues in the Visual Periphery Under Conditions of Arousal." *Journal of Experimental Psychology*, LXXX (1, 1969) 14.

65. Easterbrook, *op. cit.*

66. Carron, *op. cit.*

67. Robert M. Niddeffer, "The Relationship of Attention and Anxiety to Performance." *Coach and Athlete*, in press.

68. Rainer Martens, Sport Competition Anxiety Test, (Champaign, Ill.: Human Kinetics Publishers, in press).

69. Nideffer, *op. cit.*, 1976.

70. A. Craig Fisher (Ed.), Psychology of Sport, (Palo Alto, Calif.: Mayfield, 1976) p. 155.

71. Oxendine, *op. cit.*, p. 29.

Developmental Stages for Motivation in Sport*

John D. Lawther, Ph.D.
The Pennsylvania
State University

Sport versus Formal Exercise. Perhaps the first question to be raised when one considers the problem of motivation in sports is why one should put so much stress on sports learning and performance. Educational philosophers and leaders through the ages have advocated play and sports for the education of children. Socrates, Aristotle, Quintillian, Comenius, John Locke, even John Dewey thought physical play was essential for child education. In the early part of this century in the United States, Thomas D. Wood, Clark W. Hetherington and others led a strong revolt against artificial and mechanical exercise-programs as the content of physical education for children and youth. They felt that the strength, posture, and health aspects of fitness should be by-products — by products of exercises performed because they are natural, spontaneous and enjoyable. They wanted the physical education program *to be* the vigorous play of childhood, the hunting and chasing games, the sports and dances of the people.

Child physical activity and sport loses much of its meaning and pleasure if it becomes "prescribed work" or an obligation without real exhilaration and joy in the participation. The educational value, the recreational value, and the mental health value, not to mention the skill-attainment factor, are greatly decreased if the activity is "no fun". Many people cannot "physic away" their tensions and worries by a dose of recreative castor oil in the form of calisthenics. Much of the developmental and educational value of sports result from the vigor and enthusiasm of the participant. The boy will "shag flies" to get his legs in shape for pitching, or he will lift weights and run "wind-sprints" to get himself in shape for football; but he will not participate and persist, voluntarily over a long period of time, in arm, leg, and trunk exercises just to conform to some abstract idea of fitness (unless he is narcissistic, or perhaps a Muscle Beach devotee).

One great advantage possessed by the so-called "natural program" of physical education, based on play and sports, is the fact that the students will participate with interest and enthusiasm, and will spend a lot of their excess, out-of-school time in extra practice. In contrast with a formal

*Many of the ideas in this article were expressed previously in books written by Lawther and published by Prentice-Hall, Inc., the most recent being *Sport Psychology,* 1972, and *The Learning and Performance of Physical Skills,* 1976.

program, the motivation is much greater in sports, especially if the sports are wisely conducted or informally encouraged without great pressure to win. There is little need for a teacher to expend effort in arousing interest in activities which the community, the television and radio, the daily newspapers, and even the child's peers endow with such interest, and in which they praise and reward successes. Parental interest and enthusiasm is common and undoubtedly influences the child.

Competitive Drives and the Need for Challenge. Competition tends to crop up immediately in sports play; however the pressures to win must not be so great as to overpenalize ineffective performance, hence decrease or even remove the joy of participation. The pleasure of successes must not be removed, but neither should the activities be so elementary or so simple as to fail to challenge the child. Even with the kindergarten child, his progression, in throwing for example, can be kept challenging by having the person-catching move farther away as the shorter throws become quite successful. The child can be challenged to throw harder, higher or lower, more to the left or more to the right. In general, sports among peers promote competition, challenge and progressive improvement.

The field of sports yields not only harmless ways to express competitive urges but expression under rules of conduct which permit many desirable outcomes. The individual wants to test himself and to test himself against others. Successes foster further attempts, improve one's self-confidence and self-respect. Through such efforts, such competition, such testing in sports, the individual develops his physical skills, his emotional control, and his social adjustment. Striving for recognition and dominance starts very early in life. Greenberg reported finding it in the play activity of children between the ages of three and four, and extensive competition by the ages of six and seven.[1]

Over a generation ago, Gutteridge reported, after an extensive study of some two thousand children over fourteen states of U.S., that the school programs for kindergarten and primary-age children tended to be stereotyped and too simple; and that they failed to provide the varying opportunities appropriate to the developing abilities of the children. She said that, at the age of four or five, the children had exhausted possibilities of the equipment provided, hence turned to "stunting and adding hazards and dramatic play in order to add interest and challenge."[2]

Sport-Skill Development at Pre-school Ages. Behavior of the type reported by Gutteridge is often seen on the playgrounds. The pre-school child, after sliding down the slide several times while sitting up, tries it lying down on his back, then prone, and then head-first. Next he tries climbing up the slide itself, instead of using the ladder, or even tries climbing up the supporting pipes at the sides. Gutteridge reported the type and degree of physical development of these very young children in her extensive study. The children ranged from twenty-four to eighty-three months. She found that most of the children by the age of seven years had achieved high development in climbing, jumping, sliding, tricycling, hopping, skipping and galloping. Throwing and bouncing balls were skills attained by one-half to three-fourths of the children before the age of eight.[3] In 1968, Dayries and Davis[4] studied the development of these same skills in kindergarten and primary-school children in a city in northwestern United States. They found their sample of the children of this later generation to be slightly superior in skills to those reported by Gutteridge, and markedly superior in ball-handling skills. Such early-developed skills seem to be unit elements which the child soon combines into the more complex skills of his society as further development occurs.

Interest and Opportunity Grow with Skill. Once these beginning skills develop, opportunities for further participation are increased since both adults and peers encourage the more skillful individual's participation. The interest of the child seems to increase as his skill increases. In a society in which there are almost daily exhibitions of sports participation by both teen-agers and adults, merely having good equipment and facilities available fosters childhood imitation and participation. The children learn and enjoy learning many sports at a very early age if the environment fosters such learning. Today many youngsters of pre-school age are introduced to such sports as swimming, skating and skiing and simple gymnastics.

Basic Drives to Sport Skill. Healthy children are so full of energy that they often cannot keep still or be quiet. Furthermore they like to test themselves to see just what they can do physically; i.e., just what their potentialities are. They like to compete and to experience the risks and thrills of vigorous contests. They seek to gain recognition, approval, and prestige. They rush into sports as play, and they often do so to escape the boredom, anxieties, or just the drab routine of their daily work and duties. Remember that sport for the average child is a type of play. The healthy child, being an almost irrepressible bundle of energy, is continually expressing himself in physically active play, much of which is of a sport nature.

Sport as Pleasure, Immediate or Anticipated. The Frenchman, Michel Bouet, in his work, *Signification du Sport,* says it is evident that sport brings pleasure, otherwise it would cease rapidly to be of general interest. He says that sport is practiced proportionately to the physical pleasure derived from it, that the needs for physical exertion and movement stir up this attraction, and that sport produces a sensuous thrill — physical, perceptual, alive in one's person.[5]

Apparently one major aspect of sport motivation, therefore, lies in the fact that sport activity is often a form of play, hence pleasurable; however, this statement refers to the learner's attitude, not type of activity nor intensity of effort. Voluntary effort does not always imply immediate pleasure in sports. It often refers to the individual's anticipated successes at some distant future. Gulick said that "Play is what you do when you are free to do what you will," and that the only difference between work and play is the difference in attitude.[6]

It might be well to keep in mind two aspects of so-called play: play involving the child's immediate pleasure in the activity of the moment; and activity being carried out voluntarily and eagerly in hope or anticipation of some future success. The future goal, the dreams of future successes, social approval, admiration and prestige, and hoped-for attainment of superior abilities, all make present strenuous efforts endurable, and often eagerly carried out. The prospective athlete, voluntarily working regularly and zealously on weights to prepare himself for future success in sports, illustrates this point. Much arduous training by running is done because the athlete anticipates that it will bring him future sport success, hence pleasure. Maximum physical effort to achieve a goal, perhaps superiority to others or to some record, is often quite voluntary, hence comes under the category of play; i.e., it is effort toward anticipated or hoped-for success and resultant pleasure in achievement. Part of the motivation problem of the coach is that of keeping the learner's dreams alive and vivid.

Demonstration, Imitation, then Much Time and Practice. The common and usually successful beginning in sports teaching is for the coach or instructor to demonstrate how to perform the skill, then have the learners attempt to imitate. As noted above, many individuals arrive at the formal sports training situation with many of the basic skill units already learned (Gutteridge and Dayries studies mentioned above). Many of these individuals have already spent untold hours kicking a soccerball or football, shooting at a basketball basket, playing "catch" or softball, and whatnot. If the coach is enthusiastic; arranges facilities, equipment and practice conditions; helps learners clarify their purposes or goals; and keeps the student enjoying practice, he has solved most of the problems of learning.

Much time and patience are essential for the teaching and learning of sports by the very young individual. He should be helped and encouraged, and criticized very little. Sports learning takes much time and great numbers of trial experiences. Fortunately children at the younger ages have much free time, and tend to play at the sport in much of their free time, both in and out of season. These young sport enthusiasts profit from seeing others perform, and tend to make progress during their almost innumerable practices by trying to imitate both coach demonstrations and game performances of the older and more skilled athletes.

Verbal Explanations and Descriptions with Beginners. At the earlier stages of sport-skill learning, verbal explanation and description have little value for the learner if he has not seen a skilled performance a few times. Verbal describing of a motor act cannot be transformed into the motor act by the learner if the act, itself, is unfamiliar and has never been experienced in association with the verbal description. Besides, verbal description and explanation tend to get boring to the individual. He wants to try the skill, not listen to a lecture. The coach of the young athlete who interrupts the learner's trial attempts with long discussions, tends to reduce the motivation to learn. Perhaps the lack of ability to translate word explanations into appropriate action is what Sir W. G. Stimpson had in mind almost a century ago when he said concerning the first lessons in golf: "Let the beginner shake himself down naturally and hit. Till he has done this for a good many days, no advice has either use or meaning."[7]

Gross Patterns but not Meticulous Attention to Detail with Beginners. The young beginner should be allowed a lot of freedom in his early attempts. He will enjoy the experience more and will, more or less unconsciously, hit upon small adjustments which fit more nearly his own physical characteristics. He can, however, be held to the major aspects of the gross act — the original position, the arc of the movement, and the final position, say, if he is throwing a ball, swinging a bat, or shooting a free throw in basketball. Once he gets the general idea, major persisting errors may be pointed out to him. For example, if he is putting the shot without extending his elbow directly behind the line of the "push" (with it well out from his side as he executes the push), a mere illustration of both the error and the correct way will tend to be both helpful and appreciated. If the correction is made in a very evident intent to help, and if harsh criticism is avoided, the very correction adds to the motivation, especially if greater success seems to follow the readjustment.

Drives and Sports Learning. In a social atmosphere in which sports are given much attention by peers and adults, in which facilities and equipment are available, and in which the youth is able to use sports as a form of his physical play, his self-expression, his urge to compete with his peers, motivation tends to be adequate to stimulate learning. Motivation and incentive come from praise and criticism by the coach, and enough encouragement from his peers, his family and his instructor to reflect on his social status, his self-respect, and his prestige. Both the urge for play and physical self-expression, and the desire to compete with others seem to be innate; or at least behavior appearing from early childhood on. The coach's problem is to encourage these drives; and to arrange challenging opportunities adjusted to the skill level of the learner so that he can realize some success and pleasure, but difficult enough so that he is continually challenged to improve.

Purposeful Acts Rest for Motivation. For best motivation, the earliest beginnings in sports teaching should involve a total act — a throw toward a target (or with a person catching, perhaps); catching a thrown ball, a kick of a ball toward a target or goal; a complete swimming act (stroking and kicking), etc. A unit act such as these has a specific purpose in the mind of the child. To keep him interested and challenged, have him progress as fast as he can in combining the simpler acts into more complex units and interrelated combinations of units; for example he can dribble the soccer ball along and then try to kick it into the goal, next dribble it around an opponent in an attempt to score a goal; or pass it back and forth with a teammate in the attempt to avoid an opponent and advance toward the goal. When he needs guidance, the coach may demonstrate, using a design of performance in executing the activity which the learner has perhaps seen more-skilled performers do, and which has proved successful with previous learners at this stage of development.

Length of Practice. For greater interest, formal practices for the elementary school participant should be relatively short, and generally should involve lead-up games at the early stages; however the learner should have the facilities available so that he can do as much voluntary practicing as he wishes, on his own, outside of formal practice time. Much of the learning of the highly-skilled athlete of today is due to his untold hours of voluntary and informal practice during his long play hours both in and out of season.

Praise and Criticism. Coaches may use praise, criticism, encouragement (or even discouragement at times), reward and punishment. The relative effect of such devices depends greatly on the individual performer's interpretation, his emotional reaction and ego involvement. One must not forget that the learner's opinion of, and degree and respect for the particular instructor have great influence on his reaction to any praise or criticism.

Criticism of performance should be focused on the major error, and should make clear to the performer the readjustment which will improve his performance. The learner needs to see exactly what his mistakes were, and also see an illustration or demonstration of correct performance. Learning is proportionately greater as the quality, exactness and precision of the knowledge of results in his completed performance increases.[8]

It is questionable whether one should make a generalization about the effects of praise and criticism because too many factors are involved. The individual's past degrees of success or failure have much influence on his type of reaction. A relatively successful individual is usually helped to improve by being given justifiable criticism, especially if it is also constructive; i.e., includes specific suggestions or demonstrations of changes needed for improvement. Too much praise, particularly if it is scarcely deserved, may decrease the individual's efforts, may even produce little concern for improvement. Gerwitz and Baer experimented with children in a simple motor-skill game. Each subject of one group was isolated for twenty minutes before starting the skill. A second group went directly to the experiment. A third group was "satiated" on the way to the experimental situation by extremely solicitous and approving comments and actions on the part of the experimenter. All were praised during practice on the game. The "deprived" subjects, those who had been isolated, were superior in acquiring and performing the skill; the group that went directly to the skill ranked second; and the "satiated" group, the group that had been given extensive praise preceding the experimental activity, did the poorest.[9]

Individuals who seem to be progressing in their skill acquirement tend to profit more by a combination of praise and criticism if the praise is specific in pointing out the exact aspect improved, and if the criticism is constructive and specific. However, the effects of praise and criticism are such an individual matter that the coach must know each individual, his sensitivity, his degree of past successes, and his degree of attention to, and attempts to follow directions. The learning of a sensitive, timid beginner may be retarded by any criticism more than kindly suggested modification; whereas the relatively successful, self-confident performer may need to have his errors pointed out quite clearly and even emphatically at times, although the corrections should also be shown.

Sparks, experimenting with adolescent boys, reported best skill learning by the group which was both praised and criticized, in comparison with only-praised and only-criticized groups.[10] Again it would be well to state that individual diagnosis and treatment is essential in the use of praise and criticism because of the great variability of reactions among individuals. The same comments, the same criticisms, or even just the unsuccessful performance-attempts may disturb one subject greatly but leave another unconcerned.

Pride, Prestige, and Social Rating as Drives (Ego Involvement). The individual learner's reactions depend greatly upon his degree of ego-involvement. Ego involvement refers to the effect of the results of the performance, and accompanying remarks of praise or criticism plus audience reaction, on the performer's self-pride, his feeling of status among his peers and degree of prestige thereby gained or lost. If he feels that his social status is being affected, he becomes highly sensitive to the outcome of his performance, and to praise, criticism and peer attitude resulting. This ego involvement tends to make performance before an audience differ from performance without an audience.

Factors in Popularity of Sports in Society. Societies in general apparently play or foster sports for many reasons: for fun and self-expression; to gain prestige and honor; to uphold the honor of the school, village or nation, and to demonstrate school, community or national pride and strength; to educate youth; and of course at times for financial gain or political accalim. Sports are often an alleviating attempt of the normal person who possesses inferiority feelings and wants success, popularity and admiration from his associates. Moreover, sport success plus consequent approval and admiration bring greater group acceptance. The individual gains a feeling of security within his social group — a need very common in adolescents. Sports successes are employed by children, adolescents, and even adults in an attempt to gain popularity and prestige.

The "we-feeling", group belongingness, student-spectator group union in enthusiasm for *their* team seem to be worth-while and desirable morale factors as well as highly motivating factors in sports participation. Morale as a group characteristic is a feeling of unity within the team (and even with supporters), shared feelings, a common cause. In sports it grows with people enduring, battling, and suffering together for a considerable period of time, in the attempt to win, have a good record, uphold the prestige of the school, and achieve specific, highly desired goals. Morale means that the individual participant has a mental and emotional condition of zeal, hope and enthusiasm in work toward the group pre-conceived goals. Group morale implies teamwork, group solidarity with individual integration. Within the team, there is friendliness, comradeship and gang spirit.

Adjusting Difficulty to Stages of Learning. The early sports competitions should not be so difficult as to prevent considerable success by the competitors. One is encouraged and pursues the learning procedures more eagerly if he finds his striving successful. The degree of difficulty of the sport skills, and the standards set for achievement at the individual's particular stage of development, should be such as to permit more successes than failures in the judgment of the learner. Emotional upheaval in the early learning stages, caused by lack of success and too great pressure to perform better, retards the learning. The difficulty at the individual's particular level of development should be adequate to stimulate his best efforts, and should cause some unsuccessful attempts to enforce the challenge, but should permit observable progress and enough success to encourage the individual. In general the difficulty should be such as to permit, according to the individual's own estimate of his achievements, more successes than failures.

It becomes evident, therefore, that, at least in sport participation at lower ages and skill levels, relatively homogeneous grouping in skill levels should be arranged. Some differences in skill levels are bound to occur and are perhaps not undesirable if they are not extreme; but a beginner's attempts to compete against a very superior performer tend to be discouraging, hence not conducive to most rapid learning.

Aspiration and Attainment. The level of performance the individual undertakes to reach, often called his level of aspiration, and his degree of approach to it, produce his own subjective estimates of success. The ambitious and relatively successful individual tends to raise his level of aspiration after success. In order to improve, one must aspire to higher levels than present attainment. Complete satisfaction with one's own level of performance usually results in a ceasing of attempts to improve. Self-satisfaction and over-confidence in one's ability often result in deterioration of performance. However, new achievement records, set by one's peers, tend to help the learner re-evaluate his own performance and perhaps raise his level of aspiration. The drive to excel, to do better, to surpass one's own previous performance, the records set by others, the competitor of the moment, all are a part of human striving for maximum performance and efficiency.

Social and Environmental Factors Which Promote Sports. Sports tend to take a very important place in our society. In addition to the constant dissemination of information about sports events, sport records, and sport personalities by the newspapers, the television and the radio, we usually find members of the family[11] and close community associates attending and perhaps participating. Special facilities and equipment are often available for both formal and informal sports play. The playgrounds often have soccer, football, or baseball fields. Volleyball and basketball courts are frequently available. Many back alleys and back yards have a suspended basketball backboard and baskets available for voluntary, informal practice. Swimming pools, gymnastic apparatus, and even tennis courts are becoming more and more common. The mere fact that sports play such an important part in the activities of one's surrounding environment tends to stimulate the youngster to imitate and to participate.

The schools have cheerleaders for sports contests, organized cheers, pep meetings, bands, school songs; and perhaps even a mascot to be taken to the athletic contest. At the national and international levels, there are often formal pre-contest ceremonies (speeches, handshaking and embracing, unfurling of flags and playing of national anthems). International contests receive world-wide publicity. The winter and summer Olympics seem almost to be of universal interest.

Coach Preparation and Effectiveness. Other things being equal, the coach who has played the sport, himself, and is highly skilled, has the advantage of being able to demonstrate more accurately, plan for the next contest more wisely, and is usually considered a more competent sports teacher by his students. He should appear at sports practice in the uniform most appropriate to use in teaching the sport. Demonstration is a very important technique in teaching sports and, being dressed suitably, the coach is ready to demonstrate. The attitude he tends to radiate is affected by his own evident preparation for practice. Forcefulness and energy should characterize the coach's directions, demonstrations, and routine movements as he works. The young athletes are inclined to imitate the coach, absorb his attitudes, and feel his moods.

Summary. All down through the ages educational leaders have advocated natural, spontaneous and enjoyable physical activity, play and sports. The great advantage of play and sports over formal physical exercise is the fact that the students will participate in the play and sports with interest and enthusiasm, and will spend a lot of their excess, out-of-school time in extra practice. Sports are wide-spread in popular interest. The drive to compete with others physically seems to be almost universal in man, and a great stimulus to sports participation and achievement.

Many elementary skills, basic to sports development, have developed in most children by the time they reach primary school age. Both interest and opportunity to participate seem to increase with skill. Children are by nature physically active and eager to engage in play and sports. Sports participation tends to be a form of play and a pleasure for the child. Training for sports is often voluntarily and eagerly pursued, for immediate pleasure or anticipated pleasure in later performance and achievements.

High level in sport skills is attained only after years of motivated practice. The performer's method and form seem to be gained most rapidly from imitation of others who are more skilled and, later, to gradual adjustment of such conceived form to one's own characteristics.

Verbal direction in sports teaching is of chief advantage at the advanced-skill stage when the words have meaning in previously-experienced movement patterns.

Starting the beginner's practice with a purposeful, complete act is more interesting and usually more successful than detailed part-analysis.

Sports are common throughout society and a part of the recreational expression of most ages. The individual tends to be exposed in his developing years to sports as a means to express his drives to be active physically, and to compete with others.

Formal practices in the early learning stages should be relatively short, although voluntary and informal practice should be permitted and even encouraged by having facilities and equipment readily available. Praise and criticism are incentives which must be adjusted to the learning level, the level of success of the learner, and to his past success and present sensitivity.

Personal pride, desired social status and desired prestige are factors in motivation of the learner and his reaction to sport failures or successes.

For most rapid learning, the practice and competition should be arranged so that the learner feels that he is progressing and has more successes than failures. As he succeeds, he should be encouraged to aspire to greater achievements.

With extensive facilities available, association with like-interested peers, group promotion activities (pep meetings, cheers and songs, school letters), various sports media reporting, and the adult encouragement, motivation for sports participation is fostered.

The coach should be skilled, prepared, energetic, forceful and highly interested in his learners. Part of the coach's motivation problem is to keep the sport learner's aspirations for achievement somewhat ahead of his current performance.

REFERENCE NOTES

1. P. T. Greenberg, "Competition in Children: An Experimental Study," *American Journal of Psychology,* XLIV (April, 1932), 221-248.
2. Mary V. Gutteridge, "A Study of Motor Achievements of Young Children," Archives of Psychology, No. 244 (May, 1939).
3. *Ibid.*
4. John Dayries, personal communication.
5. Michel Bouet, *Signification du Sport* (Paris: Editions Universitaires, 1968), 468.
6. Luther Halsey Gulick, *A Philosophy of Play* (New York: Charles Scribner Sons, 1920), p. 267.
7. Sir W. G. Stimpson, *The Art of Golf,* 1887, cited by Mrs. Stewart Hanley in "The Sense of Feel in Golf," Journal of Health, Physical Education and Recreation, 8, 6 (June, 1937), 366.
8. Jack A. Adams, *Journal of Motor Behavior,* 3, 2 (June, 1971), 130.
9. Jacob L. Gerwitz and Donald M. Baer, "Deprivation and Satiation of Social Reinforcers as Drive Conditions," Journal of Abnormal and Social Psychology, 57, 2 (September, 1958), 165-178.
10. Jack Leon Sparks, Relative Effects of Various Verbal Incentives on Learning and Retention of Perceptual-Motor Skill (Unpublished Masters thesis, The Pennsylvania State University, 1963).
11. Lawrence made a study of the backgrounds of varsity lettermen at one of the Big Ten Universities and reported that 70 per cent of the athletes' fathers had played competitive sports (Robert Lawrence, personal communication).

Motivation and Performance of Sports Groups*

Alvin Zander, Ph.D.
The University of Michigan

Since the beginnings of history people in positions of authority have valued coordinated effort in a group, especially in athletic teams. Romans were excellent in social organization and every Roman city, so carefully planned, had an area set aside for sports. Where Plato and Aristotle once collaborated in Athens, just a few blocks from the parliament building, is now a basketball court. The New Testament in the Bible urges subordinates (slaves and servants) in any organization to work hard for their superior no matter how unfair he may be; thereby establishing an ethic for obedience to leaders (and coaches) that confounds us to this time. Nowadays, cooperation among members of a team is so widely respected that invocation of the idea through such terms as teamwork, team spirit, unselfish desire, clicking, or precise execution, are uttered in a reverent tone; they are especially precious virtues (next to cleanliness) in the eyes of the priests for athletics, the sports reporters.

Such concepts about team work and the nature of group-oriented motivation are familiar and practical matters to athletes, coaches, and spectators. Most psychologists, in contrast, tend to think of these notions as mystical or romantic trivia that are not worthy of study. I propose that motivation in teams warrants better psychological research than it has received thus far and I intend to give some reasons for this belief.

I have three objectives: 1) To describe the characteristics of a group-oriented motivation called the desire for group achievement; 2) to indicate the effects of this desire on team performance; and 3) to suggest ways in which this motivation may be aroused by coaches and teammates. Before taking up the desire for group achievement, however, it will be useful to remind ourselves that a sports team is a unique institution, and to review serveral methods widely used in arousing personal motivation in individuals.

An Athletic Team

An athletic team has special properties, and a special environment, that make it similar to other groups, such as a symphony orchestra, the cast of a play, a set of glass blowers creating handsome objects, or the crew of a submarine, but unlike any other organization in most respects. These

*An article published in *Psychology of Sport and Motor Behavior II*. Edited by Landers, D. M. College of Health, Physical Education and Recreation, The Pennsylvania State University, University Park, Pennsylvania, 1975. Reprinted with permission of the publisher.

qualities are worthy of attention because they press teammates and coaches in several different directions at once, thereby threatening the stability of their rationale for joint endeavor. Here are some of these properties:

1. A team conducts its major business (engaging in athletic contests) before the eyes of observers who see all that goes on and who may later also read news reports about these events. (Imagine how different some political units or business firms might be if they were monitored as thoroughly.)

2. The observers are deeply (even emotionally) involved in the team's fate. They experience as much elation after a team's success, or as much depression after a team's failure, as they would if they had been in the contest themselves.

3. The observers want a victory, not mere improvement in skill, or better development of the athletes' moral fiber. Yet, they also believe there can be too much emphasis on winning which, of course, is not everything, especially in certain unhappy seasons.

4. The observers freely provide unrequested advice to higher management (the coach) on how he should do his job, and freely blame the management (not the team) for a poor performance by the participants.

5. Observers often bypass management and direct their messages to the participants on how they should conduct themselves: the observers also give applause and rewards (often mindless) to players they like for crowd-pleasing reasons.

6. There is a rigid code of behavior that all must follow, and officials (who are at once both policemen and judges) are present to see that these rules are obeyed.

7. The team members are fully able to evaluate their performance because they repeat their major business many times and receive ample feedback after each trial, from their score, their rivals, the observers, the press, friends, and from films made during the contest.

8. The team undergoes wide extremes of emotional reaction during its existence, from boredom to pride to shame.

9. Members of the team and management are inspired by some of the above conditions to want to do well. It becomes evident to them, furthermore, that winning is indeed not the only thing that counts (except when job security is needed for certain persons). A success must be one that engenders pride, a loss must be one that causes no shame.

An athletic team, in sum, is a very public thing. Many forms of influence act upon it, and within it. These forms provide conflicting bases for the motivation of team members, which means that there are no simple and consistently effective practices for arousing motivation in all participants on all teams at all times.

Individual Motivation

Three different approaches are rather commonly used in building motivation of individuials by those who have the responsibility to do so. I do not know how frequently coaches use these approaches, or how often anyone uses them for that matter. A very brief review of them will serve to underscore the point that teachers or coaches, like business managers, use any of several styles on different occasions. None of these approaches are directly concerned with how well a team performs as a unit, only with how well each individual performs, or, what is more important perhaps, with how hard each individual works to improve his own skill and his own rewards.

The supportive approach. The logic in this method is that a well satisfied person, more than a less satisfied one, puts out more effort on the tasks assigned to him. Accordingly, in the business world he is given good pay, fringe benefits, housing, bonuses, and security. In college athletics he is given room and board, tuition, help in studies, a cash allowance, and one long distance call a week to Mom. These satisfiers are given, it should be noted, regardless of the recipient's performance, or changes in that performance. The high producer and loafer share alike, which is one of the reasons for its appeal. It is egalitarian, compassionate, and paternalistic. In the light of Title IX, it must now be maternalistic as well. This approach clearly improves the rate of recruiting and reduces absenteeism and turnover, but there is no good evidence that it affects the quality of performance. It does not help us understand, furthermore, why individual incentives work and why there are individual differences in motivation even though all individuals are treated the same.

The reinforcement approach. The logic here, as you know, is that a reward is given to a person if some agent thinks he deserves it, otherwise it is not given, or a punishment is administered instead. An important point is that the reward is contingent upon the quality of the recipient's behavior, and the rewarder sets the standard of excellence to be met if one is to qualify for that reward. In the world of work this reward is the raise in pay, the promotion, or the gold pin for good service. In the world of sports it is the star pasted on the back of the football helmet, or being named wrestling-team champion of the week. Being "benched" is the ultimate punishment, and some well known coaches are famous for their ability to terrify players by use of sarcasm and towering rages.

Reinforcements are known to enhance learning, or unlearning, and are the basis of behavior modification in psychotherapy. Over the long haul, however, the value of rewards will fade, and the price, so to speak, rises as a reward loses its value. Many costs likewise lose their sting. When these contingencies weaken, a coach must invent tailor-made appeals for the case in hand: suggesting, for example, that a player might qualify for a professional career or that a runner can set a new record if he works hard, or the coach makes changes in the schedule of reinforcements he is using. When rewards are given to some team members but not to others, they are a potential source of rivalry, not of team spirit. Because the athlete's motivation is based on things offered by another person, this approach does not account for intrinsic motivation — the zeal a person develops for himself alone. An example of the latter was the daily walk taken by former President Truman or my own daily exercises. Neither of us have taken these workouts to please someone else. The motives are private.

The pride-in-performance approach. Individuals develop personal motivations in which they seek to obtain social power, affection, nurturing, information, or other states that have significance for them. In sports, the most obvious motivation of this kind is the desire for pride in what one accomplishes, commonly called the need for achievement. We will concentrate on that need.

Psychologists usually assume that the need for achievement is learned in childhood as a result of particular parental practices. I am willing to wager, however, that this need can be developed (in principle at least) at any age, for any specific task, under appropriate conditions. What is wanted, to do this, is a task that can be repeated many times, which provides a score (in time, points, or distance) for each repetition. Gradually, a participant develops some idea about what level of accomplishment he can attain with ease, with some stretching, or not at all. He is then encouraged to see how well he can do, which ordinarily leads him to choose a goal that is a bit harder than the best level he has thus far reached. When he accomplishes that, he feels pride in his performance, and he is then asked to set a new goal. It is best if this again is a moderate challenge, not too hard. We should note that his goals become more precious to him if he knows that other persons depend on his attainments.

A coach is arousing need for achievement when he asks a player to select a private goal for each of many separate activities for the season and asks the player periodically to evaluate his behaviors in reference to each goal... Sometimes a coach and athlete jointly select a number of goals to guide the athlete in an upcoming contest because the athlete is thereby made aware of what he can reasonably ask of himself and, as a result, becomes more involved in those actions. Regardless of the source of the goals, whether they are handed down, jointly decided, or privately developed, the important thing is that the athlete use them to evaluate his own performance, which in turn determines his pride in his output. It is evident that this approach is more tasteful at an educational institution than are others.

Group Motivation

The latter two approaches stimulate personal effort because they are based on the satisfaction one derives from either a reward or a sense of pride. Such motives are clearly effective in sports, especially those in which solo actions occur, as in track, golf, swimming, or wrestling, and where much of the training is an individual effort. But there is a further kind of satisfaction that teammates can deeply value — the pride they develop in their team.

Let us consider two group-oriented motives. The *desire for group success* is a disposition on the part of a participant to experience pride and satisfaction with his group if it successfully accomplishes a challenging group task. *The desire to avoid group failure* is a disposition on the part of a member to experience embarrassment or dissatisfaction with his group if it fails on a challenging task. Either group-oriented desire is not an impulse for action; it is rather a disposition that will influence those actions that are perceived to be ways of attaining preferred consequences, that is, to attain pride in the group or to avoid shame in it. The impulse to take part or not to take part in a given activity is called a *tendency*. The tendency to achieve success is thus an inclination to have the group approach a task with interest and the intent of performing it well. The tendency to avoid group failure, in contrast, is an inclination to have the group resist performance of the activity because it is expected to lead to failure. Because a precise description of these tendencies becomes too complicated and abstract to take up here, we will devote our attention to the desire for group success and the desire to avoid group failure — assuming they invoke the appropriate tendencies (Zander, 1971, See Chapters 4 & 10).

A team, by definition, is a social unit with a task that requires a set of persons to accomplish; no individual members can do it all alone. It is perfectly reasonable, therefore, that teammates become involved in their team's outcome, not only in their individual products. This team-centered interest is most likely to develop, of course, when the team gets a score, but an individual member does not. Deep appreciation of the importance of team pride is developed as members become concerned about the excellence of their team in numerous respects, not only in its winning record. One coach I know has his team (through group discussion) set a number of challenging goals, for various statistical matters, at the outset of the season, and he presses them to be realistic about these. The goals, he says, must stretch the players but must not be pipe dreams. He does this because he wants his players to believe that winning is not the only standard of excellence and that it is important above all for him and the athletes to have pride in their team's effort in many ways. There are times when the members of a team prefer to avoid engaging in an athletic contest altogether because they expect to fail. When they are nevertheless constrained to compete, they prepare themselves and their observers to minimize the effects of failure (i.e., the noble try against impossible odds) or they set easy goals so a failure is not likely to occur. All in all, a team will be more alert when the desire for group success is stronger than the desire to avoid group failure, instead of the other way around.

Although he is a member of a team, an individual retains his own personal motive to achieve success, to some degree. I believe (on the basis of good evidence) that person-oriented and group-oriented motives are separate variables and are not the same thing at all (Forward, 1969; Medow & Zander, 1965; Zander & Forward, 1968). This means that a team member may be more interested in his own outcome than in the team's, or more interested in the fate of the team than his own, or, that both interests may be strong and additive, or that both may be weak. In some sports it is crucial that the desire for group success be stronger than the personal motive. In others it does not matter much, but it would help.

Evidence of Group-Oriented Desires

If group oriented desires are to be taken seriously in theory or in practice, we must be able to examine their effects on group behavior under various conditions. This approach requires that we are able to say with confidence whether these desires are present or absent in a group at a given time. It would be best if we did not have to ask people whether they care about their group's fate because their reports may not be credible. Fortunately, we do not have to ask because there is a behavioral measure we can use to determine the presence of a desire for group success. It is based on the observation that individuals with different degrees of the *personal* motive to approach success choose different kinds of personal goals. More specifically, a person with a strong motive to succeed chooses a moderately challenging goal, one that is neither so easy as to make success certain (because that would not be satisfying) or so difficult as to make failure certain (because that also would not be satisfying). And, individuals in which the motive to avoid failure is strong will choose either very easy goals (where success is certain to occur) or very hard goals (where failure is not embarassing). We assume that decisions about group goals are parallel to the individual choices just described and for the same reasons. That is, groups with a strong desire for group success will prefer challenging group goals, whereas groups with a strong desire to avoid group failure will prefer either very easy or very hard group goals.

My first efforts to create variations in the strength of the desire for group success, in accord with the above ideas, were based on earlier findings by Emily Pepitone (1952). She had observed that individual members of a group produce more quantity and better quality if their function is said to be important, even though all members (unknown to them) were performing exactly the same task. In accordance with this observation, we assumed that a central member of a group, in contrast to a peripheral member, would have a stronger desire for group success and that a central member, in contrast to a peripheral one, would therefore favor a more challenging goal for his group.

In an early experiment (Medow & Zander, 1965), small groups, three members in each, were asked to construct geometrical designs out of small blocks of wood. The teammates were seated at a single table but concealed from one another by screens. They were told that each member was to construct on the table before him, in a limited period of time, an exact duplicate of a design. The group's score was determined by the length of time taken for all three members to complete all three solo designs. On the wall of the room there were 14 large poster cards, each displaying a geometrical pattern. These designs varied in complexity from very simple to very hard. After each trial a group chose which design it wished to attempt on the next turn. The boys drew lots to determine who was to be the central person and who were to be the two peripheral ones. The group was told that the peripheral persons could not put a block in place until the central one had done so and had announced that fact. Thus, his actions were central in the structure of the task because he led the way and set the pace, even though all three were doing exactly the same thing at the same time.

Effective Coaching Behaviors

Zander (1975) illuminated three common approaches to the building of individual achievement motivation. Subsequently, he suggested how such approaches might be used to enhance group motivation. *The Supportive Approach* is founded on the logic that a well-satisfied person, more than a less-satisfied one, puts out more effort on an assigned task. For example, in athletics it is not uncommon to provide grants-in-aid or even room and board to incoming athletes. These benefits are provided in the hopes that the individual will perform to his optimum in the future. Thus, they are given regardless of the player's actual performance. One of the most common truisms in psychology is that rewards are capable of maintaining a desired behavior. When a desirable behavior occurs and a reward is administered contingent upon that response, then the likelihood that that same response will recur is increased. The key word in the preceding sentence is contingent. When rewards are administered noncontingently, *i.e.,* regardless of the response emitted, then no relationship should be evidenced between the reward and the emission of the desired response. The point being made is that the supportive approach violates the principle of contingency. Rewards are given prior to and not contingent upon a desired response. In the supportive approach high and low producers are treated similarly. Few would disagree with the conclusion that the supportive approach is probably not the most effective for motivating individual behavior. There is certainly no reason to suspect that a similar approach would be any more effective with groups.

The Reinforcement Approach calls for the application of rewards contingent upon the observation of a desired response. For example, a standard of excellence is set and upon achievement of that standard the performer is rewarded. Such occurrences are very common in sport settings. For example, the rewarding of stars on football helmets or athletic letters. Although the reinforcement approach has much to say for itself, it too has some problems. For instance, the coach only has so many rewards that are available to him. After awhile, the rewards lose their potency. The price keeps going up and, therefore, the desired behavior-reward contingencies tend to weaken. Within interacting team sports, another problem emerges. If rewards are administered contingent upon responses made by individuals, then inequalities are likely to occur. Rivalries among players may take place. As a consequence, social processes such as cohesion may be affected adversely.

Zander refers to the third approach as the *Pride-in-Performance Approach.* Very simply, this approach attempts to facilitate pride (positive affect) by the setting of reasonable, challenging goals. Upon the achievement of the specified goal, the person feels pride and should have increased expectancy regarding future performance. The work of the coach is to identify appropriate goals, to evaluate goal-directed behavior, and to reward positive outcomes. The pride-in-performance approach can be applied to either individual or group-oriented goals. We will turn our attention to the latter.

Group Motivation

As we have seen above, a combination of the reinforcement and pride-in-performance approaches appears to be most effective for increasing individual achievement motivation. The question then becomes that of group achievement motivation. Can a member of a sport group simultaneously maintain both an individual-oriented and a group-oriented motive to achieve? Previous research (Forward, 1968; Zander, 1968) has indicated that these two motives are both independent and additive. Therefore, one motive such as the individual-oriented motive, is not necessarily the cause of the other. Both, however, could be affected by the consequences of team sport performance in terms of success or failure.

From what we know concerning attributions for self and team, it is easy to see that a sport team member's post-competitive evaluation of himself and his group may be very different, even though both evaluations were based on the same criterion, team outcome. In the case of the Little League baseball studies (Iso-Ahola, in press-a; Roberts, 1975), a team failure outcome had no adverse effect on players' internal ascriptions for themselves. On the contrary, the results of the basketball investigation (Bird & Brame, Note 2) indicated that members of winning teams had more positive self-evaluations as compared to losers. Differences in patterns of team attributions between baseball and basketball players were also evidenced. Decreased evaluations of the team's internal qualities were made by members of unsuccessful Little League teams. That is, members of those losing teams tended to deny personal responsibility for team failure by diffusing the entire blame onto the team as-a-whole. This procedure would then allow for maintenance of consistently high self-evaluations. In the case of basketball, however, the major difference in regard to players' evaluations of winning and losing teams was that of team ability. More specifically, losers saw no difference between their own and their team's ability, while winners demonstrated enhanced positive perceptions of their team's ability as compared to their own. For interacting teams then, we see two important attribution trends occurring as a consequence of team outcome. First, the self-attributions for the internal elements appear to be tied directly to team outcome. Second, a successful team outcome appears to be explained by reference to higher team ability as compared to individual player ability. The last trend supports the notion that interacting team ability is indeed more than merely the sum of the individual abilities of the team members.

Recall that in the case of interacting teams, group structural demands require that members coordinate their efforts interdependently. Without such intermember coordination, success is not possible. No individual can achieve success unless his team does also. It seems reasonable then that teammates become quite involved in the team's outcome, as well as their own individual contribution. Further, team goal attainment is mandatory in order for a team-oriented motive to achieve to occur. The effective coach of an interacting team sport must establish group-contingent goals. After consultation with all players, realistic, challenging group goals should be identified. The expected standard of excellence must be communicated and must be accepted by the group. That is, the criterion by which or against which performance is to be evaluated must be made clear. Group attempts at goal achievement must then be evaluated. After evaluation, group achievement should be rewarded. If achievement of the goal has been found to be too difficult or unrealistic, the goal must be redefined.

The results were that the central person perceived himself as having the more responsible position and that the peripheral persons saw their jobs as less important. More significantly, the central person, in contrast to the peripheral ones, chose challenging designs reliably more often. Analysis of separate treatments that also were part of this experiment indicated that this last contrast was stronger when the central member chose the goal for the group all by himself than when the three members jointly participated in making this choice.

In a replication of this study (Zander & Forward, 1968) the central character was the only member who laid out the chosen design while the two peripheral persons provided particular pieces as the central member called for them. Halfway through the experiment central and peripheral persons changed places, in order to control on effects of personal disposition. Each design of blocks was limited to just five pieces and the goal was speed of completion, not complexity of design. Here again, a central player chose a challenging goal (time in seconds) more often than did a peripheral person. In a later naturalistic study, comparing the responses of central and peripheral members on Boards of Trustees for United Funds in 46 cities, the results were substantially similar to those found in the laboratory (Zander, Forward & Albert, 1969). Members with greater commitment to the group seemed to have greater desire for group successes.

In another early experiment to examine further if variations in the strength of members' desire for group success could be detected, weak groups were developed on the one hand and strong groups on the other (Zander & Medow, 1965). The weak groups were simply a set of strangers seated on randomly arranged chairs who were addressed as individuals ("you") during the opening instructions of the session. The members of the strong groups, in contrast, were seated tightly around a table, were addressed as "this group," were asked to choose a name for their team, and in other ways were helped to see themselves as within a single entity. Each group then performed the same task while all members were seated at a table. Here, the stronger groups chose challenging goals more often than did the weaker groups while working for many trials on an activity that required cooperative speed and accuracy.

In an additional investigation, desire to avoid group failure was generated, as was the desire to achieve group success, by telling subjects in one treatment that every group failure in a series of trials would cost them points while a success would not be rewarded at all; and, in a different treatment, that a success would be rewarded but failure would cost them nothing (Zander & Medow, 1965). As you might expect, the groups in the cost-only condition chose less challenging (and more erratic) goals than did those in the reward-only condition. It appears, in sum, as though something like a desire for group success and someting like a desire to avoid group failure may have been operating in these experiments. The crucial question now is, so what? Do groups with different degrees of desire for group success behave differently in ways that are interesting to us?

Desire for Group Success and the Performance of a Group

The effect of desire for group success upon a group's performance has been examined in nine studies, six of them in the laboratory and three in natural settings. While none of the group activities can be called athletic, they often required coordination of motor movements among members and demanded some individual skill. There is no doubt, however, that the relevance of the following results to your interests remain to be investigated.

In the laboratory, variations in the strength of the desire for group success have been created by the several methods already mentioned. In addition, variations have been sought by making the group's task more or less important to the outcomes members may obtain when they are away from the group (Forward & Zander, 1971; Thomas & Zander, 1959), by reporting that the group had succeeded or failed (when the subjects did not know these facts themselves) (Zander & Forward, 1968), or by giving questionnaires that were alleged to measure the members' desire for group success and then reporting average scores for the group on these tests (high or low) to the members (Zander, 1971, p. 148). In general, the desire for group success, created in one or another of these ways, had quite consistent relationships with one or another of the following measures of group performance.

Different aspects of group performance were investigated. In one case expenditure of energy was the central interest. Each subject held a hand dynamometer and all members were asked to "squeeze" simultaneously (Zander, 1971, p. 149). The meters were joined by wires in order, it was said, to create a group-strength score, calculated by a small and clicking "computer" to which these wires ran. In four other studies, performance was measured by speed of movement, as in making the designs of wooden blocks or in marking IBM cards (Horowitz, Exline, Goldman & Lee, 1953; Zander & Medow, 1965; Zander & Ulberg, 1971; Zander, 1971, p. 150). In another case it was persistence, as shown by the number of times a group repeated a jig-saw puzzle, working against time, when they were free to stop at any trial (Horwitz, et al., 1953). In two cases the measure of performance was greater accuracy, as in counting holes in IBM cards (Forward & Zander, 1971; Zander & Ulberg, 1971). In two unexpected instances, less accuracy accompanied more desire for group success, probably because the group task (one that required speed in ordering dominoes by number when each person had some of the necessary pieces) caused much talking and confusion as the task had not been previously rehearsed (Zander, 1971, p. 150). And finally, as just noted, stronger desire for group success caused more oral chatter among members (Zander, Fuller, & Armstrong, 1973).

In "real life" greater desire for group success was associated with more sales of insurance policies in separate districts of a large company (Bowers & Seashore, 1966), with more speed and skill when groups of military officers were on a four and a half day trek in the snow (Thomas & Zander, 1959), and with more production on 28 assembly lines (manned by women) in a factory making slippers (Zander & Armstrong, 1972).

Because, as we have noted, challenging goals are more often chosen by members who have a stronger desire for group success, it should follow that groups produce better when they have challenging goals than when they have less challenging ones. This result was observed in two laboratory experiments in which the speed of coordinated movement improved, step by step, as the group's goal was made harder, step by step (Zajonc, 1962; Zajonc & Taylor, 1963). In two studies of United Fund campaigns it was also found that goals placed just a bit harder than previous income levels generated more money than did goals placed much higher or lower than previous levels of performance (Zander & Newcomb, 1967; Zander, et al.,

1969). A goal that causes a group to stretch, but is attainable, in short, appears to stimulate a better group effort than either a very easy or a very hard goal.

Talking Among Members and Desire for Group Success

While the American team was climbing Mount Everest, Richard Emerson, a member who was interested in both team motivation and communication under stress, made standard pre-planned comments to his colleagues and recorded their answers on a small tape machine he lugged through the snow (Emerson, 1966). He found that the responses to his comments were typically such that motivation was maximized through emphasizing the chances of making it to the top were 50-50. If Emerson made a discouraging comment, they cheered him up; if he made an optimistic comment, they dampened his ardor — in both cases the future was made to appear uncertain. Talk among teammates ought, then, to bear some relevance to interest in the group's job. In athletics it is well known that "talking it up" is valuable. Indeed, in wrestling and in baseball good chatter is a true skill, an art form. Through team meetings members may also arouse one another's desire for group success and may establish a joint view that all agree to share, and live by. In a few investigations, therefore, we watched the effect of communication among team members, with these results.

1. After a group had finished its work on a group test of motor skill, in one experiment, members privately completed questionnaires that measured their feelings about their team and the work it had done. After that they had a group discussion in which they were to reach a unanimous decision on the same matters. During these discussions the participants became more approaching if that was their original inclination and more avoiding if that was their prior preference before the discussion had begun. Thus, the discussion strengthened private dispositions (Zander, 1971, p. 22).

2. Members were allowed to talk freely in one condition of an experiment and were denied any opportunity to talk whatsoever in a contrasting condition, while all participants worked on a group assignment that required very close and simultaneous coordination of motor movements. The groups that were allowed to talk set more challenging goals than did the groups that were not allowed to talk. Thus, group discussion aroused stronger desire for group success (Zander, Fuller, Armstrong, 1973).

3. Some remarks made by teammates can be conceived as *approaching* (for example, encouraging, praising, giving suggestions on how to do the group's task), while other remarks can be conceived as *avoiding* (criticizing, blaming, suggesting that less vigor be used). When remarks among members are coded under these headings we note that (Zander, Fuller, Armstrong, 1973):

> A. Members generally make more approaching remarks than avoiding ones, which means that an interesting task stimulates the kind of talk that arouses a desire for group success.
>
> B. Approaching remarks are made more often while working on the group's assignment than when discussing it during period between trials.

C. Approaching remarks caused (that is, were followed by) more approaching remarks, but avoiding remarks were followed by approaching comments as often as they were followed by avoiding ones. In general, then, avoiding remarks are avoided.

All in all, more group talk stimulates more enthusiasm for what needs to be done by a group.

Shifts in Group Goals

We have used the term *goal* a good deal in the foregoing as a shorthand way describing any of a variety of actions a person may want himself or his group to complete in accord with a given degree of excellence. Because improvement in skill and the attainment of new degrees of excellence are important in all sports, and because output on any given trial can be placed somewhere on a scale of difficulty from very easy to very hard, the term goal is a convenient way to keep all this in mind.

We should emphasize, however, that the goal teammates prefer may change over time, which is not news to those who know the literature on personal levels of aspiration. You can assume that groups will change their goals, if they have the freedom to make this decision on their own (which is not the case in most settings, including athletics) and they will make these changes in accord with the simple rule: *raise the goal after a success and lower the goal after a failure.* You can also anticipate that the tendency to raise after a success is much stronger than the tendency to lower after a failure because, as earlier implied, success on a harder goal is more attractive and failure on an easier goal is more repulsive. It follows that there are strong pressures on a group to raise its goals as its performance improves, and not to lower them as its performance worsens. Observers and others who have influence over a team also want higher goals and their desires are usually more telling on the group's choices than are the group's own scores, according to half a dozen studies into that matter. Group goals, as a result, usually tend to get harder and harder (Zander, 1971, Chapter 2).

It is interesting, then, that groups with a stronger desire for group success follow the "succeed-raise" part of the rule with greater care, because they wish to make it possible for their team to have a success and to have that success be one that is satisfying. Groups with a stronger desire to avoid group failure, in contrast, are more erratic in setting their goals, because it is not entirely clear to them how they can best avoid that failure.

How do group goals affect the personal objectives of individual members? Under what conditions are members of a group more willing to set an individual goal that is congruent with what the group expect of them? The answers to these questions are what your experience as group leaders cause you to expect. In three different experiments it was found that members are more likely to set their personal goals at levels similar to ones being pressed on them by groupmates (a) as members perceive their actions to have greater significance for the group's attainment, and (b) as members are more attracted to membership in that group. In ordinary language, if a teammate wants to be on the team and thinks what it does is important, he will ask of himself the things he knows his colleagues expect of him (Zander, 1971, pp. 164-167).

Evaluation of Group

The moment that members of a team establish a goal for their unit, they simultaneously create a criterion for evaluating their group's performance. Thereafter, when the group does better than this goal, members give the unit a favorable evaluation and when worse than this goal, an unfavorable evaluation. This practice occurs with such reliability that we can use it to judge whether the goal was internalized by the members. If the goal is used as the basis for evaluation of the team, it has really been accepted. But, if the goal is ignored and evaluation of the group is determined by some other standard of excellence instead, the goal has not been accepted — members only pretended to hold it dear. For example, a failing performance that is given a favorable evaluation reveals that the members did not employ the relevant goal for the team in making their judgment. Not uncommonly, some unexpressed aspiration is used by members as their standard of excellence (Zander, 1971, Chapter 7).

In an athletic team the importance of winning is what most often confounds matters. Clearly, being able to defeat other teams is the most laudable and visible kind of success and thus it doubtless is given most weight — especially among teams that have a winning record. Other kinds of excellence probably become more important as winning occurs less often, but I cannot think of any research that bears directly on this issue.

There are data that are indirectly related to these matters. They concern the amount of pride or shame members feel in their group, and themselves as individuals, when they try to understand a good or a poor group performance. We asked members of groups to rate the amount of pride or shame they felt in their group's score as the competence of members, and the effort exerted by them, were varied. Several findings are notable (Zander, 1974; Zander, Fuller, Armstrong, 1972):

A. An excellent performance by a group generates much more pride among members if they had tried hard than if they had not tried at all, regardless of how much ability members brought to the group's assignment.

B. A poor performance by a group generates more shame if the members are very able but did not try on the group's task than if the members are not competent but tried very hard. Thus, shame in a group after it fails is determined by the degree to which members waste their competence by not exerting themselves.

C. A success, if achieved without effort, is not a strong source of pride, if it is achieved after much effort, it is a source of pride.

D. Lack of effort is a greater source of shame in the group than a source of shame in self.

Developing a Desire for Group Success

Suppose you have by now developed some interest in the desire for group success and you wish to try your hand, more consciously than heretofore, at arousing it within a team. How would you go about it? If I were in your shoes, I would attempt to generate a commitment to the group by doing the following things. These will come at you like beads on a string, but there is no help for it. Listen to them as variations on a theme: making pride in team an important thing.

1. Emphasize the importance of pride in the group, its sources and its consequences for the team. One coach I know makes his seniors responsible for developing these ideas as well as for enthusiasm during practice and games.
2. Make sure that each member understands that his contribution to the team is valued.
3. Use various means to underscore how each teammate depends upon the work of each other for the success of their unit.
4. Emphasize the unity of the group, the score as a product of team effort, and the perception that all members are within the group's boundary.
5. Indicate to members separately how membership helps each individual, so that each will see the group as an attractive entity.
6. Take care in the selection of group goals so that these are realistic challenges, not unreasonably hard or easy ends. Set standards of excellence for all skills and activities.
7. Don't be afraid to change goals that are found to be unreasonably difficult. The warmest pride comes from living up to reasonable expectations for that group, not in failing impossibly difficult ends.
8. Once goals have been set, consider what obstacles might prevent fulfillment of these goals and how the obstacles might be overcome by the team.
9. Encourage talk in the group about how performance can be improved and how the boring parts of athletics can be made more involving.
10. Avoid fear of failure and the tendency to evade challenges that are engendered thereby.

Some Final Comments about the Desire for Group Success

When the desire for group success is strong among members, they have a keen awareness of their mutual social responsibility, which causes them to help one another, to coordinate their efforts with maximum efficiency (provided the work to be done is well practiced) and to be friendly. All members of a team, regardless of whether they are superstars or bench-riders, can attain satisfaction of a desire for group success. Society accepts it, moreover, as an appropriate and praise-worthy aspect of group purposes.

Finally, there are questions to be raised about these ideas. One is that not every person can become concerned about a group and this motivation will therefore not work for asocial types who prefer to be alone — they must be allowed to be soloists or not at all. Repeated failures by a team can make it difficult for members to arouse a desire for group success unless they have developed strong beliefs ahead of time about what they expect of themselves, aside from victories. For that matter, emphasis on winning can distract from efforts to achieve any goal other than a championship, but the distraction is not as great for a winning team as it is for a losing one. Doubtless, it is harder to develop a desire for group success in sports that require little coordination among team members than in the so-called interactive team sports that demand smooth blending of the movements of several persons.

Summary

In summary, we have taken seriously what every coach knows — the desire for success of the team as a unit can be a powerful motivating force on the participants. We have talked about the origins and consequences of this group-oriented motivation. It seems reasonable to suggest that this approach warrants further study in athletic settings. It is no panacea, but it can be useful as a means of understanding, predicting, and furthering the attainment of excellence, one of the prime values of athletics in all cultures.

REFERENCES

BOWERS, D. & SEASHORE, S. Predicting organizational effectiveness with a four-factory theory of leadership. *Administrative Science Quarterly*, 1966, *11*, 238-263.

EMERSON, R. Mount Everest: A case study of communication feedback and sustained goal striving. *Sociometry*, 1966, *29*, 213-277.

FORWARD, J. Group achievement motivation and individual motives to achieve success and to avoid failure. *Journal of Personality*, 1969, *37*, 297-309.

FORWARD, J. & ZANDER, A. Choice of unattainable group goals and effects on performance. *Organizational Behavior and Human Performance*, 1971, *6*, 184-199.

HORWITZ, M., EXLINE, R. GOLDMAN, M. & LEE, R. *Motivational effects of alternative decision making processes in groups*. Technical Report to U.S. Office of Naval Research, Bureau of Education Research, University of Illinois, 1953.

MEDOW, H. & ZANDER, A. Aspirations for group chosen by central and peripheral members. *Journal of Personality and Social Psychology*, 1965, *1*, 224-228.

PEPITONE, E. *Responsibility to Group and its Effects on the Performance of Members*. Unpublished doctoral dissertation, The University of Michigan, 1952.

THOMAS, E. J. & ZANDER, A. The relationship of goal structure to motivation under extreme conditions. *Journal of Individual Psychology*, 1959, *15*, 121-127.

ZAJONC, R. The effects of feedback and probability of group success on individual and group performance. *Human Relations*, 1962, *15*, 149-161.

ZAJONC, R. & TAYLOR, J. The effects of two methods of varying task difficulty on individual and group performance. *Human Relations*, 1963, *16*, 359-368.

ZANDER, A. & MEDOW, H. Strength of group and desire for attainable group aspirations. *Journal of Personality*, 1965, *33*, 122-139.

ZANDER, A. & NEWCOMB, T. M., Jr. Group levels of aspiration in United Fund campaigns. *Journal of Personality and Social Psychology*, 1967, *6*, 157-162.

ZANDER, A. & FORWARD, J. Position in group, achievement motivation, and group aspirations. *Journal of Personality and Social Psychology*, 1968, *8*, 282-288.

ZANDER, A., FORWARD, J., & ALBERT, R. Adaptation of board members to repeated success of failure by their organizations. *Organizational Behavior and Human Performance*, 1969, *4*, 56-76.

ZANDER, A. & ULBERG, C. The group level of aspiration and external social pressures. *Organizational Behavior and Human Performance*, 1971, *6*, 362-378.

ZANDER, A. *Motives and goals in groups*. New York: Academic Press, 1971.

ZANDER, A. & ARMSTRONG, W. Working for group pride in a slipper factory. *Journal of Applied Social Psychology*, 1972, *2*, 193-207.

ZANDER, A., FULLER, R., & ARMSTRONG, W. Attributed pride or shame in group and self. *Journal of Personality and Social Psychology*, 1972, *23*, 346-352.

ZANDER, A., FULLER, R., & ARMSTRONG, W. Communication among members during a challenging group task, 1973 (unpublished report).

ZANDER, A. Alone versus together: Attributed pride or shame in self, 1974 (unpublished report).

Assessment of Motivation in Sport and Physical Education*

Dorothy V. Harris, Ph.D.
The Pennsylvania
State University

To consider the subject of motivation is, in essence, to consider why man does what he does. The concept of motivation, specifically achievement motivation, has attracted the interest of many coaches and researchers working with athletes. Motivation appears to be the key to accomplishment, whether it be in sport, in teaching, in research, or some other challenging pursuit. Volumes have been written about the various theories of motivation, however, it is not the purpose of this paper to elaborate on all of these.

Behavior is promoted and directed by interactions and combinations of motives and emotions, some intrinsic, others extrinsic; some genetic, others environmental; some physiological, others psychological; some individual, others social, some conscious and others unconscious; and so on. Anxiety, tension, stress and other emotional states also influence the behavior of man. Motivation is an abstract concept, and exceedingly complex behavior that cannot be observed as such. Only the behavior resulting from it can be observed, measured, recorded and labeled. The understanding of what motivates an individual toward sport pursuits presents the same degree of complexity and problems as those involved in studying motivation in all human behaviors.

The achievement motive construct

Fineman (1977) provided an excellent review of the historical development of research in achievement motivation. He indicated that William James spoke of man's self-regard as being determined by self-imposed goals with achievement leading to a sense of well being, and failure producing frustration. The efforts of Murray (1938) formalized the achievement motive construct, producing a taxonomy of personality needs which direct behavior. He labeled one of these needs "achievement" and defined it as ". . . the desire or tendency to do things as rapidly and/or as well as possible. . . . to accomplish something difficult; to master, manipulate and organize physical objects, human beings or ideas; to do this as rapidly and independently as

*A paper presented at the International Symposium on Psychological Assessment in Sport. Wingate, Israel, October, 1977.

possible; to overcome obstacles and attain a high standard; to excel one's self; to rival and surpass others; to increase self-regard by the successful exercise of talent" (Murray, 1938:164).

The development of McClelland's (1951, 1955) motivational theory was strongly influenced by the work of Murray. McClelland defined need achievement as the positive or negative effect aroused in situations that involve competition with a standard of excellence where performance can be evaluated as successful or unsuccessful (McClelland, Atkinson, Clark & Lowell, 1953). McClelland's early work concentrated on developing a general theory of achievement motivation. Atkinson (1957, 1964), one of McClelland's colleagues, viewed nAch in terms of capacity for taking pride in the accomplishment. Atkinson considered not only the motive to achieve but the motive to avoid failure as well. Each of these motives is seen as a function of two situational variables: the perceived expectancy of success and the incentive value of the task being performed. Heckhausen (1967) also included two motives in his theory of achievement motivation. He included consideration for "hope of success" as well as "fear of failure."

Application of the mathematical model advanced by Atkinson (1957) and revised by Atkinson and Feather (1966) implied that individuals in whom the motive to avoid failure is stronger than the motive to achieve success would be predicted to avoid all achievement-related activities. Experimental and observational data indicate that many individuals in this category do pursue achievement oriented activities both in the laboratory and in the real world. To account for this observational discrepancy, Atkinson (1974) proposed that the concept of intrinsic motivation be included in the model. As defined, the term intrinsic refers to sources of motivation such as the appeal of the task and the tendencies to seek approval or to comply with authority that can overcome the inclination to avoid failure.

A number of other additions and modifications have been made to the basic theory in an attempt to improve the predictability and to account for behavioral variance in both laboratory and field settings. One major qualification has been to acknowledge individual differences in level of ability, skill and competence and how these differences may influence the perception of external cues defining level of difficulty, thereby mediating individual probabilities of success and failure.

An important addition to the theory was generated by the work of Raynor (1969) who considered the impact of long-term future goals on achievement behavior. This would have specific application to sport-related goals which are generally long-term. Raynor adds the concept of what he called "contingent motivation" which is aroused when the individual feels that immediate feedback of success is needed in order to guarantee opportunity to strive for some future related goal while immediate failure predicts future failure by insuring loss of opportunity to continue. Conversely, a noncontingent situation would develop if immediate success does not influence opportunity to strive for future goals and if immediate failure does not guarantee future failure. Raynor hypothesized that individuals evaluate situations in terms of their contingent or non-contingent relationship to future goals and that these contingencies and related subjective probabilities influence achievement motivated behavior. The issues raised by Raynor's insistence upon the importance of fitting a present activity into the perspective of long-range goals have broad implications for understanding both the research data and the research designs. The validity of the investigation in achievement motivation will be related to the degree that the individual is ego-involved in the task and how that task fits into the individual's life goals.

Kagan and Moss (1962) considered achievement and recognition behaviors together because the overt behaviors that appear to gratify these motives overlap to a large degree. They proposed that achievement behavior and motivation are possibly highly correlated because individuals with strong needs for mastery usually engage in achievement activities. The goal of achievement behavior is self-satisfaction for performing tasks at a level of competence that one has previously established as satisfying. The goal in recognition behavior is some positive reaction from others, a social acknowledgement of the individual's competence. Generally, mastery and competence produced feelings of self-approval; acquisition of skills also resulted in social recognition. Extrinsic reinforcement and acknowledgement produced an awareness of being esteemed by others. Kagan and Moss concluded that it was difficult to differentiate achievement and recognition motives. They indicated that perhaps their methods were not sufficiently sensitive to distinguish these or that it is impossible to measure the desire to improve one's skill apart from the need for social recognition for this mastery.

Assessing achievement motivation

While there is a great deal of variability in the notion of achievement motivation, there is even more in the measurement of such a concept. Basically, there are three major types of assessment: projective instruments; scales within personality inventories; and questionnaires designed specifically to assess achievement motivation. There are some 25 instruments which purport to measure achievement motivation, most of which have been developed since the early 1950's. It appears reasonable to expect a high statistical interrelationship among the different techniques and instruments, however, this has not been the case. Fineman (1977) surveyed the literature and prepared a table showing 78 different correlations of various instruments; 72% of the correlations indicated no significant relationship between the nAch measures.

The validity of nAch instruments has been based on the assumption that there is some relationship between nAch and performance. This is consistent with McClelland et al. (1958) who proposed that a significant positive correlation between nAch and the actual efficiency of the performance should be observed. While only a modest relationship might be expected, Atkinson & Feather (1966) suggest that this might be an oversimplification of the issue. They stated that performance and nAch will relate positively when an expectancy of satisfying the need has been aroused and when fear of failure has not been aroused. McClelland (1961) qualified his earlier statement on prediction of performance when he said that nAch will lead to more effort only when there is a chance that such effort will make a difference in the outcome.

In summary to this point, it appears that some of the studies which have demonstrated a lack of relationship between nAch and performance have reflected inappropriate situational conditions for achievement-motivated performance. It seems essential that situational factors be considered in performance predictions. Apparently, many available measures of nAch are not measuring the same construct. Further, a generalized notion of nAch may not be sufficient for specific situations. The solution appears to be to develop measures that will balance the structured nature of the questionnaire technique with the more ambiguous frame-of-reference of the respondent. When measures are designed for specific populations such as athletes, this balance between the structured questionnaire and the situation may be achieved.

The intrinsic-extrinsic motivation dichotomy

Sport situations have frequently been described as laboratories for achievement learning. Feedback is immediate, providing reinforcement contingencies. Reward systems are obvious and extensive with success being rewarded extrinsically in most competitive situations. In general, it has been assumed that individuals would be motivated to work harder to meet with greater success in order to receive the extrinsic rewards. This has been an effective means of motivating many athletes, however, continued involvement and challenge may require other aspects or intrinsic motivation as well. Obviously, many other factors must be considered. Examples include the way in which one is socialized, the value systems that exist within his social environment, the ability to perform, and so on.

The terms *intrinsic* and *extrinsic* have appeared in the discussion of motivation for sometime. Deci (1975) defined intrinsic factors as those mediated by the person himself while extrinsic factors are mediated by someone other than the athlete such as the coach, his parents, his country, etc. In other words, the athlete who is intrinsically motivated to participate in sport does so because he finds the participation itself is rewarding. On the other hand, an athlete is extrinsically motivated if he performs in sport in order to achieve some external reward.

Deci (1975) deals with human motivation and presented a cognitive perspective in attempting to account for the "whys" of voluntary behavior. He works under the assumption that most behaviors are voluntary and that individuals chose these behaviors because they desire the end result. Therefore, the individual's perceptions and cognitions are basic to his or her behavior. The operational definition of intrinsic motivation suggests that activities engaged in are ends in themselves as opposed to a means to an end. Individuals participate in activities for the feedback they get in the process and not because the involvement leads to an extrinsic reward. This concept may have relevance for the pursuit of physical activity and sport beyond the situations where extrinsic factors may be the desired goal.

Another basic premise upon which the notion of intrinsic motivation is based, is that individuals tend to be motivated to reduce uncertainty and to feel capable of dealing effectively with the environment. Deci (1975) proposed that one's need to feel competent and self-determining will produce two general classes of behavior. First, individuals will seek out situations which provide a reasonable challenge. If one is bored, one will seek a challenge; if one is over-challenged, a different situation which will provide a challenge that can be met will be sought. In essence, this suggests that the motivational mechanism operating will lead individuals to situations where they are challenged to make optimal use of their abilities.

The second class of behaviors motivated by the need for competence and self-determination that Deci described were those needs to be successful in challenge situations. Individuals are motivated to reduce dissonance when they encounter it or when they create it. Many create dissonance or incongruity just so they can have the challenge of mastery in the situation.

A complete understanding of intrinsic motivation includes both physiological and psychological motives. Whether one elects to focus on one level or the other is a matter of preference; both have a considerable amount of literature supporting their respective concept.

Relationship of intrinsic motivation and other concepts

Intrinsic motivation has been related to several concepts that have been utilized in an effort to obtain greater insight into one's involvement in sport. Rotter, (1966) in his work with social learning theory, suggested that individuals differ in the extent to which they believe that rewards are contingent on their own behaviors or attributes. Rotter's theory of locus of control suggests that those who are categorized as "internals" believe that rewards or other reinforcements follow from their behavior or attributes. Internals believe in the relationship of behavior and rewards and feel they have some control over their environment. On the other hand, those who are labeled "externals" believe that rewards are determined primarily by luck or fate; they do not believe that they have control over their environment. It would appear that Rotter's concept of internal locus of control is an essential component of intrinsic motivation. Internals feel that they can control their environment, therefore, they do many things to create feelings of competence and self-determination.

In 1959 Festinger introduced a theory of cognitive dissonance which proposed that when an individual perceived two cognitions that were discrepant, discomfort would result and the individual would be motivated to do something to reduce this dissonance. Festinger suggested that individuals preferred an absence of dissonance while Deci proposed that experiencing this incongruity provides an opportunity for facing a challenge. This, in turn, provides a sense of competence and self-determination when it is successfully met. This concept fits nicely with the whole notion of stress-seeking and risk-taking in sports activities when individuals seek out and/or create situations where challenge and dissonance are paramount for the opportunity to master and control their behaviors in the face of challenge.

Individuals' cognitive and affective behaviors are recognized as central to the study of motivation and intrinsic motivation is seen as basic to understanding behavior. Csikszentmihalyi (1975) accommodates both of the essential aspects of current motivational theory. He reports his own research attempts to get at the basis of experiencing enjoyment and fulfillment through activities for which the primary reward is in the experience rather than in any outcome following the involvement. According to Csikszentmihalyi, the individual's experience in such activities as rock climbing, dance, soccer and so on is holistic in nature and results from total involvement in the activity. He labels this state of total involvement FLOW and suggests that regardless of whether it is experienced in work or play, several commonalities are shared such as a merging of action and awareness, a centering of attention on a limited field of stimulus and a "narrowing" of consciousness; a heightened body awareness; a control of actions and environment; a coherent and noncontradictory demand for actions; and an intrinsic reward system. In short, conventional competitive sports which attempt to lure the participant toward external rewards may be removing the individual from the initial state and motives of involvement.

From Csikszentmihalyi's perspective, children seek out pleasure or FLOW naturally, however, the emphasis society places on achievement of results rather than discovery and enjoyment appears to take them away from the very experience that they seek. The irony, according to Csikszentmihalyi, is that when one focuses on exploration and enjoyment, the performance will improve without directing attention to it as such. When individuals are totally involved in the experience, their performance will be positively affected. On the other hand, when they direct their attention to external rewards and goals, their performance will be directed away from the activity and toward the reward which comes after the experience.

While Csikszentmihalyi provides some empirical basis for understanding his concept of FLOW, and demonstrates application of empirically based methodology to investigate concepts that have arisen out of humanistic psychology, he does not adequately relate his research and ideas to motivation theory in general.

Glasser (1976) has proposed the notion of "positive addiction" as a rationale for continued pursuit of physical activity, basing much of his discussion on committed runners that he says are positively addicted to running. From running, the runner gains mental strength which he uses to help him accomplish whatever he tries to do more successfully. In an attempt to understand what makes people run, Glasser began to interview runners. He was convinced that running to prevent a heart attack twenty years later would be insufficient motivation for pursuing a voluntary, painful, lonely, boring self-improvement pursuit such as regular distance running. Nor did he feel that the payoff of being trim and strong was sufficiently motivating either. What he did discover was that something "happens" to the runner that is enjoyable, so he runs again and again to re-experience this sensation. Accordingly to Glasser, it is a trance-like mental state which appears to be a process of letting your mind go, letting it spin free. It is this state that the runner becomes addicted to and is motivated to re-experience time and time again. Therefore, to avoid the undesirable experience of feeling something is missing, he runs. Glasser believes this is a form of positive addiction state of mind that exercisers reach indirectly and that those who practice transendental meditation try to reach directly. Glasser indicated that it takes time to develop addiction to such a mental state in running; most runners take nearly a year of regular long-distance running to develop positive addiction. He concluded that this type of addiction is something that individuals chose to do because they believe it has some value for them, enough to put in an hour or so a day to obtain. Glasser says that a small number of top athletes get into the positive addiction state of mind often. That they intensely enjoy the game because of the tangible satisfaction of their superior performance they get in addition to the satisfaction of the highly desirable state of mind. The idea of "getting it all together" so that it flows is most probably the same notion that Csikszentmihalyi is discussing in his concept of FLOW.

Additional factors related to motivation

Among the more consistent findings in the achievement motivation literature are those showing social class differences, generally attributed to consistent class differences in child-rearing practices assumed to stem from greater emphasis on achievement, mastery training and self-direction. However, the greatest confusion in the understanding of achievement motivation has been that involving sex differences. The initial research efforts involved primarily data gathered from males even though comparisons of male and female responses were made. Inconsistent and contradictory findings have been reported and some investigators ceased to gather data from females because they did not get good, clean, predictable data. Atkinson (1974) only devoted a single footnote to female achievement motivation and Heckhausen (1967) allotted 9 of 215 pages to the female. In short, a number of investigators have suggested that males and females differ in need stimulating achievement behavior. It has been argued that females work for love and approval rather than mastery, that achievement motivation is bound to affiliative needs. These arguments stress quite different underlying mechanisms for equivalent achievement motivation in males and females. Other differences between sexes have been related to attributions concerning performance. While males and females are equally accurate in assessing their abilities, they tend to err in opposite directions with males tending to overestimate their competence with females underestimating. Much of the theoretical and empirical discussion about social concerns over achievement and attributions about performance has centered on Horner's (1968) construct of fear of success. This construct has been fraught with methodological problems and inconsistencies in results.

Researchers in the tradition of McClelland and his followers have been single-minded in their pursuit of a unitary, fantasy-based measure of the motive to achieve success and in their rejection of other attempts to assess it by objective measures. In general, few investigators have attempted to break the motive for success into constituent parts and examine them independently even though the motive is constructed from subcategories. Other investigators who have been disenchanted with projective measures have devoted efforts to developing and validating objective measures of achievement motivation. Both projective and objective measures have demonstrated modest predictive validity in contrived laboratory studies and in predicting broader real life criteria of achievement motivations.

However, correlations between these two types of measures have been extremely low. The lack of congruence may be explained by the lack of reliability of the measurements and/or by trying to generalize to a single broad construct called achievement motivation rather than examining smaller components of behavior.

Helmreich and Spence (1977) decided that a unitary construct of achievement motivation was too simplistic to account for broad patterns of behavior in real-life settings. They also felt that important components of achievement motivation related to masculinity and femininity such as orientation toward work, striving for excellence, and concern with the reactions of others toward achievement, might operate independently of one another. Further, they hope that they could devise an achievement motivation scale that would be useful in analyzing data from both sexes. Using some original items and some derived from Mehrabian (1969), Helmreich and Spence developed the Work and Family Orientation Questionnaire (WOFO). Their multi-faceted approach included four components of achievement motivation: 1) Work Orientation — desiring to do one's best in whatever one undertakes; 2) Mastery — persistence in accomplishing tasks, of doing difficult things; 3) Competitiveness — enjoying the challenge of situations involving skill and competition; and 4) Personal Unconcern — not being concerned about what others might think. The average intercorrelation was .30, suggesting that the questionnaire was tapping components of achievement motivation which were moderately related.

Helmreich and Spence also developed a Personal Attributes Questionnaire (PAQ) which classifies individuals according to their perceived sex-role classification. Four categories are possible: 1) Androgynous — those with most desirable human characteristics some of which have been traditionally accorded to the male and some to the female; 2) Masculine — those perceiving themselves as the traditional male; 3) Feminine — those who are most like traditionally stereotyped female; and 4) Undifferentiated — those who fall below the mean for both masculinity and femininity.

		Masculinity	
		Below Median	Above Median
F E M I N I N I T Y	Below Median	UNDIFFERENTIATED	MASCULINE
	Above Median	FEMININE	ANDROGYNOUS

Source: Helmreich, R. & Spence, J. T. Sex-roles and achievement. In R. W. Christina and D. M. Landers (Eds.), *Psychology of Motor Behavior and Sport* (Vol. 2). Champaign, Ill.: Human Kinetics Publishers, 1977.

Table 1. *Sex-role classification: personal attributes questionnaire.*

Utilizing the PAQ and the WOFO instruments, female athletes including marathon and distance runners, rowers, and athletes in many other sports were tested. As indicated in Table 1, over 45% of these athletes perceived themselves as Androgynous, 23.3% viewed themselves as Masculine, 13.2% as Feminine and 17.1% as Undifferentiated.

A one by four (achievement motivation component by sex-role orientation) analysis of variance revealed several significant F ratios. The Mastery component was highly significant $F(3,233) = 7.73$, $p < .00001$. Those athletes who perceived themselves as being Masculine or Androgynous scored significantly higher in the Mastery component of achievement motivation than did the Feminine or Undifferentiated. The Work component was also highly significant $F(3,236) = 6.316$, $p < .00001$ with the Androgynous athletes scoring significantly higher than the Undifferentiated or Feminine athletes.

The Competitiveness component was observed to be highly significant $F(3,230) = 4.669$, $p < .003$, indicating that the Masculine were significantly different from the Feminine and the Undifferentiated athletes. The Androgynous athletes were also significantly different from the Feminine.

When examining the Personal Unconcern component, another highly significant F ratio was observed $F(3,203) = 3.163$, $p < .026$. The Masculine female athletes were significantly different from the Feminine.

Sex-role Classification	N	Motivational Components			
		Mastery	Work	Competitiveness	Personal Unconcern
Androgynous	109	17.9	18.4	15.7	15.4
Masculine	58	25.7	25.0	23.7	24.2
Feminine	32	13.0	13.7	11.1	12.2
Undifferentiated	41	10.1	10.9	8.9	10.1

Table 2. *Mean scores of 240 female athletes on motivational components by sex-role classification.*

The exploratory work of Helmreich and Spence followed by my own research on 240 female athletes examining the relationships of sex-role classification and achievement motivation components is promising. However, much more research is needed in this area before the model of achievement motivation can be extended to large athletic populations. Helmreich (1977) suggested that it is possible that the need to surpass others (rather than exceeding past personal attainment) might be deleterious for those in individual competitive sports. For example, the athlete whose identity is viewed in terms of individual competition may be reluctant to continue to compete with top athletes after suffering defeat because this defeat may be equated with personal inferiority. Thus, some top athletes may avoid really challenging competition because of this type of motivational problem. In any event, it appears that a multifaceted concept of achievement motivation may prove to be useful in the examination of athletes' performances.

The achievement motive concept appears to be a plausible one. Observed behaviors such as striving to do well, developing mastery and competence, making application of one's capabilities to succeed, and to evaluate this performance on the basis of one's own standards as well as be judged by others on mastery, seems to be accounted for in the notion of achievement motivation. While the Gordian knot of interrelationships among masculinity, femininity, performance, and their joint antecedents is still quite tangled, the work of Helmreich and Spence provides insight and guidance for future directions in research examining these factors in competitive sport environments.

REFERENCES

ATKINSON, J. W. Motivational determinants of risk-taking behavior. *Psychological Review.* 1957, *64,* 359-372.

ATKINSON, J. W. *An introduction to motivation.* Princeton, N.J.: Van Nostrand, 1964.

ATKINSON, J. W. & FEATHER, N. T. *A theory of achievement motivation.* New York: Wiley, 1974.

CSIKSZENTMIHALYI, M. *Beyond boredom and anxiety.* San Francisco: Jossey-Bass, Inc., 1975.

DECI, E. L. *Intrinsic motivation.* New York: Plenum Press, 1976.

FINEMAN, S. The achievement motive construct and its measurement: where are we now? *British Journal of Psychology.* 1977, *68,* 1-22.

FESTINGER, L. *A theory of cognitive dissonance.* Evanston, Ill.: Row & Peterson, 1957.

GLASSER, W. *Positive addiction.* New York: Harper & Row, 1976.

HARRIS, D. V. & JENNINGS, S. E. Self-perceptions of female distance runners. Paper presented at Conference on the Marathon: Physiological, Medical, Epidemiological and Psychological Studies, New York City, October 25-28, 1976.

HARRIS, D. V. & JENNINGS, S. E. The relationship between sex-role classification and self-esteem among female distance runners. Paper presented at the North American Society for the Psychology of Sport and Physical Activity Conference, Ithaca, N.Y., 1977.

HECKHAUSEN, H. *The anatomy of achievement motivation.* New York: Academic Press, 1967.

HELMREICH, R. & SPENCE, J. T. Sex roles and achievement. In R. W. Christina & D. M. Landers (Eds.) *Psychology of Motor Behavior and Sport* (Vol. 2) Champaign, Ill.: Human Kinetics Publishers, 1977.

HORNER, M. S. Sex differences in achievement motivations and performance in competitive and non-competitive situations. Doctoral dissertation, University of Michigan, 1968.

KAGAN, J. & MOSS, H. *Birth to maturity.* New York: Wiley, 1962.

MC CLELLAND, D. C. *Personality.* New York: William Sloan Associates, 1951.

MC CLELLAND, D. C. Measuring motivation in fantasy. In D. C. McClelland (ed.) *Studies in motivation.* New York: Appleton Century-Crofts, 1955.

MC CLELLAND, D. C. Methods of measuring human motivation. In J. W. Atkinson (ed.) *Motives in fantasy, action, and society.* Princeton, N. J.: Van Nostrand, 1958.

MC CLELLAND, D. C. *The achieving society.* Princeton, N. J.: Van Nostrand, 1961.

MC CLELLAND, D. C., ATKINSON, J. W., CLARK, R. A. & LOWELL, E. L., *The achievement motive.* New York: Appleton-Century-Crofts, 1953.

MURRAY, H. *Explorations in personality.* New York: Oxford University Press, 1938.

RAYNOR, J. O. Future orientation and motivation of immediate activity; an elaboration of the theory of achievement motivation. *Psychological Review,* 1969, *76,* 606-610.

ROTTER, J. B. Generalized expectancies for internal *vs.* external control of reinforcement. *Psychological Monographs,* 1966. *80* (1), Whole no. 609, 1-28.

Aggression in Sport

Perhaps there is no other topic in sport psychology that requires, even demands, more attention than aggression. Aggression is defined in psychology as the intent to inflict harm on another individual. Within recent years, there has been a dramatic increase in aggression in the professional sports of basketball, football, baseball and hockey. Although aggression has many connotations to players, coaches and fans, the carnage in sport must be stopped. Man's inhumanity to man has no place in athletics.

To talk about this important social problem, from practical and theoretical points of view, are three outstanding authorities. Psychologist J. P. Scott's address at the Second International Congress of Sport Psychology in 1968 in Washington, D. C. is considered to be a classic. Dr. Scott, a former athlete, covers some of the most salient topics, including the control of aggression through training. As a proponent of a peaceful and nonviolent society, Scott advocates that we must reverse the trend toward excellence in sport at the expense of participation. Sport and games participation, Scott suggests, provide effective methods for the control of undesirable aggression. You will find Dr. Scott's paper interesting, informative and thought provoking.

In "Sport, Competition and Aggression", the second paper, Leonard Berkowitz, well-known social psychologist, is not as favorable to the role of sport in the control of violence as Dr. Scott. Dr. Berkowitz is not a proponent of "bigger and better olympic games" as a way toward world peace. In contrast, Berkowitz states that athletic competition doesn't necessarily reduce the chances of violence and may even increase the probability of aggressive outbursts. Sport, Berkowitz contends, is no royal road to peace and social harmony.

In the final paper, Michael Smith, Canadian Sport Psychologist, addresses the topic of hockey violence. Dr. Smith 'pulls no punches' and 'tells it like it is'. His approach is straight forward, hard hitting and intellectually stimulating. Smith shoots down in convincing style the Campbell–Ziegler doctrine that 'fighting is an outlet or safety valve which if stopped-up would result in more vicious and dangerous behavior'. As a fan, hockey parent, former coach, and researcher, Dr. Smith is eminently qualified to address this problem.

Sport and Aggression*

J. P. Scott, Ph.D.
Bowling Green
State University

The control of undesirable violence is one of the major problems of our time. Such destructive behavior may occur on many levels of organization: between individuals, in conflicts between groups within a society (such as gang wars or riots), or in conflicts among societies on a global basis. In the following paper I shall examine the role of sports as a means of controlling violence. As you will see, sports have a major role to play in developing peaceful behavior and one which is too often forgotten.

I may add that I am speaking from personal experience as well as on the basis of objective scientific studies. As a boy and young man, I took part in many sports, particularly in track and football, and I can say from a subjective viewpoint that I have never felt more peaceful and relaxed than after a good hard game of football.

GENERAL THEORETICAL BASES

Factors Influencing Aggression

As I have shown in my book some ten years ago (Scott, 1958), fighting is affected by factors operating on all levels of organization. There are genetic or hereditary factors, physiological factors, organismic factors (including learning), social factors, and finally ecological or general environmental factors. Furthermore, each species has behind it an evolutionary history of the development of fighting, and each individual has his own personal developmental history of behavior which may or may not include fighting. In short, there is no one cause of fighting, but rather multiple causes. It follows that there is no one perfect, simple method for the control of fighting. Each of the above general types of factors may be used to either enhance or decrease the incidence of fighting between individuals. In the paragraphs below I shall summarize the major findings from each of these areas and later discuss their applicability with respect to participation in sports.

The Origin of Social Fighting

Only the higher forms of animal life show true social fighting, or agonistic behavior, but almost all animals show some sort of defensive behavior against injury by a predator: usually to turn and threaten or attack it. Social fighting probably evolved from such behavior, and it is easy to see how reflexive

*An address given at the Second International Congress of Sports Psychology, Washington, D. C., 1968. Reprinted from: *Contemporary Psychology of Sport*, (ed.) Kenyon, G. S. North Palm Beach, Florida: Athletic Institute, 1970. Reprinted with permission of the publisher.

defensive reactions could result in agonistic behavior in individual development as well as in evolutionary history. If we put two mice together, one may
start to groom the other, and if the first gets a little rough, the second may
turn around and bite. The first mouse bites back, and the fight is on. If the
two cannot escape from each other, the interaction becomes a circular one,
each animal stimulating the other to more and more violent behavior, until
serious injury results.

The same sort of behavior can be seen in nursery school children. One
child accidentally pushes another, who pushes back a little harder, the first
one retaliates, and so on, until both are crying. The problem is how to keep
this tendency toward circular interaction and ever-mounting violence under
control so that it does not become destructive.

The Physiology of Fighting

As can be seen from its evolutionary history, fighting is basically an
emergency reaction. Accompanying and following the outward behavior
there are tremendous physiological changes, all having the effect of preparing
the body for violent effort. Notice that these changes all *follow* fighting or the
stimulation to fight, rather than preceding it. There is no evidence of any
physiological mechanism that would produce a cumulative need for fighting
apart from that aroused by emergency situations. However, as so often happens in civilized life, we may be subjected to a long series of emergency
situations but have our fighting behavior totally suppressed by training. The
resulting prolonged upset physiological condition accompanied by feelings of
strong emotion can be both physiologically and psychologically harmful. We
must conclude that suppressive training by itself is not a completely satisfactory method for the control of aggression.

General Methods of Social Control

Fighting has now been studied in many different species of nonhuman
animals, both in the laboratory and under natural conditions. As we examine
these animal societies, it is obvious that there are several general methods of
the social control of fighting which apply not only to them but also appear
to be important in human societies.

In accordance with the general principle of adaptation, social fighting
tends to evolve in forms of behavior which are socially useful and minimally
harmful. If we watch two goats fighting, we see that they do this in a very
formal fashion, always in individual combat with adequate warning signals
given in advance, after which the two goats rise on their hind feet and clash
their horns together, with little harm done to either. In short, the form of
fighting is genetically *ritualized,* just as some forms of human sport such as
boxing are culturally ritualized forms of fighting.

In addition, most fighting is reduced to threats and avoidance by the
formation of a dominance order. For example, in a litter of young puppies
there is a long period in early development in which no fighting occurs.
Then the young puppies begin to playfully fight with each other, mouthing
and pawing each other's bodies. Occasionally the play becomes rough, one
animal or the other gets hurt, and the two animals then struggle with each
other for several minutes in a more serious fashion, until one gives up and

goes away. The next time the pair gets into conflict the loser quits as soon as the victor threatens, and this soon becomes a firm habit. These conflicts occur before the teeth of the young pups are well-developed, and they never do each other serious harm. The end result is a dominance relationship developed in early life and maintained into adulthood.

Another interesting animal example is that of the baboon troops studied by Washburn and DeVore (1961) in South Africa. These troops are normally composed of adult males, adult females, and large number of growing young of various ages all living together. Among the males there is a definite dominance order, with one large male being dominant over the rest. The young animals do not get into the dominance order until they begin to play with each other. This play consits of running, chasing, and grappling with each other. Occasionally it gets so rough that one small baboon will give a cry of pain. At this point one of the older males comes over and threatens all of the play group, who immediately stop their activity. The result is that the young animals learn to avoid getting too rough, and, like the puppies, learn to develop their own dominance order without doing each other actual harm. In both cases, the young animals have learned to *control harmful aggression through play*.

Dominance organization appears to be very important in all of the primate societies that have so far been studied. We can conclude that the same phenomenon should be important in human societies and raise the question of whether human play behavior brings harmful aggression under control.

The phenomenon of social dominance also illustrates the enormous importance of training in the control of aggression. When an animal is dominant, it will invariably attack or threaten the subordinate if given provocation. The same animal in a subordinate relationship with another will never attack or retaliate. The general principles are that *individuals fight in the situations in which they have been trained to fight, and are peaceful in those in which they have been trained to be peaceful.*

Training for peaceful behavior is also accomplished by another major mechanism which begins to operate far earlier in life than dominance. In any highly social species of mammals or birds, there is an early period in development when the young animal easily forms social bonds with other individuals, usually members of the same species and also other animals that may happen to be in close contact for long periods. This normally results in the formation of close attachments to particular individuals at a time when the young organism ordinarily does not fight or is physically incapable of so doing. This brings into play a control mechanism which has very great importance with respect to fighting behavior, that of *passive inhibition*. To give an example, young mice reared together in the same litter grow up peacefully as young animals, and when the time comes when they are able to fight other individuals, they continue to live peacefully together. This is explained by the principal of passive inhibition, which simply means that an animal can form habits of not fighting as well as of fighting. Perhaps an even better example is that seen in a goat flock. When two kids are born as twins and nurse from the same mother, they live peacefully together and usually maintain this habit as adults, whereas the same kids may get into conflicts with other kids of the same age and certainly with older goats and thus become part of a dominance order. There is every reason to believe that passive inhibition is very important in human beings, that young children form habits of not fighting during the time when as infants they are incapable of fighting, and that these habits persist into adult life.

Finally, one important method of social control is found only in human societies. This is the teaching and enforcement of a verbal code or codes of behavior relating to fighting. Depending on the society or the situation, the verbal code may range from one which completely forbids any form of overt violence, or even of thinking about violence, to the opposite extreme where violence and warfare are glorified by the code. These extremes of verbal models of behavior can both produce undesirable effects. If fighting is completely suppressed, abnormal behavior may result. On the other hand, the overemphasis of fighting and destructive behavior may lead to the eventual destruction of the human society involved.

These general methods of social control are so effective in any well-organized human or animal society that very little overt fighting is ever seen by the casual observer. However, social control does occasionally break down, and with the resulting social disorganization there may be a strong increase in destructive fighting.

BREAKDOWN OF SOCIAL CONTROL:
SOCIAL DISORGANIZATION

Direct interpersonal or interindividual social control is based on social relationships. It is axiomatic that a crowd of strangers who have not had time or opportunity to develop social relationships with each other, form a disorganized group compared with individuals who have either grown up with each other from birth or who have had long previous associations. Gottier (1968) recently tested the theory that social disorganization produced in this way should result in an increase in fighting. Cichlid fishes of the species known as Jack Dempseys normally fight with each other when they first meet. As a result they form a dominance order in which each fish threatens those fish which rank below him in the dominance order, and avoids those fish who stand above. Gottier compared the amount of fighting in a well-organized dominance hierarchy compared with that in which a new individual was introduced daily and found that the amount of fighting and threatening went up by 200 or 300 percent.

When we examine (Scott, 1962) the incidence of destructive violence and fighting in our society, we find that it is associated with social disorganization of various sorts. The slum areas of our large cities—no matter which nationality or race they include—often include many immigrants who are complete strangers to each other, and there are many instances of broken and disorganized families. The skidrows of our big cities are inhabited by homeless wanderers without families. Even in the affluent areas of middle class suburbia, the extreme mobility associated with industrialized life, with families moving from house to house and even from city to city every two or three years, may result in a weakened form of social organization and a loss of control which may be expressed in forms ranging from drug-taking to outright violence and vandalism.

Finally, there is a built-in period of social disorganization which normally occurs in our society. The young person, and particularly the young male, breaks away from his parental family at about the age of 18 or so, and normally does not form a new family for several years later. It is this age period between 18 and 25 in which the highest numbers of crimes and violence occur, and it is also the time when there is the highest incidence of automobile accidents. Social control frequently breaks down in men of this age, which is also the age when sport is of greatest importance in our society and when it might play a great deal more important role than it does with respect to the control of aggression.

THE FUNCTION OF SPORTS IN THE CONTROL OF AGGRESSION

Organized sports and games, whatever their nature, are a form of social organization; hence, they exert some degree of social control, both over the participants and over the spectators. It follows that sports by their very nature must counteract the factor of social disorganization as a cause of destruction and violence.

I have no wish to join the controversy concerning the definition of sport (Loy, 1968). Rather than precisely defining its boundaries, it is more important to try to subdivide what everyone considers to be sports and games into meaningful categories. One of the concepts that emerges from the work of Sutton-Smith (1968) is that games in our society belong to two cultures: one child-dominated and the other adult-dominated. In the games that children play when out of sight and control of adults, the rules are either made up by the children as they go along or are handed down from older children. Consequently, these activities are somewhat independent from adult-dominated sports and games in which the rules are written and only changed with difficulty by the adult associations which have assumed control of them.

Both these cultures have the function of preparing individuals for participation in adult life and particularly in providing ways for the control of undesirable aggression and violence. If you watch a group of very young children trying to play a game, you observe that most of their time is spent arguing about what the rules are and whether the players have conformed to them. This provides training in the practice of organized cooperative living according to rules and eventually of living according to laws. In many cases, the rules and concepts of childhood games are closely related to general concepts in our society. For example, the idea of "fairness" is very close to that of equal treatment under the law. Again, in adult-dominated contact sports, such as football and ice hockey, there are rules which define the limits of physical violence, and there are persons assigned to see that these rules are obeyed and to proscribe penalties for their violation. In short, games and sports are training grounds for the control of aggression.

THE CONTROL OF AGGRESSION THROUGH TRAINING

How important is training in the control of fighting? Can sports really have an important effect on the expression of violent behavior? First, let us see what training can do to a nonhuman animal. The common house mouse is a species which normally lives mostly upon the food which man has accumulated and within the shelters which man has designed for himself. If a wild mouse colony grows up under free conditions with plenty of food and shelter, its numbers increase very rapidly as litter after litter is born and grows up to maturity. These mice which have grown up with each other are very tolerant and show little if any fighting. Consequently, under favorably conditions, as in an old-fashioned rick or granary, mice can live together in enormous numbers in a relatively peaceful fashion. On the other hand, the same mice will attack strangers who try to move into the favorable area, and they usually drive them out. There is almost never any severe injury or death resulting from such activity because under free conditions, the mouse which is beaten is allowed to escape and can easily do so.

Using these fundamental facts about the species, we can take mice into the laboratory and, using suitable training methods, can cause them to become either entirely peaceful or to become efficient and merciless killers. Analyzing the reasons why mice that grow up together do not fight, we see that early in their development before they are able to fight they have formed habits of being peaceful through the mechanism of passive inhibition. Experimentally, we can introduce strange mice to each other and prevent their fighting during the first few meetings. The longer they have not fought, the stronger the habit of not fighting, and we can this way produce an entirely peaceful pair of mice.

On the other hand, we can take another naive mouse and train him to be a very efficient fighter. This is done by simulating an attack, by dangling a helpless mouse against the fighter, and then allowing him to apparently win. After a mouse has experienced a series of such easy victories, we can match him up with an inexperienced fighter. He attacks vigorously, soon wins because of his superior experience and initiative; and from this point on he becomes a very difficult mouse to defeat in any kind of combat. Mice trained in this way will not only attack other males on sight, but can also be trained to attack females or even the harmless young, which they normally never do.

Thus, we can demonstrate that mice have the capacity either to live peacefully together or to become blood-thirsty killers, depending on the kind of training and experience which they have received. In a normal and well-organized mouse society living under natural conditions, the mice become peaceful with respect to familiar individuals and aggressive with respect to unfamiliar ones, but do not ordinarily show either extreme of behavior which can be achieved by artificial training.

There is every reason to believe that training is equally important among human beings. We cannot make comparable experiments, for obvious reasons, but social psychologists who have experimented extensively with the expression of aggressive acts in milder situations find similar major effects of training (Berkowitz and Buck, 1967). Furthermore, we have evidence from cultural anthropology in the form of natural experiments. For instance, the Hopi and Zuni Indians were trained not only to restrain aggressive behavior completely but also taught that any kind of hostile thoughts were bad and should be repressed. At an opposite extreme, the Zulus of South Africa were trained to be efficient warriors and told that the only proper occupation of a man was to be a professional killer of people. A similar code of behavior was followed by many of our own cultural ancestors in Europe in the Middle Ages, for whom fighting, rape, and pillage were a normal way of life. One can argue that different cultures like the Hopi and the Zulu were the product of different heredity as well as different training, but this agrument falls down when we compare the behavior of the ancient Vikings with their modern descendants, the Scandinavians, who are among the world's most civilized, cultured and nonviolent peoples.

Therefore, if games and sports give training in the control of aggression, it should be effective. Perhaps the most important kind of training involves passive inhibition. Bringing groups of people together in peaceful and enjoyable activities automatically forms habits of being peaceful, and while people are engaged in these activities they cannot commit destructive acts. The games technique is particularly useful for introducing strangers, as it insures that they will begin formation of peaceful habits with respect to each other.

Furthermore, many games and sports have the effect of inducing situations which can easily lead to aggression, such as painful contact or intense competition, but training the participants to restrain themselves from violence in these situations. One of the first principles of competitive sports is that the person who loses his temper is likely to lose the game, either because he loses his judgment, or through violation of the rules.

Thus, sports and games provide powerful methods, both positive and negative, for training individuals to live together in a peaceful fashion.

THE CONTROL OF AGGRESSION IN SPECTATORS

There is a good deal of objective evidence to show that people who watch sports involving scenes of violence become emotionally aroused and consequently show more tendency to become actively aggressive thereafter. Leonard Berkowitz and his students (Geen and Berkowitz, 1966) have used an experimental situation in which college students watch one of two films, one involving a brutal boxing match and the other a film of an exciting track race. After this they have the opportunity (as they think) to deliver electric shocks to another person, and those who have watched the boxing match deal out more intensive shocks. However, the amount of punishment or pain they try to inflict depends very much on previous training. For example, both men and women will refuse to give heavy shocks to a girl, but will go ahead and punish a man severely (Taylor and Epstein, 1967).

It follows that spectators of sports involving some degree of violence will become excited to express violence themselves, but that this will ordinarily be expressed or restrained according to the training which they have previously received.

Thus, the spectator sports, and especially those involving violent contacts or intense competition, create rather than solve a problem in the control of aggression. Unless the persons who compose the crowds have been thoroughly trained in the principles of sportsmanship, violent behavior is likely to break out afterwards. It is noteworthy that most cases of this sort have involved high school night games. There seem to be two factors involved. One of these is that the students and other spectators mostly fall into an age group in which the greatest amount of violent behavior is found in our society because of developmental disorganization, and the other is that under cover of night it is less easy to detect violators of the rules. It would probably also be found that those individuals who commit violence of this sort (and many do not) have had less training in the nature of sportsman-like behavior.

THE PHYSIOLOGY OF AGGRESSION IN RELATION TO SPORTS

It has been argued in the past (usually by writers having little actual experience participating in sports) that taking part in the violent contact sports provides an outlet for the indirect expression or sublimation of feelings of anger or hostility. It has also been argued that such feelings arise spontaneously, and hence, some sort of socially approved outlet is necessary.

There is no doubt that feelings of anger and hostility do arise, whatever their cause. While the practice of using sports as an outlet for these feelings has some merit, it also has some limitations, principally that sublimation in applying violence against some inanimate object, as for example a punching bag, is never really as satisfactory as retaliating against the object or individual who was the cause of the anger in the first place. If such feelings of anger and hostility are allowed direct expression against another individual, the chief result is simply to form a strong habit of performing this kind of violent behavior, whatever it is. In the past, one solution has been to culturally ritualize such conflicts in forms which are relatively nonharmful, such as boxing matches. There is no doubt that this is a relatively effective way of settling a quarrel, but it is never an emotionally satisfactory one for the loser of the combat.

The Hypothesis of Catharsis

On the hypothesis that there is some sort of cumulative drive toward aggressive behavior, it would follow that persons who express violence should in that way get rid of their feelings and be more peaceful for a considerable time thereafter. The experiments that have been done along these lines do not bear out this hypothesis (Berkowitz, 1964). Children who become angry and are allowed to express it in some way do not become more peaceful but actually learn to be aggressive. Every time aggression is expressed, it helps to form a stronger habit, and the emotional content behind it becomes less and less necessary. Far from being a good way to control aggressive behavior, this practice actually leads to its increase.

While certain kinds of sports and athletics can be used as a controlled and non-harmful outlet for hostile feelings, this needs to be done with a good deal of care in order to be sure that harmful violence does not result. It certainly should not be considered a major use for sports. As pointed out above, most games are designed to control feelings of hostility rather than to release them. What sports can do effectively is to restore physiological behavior through violent effort, and this in turn will help to alleviate emotional disturbances.

Restoration of Physiological Balance Upset by Strong Emotion

Beginning with the work of Walter B. Cannon (1929), it has been shown that emotion of anger is very largely a phenomenon of the central nervous system, probably located in the hypothalamus. The more peripheral symptoms of anger, such as high blood pressure, have relatively little effect on behavior. The whole array of symptoms produced by anger are designed to put the body into an emergency condition ready for some sort of violent activity. If the activity is repressed as it usually is as the result of previous training, the physiological state aroused by anger may be maintained for hours. In some recent experiments with mice (Bronson and Eleftheriou, 1969), these animals remained physiologically upset for at least twenty-four hours after fighting, and such effects could be produced merely by the sight of a fighter, without any conflict taking place. This suggests that the principal physiological function of sports which include violent activity is not to sublimate the emotion of anger, but simply to provide the kind of activity which will restore the body to normal homeostatic balance.

Anyone who has competed in major sport events knows that the commonest emotion, and particularly before a contest, is that of fear or anxiety. And he can likewise remember the marvelous feeling of relief once the contest actually begins. It is probable that this kind of emotion (i.e., anxiety) is far more common under conditions of civilized living than in anger. In short, violent exercise is nature's tranquilizer.

While the hypothesis of catharsis will give an explanation for the calming effect of violent exercise, a safer and more general way to look at this phenomenon is that of restoration of physiological balance following any sort of emergency emotions.

HEREDITY, AGGRESSION AND SPORTS

With very few exceptions, male mammals are more aggressive than their female species mates. Correlated with this, males are likely to be bigger, stronger, and better equipped with offensive weapons such as horns. Among man's closest animal relatives, the primates, the condition varies from the baboons in which the males are two or three times as large as females, to gibbons in which males and females are almost equal in size. One can only guess as to what the original condition of the human species may have been, but it would appear that man falls into an intermediate group with moderate physical differences between the sexes. On the average, males are bigger and stronger than females, and more likely to indulge in overt violence, but there is a good deal of overlap between the two sexes (Scott, 1958).

In addition to these differences between the sexes, there is every indication that there is an enormous amount of variation between individuals with respect to both physical strength and aggressive tendencies, the two of which may not necessarily be correlated. In nonhuman animals such genetic differences are easily demonstrated. In dogs we have the terrier breeds which have been selected for their ability to start and win fights, and, at the other extreme, the hound breeds which have been selected for their ability to get along with strangers. Similar extreme differences in aggressiveness have been produced among the different chicken breeds.

Because of the strong effects of training, it is difficult to collect scientific data on genetic differences between human families and individuals, but there is every reason to believe that there are large genetic differences between individuals with respect to such characteristics as irritability, which may lead the individual to start fights, and physical strength which may enable him to win them.

From this evidence it follows that the need to express violent physical activity will vary a great deal from individual to individual, and that, while there are major average differences between men and women, there will be some women who have more need for violent activity than some men. It also follows that if sports are going to be a major factor in the control of aggression, we must develop both a wider variety of sports suitable to different kinds of individuals and a social or educational system which permits a much wider degree of participation in sports.

THE DEVELOPMENT OF PEACEFUL LIVING

As I have indicated above, heredity may under certain conditions cause major differences between the behavior of two individuals with respect to fighting or destructive violence. This does not mean that aggression is inherited directly, but rather that the individual has inherited certain genes which can modify his capacity to express aggressive behavior, either in an upward or downward direction. The final result comes from the interaction of these hereditary factors with various viable environmental influences including the very powerful ones of negative and positive training. As I have said above, we can use sports to develop in people habits of peaceful and enjoyable activity which automatically prevent their indulging in destructive and violent behavior and also teach them some of the rules of living in a group.

However, one cannot suddenly take an individual at the age of 15 or so when he may first begin to show possibilities of exhibiting destructive behavior and make a sportsman of him overnight. Developing a sportsman (I prefer this concept over that of developing an athlete) must start reasonably early, and here we have two psychological principles which are extremely important. One of these is the success principle. An individual who is successful in a given activity becomes motivated to perform it again, and the final peak of his motivation is the result of the number of times which he has been successful. This is, of course, derived directly from reinforcement theory. If we are going to motivate young people to take part in sports we must put them in situations in which they can be successful.

Success, in turn, is in part the result of developmental age. The second important principle is that the best age in which to start learning a particular kind of physical activity is the age at which the child can first perform it reasonably successfully. There is an optimal period for learning each kind of physical skill for each individual child. In general, one can say that most children do not achieve general physical skill and good motor control until the age of 7 or 8, when the nervous system first becomes mature. Of course, there are many exceptions, both with respect to particular sorts of skills, and resulting from variation between individuals.

SUMMARY AND CONCLUSIONS

The Current Role of Games and Sports

Games and sports can act as a powerful force for the control of destructive violence and have actually been used in this way in the past, either consciously or unconsciously, However, our society is undergoing rapid changes, many of which weaken these traditional controls.

One of the characteristics of our modern American society is geographical mobility, and this is having the effect of weakening the child-dominated games culture. For the child from a middle-income family, whose parents move every three to five years, there is less and less opportunity either to receive or to pass along the traditional games culture of children, and this function is being taken over by the parents when it persists at all. Groups of children playing by themselves are replaced by parent-dominated groups such as the Cub Scouts.

In lower-income families, mobility has similar effects, and where this is accompanied by family disorganization as well, there are essentially no controls left except those provided by the gang organizations of teenagers and young adults, which are often organized for destructive purposes. In either case, the traditional balance and connection between child and adult cultures has been upset, with a consequent weakening of games as a means for the control of aggression.

Among adult-dominated sports there is an increasing tendency to emphasize excellence at the expense of participation as these sports become professionalized and institutionalized. Baseball provides an excellent example. There are periodic attempts to change this sport, which requires a great deal of skill and is essentially a public spectacle, into a form with large numbers of participants. Softball was a game in which almost anyone could hit or catch the ball and hence could attract a large number of players. Yet, the ball was soon made harder and harder, with the result that it now takes almost as much skill to play softball as regular baseball. Little League ball was another attempt to broaden the base of participation, but it too seems to be going the way of emphasis on excellence of a few skilled players.

Why should this tendency exist? One obvious reason lies in the reactions of spectators. Watching the unskilled efforts of amateurs is unexciting, and spectator pressure demands that things be more exciting. One way to increase excitement is to get more skillful players. Another is for the promoter to deliberately increase the amount of violence in the sport, as has been done with professional wrestling. Carry this a little farther, and you have gladiatorial combats. From this point of view, professional wrestling is a decadent sport. (The same sort of result has arisen in television, where we have unusually strong competition for spectators. After hours of watching, the spectators get bored, and only scenes of slaughter and sudden death will arouse them.)

Here we have a circular situation. The more successful a sport is in attracting spectators, the more pressure toward increasing excellence and decreasing participation, with even more spectators. While watching sports provides some control over the expression of violence, it is a much weaker method than participation. Also, spectator pressure toward introducing violence into sports results in arousing increasing motivation toward disorderly and violent behavior among spectators.

Sports: An Effective Method of Controlling Violence

While the current situation in our society is far from encouraging, the fact remains that games and sports provide effective methods for the control of undesirable aggression.

First, games and sports are one way of organizing life along peaceful and non-harmful lines. This in itself combats one major cause of aggression — social disorganization.

Second, games and sports in childhood provide training in living according to rules; an essential technique for successful adult social life.

Third, rules learned in this way, plus habits of participation in sports, are particularly valuable for the control of violent behavior in the young adult age group, which represents a built-in developmental period of social disorganization in our society. (Persons working with this age group have long known that sports participation is an effective technique, but we are now beginning to appreciate the theoretical reasons *why* it works, and hence to know its limitations as well as its advantages.)

Fourth, apart from their effect in combating social disorganization, games and sports work psychologically in two different ways. One of these is through passive inhibition: the mere fact of not fighting forms a habit of not fighting in a particular situation. The other is through exposing individuals to situations that normally elicit fighting, such as intense competition or pain, and teaching them to restrain themselves.

Finally, games and sports have the physiological effect of restoring normal physiological balance through violent exercise, when this balance has been upset by strong emotions such as fear and anger. Many sports actually provoke such emotions and then relieve them, which gives the player practice in dealing with such emotions.

Thus we have a situation in which games and sports provide powerful techniques for the control of violence, but a set of general social conditions which have the effect of weakening these methods.

Positive Recommendations

What can be done to increase the effectiveness of games and sports? The answer is that we must in some way reverse the trend toward excellence at the expense of participation. If we really want to work toward a peaceful and nonviolent society we must change our goals toward encouraging every boy and girl to participate in some or many games and sports. Because of individual differences caused by heredity and experience, this means developing a variety of activities and games. We also need such activities for older people as well as young ones.

It also means developing activities with lower standards of performance; which essentially means non-spectator sports. We now have a few sports that can be both, such as swimming and skiing. The point about these sports is that competition is a non-essential part of the activity; that either swimming or skiing is an enjoyable activity in itself (or, in psychological terms, a self-reinforcing one). If ski resort operators are wise, they will continue to provide instruction, a variety of slopes, and even cross-country skiing to encourage wider participation. Fortunately, this sport is not one which lends itself to large crowds of spectators, with the resulting pressure toward increasing excellence and decreasing participation.

I have no recommendations as to how we can bring about this change in goals. Perhaps the current public awareness of the dangers of the continued trend toward increasing violence may help. And certainly the persons in our society who most clearly occupy key positions of power with respect to the future of games and sports are those educators and scientists who work with them.

REFERENCES

BERKOWITZ, L. Aggressive cues in aggressive behavior and hostility catharsis. *Psychological Review*, 1964, 71, 104-122.

BERKOWITZ, L. and BUCK, R. W. Impulsive aggression: Reactivity to aggressive cues under emotional arousal. *Journal of Personality*, 1967, 35, 415-424.

BRONSON, F. H. and ELEFTHERIOU, B. E. Chronic physiological effects of fighting mice. *General and Comparative Endocrinology*, 1964, 4, 9-14.

CANNON, W. B. *Bodily changes in pain, humor, fear and rage.* (2nd ed.) Boston: Branford, 1929, 1953.

GEEN, R. and BERKOWITZ, L. Name-mediated aggressive cue properties. *Journal of Personality*, 1966, 34, 456-465.

GOTTIER, R. The effects of social disorganization in *Cichlasoma biocellatum.* Unpublished doctoral dissertation, Bowling Green State University, 1968.

LOY, J. W., JR. The nature of sport: A definitional effort. *Quest*, 1968, Monograph 10, 1-15.

SCOTT, J. P. *Aggression.* Chicago: University of Chicago Press, 1958.

SCOTT, J. P. Hostility and aggression in animals. In E. L. Bliss (Ed.). *Roots of behavior.* New York: Harper, 1962.

SUTTON-SMITH, B. Play, games and controls. (Manuscript in preparation, 1968).

TAYLOR, S. P. and EPSTEIN, S. Aggression as a function of the interaction of the sex of the aggressor and the sex of the victim. *Journal of Personality*, 1967, 35, 474-486.

WASHBURN, S. L. and DE VORE, I. The social life of baboons. *Scientific American*, 1961, 204, 62-71.

Sports Competition and Aggression*

Leonard Berkowitz, Ph.D.
University of Wisconsin -
Madison

You might remember General MacArthur's farewell speech. "Old soldiers never die," he said, "they just fade away." Every once in a while I have the impression that the same thing can be said about certain psychological notions, especially in regard to aggression. Old ideas never die, apparently. They may fade away occasionally, but someone is bound to resurrect them and proclaim them as a newfound truth. This certainly seems to be the case with ventilative conceptions of aggression. We're repeatedly told that civilized man does not have sufficient outlets for his supposedly pent-up aggressive urges. Society would be improved by providing him with safe opportunities to discharge, or sublimate, his aggressive energy. In ventilation there is health.

Sports, and competitive games generally, are frequently recommended as an effective purge. The basic thinking here, as you know, is that an aggressive drive continuously presses for discharge and must have an outlet, either in attacks upon others or against the self, or in efforts to achieve mastery. Sports presumably can furnish this needed release. As an example, one of the leading contemporary exponents of the notion of a spontaneously generated aggressive drive, Konrad Lorenz, has this to say in his recent book On Aggression (1966):

"...the main function of sport today lies in the cathartic discharge of aggresive urge..." (p. 280).

Extending this reasoning to international relations, he and others believe that international games can promote peace:

"The most important function of sport lies in furnishing a healthy safety valve for that...most dangerous form of aggression that I have described as collective militant enthusiasm...The Olympic Games are virtually the only occasion when the anthem of one nation can be played without arousing any hostility against another." (p. 281).

The tragic events at the Olympic Games in Munich this past summer must make us wonder about sport as an outlet for "collective militant enthusiasm."

Conventional psychodynamic theorizing also holds that the aggressive

*An article published in the *Proceedings Fourth Canadian Symposium: Psycho-Motor Learning and Sports Psychology.* (ed.) Williams, I. D. and Wankel, L. M. Waterloo, Ontario: The University of Waterloo, October, 1972. Fitness and Amateur Sport Directorate, Department of National Health and Welfare, Ottawa, Canada. Reprinted with permission of the publisher.

"drive," whether it is instinctive or the product of earlier frustrations, can safely be discharged through athletic competition. Writing about 25 years ago, as an illustration, William Menninger (1948) contended that play brings about a healthy release from the tensions supposedly created by "instinctive" aggressive impulses. He also claimed that "competitive games provide an unusually satisfactory social outlet for the instinctive aggressive drive," but believed that some discharge could also be obtained through sports involving "sedentary intellectual competition," such as chess and checkers (p. 343).

It's easy to understand this type of reasoning. We can readily grasp the metaphor of a reservoir of aggressive energy pressing for discharge, like a boiler full of steam, and the idea of games as an outlet for this energy seems to coincide with our experience. But this ease of understanding is a misleading trap. The fit between metaphor and experience is more apparent than real and largely arises from incomplete analyses. A growing body of carefully collected evidence indicates that athletic competition doesn't necessarily reduce the chances of violence and may even increase the probability of aggressive outbursts under some circumstances. Sport is no royal road to peace and social harmony.

In considering the impact of sports it's important to distinguish between the mere observation of a game or competition and active participation in it. Even though some writers suggest that the audience can find a satisfactory release for its pent-up aggressive urges through watching others beat each other up or through observing competition (Lorenz, 1966; Storr, 1968; Feshbach, 1961), observed sports may not have the same results as actual participation in the game. The individual who only sees the encounter may not enter into it as fully as the actual player, and therefore might not obtain as complete a "release."

EFFECTS ON THE SPECTATORS

Well, what are the effects of watching some competition? There's clearly no single answer to such a question, but on looking at the evidence one thing is puzzling. There are so many reports of spectators becoming violent as a consequence of an athletic match, we have to wonder why the notion persists that the viewers will discharge their aggressive inclinations by seeing the game. Here's a sampling of these reports:

In May, 1964 a referee's decision at a soccer match in Lima, Peru caused a riot, leading to the death of a number of spectators (reported by Goldstein & Arms, 1971, p. 83).

According to some analysts (Lever, 1969), a war between El Salvador and Honduras was precipitated by a soccer game between teams representing these countries.

Athletics didn't improve the relations between Czechs and Russians shortly after the Russians had suppressed the Czechs' attempt to liberalize their government. In March, 1969 when a Czech hockey team defeated the Russian team in the world championship tournament, exuberant Czechoslovakian youths ransacked the Prague offices of the Russian airline;

instead of being satisfied, the excited Czechs attacked symbols of those they hated.

In this country, among the many incidents that could be cited, a high school basketball game in New Jersey stimulated a riot in the audience, while another game the same week in a neighboring community brought on a fight between the opposing cheerleaders (Turner, 1970).

Quantitative investigations also show how witnessed athletic contests can arouse hostility in the spectators. Goldstein and Arms (1971) interviewed men at the 1969 Army-Navy football game in Philadelphia and found a significant rise in feelings of hostility from right before to just after the game regardless of which team the men favored and which side had won. By contrast, spectators at the Army-Temple gymnastics meet held during the same month did not exhibit this increase in hostility.

In this case watching a contact sport had led to heightened aggressive inclinations. This needn't always happen. The tens of millions of people seeing televised football games every Autumn week-end aren't necessarily provoked to violence (unless, of course, they had bet heavily on the outcome of the game and lost). What happens depends upon a variety of factors. I have suggested, for example, that the witnessed event can serve as a stimulus that will elicit semantically-associated responses, but just what reactions occur is a function of the meaning of the stimulus to the observer. If the scene is interpreted as an *aggressive* encounter, in which the competitors presumably are deliberately trying to hurt each other, it is a stimulus having *aggressive* meaning and can then elicit aggressive reactions. Take a football game or a prize fight. A spectator doesn't really have to think of this as an *aggressive* contest, although it is obviously easy to do so. He might regard the opponents merely as players who are trying to win for the money or prestige the victory would bring. When one player knocks someone else down this is viewed as a demonstration of superior strength or skill. The same scene becomes an aggressive match, on the other hand, when the observer believes the contestants want to hurt each other as well as win. However broad or subtle our own definition of "aggression" might be, it's the viewer's interpretation that really matters; the scene isn't really an aggressive stimulus unless he thinks of it as aggression, as the deliberate injury of others.

An experiment by myself and Alioto tested this reasoning using college students as subjects. Each man, who had first been insulted by a paid accomplice, was shown a brief movie either of a prize fight or a professional football game. The introduction to this film "explained" the background of the contest, and portrayed the opponents either as players unemotionally engaged in their professional roles or as aggressors trying to hurt their enemy. When the subject was given an opportunity to shock the insulting confederate at the end of the film, he attacked this person more strongly if he had watched a scene having the aggressive rather than nonaggressive meaning. This was true for both the prize fight and football game. Moreover, only the men seeing the *aggressive* contest were significantly more punitive to the confederate than a similarly provoked control group shown an exciting but nonviolent film.

This experiment indicates, then, that the spectators' interpretation of a game effects their reactions to it. The contest is more likely to have aggressive consequences if it is regarded as an aggressive encounter. But other factors are also important. In our research at Wisconsin, for example, we have found that the observer's readiness to act aggressively at the time he watches the movie influences the probability that he will exhibit overt aggression at the end of the film. This means, obviously that the aggressive game will be most likely to evoke open violence from those spectators who are already inclined to be aggressive.

But again, I don't think this is all. We also have to consider other things such as the spectators' feeling of anonymity (which would lower their fear of being punished for aggression) and especially now, excited as they are. This excitement theoretically should "energize" the aggressive reactions elicited by the aggressive scene, heightening the chances of open violence. Geen and O'Neal (1969) demonstrated that noise can have this arousing effect. Their subjects who watched our standard prize fight scene and then were exposed to a burst of moderately loud noise were subsequently more punitive towards a fellow student than other subjects not given the noise or who didn't see the film. The arousing noise had evidently strengthened the implicit aggressive reactions elicited by the witnessed prize fight, leading to the stronger attacks right afterwards.

All in all, this evidence clearly shows that people watching some athletic event are unlikely to drain their supposedly pent-up aggressive urges. The game might even heighten the probability of violence under some conditions. If the spectators are less aggressive afterwards, I would say they either feel good because their team won or they were so distracted by the exciting contest that they forgot about their troubles for the time being and, in not brooding, stopped stirring themselves up.

EFFECT OF PARTICIPATING IN COMPETITION

Earlier I noted the possibility that actual participation in an athletic competition might produce a more satisfactory "release" than the mere observation of such an encounter. In actuality, however, it seems that the persons who take part in the game can also become more aggressive as a consequence of what they see and do.

One reason for this is that the game is exciting, and we just saw, excitement can energize whatever aggressive tendencies might be operating at the moment. Zillmann, Katcher and Milavsky (1972) have recently reported that the excitation created by two and a half minutes of strenuous physical exercise (bicycle riding) increased the intensity of the punishment university men administered to a peer. This happened whether or not the subjects were angry with this other person, but the energizing effect was stronger when the men had been provoked by him earlier and now had an opportunity to retaliate. The nonangry men were evidently ready to punish the other person and were therefore already somewhat inclined to attack him when they engaged in the brief exercise. The excitation then strengthened their aggressive inclinations. Needless to say, the angry subjects were even more intent on attacking this other person, and the exercise-created arousal strengthened their aggressive inclinations even more. The angry men didn't discharge their hostile urges through the vigorous physical activity, but instead, became somewhat more violent.

The competition inherent in the game can also be exciting, and again, this can intensify the players' aggressive tendencies. We have some suggestive data in a study of children's play carried out by Christy, Gelfand and Hartmann (1971). The first- and second-graders in this experiment first watched an adult engage in either aggressive-like play (punching and kicking a Bobo doll) or vigorous but nonviolent action (such as jumping around) and then were placed in either a competitive or noncompetitive situation. The arousal created by the competition energized the behavior tendencies activated by the adult's conduct. Whether they had won or lost, the children who had experienced the competition were most likely to imitate the adult's earlier behavior in their own play immediately after the competition. So, if someone starts acting violently for one reason or another, any other people around who are excited because they're competing against others should be particularly likely to do the same thing. The competition heightens, not lessens, their susceptibility to aggressive influence.

I've long suspected (Berkowitz, 1962, 1969) that competition also has some frustrating aspects if there isn't any clearcut victory in sight and especially if the individual loses, and have argued that this frustration can also create a readiness for aggression. This means that competition could increase the chances of aggression specifically as well as heighten the players' susceptibility to external influences generally. There's been a good deal of controversy about this, as you undoubtedly know, but some experimental findings do point to a competition-increased probability of aggression. As just one illustration of this, the well-known "Robber's Cave" experiment (Sherif et al., 1961) dramatically demonstrates how competition between groups of teenage boys can lead to outbreaks of violence. The frustration should be even stronger, obviously, if a person is defeated in the competition, and this thwarting could produce an even greater pre-disposition to aggression. We can see this, as an example, in the research on children's play conducted by Gelfand, Hartmann and their students. In the experiment with Christy that I mentioned earlier as well as in the case of the young boys in an earlier, similar study (Nelson, Gelfand and Hartmann, 1969), those children who had not been subjected to strong environmental influence but then suffered a loss in the competition were especially apt to engage in aggressive-like play afterwards. The pain of the defeat heightened their readiness for aggression.

In all of this I've focused on the temporary impact of sports: the excitement and the aggressive stimulation that might arise. Nothing has been said about more persistent learning, but there's also some suggestive evidence that the aggressiveness learned in play can generalize to other situations as well. In one study (Walters & Brown, 1963) the children given intermittent reinforcement for punching a Bobo doll behaved more aggressively than the controls in a competitive situation some days later. We recognize that this kind of learning may not always occur or may not always become apparent; the reinforced aggression might not transfer to other situations if the reinforcement schedule isn't appropriate and especially if the person learns to discriminate between play and the real world. Prize fighters and football players know that it's alright to knock their opponent down in the ring or on the football field but not in the street or house. Still, I would bet that if they happen to be angry and not thinking on some occasion, the reinforcements they had previously received for aggression in competition will increase the chance that they will act violently in this other setting as well.

The discriminations the individual learns and the inhibitions he acquires also help restrain the temporary aggressive reactions stimulated by the sight of aggression in the game or by the frustrations in the situation. Those aggressive reactions are usually fairly weak and relatively short-lived (more so in the spectators than in the players, I would guess), and prior learning controls these responses so the people don't attack the others around them indiscriminately. But if these persons are excited enough, stimulated enough, and sufficiently uninhibited at the moment, they could act violently. The game they played or watched has not drained their aggressive energies. Sport has considerable value for our society, but we shouldn't justify it as a safe outlet for pent-up violent urges.

REFERENCES

BERKOWITZ, L. *Aggression: A Social-Psychological Analysis.* New York: McGraw-Hill, 1962.

BERKOWITZ, L. "The Frustration-Aggression Hypothesis Revisited." In L. Berkowitz (Ed.) *Roots of Aggression.* New York: Atherton Press, 1969, pp. 1-29.

CHRISTY, P. R., GELFAND, D. M., and D. P. HARTMANN. "Effects of Competition-Induced Frustration on Two Classes of Modeled Behavior." *Developmental Psychology,* 1971, 5. 104-111.

FESHBACH, S. "The Simulating Versus Cathartic Effects of a Vicarious Aggressive Activity." *Journal of Abnormal and Social Psychology,* 1969, 63, 381-385.

GEEN, R. G. and E. C. O'NEAL. "Activation of Cue-Elicited Aggression by General Arousal." *Journal of Personality and Social Psychology,* 1969, 11, 289-292.

GOLDSTEIN, J. H. and R. L. ARMS. "Effects of Observing Athletic Contests on Hostility." *Sociometry,* 1971, 34, 83-90.

LEVER, J. "Soccer: Opium of the Brazilian People." *Trans-Action,* 1969, 7, 36-43.

LORENZ, L. *On Aggression.* New York: Harcourt, Brace and World, 1966.

MENNINGER, W. C. "Recreation and Mental Health." *Recreation,* 1948, 42, 340-346.

NELSON, J. D., GELFAND, D. M. and D. P. HARTMANN. "Children's Aggression Following Competition and Exposure to an Aggressive Model." *Child Development,* 1969, 40, 1085-1097.

SHERIF, M., HARVEY, O. J., WHITE, W. R. and C. W. SHERIF. *Intergroup Conflict and Cooperation: The Robber's Cave Experiment.* Norman, Oklahoma: University of Oklahoma Book Exchange, 1961.

STORR, A. *Human Aggression.* New York: Atheneum, 1968.

TURNER, E. T. "The Effects of Viewing College Football, Basketball and Wrestling on the Elicited Aggressive Responses of Male Spectators." *Medicine and Science in Sports,* 1970, 2, 100-105.

WALTERS, R. H. and M. BROWN. "Studies of Reinforcement of Aggression: III. Transfer of Responses to an Interpersonal Situation." *Child Development,* 1963, 34, 563-571.

ZILLMANN, D., KATCHER, A. H. and B. MILAVSKY. "Excitation Transfer from Physical Exercise to Subsequent Aggressive Behavior." *Journal of Experimental Social Psychology,* 1972, 8, 247-259.

Hockey Violence:
Interring Some Myths*

Michael D. Smith, Ph.D.
York University

"A lot is made of it [violence] that doesn't need to be. We put men on the ice who are skating at full speed; the use of the body is an important part of the game; the players are surrounded with hard boards and they play at an intensity that, when they're out on the ice, is not demanded by any other sport." Thus spoke John Ziegler, the new president of the NHL, at a recent gathering in New York City. "I do not find it unacceptable," he went on, "in a game where frustration is constant, for men to drop their sticks and gloves and take swings at each other. I think that kind of outlet is important for players in our games." (Oh!) This is what's known as a recycled speech. Ziegler's predecessor, Clarence Campbell, made it regularly for decades.

What's hard to believe is that there are still listeners. But from my vantage points (as fan, hockey parent, former coach, hockey association executive, member of two Ontario Hockey Council subcommittees, researcher) this much is evident: Though many condemn illegal violence in both professional and amateur hockey as unnecessary and undesirable, as many cling to the Campbell-Ziegler dogma that fighting, stick swinging, and the like are inevitable by-products of the "speed," "body contact," "intensity," and/or "frustration" inherent in the game and that fist fighting is an "outlet," or safety valve, which stopped up would result in more vicious and dangerous behaviour. That these notions fly in the face of what social scientists have learned about violence in general is of no avail; there has been almost no directly relevant research on hockey violence to dislodge them from the public mind (the conclusions of the 1974 Mc Murtry Report notwithstanding). Yet until the Campbell-Ziegler orthodoxy is permanently put to rest the major overhaul hockey needs, at all levels, will surely not take place.

Let's start by refuting the "speed-contact-intensity-frustration" foolishness. In some cultures where hockey is seriously taken and performed with "intensity" fouling is rare — or was, before Canadianization. Occasionally even North American pros show they can restrain themselves, when it is crucial that penalties be avoided. Large individual and team differences in illegal violence exist in professional and amateur leagues. Were the

*An article published in Canadian Dimension, 13, No. 6, 1978. Reprinted with permission of the publisher.

Campbell-Ziegler arguments true we would expect to find violence fairly evenly distributed throughout the game, unless one were to contend that the Philadelphia Flyers, say, annually experience more frustration than other teams, or are somehow compelled to respond to frustration with aggression, whereas others are not. As for the "outlet" argument that prohibiting fisticuffs leads to an increase in stickwork, this may be true. But not for the reason implied. At almost every level of hockey, illegal violence, whether by fist or stick, *pays* in one form or another; it will continue as long as it pays, *not* because it is in the nature of the game.

Underlying the Campbell-Ziegler claims seems to be a pastiche of several folk theories of aggression: (a) the theory that it is instinctive, a residue probably of our brutish beginnings; (b) the theory that it is caused by frustration; (c) the theory that it cathartic, draining away aggressive energy previously generated under (a) or (b). Modern research repudiates instinct theory. Men — and beasts generally speaking — *learn* to be aggressive and use aggression for specific purposes, usually to get or keep something they want. Frustration theory has a scientific basis, but even its chief proponents don't claim that frustration always leads to aggression or that aggression is always caused by frustration. Anthropologists have shown that people in some societies simpler than ours are willing to suffer frustration infinitely without ever resorting to aggression. Like most human behaviour, responses to frustration are contoured by learning and culture. Violence in hockey undoubtedly is sometimes a response to frustration — but because it's tolerated, not because it's in our genes. Finally there's almost no reliable evidence in support of catharsis (or "flush toilet") theory; on the contrary, numerous studies show that behaving aggressively, or viewing others behaving aggressively, tends to lead to more aggression, not less. This said, how *is* violence in hockey to be explained?

Following are some findings from a study conducted under my supervision at York University. These data come mainly from interviews with over 600 randomly sampled Toronto amateur hockey players (house league Peewees to Junior A "junior pros") and sixty NHL'ers. They are augmented by the observations of six field workers, myself included, who attended hundreds of hockey games in what seems like every arena in the province. For this I received a permanent case of the sniffles.

The chief source of amateur hockey violence — I'm referring to illegal physical assaults of all kinds — is the professional game, not surprisingly. Its influence seems to operate in two main ways. The first has to do with the structure of the "system." North America's pro teams depend upon junior professional leagues for a steady output of talent. Most of the ablest boys are strongly motivated to advance through minor to junior hockey and thence to professional. But en route, the number of available positions progressively diminishes, and competition for spots gets increasingly intense. Professional standards determine who moves up and who does not. One of the most important of these is the willingness and ability to employ, and withstand, illegal physical coercion.

All the pros we talked to acknowledged this. "It's an extra skill almost," explained one, "it's like having a hard shot." Most accept it without protest.

Pugilistic encounters, in particular, are not big deals. Said another: "They're getting cut and stuff like that but they're not giving guys brain tumours and stuff like that or pounding their heads to a pulp until their heads puff up." Even "goons," or designated fighters, are tolerated, if not highly esteemed. Asked how they felt about someone like Dave Schultz, at one time professional hockey's preeminent hit man, most players responded like this one: "I've got nothing against Schultz because he's trying to make a living and it's not his fault that he's there in Philadelphia [he's now moved]. That's the type of player they wanted there and he's that type of guy so they put him in there and he's going to do the job. If they're paying you eighty or a hundred thousand a year, or whatever, it's pretty hard to turn that down." Only ultra-violence is "violence" in the world of big-time hockey. A veteran goalie put it this way: "Let me tell you what *violence* is. Violence is when the guy is standing there and he gives you a spear, OK, and you don't think anything of it, but you just hammer him over the head with a stick and down he goes. He's unconscious for five minutes. That might be violence. What do you get? You get a five minute penalty. I know, because it happened to me. A guy came up and he speared me. Standing in the goal crease, he speared me. I just upped and hammered him over the head with my goal stick." Stickwork of this sort is generally feared and hated but occurs nonetheless. When lesser assaults are tolerated and encouraged, it's hard to draw a line.

We found ten-year-old Atoms who could handle heavy bumping, picked for teams over other more skilled, but less tough (and usually smaller). aspirants. Fourteen-year-olds with marginal playing ability are upwardly mobile in the Metropolitan Toronto Hockey League's elite AA division primarily because they can fight. One such was the "Animal," as he was known to other players around the circuit. When opposing coaches prepared for games against the "Animal's" team, they always made special plans to "handle" him. The Flyers' (a fictitious name) plan on one occasion was explained by their coach in a pregame talk, which we tape recorded: "Look, if this character starts anything, take him out early. We can't have him charging around hammering people. Somebody's going to have to straighten him out. Just remember, get the gloves off and do it in a fair fight. If you shake him up early he can't keep it up. Besides, it's best to take the penalties early in the game before we get too tired to kill them effectively." The adolescent bully is hardly a recent social phenomenon, but his sponsorship by adults on the scale evident is minor hockey may be somewhat unique.

The kids know what's required. Seventy-six per cent of the 274 select players (they "try out" for teams) in the survey and 55 per cent of the 330 house leaguers agreed that this statement applied to their leagues: "If you want to get personal recognition in hockey it helps to play rough. People in hockey look for this." Sixty-eight per cent of the select players agreed that in their leagues "To be successful most hockey teams need at least one or two tough guys who are always ready to fight"; 45 per cent of the house league boys felt this way. Agreement with these statements increased with age in both leagues.

The question is: Do youngsters accept these facts of hockey life as stolidly as the pros? It seems not. The majority of players on select teams (where most of the violence occurs) wished there were less fighting in their games and less stickwork. Some simply quit hockey. A junior pro talked about one, a seventeen-year-old former teammate who was being groomed for the goon role: "I really felt sorry for him. He was really a good guy. He knew why he was scouted. They knew he could fight and he knew. He was a good hockey player but he knew he was there to once a game go out and get somebody."

There's more to violence, of course, than its utility as an occupational skill. It has a strong macho underpinning, a state-of-affairs not confined to hockey, needless to say, but exaggerated there. Where else can you see grown men threatening and posturing and scuffling schoolyard-style? Respect is the thing. You lose it if you are intimidated, especially if this effects your teammates. A professional player put it like this: "If you don't stand up for your rights, the players will look down on you because in this game you got to have a lot of guts and you got to stand up for your rights. As far as helping your teammates out, if you see somebody getting beat up in the corner you got to get in there and try to help him. I think you get a lot of respect by doing that. Even if you're not a fighter you shouldn't shy away from things and stuff like that. You either stand up for your rights or suffer."

The second way that pro hockey influences amateur hockey is through the communications media. Our consumption of the professional game in one form or another has for decades been nothing short of voracious. Small wonder it is more or less the model for the rest of hockey in Canada. Consider just a few of the ways in which the violence motif is conveyed: attention-grabbing newspaper pictures of fights (one recent Toronto Star photo shows Philadelphia's Harvey Bennett punching the big bag in preparation for the season); radio and television "hot stove league" commentary (chuckles about Gordie Howe's legendary elbows, a breathless report that a new penalty record has been set); newspaper and magazine pieces ("Why the Old Time Fights Were Better," "Hit Man"). Think of the sheer amount of attention given hockey's enforcers and tough guys. Leaf's "Tiger" Williams is a media *celebrity*. Then there's the Better T Shirt Company. It produces shirts emblazoned with scenes of Neanderthal players gleefully performing various dirty work. "Hooking," "Charging," the captions read. I got mine last winter at an Atom tournament in Peterborough, Ontario. They were being sold in the arena lobby. Even the National Film Board is in the violence business. "Blades and Brass," its award-winning short on pro hockey, highlights bloody faces and body thumping (to rousing Tihuana Brass tunes). Check out the biographies on the backs of your kids' bubble gum cards. Here's one: "Nicknamed 'Battleship,' he's one of the NHL's toughest competitors. Second high on Penguins in penalty time last year." (Will anyone be surprised when the Reggie Fleming Trophy for the most penalties in a single season is announced?) One could go on. Clumsy or artful, cynical or unwitting, the message is clear.

So we've been sold pro hockey's ethos of violence, which helps explain why much of minor hockey is the big league in miniature. But do kids actually learn dirty tricks from watching the big leaguers? Research shows that conditions for learning violence via TV, for example, are almost laboratory-perfect: big league models who get money and attention for acts of violence, young hockey playing viewers who can expect rewards for the same behaviour, close similarity between the social situations portrayed on the screen and encountered subsequently by the observers. Remember the rash of head-butting (a relatively novel form of assault) in minor hockey a few years ago, introduced on TV by Schultz?

Seventy per cent of our amateur interviewees watched television pro games at least once a week. We asked them this: "Have you ever learned how to hit another player illegally in any way from watching pro hockey?" Fifty-six per cent said yes. Here's a small sampling of what they said they learned:

— Sneaky elbows, little choppy slashes Bobby Clarke style.
— Hitting at weak points with the stick, say at the back of the legs.
— Coming up from behind and using your stick to hit the back of his skates and trip him.
— Put the elbow just a bit up and get him in the gut with your stick.
— Giving him a shot in the face as he is coming up to you. The ref can't see the butt-ends.
— How to trip properly.
— Like Gordie Howe, butt-ends when the ref isn't looking.

Learning is not necessarily doing, to be sure. But when asked how many times during the season they had actually hit another player in this way, 60 per cent of the boys replied "at least once"; 20 per cent said "at least five times" (mostly Midgets, Junior B's and A's). Official game stats verified these responses; those who stated they perpetrated these indecencies actually received more major and minor penalties.

It would be convenient to pin the entire responsibility for minor hockey violence on professional hockey and its media cheerleaders. But misleading. There's a pervasive support system that goes far beyond the pro game. It starts early. The most penalized player on an Atom team in the Ontario Minor Hockey Association, following a game in which he'd racked up three more minors—one for a semi-fight—walked into the arena lobby and over to his parents who were talking to the coach. I was close enough to hear his father say, "We've got a regular Tiger Williams here!" General laughter. Sheepish grin. Or there's the conversation that occurred at an MTHL AA Bantam parent's party: Parent One (father): "There's nothing wrong with a good fistfight in hockey as long as everyone drops their gloves and sticks fist. Having skates on is the great equalizer anyway. No one is really going to get hurt during a hockey fight. If the referees see that one guy is killing another guy they'll step in and break it up fast enough." Parent Two (mother): "I agree. The fights seem to do some good. The boys get it out of their systems and they usually end up playing better hockey in the long run." Parent Three (father): "I think if the boys had dropped their gloves earlier in the game the other night, that number 5 wouldn't have gone after _____ with his stick." Parent Four (father): "That's the sad part now. Kids today don't know how to get the gloves off and get the fists up. Everyone is hitting everyone else with their sticks. I think fighting with the fist is a good way to toughen a boy up. He's got to learn to take his lumps as well as give them out. The problem is that everyone in hockey is so sneaky now. They hit you when you're not expecting it. I haven't seen a good fist fighter in two years in the MTHL."

What do players think their parents and others think about fighting? We asked them if they felt their (a) mothers, (b) fathers, (c) coaches, and (d) teammates would approve or disapprove of a "minor hockey player punching another player" in the following situations: (1) if he had been. "ridiculed and made fun of," (2) "shoved," (3) "challenged to a fight," (4) "punched" by the other player. From the responses to these items an Approval of Hockey Fighting Index was constructed. Scores ranged from 0 (for four "disapproves") to 4 (for four "approves") for each of the persons above. Here's a selection of "high" scores (three or more "approves"); for instance, not one house league player thought his mother would approve of fighting in three or more of the situations, but 58 percent thought their teammates would approve in at least three of the situations.

	House League	MTHL AA	Jr. B	Provincial Jr. A
Mother	0	6	7	15
Father	6	21	46	49
Coach	8	26	50	73
Teammates	58	63	86	84

The data are clear: the greater the social support, the more violent the hockey, a correlation applying also to individual performers at all levels.

Paste the speech in your scrapbook, John, under "Myths and Folklore." When it finds its way into the Hockey Hall of Fame (to a glass case, perhaps, next to "cyclone" Taylor's skates), visitors can marvel.

Humanism in Sport

Historically, there have been two major forces in psychology. First, Sigmund Freud popularized his psychoanalytic theory in which life (libido) and death (thantos) instincts played a major role and attention was focused on unconscious processes as motivators of behavior. Second, drawing on the early work of Ivan Pavlov and Edward Thorndike, John Watson became the leading proponent of behaviorism. In contrast to psychoanalysis, behaviorism rejected introspection as a viable approach to scientific inquiry. Psychology under Watson, and later popularized by B. F. Skinner, was to become an objective science — a discipline which centered attention on overt rather than covert behaviors.

There is a third force emerging in psychology which rejects both psychoanalysis and behaviorism. That force is humanism. Humanistic, or third force psychology, was initiated by Abraham Maslow. Maslow, The Father of Humanism, thought that both psychoanalysis and behaviorism were pessimistic views of man. Freud, for example, saw man as being essentially evil and in ·continual conflict with societal mores. Behaviorists, particularly Skinner, viewed man as being buffeted to and fro by environmental stimuli. According to Skinner, in order to produce the desired behavior all you have to do is "shape" the environment. Under this system, man was not given credit for being a thinking organism. Behaviorism, so to speak, beheaded man.

In contrast to both psychoanalysis and behaviorism, humanism envisions man as being essentially good and striving for self-actualization. The development of human potential is the salient feature of this approach.

Largely ignored by sport psychologists, coaches and physical educators, concerted efforts to bring humanism to sport have not taken place. George Sage, author of the article in this section, traces the historical milestones in the rise of humanism in psychology and sociology. Sage talks about traditional sport practices and then shows how third force psychology may be applied systematically to athletics. Becoming all one is capable of becoming through sports participation is an integral part of Sage's message. Sage is systematic and thorough in his approach and his article provides 'food for thought' for those of us who have studied sport as it is, and thought about what it ought to be.

Humanistic Psychology and Coaching

George H. Sage, Ed.D.
The University of
Northern Colorado

To examine the relations between the concepts of humanism and sport, I have structured my observations around four topical areas:

1. Humanistic Developments in the Social Sciences
2. Basic Principles of Humanism
3. Traditional Practices and Value Orientations in American Sport
4. Humanism Applied to Sport

HUMANISTIC DEVELOPMENTS IN THE SOCIAL SCIENCES

There are some rather dramatic events going on in the social sciences, and these activities have already had an impact on the basic disciplines out of which they have evolved, and they are also having an enormous impact in applied fields such as education, business management, religion, and other "people oriented" professions. These events are related to new theories about humanity and methods of interpersonal relations which have emerged in the social sciences over the past couple of decades.

The essence of the new ideas is a more optimistic, democratic, humanistic conception of human beings. In psychology this movement has been called Third Force or Humanistic Psychology. In sociology the new wave has been given various names: Symbolic Interactionism, Ethnomethodology, Phenomenological Sociology, and Existential Sociology. In business management the more humane form of management leadership has become known as "Human Relations" management. I shall describe each of these developments briefly.

A. Humanism in Psychology

In psychology, throughout most of the 20th century, psychologists have primarily traced their thinking to either Sigmund Freud or John B. Watson. Freudism and Behaviorism (Watson's contribution) are deeply embedded into much of the psychology which is taught in American universities and applied throughout much of American child rearing, formal education, and other activities in which there is frequent interpersonal relations. Thus, most of you as well as most coaches and other educators, have had a heavy indoctrination in these approaches to human personality and behavior.

An essential theme of both of these approaches is basically a pessimistic view of humanity—it permeates these theories. For Freud, man was an animal and only an animal. In his book on *Creativity and the Unconscious* (1958) Freud wrote:

> In the course of his development toward culture, man acquired a dominating position over his fellow creatures in the animal kingdom. Not content with this supremacy, however, he began to place a gulf between his nature and theirs. He denied the possession of reason to them, and to himself he attributed an immortal soul, and made claims to a divine descent which permitted him to annihilate the bond of community between him and the animal kingdom . . . (but) we all know that . . . the researches of Charles Darwin, (and) . . . his collaborators . . . put an end to this presumption on the part of man. Man is not a being different from animals or superior to them; he himself originates in the animal race and is related more closely to some of its members and more distantly to others.

From his animal origins, according to Freud, came basic human instincts, which Freud divided into two major categories: the life instinct and the death instinct—the first is exemplified in the sex drive and the second is the aggression drive. That humans are basically an aggressive, dominating animal is central to Freud's theory. In the *New Introductory Lectures on Psychoanalysis,* (1933) he describes this basic hostility of persons towards each other. He says: "Culture has to call up every possible reinforcement to erect barriers against the aggressive instincts . . . its ideal command to love one's neighbor as oneself is really a hoax since "nothing is so completely at variance with human nature as this." In another place he proclaims: "Hatred is at the bottom of all relations of affection and love between human beings . . . (Brown, 1963)."

Behaviorism, the second force in psychology, had its origins with Ivan Pavlov and Edward Thorndike near the beginning of the 20th century and bloomed into a full theory of Behaviorism under John B. Watson. Behaviorists excluded the subjectivism of Freud and placed their emphasis on a dispassionate observation of behavior. "The Behaviorist," said Watson (1930) "dropped from his scientific vocabulary all subjective terms . . . even thinking and emotion as they were subjectively defined." With regard to morality, Watson declared: "The Behaviorist is not interested in (man's) . . . morals, except as a scientist; in fact, he doesn't care what kind of man he is." Humans, thus, are considered to be flexible, malleable, and passive victims of their environment, which determines their behavior. In his book, *The Broken Image,* Floyd Matson (1966) quotes Watson as saying: "In short, the cry of the Behaviorist is, 'Give me the baby and my world to bring it up in and I'll make it crawl and walk; I'll make it climb and use its hands in constructing buildings of stone or wood; I'll make it a thief, a gunman, or a dope fiend. The possibilities of shaping in any direction is almost endless!"

Like Freud, and Darwin before him, the Behaviorist saw humans as merely another type of animal, with no essential differences from animals and with the same destructive, anti-social tendencies. Watson (1930) stated: "We believed then (1912) as we do now, that man is an animal, different from other animals only in the types of behavior he displays (and)...the extent to which most of us are shot through with a savage background is almost unbelievable." B. F. Skinner, the modern spokesman for Behaviorism says: "The only difference I expect to see revealed between the behavior of rats and man (aside from the enormous differences in complexity) lie in the field of verbal behavior" (Matson, 1966).

Starting in the 1930's, but not gaining any real recognition or momentum until the past decade, a new theory in psychology is advancing which provides a viable alternative to the first two major forces. This approach has become known as humanistic, or Third Force, psychology and the generally acknowledged founder of this movement is Abraham Maslow. This approach is different in many ways to the previous psychological theories, but its most unique and central difference is an entirely different perspective of the nature of humanity. It views humans optimistically, and having the potential for truly remarkable behavior. Maslow (1970) says: "What is happening now is a change in the image of man . . . . In the case of the humanistic and Third Force image, which shows so clearly that we have been selling human nature short throughout the whole of recorded history, this is certainly . . . a revolution in terms of its consequences. It can and will change the world and everything in it."

2. Humanism in Sociology

As sociology emerged as a unique discipline in the first half of this century "structural-functionalism" took over the theory side of most sociology departments. This theoretical orientation is best personified by the work of Talcott Parsons at Harvard and Robert Merton at Columbia. Just as with psychology, most persons who have taken sociology classes have received the dominant perspective.

Structural-functionalism views society as a set of institutions serving its functional needs; it ignores historical perspective, and sees change and conflict as deviations rather than as inherent social processes. The dominant concern of structural-functionalism is with order in society—an order based on conformity to shared values, and one in which joy, freedom, and self-fulfillment, usually do not appear.

Structural-functionalism is basically an amoral, conservative approach to social behavior, with an emphasis on social order; social change is virtually neglected or treated as pathological or abnormal. Change agents are labeled deviants. Recent critics of structural-functionalism have argued that too often the effect of this perspective is to label all non-conformist behavior as aberrant, no matter what the person's intention.

This theory is both implicitly and explicitly conservative and justifies the status quo. It focuses on human adjustment to society, on conformity and adaptation, on an individual as a controlled product of society and culture rather than as a determiner of his own fate. The model of humanity, often not explicit in the theory, resembles the Freudian and Behavioristic models.

Although structural-functionalism has had the most visible position in sociology, several new perspectives have been gaining ground rapidly and show many indications of displacing structural-functionalism. The most prominant of these alternative groups is the Symbolic Interactionists. The Symbolic Interactionist views humans as living in a symbolicly meaningful world and he recognizes that the meanings that guide conduct are not inherent in the actions of institutions, but are created by persons through their choices and their definitions of their life situations. It is through our choices that we endow selected aspects of "reality" with significance (Staude, 1972). This perspective clearly takes an optimistic view of humanity because it affirms that humans are a thinking animal, rational, and essentially in control of their own situation; they can make their own future.

For the Symbolic Interactionist, human beings are neither creatures of impulse nor heedless victims of external stimulation. They are active organisms, guiding and constructing their lines of action while continuously coming to terms with the demands of an ever-changing world as they interpret it. This is a perspective that encourages sympathy for the non-conformist, the outcast, and the downtrodden.

Another of the new approaches in social theory is an approach called ethnomethodology. This is the study of the methods used by members of a group for understanding communication, making decisions, being rational, accounting for action, and so on. Ethnomethodologists study the routine grounds of everyday activities. The focus is on the individual, how he interacts with his environment—especially the meanings which he derives from interaction.

The Symbolic Interactionists and the Ethnomethodologists represent only two groups of several which are currently active within sociology that clearly reject a worship of science and have an empathetic concern for humanity.

3. Business Management and Humanism

Business management theory and practice has undergone some significant changes in the past generation too. The latter 19th century witnessed the enormous growth of large bureaucratic business and industrial enterprises with the merger of industrialization and technological know-how. At the turn of the 20th century, a bustling time of population growth and industrial expansion, managements were faced with the problem of bringing large numbers of workers, many of whom were unskilled and untrained—together into a cooperative enterprise. At this time, the core ideas for a system to increase productivity through better utilization of manpower took shape through the writings of Frederick Taylor. This management theory, often referred to as Scientific Management, was enthusiastically adopted by American business and industrial organizations and has over the past 60 years been used by various industrial as well as non-business organizations such as schools, the military, and sports.

The underlying notions about the nature of humans, from the Scientific Management perspective, have been enumerated by Douglas McGregor (1957):

    a. The average person is by nature indolent — he works as little as possible.

    b. He lacks ambition, dislikes responsibility, prefers to be led.

    c. He is inherently self-centered, indifferent to organizational needs.

    d. He is by nature resistent to change.

    e. He is gullible, not very bright, the ready dupe of the charlatan and demagogue.

The overriding notion is that workers in the mass are economic creatures, each impelled by an irresistible force to seek the maximum wage at a minimum effort.

Beginning with the research of Elton Mayo at the Hawthorne plant in the 1920's, which showed that when people are treated as important human beings they are more productive and happier, an entirely new approach to organizational leadership has been formulated and supported with experimental findings. It is called Human Relations management theory.

There are several key elements to Human Relations theory:

1. People are not by nature passive or resistent to organizational needs. They have become so as a result of experience in organizations; the motivation, the capacity for assuming responsibility, and the readiness to direct behavior toward group goals are all present in people.

2. It is deeply concerned with attitudes, values, emotional reactions of individual group members.

The Human Relations approach differs from Scientific Management in that it emphasizes that external control will not motivate persons to apply all their talents in behalf of group goals. The emphasis is non-authoritarian styles of leadership, member participation in group decision making, and the encouragement of organizational activities in the service of individual needs. In short, this approach promotes individual autonomy and intrinsic motivation.

Organizational research over the past 20 years has convincingly shown that when employees are given an opportunity to participate in the organization's decision structure and when they are treated in such a way as to recognize their uniqueness and humanness, they achieve greater production and are more satisfied with themselves and with their jobs. There is growing evidence that strongly suggests that Human Relations values are not only resonate with an increasing number of people in today's world, but are also highly consistent with the effective functioning of organizations built on the new view of humanity.

Basic Principles of Humanism

The basic foundations of the humanistic orientation that is now sweeping the social sciences is a fundamental concern for the human person as an entity having a measure of autonomy, choice, and self-determination. There is a fundamental conviction that "best" individuals are those who possess a positive self-concept and accept themselves in an appreciating way. There is a belief that one cannot function to his fullest capacity without believing in and accepting the totality of himself. There is a belief that individuals possess a dignity and integrity which should be respected; that they are basically able to make their own decisions and deal with events. As one humanistic psychologist says:

An essentially positive view of the self permits adequate people to be effective without the worry about conformity or nonconformity. . . . It provides a kind of security that permits the owner a freedom he could not have otherwise. . . . This permits him to be creative, original, spontaneous. . . . Feeling he is much more, he has much more to give (Combs, 1962).

The acceptance of one's self is also expended into feelings of oneness with one's group. Humanists confirm that this feeling is necessary to their conceptions of the adequate person. Combs (1962) states:

Truly adequate people have a greatly expanded feeling of self. . . . It is a feeling of unity or oneness, a feeling of sharing a common fate, or striving for a common goal . . . most adequate men and women . . . seem to reach a point where they identify with great blocks of mankind, with 'all' mankind, without reference to creed, color, or nationality.

Humanism posits an expanded awareness, a willingness to accept all facets of reality and perception. Maslow (1970) notes: "Self-actualizing people have the wonderful capacity to appreciate . . . freshly and naively, the basic goods of life, with awe, pleasure, and wonder, and even ecstasy, however stale these experiences may have become to others. . . ." Finally, humanism views "life success" differently than has been traditional; it views success not so much with making a living as making a life.

Accompanying and supporting a great deal of the theoretical structure of the humanistic perspective is a strong disillusionment with values and interpersonal relations as manifested in corporate organization values and behaviors and traditional ethics. While corporate organization and the Protestant Ethic were central themes of an industrial society, humanism addresses itself to a post-industrial society. The emphasis on basic needs gives way to a focus upon what Maslow calls the growths or meta needs. The enhancement of human potential receives more of our attention as basic survival needs are satisfied more easily (Podeschi, 1974).

Although humanism recognizes the environmental demands upon individuals, it views human beings as having an intrinsic nature and it views them optimistically, concentrating on healthy, self-actualizing persons who are fulfilling their idiosyncratic as well as their universal human potential (Podeschi, 1974). In his essay "The Theoretical Foundations of Humanistic Sociology," John Staude (1973) notes that the humanistic orientations restores the individual person in his rightful place as the principal agent of action. The humanists see men and women as the creators of their own acts, with all the uncertainty, ambiguity, dread, anxiety, and responsibility that such freedom, choice, and decision imply.

This movement has already had an impact upon a broad spectrum of American life. Witness the influence it has had upon the educational system, religion, minority rights, women's rights, and the freedom of greater choice in individual life styles. There has also been an awakening among the masses of blue-collar workers, whose financial responsibilities tie them to meaningless jobs. The dissatisfaction with the endless rat race is surfacing more and more, and employers are going to have enormous problems if change does not occur.

TRADITIONAL PRACTICES AND VALUE ORIENTATIONS
IN AMERICAN SPORT

Before discussing applications of humanism to American school sports, it is necessary to describe in some detail the traditional practices and value orientations of American sports practices. This will illuminate present conditions and then I can contrast the humanistic approach as it applies to sports. Although most of what I will have to say applies to boy's and men's program, the current direction of the women's sports movement suggests that it may soon model that of the men in every respect.

Inter-school sports began in the latter 19th century and was a creation of college students. Until the beginning of this century, intercollegiate sports were basically student affairs, with little faculty of administration intervention. However, by the early years of the 20th century control of the programs was taken away from the students, for all intents and purposes, and became vested in the alumni, faculty, and administrators. Now colleges began using athletics to publicize the institution and what started as student recreation became public entertainment and big business for the colleges. True to the patterns of American education, high schools adopted the practices and procedures of colleges, and secondary school athletic programs mirrored, in many details, the collegiate programs.

Once the entertainment and public relations functions of school sports became dominant, the need for experienced coaches arose. Whereas previously the coaching functions were performed by older players or by adults in their spare time, now coaching became a serious business and teachers of athletics (coaches) were employed to direct the athletic teams. Thus, there developed a vocation out of what was, and indeed still is throughout most of the world, an avocation—teaching games. There were several consequences of employing full-time coaches and using school sports for entertainment and publicity.

Once coaching became an occupation, performance criteria became associated with competence. Although inter-school athletics have always been justified as an educational enterprise, objective, marketplace criteria have become virtually the only measure of coaching ability, and "win" has become synonymous with success and "lose" has become associated with failure. Prestige in coaching has been based upon won-loss records. A coach, according to all accepted standards, must win in order to have coached well. One college coach recently proclaimed: "I'd give anything—my house, my bank account, anything but my wife and family—to get (an undefeated season)."

I think that it is easy to see how this system may produce coaching behavior which emphasizes the treatment of players for what they can do for the coach—win—rather than the treatment of players based upon what coaches can do for the personal-social growth of athletes as individuals.

With the rise of increasingly institutional and codified school sports, the characteristics of the enterprise closely modeled the older psychological and traditional value perspectives. The emphasis on intensive competition and a "Winning is the only thing" ideology, which for many has become the norm, is grounded in the idea that we must struggle against others to get ahead. If one has to be ruthless and unscrupulous in accomplishing the objective, it follows that the important thing is beating out the opposition.

Leadership practices commonly employed by coaches in American sport are firmly based on the older psychologies, sociology and business management theory. Corporate organization and traditional values have made sport an element for the promotion of these systems. There is an acceptance of the priority of institutions and organizations and a belief that the individual must subordinate his will to them. It is consistent with this orientation, but an example of its consequences, that almost unanimously the public has risen up in righteous indignation against Bill Walton because he has spoken out in defense of personal freedoms and individual rights while this same public has reacted to violations of NCAA policies and unethical coaching behavior with a shoulder shrug and a response that "after all one has to win to have a successful program, and besides everyone else is doing it." The organization must be served. The moral stance of basketball coach, Bill Musselman, who just departed the University of Minnesota for the pros just as the NCAA was poised to charge Musselman with numerous violations is symptomatic of this value orientation. When he was asked how he felt about the charges against Minnesota, Musselman replied, "I'm not a member of the university staff anymore, so my conscience is clear." Where is the public outrage against this behavior? Where is the public outrage against coaches who change transcripts?

The individual player is expected to do his best to fit himself into functions which are needed by the organization. This is vividly exemplified in the popular locker room slogan: "There is no I in team." A system of incentives and rewards, i.e., letter awards, helmet decals, etc. are instituted to "motivate" athletes to perform. In this approach decisions are made by management (the coach), after a thorough cost efficiency analysis, and the players are expected to carry out the will of the coach for the accomplishment of organizational goals (Sage, 1973). This is precisely the kind of behavior that is sought after in an efficiency-conscious business society.

Instead of coaching from the expressive foundation of personal fulfillment, coaches often adopt a production profile in working with athletes. Victories, fame, or whatever become products designed to satisfy felt insufficiencies; and obviously, one's athletes then become a necessary cog in the chain of production. Under the banner of efficiency, personal relationships give way to distance and manipulation.

The most important foundation of both American sport and corporate organization is authority. In both activities rigid and bureaucratized hierarchy controls more and more aspects of the workers' and athletes' lives both on and off the job or, in the case of sports, the field of play. As Hoch (1972) says:

> In football, like business...every pattern of movement on the field is increasingly being brought under the control of a group of non-playing managerial technocrats who sit up in the stands...with their headphones and dictate offenses, defenses, special plays, substitutions, and so forth to the players below.

The relation between school sports and the business world can be seen very vividly when one realizes that coaches typically justify school sports programs on the basis that they help prepare youth for the highly competitive business-industrial ideology of American corporate capitalism in which they will live as adults — thus sports become a means for socializing youth for adulthood.

Paul (1974) says: "The much maligned 'old coach' often, if not always, felt that by developing in his players tenacity, aggressiveness, and a will to win, he was providing them with the psychological armor that would sustain them against the assaults of a competitive, hostile world (Paul, 1974)." It makes one wonder if this is the kind of training which prepares persons for a Watergate; or prepares persons for business positions that when their corporation is caught violating federal laws, as IBM recently was, the chairman of the board says: "We don't train losers (IBM)." Presumably they train executives to win at any cost, and the hell with federal laws — winning is everything, you know. But perhaps they didn't have to train them at all. They might have already possessed this ethical norm — learned from inter-school sports participation.

It is clear that the dominant approach in current institutionalized sport is an authoritarian, product oriented enterprise. The basic concern is with athletes subjecting themselves to the will of the coach whose primary concern often becomes winning athletic contests. The rise of increasingly institutionalized and codified sports teams has caused many coaches to view team members as objects in a machine-like environment who need to be conditioned to perform prescribed, fragmented tasks as instrumental to team performance. Thus, the players become another person's (the coach's) instrument, and are used to reach the objectives and goals of the organizational collectivity; they are reduced to cogs in the organization's machinery.

Now you may not like the summary of institutionalized inter-school sport which I have made; but like it or not, basically it is correct.

HUMANISM APPLIED TO SPORT

What is a humanistic approach to sport? Well, I think you have probably already ascertained several clues to the applications of humanism to sport, but I wish to suggest more specific practices and procedures now. First, the humanist rejects the traditional sex-role stereotypes; and with regard to sport, sees it as a human province, not as either masculine or feminine. It is believed that sport has the same potential for personal growth and self-actualization for females as it does for males. I hasten to add though, it still possesses the same dangers of exploitation and subjection of the individual. I hope female coaches will mark this well in their quest to model women's sports after men's programs.

The ideology of humanistic leadership gives emphasis to an empathetic identification with others, an openness to experience, acceptance of a wide and rich perceptual field for information from which to draw, and a commitment to enhancement of a positive self concept of those with whom the leader comes in contact. In this approach, leadership is perceived as one of freeing people to be more open to their experiences. The leader sees her task as one of releasing, facilitating, and assisting, not one of manipulating, coercing and appeasing in order to "shape" appropriate behavior. Leader behavior is flexible and open to revision in view of long term issues and consequences rather than focused on immediate goals and short term, current consequences. Finally, the leader perceives her task as beginning from a clear acceptance of other persons and their current ways of thinking, feeling, and behaving. She believes that her own acceptance and openness will in turn promote acceptance and openness in others. The importance of these viewpoints for sport are particularly related to coaching and management methods which most effectively facilitate these goals.

The traditional coaching model, with its emphasis on relatively rigid structure, imposition of conformity through requirements, direction and control exercised through a formal hierarchy of authority — with the coach as the all-powerful authority figure — a fixed system of rights, duties, and procedures, and relative impersonality of human relationships is proving dysfunctional to contemporary realities. No matter how much emphasis is placed on such other qualities in coaching as coaching technique, technology, equipment, facilities, the humanity of the coach is the vital ingredient if athletes are to learn self-identity, self-responsibility, self-direction, and self-fulfillment. Traditionally, many coaches have defined coaching as analogous to sculpturing — making the players what the coaches want them to become. Thus, we have two sport psychologists, Bruce Ogilvie and Thomas Tutko (1966), labeling athletes who will not be molded in the ways coaches wish as "problem athletes." The humanistic coach views the coaching experience as gardening — helping athletes grow and find what they want to be.

The goal of school sports, and all of education, for the humanist, is the production of increasing uniqueness and independence, and this cannot be achieved in an autocratic atmosphere in which the team is built around an omniscient authority figure where all decisions are made by the coach while players are relegated to passive followers of orders. A common sense principle of school sport, then, is that it should promote the fulfillment of the individuals engaged in and influenced by it; thus the real goal of sport, or any educational venture, is seen to encompass nothing less than the fulfillment of the student. In the sense I am using it here, fulfillment implies the actualization of the full potentialities for personal-social growth latent in the individual.

With regard to school sports programs, the humanistic coach starts with the basic premise that the sport is for the players, not the coaches. She believes that it is a serious mistake to adopt business-industrial practices and values in an area whose primary purpose is human expression. She believes that educational endeavors must measure efficiency not in terms of so many work hours per product but they must measure their efficiency in terms of increased humanism, increased power to do, and increased capacity to appreciate. The coach, then strives to be more a resource person than an authority figure. She strives to make her players free of her, able to make their own decisions, self-reliant, responsible for their actions (Laughlin, 1974).

Statements like the following one which was recently made by the former University of Wyoming football coach, Fritz Shurmer, are completely rejected by the humanist for the hoax that they are. In talking about the development of self-discipline in sports, Shurmer said: "...establishing a pattern of discipline to the extent of telling a player when to go to breakfast, when to cut his hair, and how much hair he can have will help a player develop self-discipline (Shurmer, 1973)."

The humanist coach acknowledges that contemporary society requires self-directing, responsible adults who are capable of independent behavior but she believes that athletes learn to control themselves by being given opportunities to make their own decisions. Self-discipline comes from practice in disciplining oneself, not by being obedient to others' demands. If, as humanists argue, choice is a basic fact of human existence, then athletes should be given the opportunity to make choices. They cannot be expected to develop the ability to choose wisely if all choices are made for them (Laughlin, 1974).

The traditional pattern of training for self-discipline is exposed for the joke that it is by former All-Pro football player George Sauer (See Scott, 1971) who said:

> It's interesting to go back and listen to the people on the high school level talk about sport programs and how they develop a kid's self-discipline and responsibility. I think the giveaway, that most of this stuff being preached on the lower levels is a lie, is when you get to college and professional levels, the coaches still treat you as an adolescent. They know damn well that you were never given a chance to become responsible or self-disciplined. Even in the pros you are told when to go to bed, when to turn your lights off, when to wake up, when to eat, and what to eat.

It is ironic, but pitifully illustrative of how traditional sports practices, which claim to develop self-discipline, keep those who have been exposed to these methods the longest, the pros, in virtual bondage. Note that freedom for the players has been a key issue in the negotiations between the NFL players association and the owners. That is, professional athletes are asking for freedom from curfews, fines, and other silly rules. These are grown men asking for their individual freedom, not adolescents!

If sports helps kids build character, as coaches claim, then players need a chance to make their own choices. In a way, character is composed of the choices one makes. So if coaches make all the decisions they are stunting character development, not nurturing it (Laughlin, 1974). Moreover, coaches are not military leaders, fashion designers, or judges and the preoccupation with rigid standards of personal appearance, political beliefs, interests, and private behavior is misplaced. Coaches should realize that clothes, hair cuts, personal likes and dislikes are not valid criteria for judging people and their worth to society (Mosston and Mueller, 1974).

While humanism gives preference to cooperation over competition, it does not reject competition in a sport context. Competition, within limits of sport, is accepted for its own pleasure. But, except when carried out as fun, there is a belief that intensive competition has the danger of generating conditional self-worth, role-specific relationships, excellence based on competitive merit, self as a means, and subjection of self to external control (Schafer, 1971b). Perhaps Leonard (1973) best summarizes the humanistic perspective with regard to competition: he says, "There is nothing wrong with competition in the proper perspective. Like a little salt, it adds zest to the game and to life itself. But when the seasoning is mistaken for the substance, only sickness can follow. Similarly, when winning becomes 'the only thing,' it can lead only to eventual emptiness and anomie." One does not have to search far for examples of the consequences of "win at any cost" mentality: Basketball scandals of 1950's and 60's, recruiting violations in the past two years by Oklahoma, Southwest Louisiana, Long Beach State, Minnesota, and numerous others, the 1973 Ohio State-Minnesota basketball game, and even Watergate.

Invariably, when anyone criticizes the "winning is the only thing" ethic traditionalists smugly counter with: "If winning is not important, why keep score?" For the humanist, it is not a question of whether a score is kept; of course a score is kept in sport competition, and it is important. It is important for measuring one's quality of performance; it is a means for ascertaining the skill which one displayed during competition. But it is not an end; it is a means! The end in sport is the joy, exhilaration, and self-fulfillment that one obtains from movement; it is the display of skill, the challenge of matching tactical wits with competitors, and the sensual feelings that arise in competition. Using victory as the only end, the goal of sport competition, is too limiting, confining, too shallow, too short-sighted for humanism. One reason winning is so overvalued is that we haven't been taught to enjoy the doing — the process — of whatever it is we are attempting.

Miller (1970) suggests that individuals who play games in order to win are actually not "playing" games, they are working at them. Thus, they do not win anything of value. In a program which is ends-oriented, the game is for winning; in the means-oriented program the game is the game; it is for playing. In the first program the player cannot be happy unless she is winning, is successful, whereas in the second, if one is satisfied and happy with the play she is successful. In this second program the expressive nature of sport is emphasized, and, as Ingham and Loy (1973) say: "sport needs no other justification than that it provides a setting for sociability and fun." So it goes without saying that the "winning is the only thing" ethic is rejected by humanism since it so severely restricts the rich potential for human growth, development of a positive self concept, and opportunity for peak experiences through competition.

The humanistic coach places individual expression above group conformity, self-discipline above authority, independence above dependence. She makes concerted effort to give attention to every player on the team, not just the starters. She might even develop a system whereby every player plays a part of every game. She makes an effort to treat opponents as worthy competitors; she has empathy for the weak opponent and will not try to pour it on when she has this opponent out-classed. In short, the coach cares, really cares, about each and every sports participant, not just her own athletes, but *all* athletes. In a sense, opponents are viewed as extended teammates, for if they had decided not to compete there would be no contest; they, in effect, cooperate so that the contest can be enjoyed together.

By now you may be saying: "But the humanistic coach will have no authority, no control." It is true that as one becomes more concerned with individuality and the processes of living there may be an overreaction where impulsiveness and spontaneity runs in circles chasing itself (Podeschi, 1974). However, there is no suggestion in the humanist perspective that directive and dynamic leadership is to be abandoned to complete equalitarianism. Of course the coach needs authority but it is to be exercised in a humane and supportive way. Maslow (1965) noted that the great leader is one who has just the right combination of humility and flexibility while at the same time possessing the strength of character to stand alone when an important principle is involved. He says: "The kind of person who must be loved by all probably will not make a good leader."

A critical factor with regard to the legitimate use of authority by the coach is the scope. In this regard, Schafer (1971a) says:

> Authority ought to be narrow rather than broad in scope in that it is exercised over behavior clearly and directly related to training and performance. Determination of the precise limits of authority in the end must depend upon the good judgment of the sensitive coach, although athletes can hardly be faulted for increasingly resisting the authority of the unnecessarily intruding and controlling coach and for demanding that he stay within his justifiable limits in controlling their lives.

Edwards (1972) has noted that "...America would gain far more than she would lose through initiation of...an alternative sport structure...in which the younger generation can be socialized with values stressing cooperation rather than antagonism, participation and self-actualization rather than confrontation and domination." One can hope that the basis of the women's sports movement is more than an effort to gain entry into the American sports system and is instead a desire to totally overhaul our sports system.

Perhaps John Stuart Mill, the 19th century philosopher, who certainly knew nothing about inter-school sports but a lot about human nature, best expresses what might be a guiding humanistic principle for sports programs. In his essay "On Liberty" he says:

> Human nature is not a machine to be built after a model, and set to do exactly the work prescribed for it, but a tree, which requires to grow and develop itself on all sides, according to the tendency of the inward forces which make it a living thing (In Commins and Linscott, 1974).

Will the humanistic movement be adopted in the field of sport as the dominant model? No one knows for sure. There are many reasons to expect it won't but there are encouraging signs that it might. Perhaps humanism is an idea whose time has come. Podeschi (1974) believes that the greatest effects of the humanistic perspective will produce their greatest effects in the coming century. Only time will tell.

REFERENCES

BROWN, J. A. B., *Freud and the Post-Freudians,* New York: Cassell, 1963.

COMBS, A. W., "A Perceptual View of the Adequate Personality," in A. W. Combs (ed.) *Perceiving, Behaving, Becoming,* ASCD Yearbook, Washington, D.C., 1962.

COMMINS, S. and LINSCOTT, R. N., (eds.) *Man and the State: The Political Philosophers,* New York: Random House, 1974. ("On Liberty" by John Stuart Mill reproduced in its entirety, pp. 135-260).

EDWARDS, H., *Sociology of Sport,* Homewood, Ill.: Dorsey Press, 1973.

FREUD, S., *New Introductory Lectures on Psychoanalysis,* New York: W. W. Norton, 1933.

FREUD, S., *On Creativity and the Unconscious,* New York: Harper and Row, 1958.

HOCH, P., *Rip Off the Big Game,* Garden City, New York: Doubleday, 1972.

IBM: "Time to Think Small," *Newsweek,* October 1, 1973, pp. 80-84.

LAUGHLIN, N. T., "Existentialism, Education, and Sport," In G. H. McGlynn (ed.) *Issues in Physical Education and Sport,* Palo Alto, California: National Press Books, 1974, pp. 169-180.

LEONARD, G. B., "Winning Isn't Everything, It's Nothing," *Intellectual Digest,* 4 (October): 45-47, 1973.

MC GREGOR, D., "The Human Side of Enterprise," *The Management Review,* 46: 22-28, 88-89, 1957.

MC GREGOR, D., *The Human Side of Enterprise,* New York: McGraw-Hill, 1960.

MC GREGOR, D., *The Professional Manager,* New York: McGraw-Hill, 1967.

MASLOW, A. H., *Eupsychian Management,* Homewood, Ill.: Dorsey Press, 1965.

MASLOW, A., "Personal letter to Frank Goble, February 6, 1968," Published in F. Goble, *The Third Force,* New York: Grossman, 1970.

MASLOW, A. H., *Motivation and Personality,* (2nd ed.) New York: Harper and Row, 1970.

MASLOW, A. H., *The Farther Reaches of Human Nature,* New York: Viking, 1971.

MATSON, F., *The Broken Image,* New York: Doubleday, 1966.

MILLER, D. L., *Gods and Games: Toward a Theology of Play,* New York: World, 1970.

MOSSTON, M. and MUELLER, R., "Mission, Omission, and Submission in Physical Education," in G. H. McGlynn, (ed.) *Issues in Physical Education and Sport,* Palo Alto, California: National Press Books, 1974, pp. 97-106.

OGILVIE, B. and TUTKO, T. A., *Problem Athletes and How to Handle Them,* London: Pelham Books, 1966.

PAUL, W., "Authoritarianism in Physical Education and Sports," In G. H. McGlynn (ed.) *Issues in Physical Education and Sports,* Palo Alto, California: National Press Books, 1974, pp. 194-205.

PODESCHI, R. "The Farther Reaches of Physical Activity," *Quest* XXI (January): 12-18, 1974.

SAGE, G. H., "The Coach as Management: Organizational Leadership in American Sport," *Quest* XIX (January): 35-40, 1973.

SCHAFER, W. E., "Sport, Socialization and the School: Toward Maturity or Enculturation?" Paper presented at the Third International Symposium on the Sociology of Sport, Waterloo, Ontario, Canada, August, 1971(a).

SCHAFER, W. E., "Sport and Youth Counter-Culture: Contrasting Socialization Themes," Paper presented at the Conference on Sport and Social Deviancy, SUNY, Brockport, December, 1971(b).

SCOTT, J., "The Souring of George Sauer," *Intellectual Digest,* 2 (December): 52-55, 1971.

SHURMER, F., Quoted in *Greeley Tribune,* September 12, 1973.

STAUDE, J. R. "The Theoretical Foundations of Humanistic Sociology," In J. F. Glass and J. R. Staude (eds.) *Humanistic Society,* Pacific Palisades, California: Goodyear, 1972, pp. 262-268.

WATSON, J. B., *Behaviorism,* Chicago: University of Chicago Press, 1930.

Attention and Anxiety

In sport psychology texts written to date, few authors have covered the psychology of attention. Only in *The Inner Athlete* does R. M. Nideffer give extensive coverage to this important topic. Dr. Nideffer, author of the paper in this section, has developed a model for conceptualizing attentional focus in sport. Once attentional style is determined, Nideffer maintains that it is possible to predict athletic performances in a variety of sport situations.

In analyzing sport situations, it is important to think of attention on the basis of both width and direction. The width dimension is seen in Nideffer's models as existing on a broad to narrow continuum. The athlete who possesses a narrow focus has the ability to shut-out anything that might distract. This kind of concentration is needed, for example, in hitting a baseball or driving a golf ball from a tee. A broad focus of attention is required for positions such as quarterback, linebacker or leading a three on two fast break in basketball.

The direction dimension also exists on a continuum from internal to external focus. Players who are classified as 'internal' are involved in their own thoughts and feelings. Bill Morgan, University of Wisconsin sport psychologist, found that world-class marathon runners monitored their body processes as they ran whereas lesser skilled runners attempted to disassociate or focus on factors outside themselves.

Quite obviously, the demands of the sport and the particular position played will dictate the particular attentional style that will produce the best performance. The quarterback, for example, who possesses 'tunnel vision' is not going to function well picking-up secondary receivers in the open field.

For best results, Nideffer suggests that athletes should maintain a balance between attending to external and internal processes. And, they should be able to switch from one style to another as the situational factors change. Nideffer's rule is: the more complex and rapidly changing the situation, the more external focused your attention must be.

In Dr. Nideffer's paper within this section, he establishes the relationship of attention and anxiety to performance. His excellent sport examples of situations requiring different perceptual and attentional styles makes the article interesting and informative. Nideffer's strength is his ability to combine the theoretical and practical aspects of sport psychology.

The Relationship of Attention and Anxiety to Performance*

Robert M. Nideffer, Ph.D.
President, Enhanced
Performance Associates

To be able to teach effectively, the coach of an athlete must have a framework for conceptualizing the demand characteristics of a particular situation. With respect to the physical aspects or demands of a sport, most of the parameters have already been identified. Our understanding of the mechanics involved in a sport (e.g., gymnastics) have reached the point where we can analyze a particular move and point out the mistakes. Unfortunately, we are only beginning to understand why the mistake was made in the first place. It is in examining the mental aspects of performance (why the mistake was made) that our diagnostic skills and understanding are most lacking. A major purpose of this article is to offer a framework for beginning to understand and to define the relevance of mental factors to complex physical activity. In this way we can begin to understand why the mistake was made.

The idea that attention, the ability to direct our senses and thought process to particular objects, thoughts, or feelings, is important in being able to perform effectively is not new. Unfortunately, we have not clearly defined what we mean by attention, or what the attentional demands for a particular situation are. Very often we infer the individual was attending properly if they were successful and improperly when they were not. This lack of definition does little to assist either the athlete or the coach in understanding what went wrong. Shouts such as "keep alert," "use your head," "pay attention" and "open your eyes" offer little in the way of concrete corrective information. To be able to teach and communicate effectively, the coach must be able to define the attentional demands of a particular situation, to be able to point out the specific "mental errors." To perform effectively, the athlete must be capable of responding to those attentional demands.

In talking about the attentional demands of a particular situation (e.g., shooting a free throw), it is necessary to define attentional process on two dimensions. First, attentional width is important. An individual's attention may be described as falling at some point along a continuum ranging from very narrow (like a beam of light) to very broad. Most individuals (within limits) are able to broaden or narrow their attention as the situation demands. The second attentional dimension has to do with the direction of focus. Again, attentional processes can be placed on a continuum with an extreme external focus (looking at objects in the world) at one end and an extreme

*An article published in *Coach and Athlete*, 1974. Reprinted with permission of the publisher.

163

internal focus (looking at your own feelings, thoughts and ideas) on the other. Under normal conditions, most of us attempt to maintain some kind of balance between our thoughts and ideas on the one hand and what is going on out in the world on the other.

At any given point in time, a person's attention can be thought of as falling at some point along the width and direction continuums. Thus, at that particular instant they may be described as having either a broad internal focus, a broad external focus, a narrow internal focus, or a narrow external focus. Just as individual attention is defined in terms of width and direction of focus the environmental situation will demand a certain type of attention. If the individual's attention corresponds to the environmental demands, they will function effectively; if not, they will make mistakes. The importance of these concepts can be emphasized by suggesting that individuals have particular attentional styles (e.g., some people tend to have a broad external focus, others a narrow internal one) and that specific sports demand certain styles or a certain amount of flexibility (movement along the continua).

To highlight what I have been saying, let me present a couple of examples of the attentional demands of particular situations. First, imagine a quarterback with a third and long yardage situation. This particular quarterback calls a pass play and we pick up on the play just as he is dropping back. Ideally, the quarterback will have a broad external attentional focus. He needs this particular attentional style because he must dodge incoming linemen, watch for a blitz, as well as look downfield for both primary and secondary receivers. If the quarterback narrows his attention too much, he may fail to look for his secondary receiver. When the primary receiver is open, he can get away with a narrow focus, but when he's covered, the quarterback fails to find the open man and gets tackled or throws an interception.

Contrast the demands placed on a quarterback with the demands placed on a golfer who is putting out on the 18th, and who is in a position to win the match by sinking the putt. Here the demand is for a narrow external focus. For the golfer to let his attention broaden and focus on the crowd, or to become internally directed, perhaps at his own fear, would be disastrous. He would become overloaded with irrelevant stimuli and his concentration would be destroyed. Each sport makes demands on the participant with respect to these attentional variables. Some sports, such as football, may demand a variety of attentional focuses, while others such as golf may demand less. Not only are there differences across sports, but there are differences within sports depending on the position and the particular situation. An interior lineman, for example, may need a narrow external focus, moving to execute a specific block, while the quarterback needs a broad focus.

To facilitate defining the attentional styles needed for a particular situation, it is useful to describe how each of the four focus may be employed. A broad external focus is useful when the individual needs to be aware of and able to respond to a complex rapidly changing environment. In addition to the quarterback example, a three on two fast break in basketball, a double play in baseball, or playing linebacker in football would all demand the ability to have a broad external focus. Situations where a narrow external focus would be useful would include hitting and pitching in baseball, golfing, bowling, etc. In almost any situation where only one stimulus (e.g., a ball or pins) is relevant, an internal focus can be important for rehearsal of tasks, reflection and preparation for a game, as well as for endurance. For example, distance runners can use the ability to narrow their attention and focus internally as a means of directing thought to the mechanics of running (to a rhythm), thus increasing pain tolerance by not attending to the painful cues. Coaches and athletes need a broad internal focus to prepare for a game. Such a focus is reflective, it allows you to learn from mistakes, to analyze situations, plan strategies, and to predict an opponent's moves. The quarterback calls an audible at the line because he notices a change (external) in alignment and because he remembers earlier plays or pre-game strategy (internal).

At the University of Rochester we have begun to develop a test designed to measure an individual's attentional style. We are using the subjects' responses to specific questions on the test in order to plot an attentional profile. First, it provides an indication of how capable the individual is of developing a broad internal, and/or broad external focus when these attentional styles are called for. In addition, it provides an indication of how often mistakes are made because the person becomes confused and overloaded by letting in too many external and/or internal stimuli. Finally, the test provides information about the individuals' ability to appropriately narrow their attention (e.g., in order to read) as well as indicating their tendency to make errors of underinclusion because their focus is narrow when it should be broad. Recently, this test was administered to the University of Rochester swim team in an attept to examine the relationships between these attentional variables, anxiety, and swimming performance.

The swim team coach was asked to rate the performance of those swimmers he had coached for over a year (10 swimmers). He scored each swimmer on a five point scale on each of 30 items designed to evaluate swimming performance. He evaluated their performance in practice and in a variety of meet situations. In addition, he rated their tendency to "choke," to make mistakes early and fall apart vs. making mistakes early and then warming up. Independent of the coaches ratings the swimmers were given the Test of Attentional Style and the State Trait Anxiety Index (STAI). The test was administered to the swimmers in a group with the total time for test administration being approximately 45 minutes. Once the data were collected, the swimmers scores on the attentional scales and on both state (situational) and trait (general) anxiety were correlated with the coaches ratings of performance. Statistically significant correlations (.50's, .60's, .70's, .80's) suggested the following relationships.

Swimmers who score high on the overload scales tend to have inconsistent performance. They are impulsive and not only is the performance inconsistent, but the level of performance is generaly low. It is almost as if the individuals react to anything in order to reduce the stimulus overload. In contrast, swimmers who are able to develop an effective broad internal focus are consistent, high level performers. Consistent performance is also a characteristic of swimmers who are able to effectively narrow their attention, though the level of performance varies from swimmer to swimmer. It may be that individuals with a broad internal focus are more capable of analyzing and rehearsing their performance than other groups.

The tendency for a swimmer to make errors of underinclusion, due to an inappropriately narrow focus, is associated with poor performance both in practice and in meets. In addition, these swimmers let early mistakes disrupt subsequent performance. They focus on their mistakes and fail to respond to their environment. They have a tendency to choke in pressure situations, they are unable to adapt to changes in meet strategy, they have difficulty planning ahead and they are unwilling (or unable) to listen to suggestions their opponent may offer. Similar relationships are found between performance and anxiety.

State anxiety refers to the tendency of a person to become anxious in particular, arousing situations; trait anxiety refers to the tendency of an individual to maintain a high level of tension (arousal) across situations of varying intensity. High scores by swimmers on either of these scales is associated with poor performance. In addition, high scorers tend not to be team leaders. Those individuals high on trait anxiety have difficulty planning ahead and are poorer with respect to physical skill. Finally, a high score by swimmers on the state scale is associated with choking under pressure and being unable to adapt to changing competitive situations. It appears as if anxiety is associated with a narrowing of attention leading to the types of problems and mistakes that characterize swimmers who make errors of underinclusion.

The nature of the relationship between anxiety, attention and performance (should it hold up in future studies) has rather extended consequences for athletics. For years psychologists have been emphasizing that increases in anxiety and arousal act to narrow attentional processes. Should this narrowing be appropriate in that few cues are needed then arousal can act to improve performance. On the other hand, if a broad focus is required or if attention is directed to internal stimuli (thoughts and feelings) when it should be directed externally, performance will be impaired. The data presented here on the swimmers tends to substantiate the hypothesized relationship between attention, anxiety, and performance. Let me provide a couple of examples of how these relationships might affect coaching practices.

Our quarterback from a few paragraphs back failed to make the third down play because he narrowed his attention and didn't see that his secondary receiver was wide open. He became upset and angry at himself as he walked to the bench. The coach, too, was angry and immediately told him how stupid he was. Rather than helping by relaxing him and letting his attention broaden, this served to arouse him more, further narrowing attention. For this particular quarterback, a better approach would have been "it's OK" and to then begin talking about something else (e.g., plans for the next series of downs). In contrast, some athletes may need their attention narrowed, and their level of arousal increased. A long jumper like Bob Beamon needs to put all his energy into one effort and needs his attention riveted to one spot, the take off point. If he is overly broad in focus, attending to the crowd, etc., a yell from the coach might help.

To the extent that the variables of attentional style and anxiety interact and assume the importance outlined above, we are in a position to be able to dramatically improve an individual's performance. As we are able to define the attentional demands of situations and the attentional styles of individuals, our ability for putting the right player in the right position or situations, at the right time improves. In the future, not only will we be able to select athletes for particular events, but we will be (and I believe are) able to offer specific suggestions and exercises to help athletes gain control over their attentional processes. For example, hypnosis, relaxation procedures, meditation, and self control instructions can all be used to lower anxiety and help an individual broaden attention as well as control the direction of focus.

Psychologists and coaches are just beginning to become aware of the ways they can work together. Hopefully, as they begin to cooperate more fully and are able to respond more directly to each others needs, we will see some dramatic improvement in performance. Great athletes and great coaches seem to already respond in ways consistent with many of the things that have been presented here. They implicitly seem to recognize and respond to the demands of situations. Perhaps as the relationships become clearer and our teaching skills improve, more coaches and athletes will approach greatness.

Meditation and Sport

Within recent years, a great deal of attention has been given to meditation based upon the Hindu discipline of yoga. The practice known as transcendental meditation (TM) has attracted hundreds of thousands of practitioners. Many athletes, including Bill Walton and Craig Lincoln, former Olympic diver, have practiced TM.

The proponents of transcendental meditation claim that TM rejuvenates and normalizes the function of the nervous system, eliminates mental stress, promotes clear thinking and comprehension, enriches perception and eliminates discord. Best-selling books have been written on the subject and most of the major cities now have TM Centers. Although some sport psychologists are convinced of its usefulness, others state that some TM promoters offer false promises or misinformation. They claim that it is too early to evaluate the affect of TM on athletic achievement.

The American Foundation for the Science of Creative Intelligence, the promoters of TM, have recently founded a special division for sport. Through TM training, they hope to show that athletes will feel better, learn faster, be more relaxed and have more energy. TM is also said to provide relief from a wide variety of the so called stress diseases, e.g., high blood pressure, peptic ulcer, heart disease, insomnia and drug addiction. It is in the area of improved performance, however, that coaches are most concerned with transcendental meditiation.

The author of the article in this section, Emma McCloy Layman, is an excellent authority on meditation. Dr. Layman, in a penetrating analysis of the research and conceptual literature, agrees with Robert Nideffer that TM may be beneficial to athletes, particularly in calming the mind and reducing hyper-arousal. In her coverage, Dr. Layman discusses the physiological and psychological correlates of meditation and the improved concentration that may result from its use.

As Layman cogently points out, much that has been written about yoga and zen seems vague and esoteric. There is, however, growing evidence, particularly clinical studies, to suggest that meditation may be beneficial to the athlete psychologically and to his/her performance.

Meditation and Sports Performance

Emma McCloy Layman, Ph.D.
Iowa Wesleyan College

Since the fourteenth century, Japanese martial arts like judo, karate, aikido, and archery have been linked with Zen philosophy and meditation. Recognizing this linkage, Eugen Herrigel, a German philosopher, spent six years studying archery under a Japanese Zen master, hoping to gain an understanding of the essence of Zen as well as to perfect his skills in archery. He described his experiences in a little book entitled *Zen in the Art of Archery*.[19] Although Herrigel's book, published in 1953, is now considered a classic in its field, it has been only in the last decade that European and American coaches and athletes have begun to realize a possible relation between Oriental "spiritual" disciplines and what we call "sport." Now we're advised that running, tennis, and golf are forms of meditation, and that the New York Jets and Los Angeles Rams benefit from the regular practice of Transcendental Meditation.[36] It's suggested that application of the wisdom of the Orient can take strokes off one's golf score, improve one's tennis backhand, increase one's running speed, or raise one's batting average, as well as reducing the stress in athletic competition and making sports participation a lot more fun. But are ancient Oriental spiritual disciplines *really* related to sports learning and performance? If so, *how* are they related? It is these two questions which we shall be exploring in this chapter.

Non-Western Approaches to Meditation

Most non-Western approaches to meditation had their origins in India, more than 4,000 years ago, although some currently-used techniques have reached their fullest development in more recent times. The different systems — such as those of Yoga, Zen, and TM — utilize different devices for attaining their goals. These devices include such varied techniques as concentration on breathing, visualizing an object, imagining the sound of a Sanskrit syllable called a *mantra,* working on a paradoxical riddle called a *koan,* or "just sitting." Each system emphasizes one or more of these or other techniques.

The majority of Oriental approaches to meditation use principally sitting meditation, with the meditator sitting cross-legged, preferably in the lotus position. However, Zen masters advise that meditation may be done also while sitting on a chair, standing, walking, working, or playing; and Transcendental Meditation (TM), in its adaptation to Western ways, has the meditator concentrate on an assigned mantra for 20 minutes twice a day while sitting comfortably in a chair.

Although followers of different meditational schools may use different techniques, all of the Oriental approaches to meditation have certain features in common. As far as technique is concerned, all stress the importance of an erect posture permitting deep and easy breathing, and all state that the meditative position should be a relaxed one. All stress that meditation is in terms of contemplation of concrete sensory images rather than engaging in reflective thinking or logical reasoning. All seek to develop awareness of the present, with lack of concern for the past and future, and all provide training in concentration of attention. All are based on a theory of the unity of all aspects of the universe, and see meditation as a means of increasing awareness, eliminating illusory thinking, stilling the mind, stabilizing the emotions, and making more energy available for the activities of life. All of the well-known meditational systems with the exception of Transcendental Meditation have developed in a religious context, but adherence to a particular system of religious belief is not necessary in order to benefit from any of these techniques.

Physiological and Psychological Effects of Meditation: Research Findings

The physiological effects of meditation are well-established, through well-planned research with adequate controls. The majority of this research has been concerned with the effects of TM, but some has involved Zen or yogic meditation. Among the most frequently reported physiological effects of meditation are the following: brain-wave changes consisting of the appearance of Alpha waves in the early stages of meditation, with Theta waves appearing later; lowered metabolism; lowered heart rate, respiration, and blood pressure; decrease in concentration of arterial lactate; decreased galvanic skin response; and increased blood flow in the skeletal muscles. [2, 4, 7, 16, 24, 27, 39] Allison[2] and Orme-Johnson[27] report findings indicating reduced hyper-arousal of the sympathetic division of the autonomic nervous system and activation of the energy-restoring parasympathetic division. Banquet's[4] summary of brain-wave studies shows not only the usual Alpha and Theta waves, but synchrony between the dominant and non-dominant cerebral hemispheres as well as between higher and lower brain centers.

Many researchers, in commenting on the physiological studies, have pointed out that the changes reported are the reverse of those associated with the stress syndrome.[7] The significance of the findings from the standpoint of integrated, harmonious functioning and energy conservation also are often mentioned. Some have pointed out that the physiological changes are similar to those associated with relaxation not involving meditation, or just sitting quietly. [16, 24]

Neurological research suggests that meditation of the type we are discussing involves activation of the non-dominant hemisphere of the cerebral cortex. [28, 29] There has been a great deal of theorizing and speculating about brain functions, but most researchers concur in the conclusion that the dominant hemisphere is mostly involved in logical reasoning, abstract thinking, symbolic speech, and mathematics, whereas the non-dominant hemisphere is more active in intuitive thinking, perception, kinesthesis, motor adjustments to space, and sense imagery, as well as in musical and artistic functions. [28, 29] If these conclusions are supported by future research, they will clarify to a considerable degree the relationship between meditation and athletic performance, since sports certainly involve spatial adjustments and kinesthesis, as well as visual perception and imagery.

The psychological research on the effects of meditation shows improved academic performance [10, 33], increased productivity on the job[13], improved reaction time[35], and improved verbal learning of paired associates[1]. Several studies [17, 18, 30, 33] report improved concentration, sensitivity to internal cues, and sensory discrimination, but Williams and co-workers [40, 41, 42] indicated no effect or a negative effect of meditation on fine perceptual-motor skills.

A number of studies show personality changes resulting from meditation. [13, 20] Lesh[23] found that Zen meditation produced greater empathy in prospective counselors. Seeman and others[33] found that TM improved self-actualization and resulted also in increased spontaneity, self-regard, acceptance of aggression, and capacity for intimate contact. Cowger[11] and Marron[25] reported that meditation creates a feeling of peace and calm, and reduces anxiety. Marron[25] also found that meditators differ from non-meditators in having more creative interests, being more open to mystical experience, resisting cultural conformity, having a need for privacy and detachment, having a more democratic character structure, and being more tolerant of ambiguity.

Many studies have explored the usefulness of meditation as a psychotherapeutic adjunct or technique.[20] Reviewing a number of such studies, Smith[39] says, "Without exception the studies reviewed show the regular practice of meditation to be associated with decrements of psychopathology, particularly anxiety, over a period of time ranging from 4-10 weeks" (p. 564). However, he points out that most studies resemble solicited testimonials, populations are sometimes not comparable, and there are no controls for "just sitting," and for expectation of relief. In an experiment performed after writing his review, Smith[38] found that when a group treated with periodic somatic inactivity was compared with a group practicing TM, there were no significant differences between the groups.

Several studies report TM as being effective in decreasing drug abuse[5, 8, 22, 34, 43]. Some of these studies are not adequately controlled, however, so we must consider them as only suggestive rather than as definitive.

Applications in the Field of Sport

1. Effects of Meditation on Performance in Sport

What does meditation do for the athlete? Here we have little well-designed research to give us the answers. However, the attitude implicit in the eastern philosophies suggests an attitude which can be applied toward sport, and general research provides us with some facts and principles which may find applications on the tennis and basketball court, on the golf course, or on the athletic field. We also have reports of personal experiences of athletes and coaches.

Many writers have mentioned the destructive effect on athletic performance of brooding over past mistakes or trying too hard, and have claimed that meditation will help by its calming effect, as well as by the fact that it improves concentration which is badly needed for bodily control, forces attention on what is going on in the present, and conserves energy, making it possible for the athlete to put forth maximal effort without getting "up tight" about it.[7, 9, 14, 15, 31, 32, 36]

Iowa Wesleyan College athletes who have participated in competitive sports with teams from Maharishi International University have observed that MIU athletes (all meditators) are aggressive players who seem not to tire easily, remain calm throughout the game or match, and do not get upset if they lose or make mistakes. This is generally confirmed by the MIU players. An MIU professor observes also that he is struck by how much enjoyment the MIU athletes seem to find in playing.[3]

Coaches sometimes report that they have their players concentrate on their breathing between plays.[9] This, of course, is a form of meditation. Gallwey[14] and Colletto[9] see this as a means of assuring that players remain focused on what their own bodies are doing at the present moment, and enables them to avoid dwelling on past mistakes.

Considerable publicity in the media has been given to reports of professional athletes who believe they have been benefitted by Transcendental Meditation. These athletes testify that TM has made them feel better physically, has made them happier persons, has made them less anxious, and has improved their athletic performance.[24] These reports, of course, are not based on scientific research, so must be considered as only suggestive.

Reddy and co-workers[31] conducted, as far as the writer is aware, the most careful and objective investigation of the effects of a TM program on athletics published to date. Male Indian athletes wishing to learn the TM technique were randomly assigned to an experimental group and a control group, each with 15 subjects. Each group was composed of university students and government workers. Athletic performance tests, physiological tests, and an intelligence test were administered to both groups before the experimental group was taught and again six weeks after the experimental group received instruction in TM. During the six weeks, both groups participated in a general athletic conditioning program. While members of the experimental group were meditating for 20 minutes twice a day, members of the control group spent the 20 minutes resting with eyes closed, either sitting or lying down. (Their instruction in TM was postponed until after the conclusion of the experiment.) The meditating athletes improved significantly more than the nonmeditating control group in the 50 meter dash ($p < .001$), the East German Boomerang Agility Test ($p = .0025$), the standing broad jump ($p = .0056$), and a reaction time and coordination test ($p < .001$). The meditators also improved more than nonmeditators in the shot put and a strength test, but the differences in these were not significant. The physiological improvement of the experimental group was superior to that of the control group on all measures: cardiovascular efficiency as measured by the step test ($p = .0011$), respiratory efficiency as indicated by the vital capacity (p .001), systolic blood pressure ($p < .001$), diastolic blood pressure ($p = .0011$), and hemoglobin ($p = .048$). The meditators also showed a greater increase than the non-meditators in intelligence as measured by Bhatia's battery ($p < .001$). The investigators concluded that the Transcendental Meditation program helps the athlete to develop a broad range of qualities essential to his performance: agility, speed, endurance, fast reactions, and mind-body coordination.

2. Sport as Meditation

It has sometimes been stated that sport can be a form of meditation.

Fred Rohe, a runner, says that running is a form of meditation.[32] He suggests running in harmony with the breathing rhythm, running relaxedly, and running with complete awareness of what one is doing, claiming that being aware of the details of one's running gives the runner economy of energy leading to purity of movement.

Quoting a mystically-oriented Scottish golf pro, Murphy[26] describes how golf may be used in meditation to develop concentration and stillness of mind, and incidentally to learn how to keep one's eye on the ball. He says, "Imagine a golf ball. Make the image of it as vivid as you can. When anything intrudes upon the image, let it pass. If the golf ball disappears, imagine it again. If it wavers, make it steady...If you cannot get something out of your mind,...get to know the intrusion" (p. 180). Then he goes on to state that the most basic kind of meditation during a round of golf is the visualization of our shot as we stand up to the ball. "An image in our mind," he says, "can become an irresistible path" (p. 180).

Much of what has been written about sport as Yoga or Zen seems vague and esoteric. However, Timothy Gallwey, a tennis pro, has tried to translate the meditational attitude into readily understandable specifics in the learning and teaching of tennis.[14] [15] Most of what he has to say is equally applicable to other sports.

Gallwey states that every game is composed of two parts, an outer game and an inner game. The outer game of tennis concerns itself with correcting errors of grip, stance, backswing, follow-through, shifting of weight, etc. after conscious analysis of what one is doing right and wrong. In contrast, the inner game uses the "unconscious" mind and the natural wisdom of the body. If one plays the "inner game," what happens? Gallwey says, "The player of the inner game...learns that the secret to winning any game lies in not trying too hard. He aims at the kind of spontaneous performance which occurs only when the mind is calm and seems at one with the body"[14] (p. 13).

Gallwey reminds us of what every good coach knows — that often verbal instruction *decreases* the probability of the desired correction occurring, and that images are better than words in correcting errors and teaching new skills[14] (p. 19).

In saying that the player at the top of his form plays "unconsciously," Gallwey does not mean that he plays without consciousness. "In fact," he says, "someone playing 'out of his mind' is more aware of the ball, the court, and, when necessary, his opponent. But he is not aware of giving himself a lot of instructions, thinking about how to hit the ball, how to correct past mistakes or to repeat what he just did. He is conscious, but not thinking, not *over-trying*"[14] (p. 20).

Gallwey says that every individual has two "selves" — Self 1, which is the conscious, analytic teller, and Self 2, which is the unconscious automatic doer. In connection with these so-called two selves, he makes five points: (a) The key to improving performance in any sport lies in improving the relation between the two selves so that they function as one harmonious whole[14] (p. 25). (b) Most people are controlled by Self 1, and try too hard[14] (p. 25). (c) Harmony and unity between the two selves exists when the mind is still, and only then can one's peak performance be reached. (d) When a tennis player is 'on his game,' he is not thinking about how, when, or where to hit the ball. It seems to go where it should automatically, without conscious direction[14] (p. 31). (e) When the two selves are together, the action flows smoothly and freely and the player is concentrating without *trying* to concentrate.[14] (p. 32).

Gallwey recommends meditation for "stilling the mind," but has two principles to be applied in the sports situation itself. These are, first, to learn to be non-judgmental, and second, to learn to trust your body[14] (p. 33). In developing the skill of non-judgmental awareness, he says that the player should first of all try to see and feel his or her strokes as *they are,* rather than as right or wrong[14] (p. 44-45). In learning how to trust his or her own body, the player is advised to visualize how to do it, then copy the visual image, letting the body do what it does naturally rather than telling it *what* to do.

Gallwey emphasizes concentration on the 'now' or one-pointedness of attention as essential to calming the mind. He applies this to the tennis situation. He says that, in tennis, concentration means *watching* the ball rather than *thinking* about it[14] (p. 91), suggesting that the focus should be on something subtle about the ball, such as the pattern made by the seams as it spins. The player should concentrate on *seeing* the ball, *listening* to it, and *feeling* the hand and arm as they move[14] (p. 91).

Summary and Recommendations

General research on meditational yoga, Zen, and Transcendental Meditation indicate physiological and psychological benefits which should result in better athletic performance. The study by Reddy and coworkers on the effects of TM on athletic performance confirms the results anticipated on the basis of more general research.

Gallwey's attempts at translating attitudes based on Oriental philosophy and meditational approaches into specific methods of learning and teaching athletic skills have resulted in principles and procedures which, for the most part, seem psychologically sound. One might question the concept that the correct techniques for skilled performance are pre-programmed in the unconscious, and it may be that the significance of "calming the mind" is a bit overdrawn. However, Gallwey's stress on concentration of attention for bodily control, use of visualization and kinesthesis to enhance learning, not trying too hard, and substitution of knowledge of *what* one is doing for *judgments* of it as good or bad cannot be criticized from the psychological standpoint.

At this point, it appears that we have enough preliminary evidence that meditation may be beneficial to athletic performance to make it worth trying. However, we also need to translate the preliminary evidence into hypotheses which can be thoroughly tested in the sport situation. We need to plan research with a pre-posttest design, suitable comparison groups, larger numbers of subjects, and control for expectation of improvement. With respect to Gallwey's suggestions, these need to be tried with other sports, and also should be subjected to more systematic, careful research.

REFERENCES

1. Abrams, A. I. Paired associate learning and recall. In D. W. Orme-Johnson, L. H. Domasch, and J. T. Farrow (Eds.), *Scientific Research on Transcendental Meditation: Collected Papers.* Los Angeles: M.I.U. Press, 1974.

2. Allison, J. Respiratory changes during Transcendental Meditation. *Lancet,* No. 7651. April 18, 1970, 833-834.

3. Aron, Arthur. Personal communication.

4. Banquet, J. P. EEG and meditation. *Electroencephalography and Clinical Neurophysiology.* 1973, Vol. 35, 143-151.

5. Benson, H. and Wallace, R. K. Decreased drug abuse with Transcendental Meditation: A study of 1862 subjects. In C. J. D. Zarafonetis (Ed.), *Proceedings of the International Symposium on Drug Abuse.* Philadelphia: Lea and Febiger, 1972, 369-376.

6. Blasdell, K. The effects of the Transcendental Meditation technique on a complex perceptual motor task. In D. J. Orme-Johnson and I. Farrow (Eds.), *Scientific Research on the Transcendental Meditation Program,* Vol. 1. Weggis, Switzerland: MERU Press, 1976.

7. Bloomfield, H. H.; Cain, M. P.; Jaffe, D. T.; Kory, R. B. *TM: Discovering inner energy and overcoming stress.* New York: Dell Publishing Company, 1975.

8. Brautigam, E. *The effect of Transcendental Meditation on drug abusers.* Research Report, City Hospital of Malmo, Sweden, Dec. 1971.

9. Colletto, J. with Sloan, L. J. *Yoga conditioning and football.* Millbrae, Cal.: Celestial Arts, 1975.

10. Collier, R. W. The effect of Transcendental Meditation upon university academic attainment. *Proceedings of the Pacific Northwest Conference on Foreign Languages,* Seattle, 1974.

11. Cowger, E. L. The effects of meditation (zazen) upon selected dimensions of personal development. *Dissertation Abstracts International,* 1974 (Feb.), Vol. 34 (8-A, Pt. 1), 4734.

12. Ferguson, P. C. and Gowan, J. C. Psychological findings in Transcendental Meditation. *Journal of Humanistic Psychology,* in press.

13. Frew, D. R. Transcendental Meditation and productivity. *Academy of Management Journal,* 1974, Vol. 17 (2), 362-368.

14. Gallwey, W. T. *The inner game of tennis.* New York: Random House, 1974.

15. ---------------. *Inner tennis: playing the game.* New York: Random House, 1976.

16. Goleman, D. J. and Scwartz, G. E. Meditation as an intervention in stress reactivity. *Journal of Consulting and Clinical Psychology,* 1976, Vol. 44 (3), 456-466.

17. Graham, J. Auditory discrimination in meditators. In D. W. Orme-Johnson, L. H. Domash, and J. T. Farrow (Eds.), *Scientific Research on Transcendental Meditation: Collected Papers.* Los Angeles: M.I.U. Press, 1974.

18. Hendricks, C. G. Meditation as discrimination training: A theoretical note. *Journal of Transpersonal Psychology,* 1975, Vol. 7 (2), 144-146.

19. Herrigel, Eugen. *Zen in the art of archery.* New York: Pantheon Books, 1953.

20. Hjelle, L. A. Transcendental Meditation and psychological health. *Perceptual and Motor Skills,* 1974, Vol. 39, 623-628.

21. Institute for Fitness and Athletic Excellence. *Excellence in action.* Livingston, N.Y.: MIU Press, 1975.

22. Lazar, Z.; Farwell, L.; and Farrow, J. T. The effect of the Transcendental Meditation program on anxiety, drug abuse, cigarette smoking, and alcohol consumption. In D. J. Orme-Johnson and I. Farrow, *Scientific Research on the Transcendental Meditation Program:* Collected Papers, Vol. 1 Weggis, Switzerland: MERU Press, 1976.

23. Lesh, T. V. Zen meditation and the development of empathy in counselors. *Journal of Humanistic Psychology,* 1970, Vol. 10 (1), 39-83.

24. Malek, J. and Sipprelle, C. N. Physiological and subjective effects of Zen meditation and demand characteristics. *Journal of Consulting and Clinical Psychology,* 1977, Vol. 45 (2), 339-340.

25. Marron, J. P. Transcendental Meditation: a clinical evaluation. *Dissertation Abstracts International,* 1974 (Feb.), Vol. 34 (8-B), 4051.

26. Murphy, M. *Golf in the kingdom.* New York: Dell Books, 1973.

27. Orme-Johnson, D. W. Autonomic stability and Transcendental Meditation. *Psychosomatic Medicine,* 1973, Vol. 35 (4), 341-439.

28. Ornstein, R. E. *The psychology of consciousness.* San Francisco: W. H. Freeman, 1972.

29. Ornstein, R. E. and Naranjo, C. *On the psychology of meditation.* New York: Viking Press, 1971.

30. Pelletier, K. R. *Altered attention deployment in meditators.* Berkeley: Psychological Clinic, Univ. of California, 1972.

31. Reddy, J. K., Bai, A. J. L., and Rao, V. R. The effects of the Transcendental Meditation program on athletic performance. In Orme-Johnson, D. J. and I. Farrow, *Scientific Research on the Transcendental Meditation Program: Collected Papers,* Vol. 1. Weggis Switzerland: MERU Press, 1976.

32. Rohe, F. *The Zen of running.* New York: Random House, 1974.

33. Seeman, W., Nidich, S., and Banta, T. The influence of Transcendental Meditation on a measure of self-actualization. *Journal of Counseling Psychology,* 1972, Vol. 19 (3), 184-187.

34. Shafii, M., Lavely, R., and Jaffe, R. Meditation and prevention of alcohol abuse. *American Journal of Psychiatry,* 1975, Vol. 132 (9), 942-945.

35. Shaw, R. and Kolb, D. One point reaction time involving meditators and non-meditators. In D. W. Orme-Johnson, L. H. Domash, and J. T. Farrow (Eds.), *Scientific Research on Transcendental Meditation: Collected Papers.* Los Angeles: M.I.U. Press, 1974.

36. Smith, A. Sport is a western Yoga. *Psychology Today,* Oct. 1975, 49-51; 74-76.

37. Smith, J. C. Meditation as psychotherapy: A review of the literature. *Psychological Bulletin,* 1975, Vol. 82 (4), 558-564.

38. -------------- Psychotherapeutic effects of Transcendental Meditation with controls for expectation of relief and daily sitting. *Journal of Consulting and Clinical Psychology,* 1976, Vol. 44 (3), 630-637.

39. Wallace, R. K., Benson, H., and Wilson, A. *American Journal of Physiology,* 1971, Vol. 221, 795-799.

40. Williams, L. R. T. and Herbert, P. G. Transcendental Meditation and fine perceptual-motor skills. *Perceptual and Motor Skills,* 1976, Vol. 43 (1), 303-309.

41. Williams, L. R. T., Lodge, B., and Reddish, P. A. *Research Quarterly,* 1978, Vol. 48 (1), 196-201.

42. Williams, L. R. T. and Vickerman, B. L. Effects of Transcendental Meditation on fine motor skill. *Perceptual and Motor Skills,* 1976, Vol. 43 (2), 607-613.

43. Winquist, W. T. *The effect of regular practice of Transcendental Meditation on students involved in the regular use of hallucinogenic and 'hard' drugs.* Los Angeles: Department of Sociology, University of California at Los Angeles, 1969.

Social & Cultural Aspects of Sport

Traditionally, sport has been male-oriented and male dominated. Within recent years, however, women have become an integral part of the sports-world. Mandated by Title IX, women now enjoy nearly the same opportunities for participation in a wide variety of sports as men. Although research shows that sport participation has different meanings for males and females, it is likely that both sexes receive the same physiological and psychological benefits. It is in the sociological area, however, that women usually find greater satisfaction from participation.

To talk about this important topic, papers are included from three outstanding authorities. In the first article, Frank Reis and Beth Jelsma examine sex roles from a social psychological perspective. They consider two issues central to the question of sex differences in sport. They are: femininity-masculinity, and the differential meaning of sport for males and females. Contrary to popular opinion, they do not consider femininity and masculinity as bipolar traits. That is to say, it is possible to possess both characteristics. Sport participation, Reis and Jelsma postulate, may produce individuals who embody more of the desirable features of both sex-role orientations.

Dorcas Susan Butt, clinical psychologist and former world-class athlete, calls for drastic changes in sport to curb what she called the "aggression, militarism and dehumanization" features of the game. In brief, Dr. Butt hopes the "madness" in sport will cease.

The commitment, Butt contends, should be to community and solidarity between people and groups rather than to individualism and status. Women, according to Butt, are in a unique position to encourage all of the positive values which have tended to be neglected in sport. In a word, Butt feels that cooperation should replace competition as the primary motivation in sport.

In the final paper, Roscoe Brown has written a provocative article about the role of the black athlete in sport. Brown contends that the "jock-trap" is seductive and produces many deleterious affects. He talks about some of the stereotype images of the black athlete, the phenomenon of "stocking" and the failure of many black players to complete college or university degree requirements. In brief, Brown's message is that the athlete is not a gladiator.

Dr. Brown's remedy for the "jock-trap" has been called too radical and unfeasible. Becoming a professional while participating in intercollegiate athletics appears to be unrealistic to conservative members of the sport establishment. Perhaps Brown is ahead of his time.

Justification for professionalizing collegiate athletics, Brown suggests, comes from two sources. First, it would eliminate the hypocrisy; and second, athletes would gain respect for the real value of an education.

In summary, this section of the text focuses on important social problems in contemporary society. Perhaps sport participation will lead to greater harmony among men and women and promote better human relations among people of diverse ethnic backgrounds. All members of the sportsworld should work toward the realization of this worthy goal.

A Social Psychology of Sex Differences in Sport*

Harry T. Reis, Ph.D.
Beth Jelsma, B.A.
The University of Rochester

The application of psychological principles and theories to the under-standing and motivation of the individual athlete has blossomed in recent years. Most of these endeavors revolve around two fundamental themes: the description and location of the "successful personality type," and the outlining of motivational dynamics. Coaches aware of the relationship between personality and situations might select those athletes whose per-sonality styles are most appropriately matched to the requirements of a given sport or position. Similarly, coaches aware of motivational dynamics, might tap those underlying factors and coax a higher-than-expected level of performance out of an individual athlete. What these approaches have in common is their reliance on stable, enduring structures residing within the person, structures over which he or she would seem to have little active, aware control. Neither approach takes into account the social context in which sporting activities are conducted.

Social psychology affords a third and quite different perspective. Social psychology is concerned with how people are influenced by, and in turn exert an influence on, their social environment. The "social environment" refers to the entirety of a person's surroundings: peers, authorities, institu-tions, societal stereotypes, and the vast array of stimuli and situations with which we are confronted daily. The social psychologist studies how people perceive their social environment, and how these perceptions affect their beliefs, intentions, interests, self-conceptions, and behavior. In particular, the social psychological vantage point allows us to consider a person's current behavior from the standpoint of his or her previous life experiences, and how he or she actively develops and maintains certain impressions of the present.

Our purpose in this chapter will be to examine from a social psycho-logical perspective differences in the organized sports activities and interests of females and males. Such an assessment appears vital in an era when old truths are being re-examined, and changes in age-old sex-typed attitudes

*We would like to express our appreciation to the following individuals for their generous assistance in conducting the research reported in this chapter: Bill Boomer, Sue Gelman, Becky Iwata, Helen Katz, Jean Merenda, Jane Possee, and Steve White.

and institutions are being sought. In responding to these forces for change, it must be asked: Does sports participation have the same meaning for females and males? To the extent that there are differences, the failure to articulate them and include them in planning will result in activities which are not growth-producing, or intrinsically satisfying for the participant, as well as less than optimal performance. As someone once said, "Equality is the most unequal inequality of all."

It should be made clear at the outset that we are not speaking of differences which have their origin in innate or biological factors. Rather, they stem from social processes, which may be derived from at least three currently dominant psychological theories: cognitive-developmental theory (Kohlberg, 1966); psychoanalytic theory (Erikson, 1950); and social learning theory (Bandura and Walters, 1963). These theories are too lengthy to be detailed presently (the interested reader is referred to the references cited above. Deaux (1976) also provides a useful, eminently readable presentation). In barest bones, we would stipulate the following. Organized sports are presently a highly sex-typed, male-oriented pursuit. Because sex-role stereotypes are of great importance to people in our society, the way in which sporting activities are learned corresponds to their appropriateness for one's sex. Such sex-specific learning entails numerous aspects of the learning process. In general, parents, teachers, coaches, and peers may respond to an athlete in a manner consistent with their belief that various athletic behaviors are more suitable or fruitful for one sex or the other. Furthermore, people, including children, are active processors of the information contained in their social environment. They are likely to perceive prevailing patterns of sex differentiation and come to value more highly those activities or attitudes usually associated with their own gender. Therefore, the existence of stereotypic sex differences in sports in the present fosters its renewal. This is the phenomenon of the *"self-fulfilling prophecy,"* that is, a prediction which comes to pass solely because people believe it. After all, what we learn reflects the standards and activities of our models. To the extent that there presently exist sex differences among athletes, people will learn these differences as they learn anything else regarding sport. In particular, two dimensions of difference stand out: one is *familiarity,* or previous experience with sporting activities, and the other is *ego-involvement,* the extent to which sports are a personally important, valued pastime. We will refer to these later.

The advantage of such a psychological model is that it offers readily specifiable directions within which we might modify prevailing experiences. Instead of describing sex differences as inherent, immutable, and seemingly unchangeable, we will describe them as behaviors which have been learned within a given context and which are as flexible and amenable to change as the people they characterize. Let us now use this framework to discuss two issues central to the question of sex differences in sport: femininity-masculinity; and differential meaning of sports to females and males.

Femininity-Masculinity
There is perhaps no myth so firmly rooted within the traditions of

American sport as that which asserts that the athlete is somehow more masculine and less feminine than the non-athlete. To begin, it is necessary to clarify what is meant by these terms. It is one thing to state that males are more likely to engage in organized sporting activities. It is quite another to imply one's willingness or reluctance to participate hints at certain inner psychological characteristics. Two fallacies are involved in the second statement. First, it is apparent that individuals possessing most any set of personality traits are capable of enacting most any behavior when the situation calls for it, and when it is sufficiently rewarding for them to do so. That is to say, although inner states may predispose a person to respond in a given fashion, situational factors are capable of altering all but the most insistent needs. Second, it has long been presumed that femininity and masculinity are bipolar opposites — that if one is *high* in masculinity, by definition one has to be *low* in femininity. There is now considerable evidence documenting how misleading this position may be (e.g., Constantinople, 1973). This becomes apparent if we divest the concepts of the gravity which the terms *masculine* and *feminine* engender, and instead consider the actual psychological characteristics in themselves. In the typical study (e.g., Spence and Helmreich, 1978), masculinity tends to encompass such instrumental dimensions as independence, competitiveness, "stick-to-it-ness," and standing up under pressure. Femininity is comprised of expressive or affiliative traits such as helpfulness, awareness of the feelings of others, warmth, and understanding. Nothing in either of these trait clusters pre-cludes the other; they are independent, and individuals are capable of possessing greater or lesser amounts of both. The traditionally masculine character is that person of either biological gender who is high in instru-mentality and low in expressiveness, while the traditional feminine person-ality consists of a high degree of expressiveness combined with low instru-mentality. But an individual may be high in both characteristics as well, an amalgam which has been labelled androgyny (Bem, 1974; Spence, Helmreich, and Stapp, 1975). The androgynous person literally has the "best of both worlds," being both instrumental and expressive, and of course is theoretically equally likely to be a biological female or male. What is most important, however, is that while the notion of masculinity and femininity as bipolar opposites precluded such a duality, independent consideration highights both their desirability and complementarity.

Interestingly, what little data we now have on female athletes supports our confidence in the advantage this perspective affords. Spence and Helmreich (1978) report that 39% of a sample of University of Texas female varsity athletes fell into the androgynous category, in contrast to only 10% in the traditionally feminine category. For a comparable group of non-athletic female students, the numbers were reversed: 32% were feminine while only 27% were androgynous. Harris and Jennings (1977) reported similar percentages in a sample of female scholastic and club distance runners: 17.6% feminine, 33.8% androgynous (unfortunately, they did not report a control group). What these figures tell us is that athletic participation among females does not incur liabilities to their expressiveness, or femininity. Rather, it seems to enhance their instrumentality, or masculinity, producing individuals who embody more of the desirable components of *both* sex-role orientations. From these data, we see that the usual stereotypes of what sports cost the female athlete fall wide of the mark.

Differential Meaning to Females and Males

Let us begin this section with a simple question: Does participation in an organized sport have the same personal meaning to males as it does to females? That is, does success and failure have the same personal and social implications for them? Is their performance equally relevant to their self-concept? Is the day-to-day interaction with other team members working toward a common goal equally important? We will first present evidence indicating that sports have differential meaning for females and males, differences which derive from two interdependent factors: the status of sports as a stereotypically male sex-linked activity in American society, and the varying styles with which females and males interact with others.

The first of these factors beings with a rather obvious statement. Until quite recently, engaging in sports, particularly organized sports, was thought of as the province of males, with only a comparatively small number of women in a handful of sports deviating from this norm. Although this exclusivity is changing rapidly — witness the pressure brought to bear on educational institutions by Title IX — the notion of sports as stereotypically male-linked is still essentially valid. Stereotypes, particularly sex-role stereotypes, have important consequences for the way in which people learn and invest value in the various aspects of a task. In essence, they often serve as guideposts, helping people define just which pursuits will be fruitful, appropriate, or rewarding for them, and which will not. (As we have stated earlier, these stereotypes are frequently "self-fulfilling prophecies" — predictions which, by guiding and encouraging some people into one domain and others into another, guarantee their perpetuation, regardless of any underlying kernels of truth which may or may not exist.) Another way to state this is to note that stereotypes provide *information* (which may be right or wrong) about the prior experiences of others and what our own experiences are likely to entail. What we make of this information *motivates* us to seek or avoid the questioned activities. Through this process, the male sex-linked status of sports yields two general classes of consequences. First, we would expect males to be more *familiar* with sports, by virtue of having more, and more varied, past sporting experience. Second, sports will be more *ego-involving* for males, that is, success will be more important to them, and will have greater implications for their self-concept. In its extreme, this term refers to the need to win, as opposed to the desire.

The implications of familiarity and ego-involvement for the motivation, performance, and self-perceptions of an athlete are considerable. However, let us defer their discussion momentarily, pending the presentation of the second major factor and a set of relevant data. This second research direction has been founded upon the premise that females and males prefer different styles of interacting with others. In the clearest statement of this distinction, Kay Deaux (1977) argues that in social situations, males generally opt to seek and assert status differentials, typically striving to demonstrate their superiority over others while minimizing any personal deficiencies. Females, on the other hand, are seen as more frequently choosing affiliative behaviors which reduce status differentials and instead concentrate on developing and maintaining equalitarian relationships with others. As in our previous discussion, these are general orienting predispositions, rather than hard and fast rules. Either sex is capable of selecting either disposition when the situation is right. However, in general, males are more likely to choose the status-asserting alternative, and females the affiliative option. In particular, as Deaux states, the more "social" the setting, the more likely these tendencies will be evidenced. Thus, we are more likely to see sex-stereotypic behavior in front of an audience than in a small group of same-sex peers.

Putting these two lines of reasoning together suggests an interesting, central hypothesis. Males should be relatively more concerned with the competitive aspects of winning an athletic event. For them, the predominant focus of attention and energy is competing, winning, and beating their opponent. To females, these factors may not be as salient as the more participative elements of sports: interacting and working with other team members both in preparation and in competing. Either of these profiles may be consistent with striving for excellence, if this is defined in terms of meeting and surpassing personal standards, rather than simply winning or losing. These hypotheses are fundamental representations of our original assertion: that sports participation has different meaning to females and males. We therefore decided to survey a group of college varsity athletes in order to assess their validity.

Ninety-five student athletes at the University of Rochester, a medium-sized, private institution with a low-keyed emphasis on sports (no athletic scholarships are given), were asked to complete a brief questionnaire describing their sporting experiences, and their feelings, opinions, and reasoning about their present participation. Forty-eight males and forty-seven females evenly distributed among four athletic teams were polled: 21 basketball players, 34 lacrosse, 29 swimming, and 11 tennis. The questionnaires were anonymous and administered by one of the authors or by a manager/captain of the team. So that demand characteristics would not be a factor, there was nothing in any of the questions to imply that we were interested in sex differences. It was emphasized that we were interested in their personal opinions, regardless of what others might think, and that there were no "right" or "wrong" answers to any of these questions. All items were constructed as standard 1 to 7 scales, in which respondents are requested to circle that alternative which most nearly describes their own feelings. As an example, the first question asked of basketball players was: "How much do you enjoy basketball?" and was labelled (1) not very much... (4) moderately...(7) a great deal. The four teams sampled were picked because they encompassed a variety of issues: traditionally acceptable vs. not previously acceptable for females, individual vs. team performance centered, contact vs. non-contact, etc.

The primary questions subdivided into three major categories: reasons for one's own participation, how one personally defined a successful performance, and ego-involvement in particular aspects of engaging in sports. The specific items and the mean replies of female and male athletes are

Question	Females	Males	F
Reasons for Participating			
Inherent enjoyment	6.45	6.34	<1, not signif.
Status of team	2.77	3.68	5.14, p<.05
Enjoying competition of game	5.32	6.02	6.54, p<.05
Winning the competition	4.26	5.34	10.96, p<.001
Everyday interaction with team members	6.15	5.94	3.60, p<.06
Task-oriented group with common goal	5.67	5.09	10.48, p<.005
Performing as well as I can	5.91	5.85	<1, not signif.
Health benefits	6.07	4.93	10.65, p<.005
Definition of Success			
Playing well myself, regardless of team	5.09	5.04	<1, not signif.
Entire team playing well, regardless of winning	6.57	6.04	15.81, p<.001
Enjoying the game, regardless of winning	6.25	5.41	8.69, p<.005
Winning the game	4.32	5.09	6.88, p<.01
Playing better than my individual opponent	4.74	5.50	3.75, p<.06
Interacting with other team	5.62	4.83	12.63, p<.001
Ego-Involvement in:			
Performing as well as you can	18.38	18.30	<1, not signif.
Beating your opponent	12.68	14.34	4.79, p <.05
Working with others to a common goal	19.11	18.54	<1, not signif.
Everyday interaction with other team members	17.36	16.09	3.80, p<.06
Enjoyment of the sport	6.40	6.54	<1, not signif.
Amount of past experience	4.57	5.15	1.20, not signif.
How well did you do this year?	4.43	4.38	<1, not signif.
How well do you expect to do next year?	5.36	5.71	<1, not signif.

Note. All analyses have 1,88 degrees of freedom. Higher scores indicate greater rated importance.

Table 1. *Questionnaire responses by female and male athletes.*

shown in Table 1. (The final column refers to an analysis of variance, a statistical procedure which tests if the differences between females' and males' mean responses is larger than that which could be expected by chance alone. The particular analysis was an unweighted means analysis, which controls for disparities in the number of athletes sampled from the four sports. Differences among the sports were, with one notable exception to be discussed below, minor, and will not be reported. (They are available from the senior author upon request.) The tabled ego-involvement scores each represent the sum of three similar questions, and therefore should be thought of as 3-21 scales.

The results of these analyses are clear and consistent. On all questions dealing with competition, winning, and beating one's opponent, males scored significantly higher than females. Items concerned with participating in the game, interacting with one's teammates and opponents, and everyday socializing, revealed the opposite pattern: females rated them as more important than males. A final interesting point found in these data indicated that there were *no* significant differences in enjoyment of the sport, nor in the desire to perform well. Both females and males were highly, and equally, concerned with playing well and enjoying it.

Consequences of the Competitive/Participative Distinction

There is therefore evidence for a basic difference in the meaning which females and males affix to their reasons for engaging in sports in the first place, and their definitions of success. The distinction having been established, we now need to ask about its consequences. The most apparent of these is performance level. Obviously, performance must be referred to same-sex standards, since physiological differences in the sexes' physical capacities makes direct comparison unreasonable. Unfortunately, we are aware of no data relating an athlete's attitudes on either of these dimensions to performance. There are some studies which demonstrate that athletes have more competitive "personalities" than non-athletes, and some that find achievement needs related to accomplishment. However, achievement and competitive needs are not one and the same, as the innovative work of Spence and Helmreich (1978) has shown. They posit a theory of achievement motivation with four components: Mastery (the desire to overcome difficult obstacles); Work Orientation (the willingness to work hard); Competitiveness (the desire to beat other people); and Personal Unconcern (lack of interest in the negative responses of others to succes). A central element of their research examines the relationship of these four factors to professional success among college students (measured by grades), scientists (measured by scholarly citations), and businessmen (measured by salary). Consistently, the most successful individuals are those high in Mastery and Work Orientation, and low in Competitiveness; the least successful people are low in Mastery and high in Work Orientation and Competitiveness. Only when Work Orientation is low does Competition reveal a positive correlation with achievements. These findings must, of course, be verified with athletes as well. However, if we may extrapolate to our athletes, it may be argued that the more competitive orientation of males would not predispose them to superior performance. The mastery-type questions in our survey which imply concern for greater accomplishments show no differences between females and males. Perhaps the pattern stems from the very nature of the goals themselves and the possibilities for goal attainment. Success at competition is available only to a small handful of participants and is always challenged, usually by more and more skilled competitors. A personally skillful performance, exceeding one's previous levels, is however virtually always accessible to all athletes. The Mastery-oriented athlete therefore stands a considerably better chance to come away from a performance satisfied than the Competitively-oriented athlete. Such satisfaction obviously relates to one's willingness to train and continue developing. More importantly, it has a major bearing on one's intrinsic motivation.

According to Deci (1975), intrinsically motivated activities are those undertaken for the enjoyment of the activity itself. Extrinsic rewards, such as money or medals, are thought to have two types of effects: informational, signifying the individual's competence and skill; and controlling, denoting their use by others to encourage higher levels of performance. Deci has demonstrated that unless an extrinsic reward provides continued feedback about one's competence, it will have a detrimental effect on intrinsic motivation, since one presumably perceives oneself partaking for the reward, not the activity. The clearest evidence of this undermining of intrinsic motivation is the cessation of participation once the extrinsic rewards are taken away. Winning an athletic event, particularly as a team member in a school or other such institution, is accompanied by extrinsic rewards which obviously connote competence. As long as a competitively-oriented athlete keeps winning, and as long as the extrinsic rewards usually associated with winning (e.g., medals, college scholarships, the praise and esteem of coaches, parents, teammates, and schoolmates) continue, the participant's sense that he or she is a competent, able individual will likely remain stable and even grow. However, as one progresses, these rewards inevitable diminish, be it through higher levels of competition, aging, changing values in one's peer group, or a general dulling of the same reward's impact. Sooner or later, intrinsic motivation will suffer, if the meaning of one's sporting activities centered on the results of competition. For many, these were never accessible, failure at sports competition being far more likely than success.

A participative orientation is, of course, extrinsic also. However, the picture is rosier here, because success is available to all participants, not merely the winners. The team may lose, but a player may nonetheless experience a successful performance. Referring back to Table 1, we might remember that females were more likely to define success in terms of "playing well, regardless of winning" and "enjoying the game, regardless of winning". Those athletes with a more participative focus for their endeavors, as we have generalized females here, are more likely to experience a sense of personal competence and task mastery, factors conducive to intrinsic motivation. We can expect the intrinsically motivated athlete to persist longer, notably after the school years when many of the extrinsic gratifications which sports provide are no longer available or important.

Much of this appears to violate common sense notions about the necessity of a competitive spirit in the successful athlete. Some competitiveness would seem important. However, the potentially disruptive effects of excessive competition on a group's performance and morale have been documented frequently, particularly when individual status within a group (the "starring" role) is a relevant issue. Certainly many team sports require players to sacrifice personal gains to the team goal. Furthermore, although competition may yield short-term or sporadic benefits, it does not necessarily imply enhanced performance in the long run. Successful athletics require a sustained effort at preparation and training which is essentially unrelated to the competition of the event or game. We might even speculate that the participative individual would devote more attention to the mundane aspects of daily training, since such a person enjoys the steady interaction with teammates. These benefits would be conducive to group cohesiveness and teamwork, as well as individual performance. Of course, more research is needed to draw firmer conclusions. However, there is no evidence to indicate that a competitive style is necessarily more advantageous than a mastery of participative attitude.

There are other aspects of social psychology which might provide further interesting generalizations toward understanding the self-perceptions of female and male athletes. One of these is attribution theory, an area concerned with how people perceive the causes of their own successes and failures. In numerous studies, it has been shown that the more ego-involved one is in success (that is, the more important it is to succeed), the more likely one is to take credit for success and deny blame for failure. This usually takes the form of attributing success to an internal cause (my ability, my effort), and failure to an external cause (the difficulty of the opposition or the conditions, luck). This is a pattern of response to competition which Robert Levine and the first author labelled "fear of failure" (Levine, Reis, Sue, & Turner, 1976), since it is a way of evaluating a performance which allows one to incorporate positive information into the self-concept, while excluding negative information. Attributing a failure externally may contribute to feeling helpless, wherein one feels incapable of having any meaningful effect over what happens. Putting energy into improving requires a sense that one's efforts *do* have a meaningful effect. Of course, "fear of failure" may be an overly embellished term; the concept refers to how a person integrates a given outcome at an ego-involving game one wants (needs) to win. Certainly, the external pressures brought to bear on many athletes by others ("You've got to win") make this understandable. If one must win, how can one take responsibility for not?

What the literature also shows is that ego-involvement, together with these attributions, is more likely on appropriately sex-linked tasks. On opposite sex-typed activities, we often see evidence of "fear of success" (Horner, 1972). Although Horner's original notion that females generally possess more fear of success as a personality trait has been fairly well rejected, it still remains a valid concept to describe a pattern of taking the blame for failure (lack of ability) and denying credit for success (luck, easy task). Since sports is an opposite sex-linked task for females and competition is less ego-involving, we might see more "fear of athletic success" among female athletes than males. Furthermore, a number of researchers have reconceptualized fear of success as "fear of the social consequences of success at an opposite sex-linked task." In the previous section on masculinity-femininity, we have discussed stereotypic beliefs about some of these social consequences, rooted in the loss of femininity, both in one's own eyes and the eyes of significant others. Such a belief is of course sufficient to produce the effect.

Postscript

In the preceding pages, we have posited the essentially different meaning which sports have for females and males. These differences can be seen as the result of stereotypes which define organized athletics as a male-oriented domain in American society, and not any inherent differences in females and males. Essentially, we argued that as a result males are more in tune to the competitive, status-asserting elements, while females are more concerned with the affiliative, participative aspects. For both sexes, performing skillfully while enjoying it seem to be equally salient.

Of course, these are only general tendencies, which are descriptive of larger groups, and not individuals. This should be most clear in the mechanisms we utilized earlier to account for our position. If sex differences in such stereotypic effects can be explained in terms of past familiarity and ego-involvement, then individuals with atypical past experiences should in fact show atypical and contrasting patterns of interest and understanding. Strong evidence for this contention arises from our data. Swimmers were included in the sample so that we might examine the self-perceptions of athletes in a sport which has encouraged female participation for quite some time. Swimming was the first women's sport to enter the Olympics (1912). Further,

Metheny (1974) noted that females have generally not been excluded from sports involving no body contact or aggression, and which embody graceful, aesthetically pleasing notions. Swimming clearly fits this bill, and it is interesting to note that of the four sports we polled, the swimmers showed the fewest sex differences. (By and large, female swimmers indicated only minimally less competitiveness than males, although their participative interests remained significantly greater). It is revealing that a sport in which the sex-typing pressures are least should also yield the smallest differences between its female and male participants. Defining a sport as sex-appropriate for females allows them to focus their attention on the ego-involving aspects of winning or losing, since the skills involved in swimming well are personally valued. Conversely, since a sex-inappropriate sport is less likely to raise such concerns, one might attend less to winning and losing, and more to the social relations surrounding the activity.

There is nothing in any sport which makes it inherently "male" or "female". Nothing, that is, except for the existence of that stereotype in American society today. If the mere existence of a stereotype helps perpetuate it as a self-fulfilling prophecy, then the energies being exerted today toward change *are* clearly in the proper place. The discriminatory effects of stereotypes do not disappear by ignoring them. Rather, acknowledging them as stereotypically produced readily locates the means for effecting change. With time and experience, we should see sports emerge as a less sex-linked pursuit, and consequently fewer differences of the sort documented in this chapter.

Certainly the research we have described only begins to construct a general understanding of the social psychology of sport, applied to sex-role factors. Much, much more research aimed at unravelling cause and effect is needed. But there is nothing in the evidence we have reviewed which indicates any superiority for the competitive orientation. In fact, it would seem that the more participative orientation is conducive to greater satisfaction, and an engagement in athletics which is more likely to persist beyond early adulthood. One might hope that in this period of change, we offer males the opportunity to participate in sports as females do, rather than vice versa. Regardless of our own bias, however, we must understand athletes' understanding of their own activities in order to work with them.

BANDURA, A., & WALTERS, R. H. *Social learning and personality development.* New York: Holt, Rinehart, & Winston, 1963.

BEM, S. L. The measurement of psychological androgyny. *Journal of Consulting and Clinical Psychology,* 1974, *42,* 155-162.

CONSTANTINOPLE, A. Masculinity-femininity: An exception to a famous dictum? *Psychological Bulletin,* 1973, *80,* 389-407.

DEAUX, K. *The behavior of women and men.* Monterey, Calif.: Brooks/Cole, 1976.

DEAUX, K. Sex differences. In T. Blass (Ed.), *Personality variables in behavior.* Hillsdale, N. J.: Erlbaum, 1977.

ERIKSON, E. H. *Childhood and society.* New York: W. W. Norton, 1950.

HARRIS, D. V. and JENNINGS, S. E. Self-perceptions of female distance runners. *Annals of the New York Academy of Sciences,* 1977, *301,* 808-815.

KOHLBERG, L. A cognitive-developmental analysis of children's sex-role concepts and attitudes. In E. E. Maccoby (Ed.), *The development of sex differences.* Stanford, Calif.: Stanford University Press, 1966.

LEVINE, R. V., REIS, H. T., SUE, E., & TURNER, G. Fear of failure in males: A more salient factor than fear of success in females? *Sex Roles,* 1976, *4,* 389-398.

METHANY, E. Symbolic forms of movement: The female image in sport. In G. H. Sage (Ed.), *Sport and American Society.* Reading, Mass.: Addison-Wesley, 1974.

SPENCE, J. T. and HELMREICH, R. L. *Masculinity and femininity.* Austin, Texas: University of Texas Press, 1978.

SPENCE, J. T., HELMREICH, R., & STAPP, J. Ratings of self and peers on sex-role attributes and their relation to self-esteem and conceptions of masculinity and femininity. *Journal of Personality and Social Psychology,* 1975, *32,* 29-39.

New Horizons for Women in Sport *

Dorcas Susan Butt, Ph.D.
University of British Columbia

In this article, I would like to talk about sport, social values and our future. Among the issues reoccuring during this conference have been: the problems associated with the teaching of physical culture in our schools, the unfair distribution of sporting facilities and support generally existing between men's and women's athletics, the negative competitive values associated with much organized sport, the constrictive social role many women are forced into by the status quo and the great difficulties encountered in initiating change when change is so obviously needed. Some have mentioned that the problems being discussed here are the same as those discussed 30, 40 and even 50 years ago by those involved in sport and recreation. Why should we be any more successful in finding new ways and effectively introducing improvement?

Let me digress to the sources of some of the problems noted in the larger culture outside of sports and recreation. In Canada and in many other countries, the way in which most of us live has, to an unfortunate extent, been dominated by economic interests, by growth type values and by external standards of achievement being forced upon us during our socialization. The average family operates upon the premises that it must look after its own economic welfare and that its members, for the most part, need not concern themselves directly with governmental and even community affairs. The family is thought to be doing well provided there is room for its material advancement from year to year and the individual is seen to be doing well if school grades are high or if salary is increased. Social approval, prizes or money, and sometimes applause are the rewards for doing "better" than others. These competitive values in which one strives for external reward, in the process excluding others, are unfortunately often the dominant values communicated to our children in the schools where they learn, on the sporting fields where they play and over much of television in front of which the average child sits for at least 20 hours a week. The children see before them a world in which the victors in competition become those of high power and thereafter judge and exert influence over the vanquished and over those who have done less well. It is not surprising that these values are emphasized in the socialization of children for even on an international level the same values prevail. The wealthy and powerful nations have traditionally

*Invited Paper Presented at: *Women in Motion: Health, Sport and Recreation,* International Women's Year Conference, University of British Columbia, October 24-26, 1975.

dominated the poor ones and differences have been solved through various manifestations of force. Here too, economic expansion and the pursuit of mastery over others, material luxury and opulence have been practiced.

Internationally, nationally and even individually I hope, along with others, that we are now in a process of change. This change is being brought about by the fact that the values which have traditionally been pursued by the privileged and the powerful threaten the survival of all. I refer to the consequences of the maintenance of power: to the weapons which have been developed, to the consumption of natural resources which are limited in supply and to the emergence of large numbers of alienated and under-privileged people who may eventually demand their rights at any cost. Whereas in the past these consequences could sometimes be avoided, today we are all involved and may all have to pay for the debts accumulated. Everyone on this planet is in a vulnerable position and this widespread vulnerability depends for the first time in history upon the behaviors of other humans. Our welfare, our quality of life and our survival are not to be taken for granted unless there is a massive shift in values in which negotiation and mutual consideration take the place of force when there is conflict, in which cooperation between peoples takes the place of competition and in which broad communal identities with nature and fellow humans take the place of narrow individualistic and self-centered identities.

As a generation we have been very critical of our parents. I suspect that our children will be even more critical of us, not that we failed to identify the problems and the changes needed in our times, but that we failed to act on them.

What, you may ask, has all this to do with *Women in Motion*? Let me comment from a few findings in the social sciences in order to link the relevance of broad social values to physical activity. First, we know that the ways in which young children and young animals play provide a blue print for their later behavior. Animals and children rehearse, practice and experiment with the competencies they will use in their later lives. If a child is rewarded for winning against others and obtains reinforcement for striving to outdo others, then competitive behaviors and values are encouraged. If a young girl is socially disdained for her efforts to develop physical competence, if the facilities are not available for her to practice at school and if her mother provides an alternative model of being inactive, submissive and uninvolved outside the home, so is that pattern encouraged and made probable for the child as she develops. Second, all cultures tend to preserve their social structures through value systems which are justified and passed on not only through social reinforcement but through the myths, cultural products and folk models of the culture. It is no accident that in our culture the multi-national corporations and other economic interests are supporting sport as a folk model. It is no accident that professional athletes compete to the tune of 100,000 and 200,000 dollars a year or that skilled promotion can result in a single purse of one million dollars and more. It is also no accident that the general public will throng 50 and 100 thousand strong into a stadium to witness a win-lose type struggle in which aggression, militarism and dehumanization are the features of the game.

I hope that such 'madness' will cease and that sports and games will change their course. For they are presently keeping alive in front of our people, and more importantly our children, values which could lead to self-destruction. It is in a shift from these values that I suspect most of the people in this room are interested. Comments have been made on the difficulties met in attempting to change the status quo in our school, on the frustration of trying to teach gymnastic skills to 30 youngsters at one time and on the destructiveness of the competitive system in which large numbers became non-participants, uninvolved and passive.

Why should such issues be important at a conference on *Women in Motion?* And, how are reforms to be put into effect?

First, why women? For the injustices women have suffered in the past, they now find themselves in a privileged position because many are well schooled in the values of community and cooperation. They have insights into and experience of the personal and subjective side of human behavior. These competencies are in demand. Because social systems operate on homeostatic principles, the status quo which has been emphasized and which has been the reserve of men is now searching for and endorsing the corrective influence and contributions of women. Thus women have perhaps more than ever before the opportunity to develop and use both competence and insight.

As a result, women are placed in an interesting dilemma when called upon: Shall I accept the position of privilege open to me and work within the old framework thus preserving the status quo? Or, shall I sacrifice all and work for the reform I know is needed? How much, for example, should anyone here stake in reform to the problems s(he) has posed? Does one resign from the committee which continually bases its decisions upon a rigid hierarchical structure? Does one refuse to teach if the size of one's class is not reduced? Does one continue to behave cooperatively in the face of continued competition? In other words, how much should one live by ideals and teach by life style?

We note that reform is not confined to women. Many men are equally in a position to offer constructive changes and unique insights. However, on the whole, women are in the position of greatest potential because they have not been as invested in the status system of the competitive society as have men. The uncommitted always have a greater potential for inducing change and in addition women are well versed in the broader communal identity which is the need of the future. Women are well acquainted with the joys and the sacrifices of group living. For they have had to consider the social and psychological welfare of their children and they have placed the development of the family as a group ahead of their own individual advancement. At the same time many a woman has been made well aware of the follies of competition as she has seen her child return crestfallen from school having not made the team or harboured her retarded child in the home because the child was not welcome or wanted in the system. When she wished to return to the work force at age 40, she has experienced what it is like to be turned away because she did not have the mechanical skills of the market place. She has lived with her husband who has sought to preserve his place in an economic system that may no longer need him and many a woman has seen her husband give up the struggle to heart problems, ulcers or alcohol or just plain unhappiness and lack of fulfillment. In summary, many women are able to initiate change because they are not locked into the prevailing status system and their commitments are to community and solidarity between people and groups rather than to individualism and status.

Are women also more cooperative than men? Although studies are not definitive, it seems likely the answer to this question is "yes". At first women enter social situations with more cooperative intentions than men. But if crossed they become even more competitive as a form of self protection. We must find ways in which women may use their cooperativeness in the service of all.

Having dealt with the question, Why women?, let us turn to the second, Why sports? Women in sports and physical recreation are more able to encourage positive social change than many other groups. Much of their work is with youth and with the personal and social development of adults. What one learns through activity one applies elsewhere. In emphasizing competence as a basic personal motivation and encouraging the participation of all across age and sex groups the greatest personal growth and knowledge about others is promoted. I am not in favor of coralling the men to look after the babies while the women play football, but in making our own sporting experiences with the children so attractive that the men will plead for inclusion. Women are in a position to encourage all of the positive values which have tended to be neglected in sports: mutual understanding and the enjoyment of competence, self-exploration and new definitions of excellence. In educating our children in sports, we must remember that we are preparing them for future personal adjustments as well as for social participation. Large numbers should not be excluded either because of sex or lack of the so-called competitive instinct. We must also remember that studies indicate animals and children have the potential for both cooperative and competitive behaviors and that these behaviors are socially induced and supported. We want to encourage personal competence and social cooperation, not personal avariciousness and social competition.

There are several major directions in which women might consider investing their energies and potentials in sport. Let me describe five of these as I see them.

1. Women must become increasingly involved and responsible in community, school, and governmental programs. The more women read, discuss and participate the better. We should not isolate ourselves from the men, from the children or from the ideas and approaches of different cultures. There are now funds available for the running of community, national and international programs in sport and recreation. Not only do these programs have to be operated but they have to be conceptualized, planned and administered. All of these levels and responsibilities need the contributions of women.

2. Women must be prepared and willing to offer leadership in the area of physical culture. I do not think this should be orthodox leadership, but exploratory, innovative and even radical. It is important that in situations

which are unstructured or in which creativity is needed, a facilitative type of leadership is usually most productive. A directive, system-locked, inflexible leadership is not. For this reason, women who are now leaders should be aware of and search for future talent and give such people a free rein. We must keep in mind that the most able and innovative leaders of the future are not necessarily those with the most degrees, the most medals or even the most formal experience. Let us also look in the homes for women who are responsible and experienced in other ways and who have not become locked into our usual academic programs. For we need people to prod the universities, to prod governmental and sporting bodies and to encourage everyone to greater goals. Leaders should be sought out and asked to assume responsibilities. They should have their positions thrust upon them and give them up readily to others rather than grab them and seek to preserve them. We must also spend time on one to one leadership, or on the coaching relationship, in which individuals develop most significantly.

3. Women must make it easier for those women who do not participate in organized physical activity for practical reasons to do so. We must seek them out and build on the potential which is there. They too have basic motivations to experience and to develop competence. They too will enjoy programs which are not based upon competition but on competence, which are not modelled after the homogeneous sports culture of the commercial male world but after the multi-age multi-sex culture of the world in which they live.

4. Women must preserve their objectivity when they become involved in institutions of any sort and not be carried away by the special privileges which will be offered. It is very easy to accept what our status offers us and to forget the plight of others. We must be skeptical of the prizes and the privileges and of the money and the awards offered in order to remain true to ourselves. When privileged we should use that privilege for the education of all. I would like to see more professional athletes channelling their winnings into helping the disadvantaged rather than into land speculation just as I would like to see athletes defaulting on match point or retiring before the game has ended in order to emphasize the importance of competence over the final victory.

5. Women must gather information on the sporting experience through social experimentation. In social experimentation one tests out an idea on a small scale to see what happens when a new policy, idea or method is put into effect and keeps an accurate description of what results so that it will be of value to others. There are very few government agencies, school principals or supervisors who will turn down a well thought out experimental program in which all interested parties can learn from the failures as well as from the successes. In initiating such programs we must be responsible and must report the results. By responsible, I mean we should not try to escape from our ordinary duties to play with our pet projects but rather do both. By report, I mean we should keep records which can be used to communicate what we have done and what we have learned to others.

I look to women and to sport with great hope for the future. Women are posed to contribute much and the social climate is right to accept that contribution. I am reminded here of a statement made by Elizabeth Cody Stanton to the International Council of Women in 1888:

> "Thus far women have been the mere echoes of men. Our laws and constitutions, our creeds and codes, and the customs of social life are all of masculine origins. The true woman is as yet a dream of the future".

Perhaps sport is one avenue through which this true woman may be realized.

The "Jock-Trap"— How the Black Athlete Gets Caught!*

Roscoe C. Brown Jr., Ph.D.
President, Bronx Community
College of the City University
of New York

The "jock-trap" is an allegorical and somewhat humorous way of referring to the trap into which so many college athletes fall. This trap which is
reminiscent of the gladiators of the Roman empire results in many athletes
being left without an education after the college has benefitted from their
their physical skills. Unfortunately, the Black athlete gets caught in the
"jock-trap" more frequently than the white athlete. Certainly one should
condemn a system that develops a "jock-trap" for both Blacks and Whites,
but the impact on Black youth is even more serious because there is only a
limited number of Black youth in college and the Black community des-
perately needs the skills and commitment for social change that should
result from a college education.

Let us look at the "jock-trap" and how it "runs its game" on the Black
athlete. It begins at the instant of selection — selection of the sport in
which he chooses to participate and selection of the position the coaches
choose for the athlete. Is the predominance in certain sports such as basketball, football, track and field and at certain positions such as cornerback,
split end, defensive end or in certain events such as the sprints or jumping
events in track due to a *natural propensity* of Black athletes to excel in
these sports or positions, or is it due to some form of *selectivity* based on
social and economic considerations? My thesis (and I believe the thesis of
most anthropologists) is that there is no particular physical characteristic that
makes the Black more proficient in one sport than another. The reason why
Blacks tend to cluster in certain sports or in certain positions is sociological;
there is a kind of social conditioning, based in part on the racism that affects
everything that involves Black people in our society, that leads Black youth
to try to emulate Black athletes who have been successful. Probably the
best example of this is boxing. During the heyday of Joe Louis and Sugar
Ray Robinson literally thousands of Black youth explored the path to
success through the field of boxing. With the acceptance of Blacks into major
league baseball beginning with Jackie Robinson's entrance into baseball in
1946, and the fantastic successes of Bill Russell in basketball and Jim Brown

*Delivered at the Maryland State Association of Health, Physical Education and Recreation
Meeting, October 19, 1972.

in football, hordes of Black youth have been attracted to these sports instead of boxing. Now it is the Puerto Rican and the Hispanic youth who are being attracted to boxing because this is where they have some role models. The same thing might be said about the attraction of Hispanic youth to baseball because of the presence of heroes like Juan Marichal and Roberto Clemente. My hypothesis is that Blacks can be successful equally in proportion to whites in any sport in which they have the opportunity to participate with high quality competition and excellent training.

Some studies have suggested that Blacks' body types are not conducive to a high level of buoyancy, and thus, Blacks do not swim well enough to be champions. I am sure that there are Blacks who have the same body type as white championship swimmers and can excel in swimming, if given the chance. One of the really interesting questions is "why there is no top flight Black professional quarterback at this time?" There are probably some on the horizon, but they haven't arrived as yet. Possibly, one reason for this is that traditionally quarterbacks are taught by former quarterbacks and there have been relatively few former really great Black quarterbacks. Black youth who have played on the predominately Black teams have not had the coaching needed to develop the excellence that it takes to be a pro quarterback. With the integration of teams all over the country and with the moving into the pro ranks of star quarterbacks who are Black like Joe Gilliam, Jr. of the Steelers and Eddie McAshan of Georgia Tech, I look forward to the correction of this omission in terms of Black QBs. The same pattern of omission of Blacks can be seen in the position of offensive center in football or catcher in baseball. The suggestion has been made by John Loy in a study that the majority group (white athletes) gravitates to the central positions in sports. This is supplemented by Harry Edwards' hypothesis that the central positions involve thinking and decision making. Since many whites accept the stereotype that Blacks cannot function in the intellectual realm, this leads some coaches to avoid placing Blacks in central positions, or even to encourage them to try these positions. This is further complicated by the phenomenon of "stacking" where on some teams Blacks are made to compete for the same positions in order to keep the "racial" balance on the team. Just because a pro-draftee is drafted for a particular position that doesn't mean that he has to stay there. Changes occur all of the time with white personnel. Thus, there is no reason to expect that Blacks couldn't change their positions, too.

Another aspect of the "jock-trap", and probably the most tragic, is the fact that so many Black athletes simply do not get the education that they are entitled to, either in high school or in college, while they are being lionized as athletic figures. The athletic system as it is presently conducted in our major high schools and major colleges, tends to victimize the Black athlete in terms of his education. All athletes, Black, White and Brown deserve the opportunity to get a good education, an opportunity which is being denied to them because of the way the athletic system works. It is well known that requirements for academic achievement and performance are not generally as high for athletes in most high schools and colleges where athletics are employed. In many of the "athletic factories" the athlete on scholarship usually takes only a twelve point load. (We should note that it takes a fifteen point load each term to get a degree in four years.) While some athletes go back to get their degrees after the fourth year, in far too many places there is no financial aid for tuition and maintenance to support athletes after they have completed their years of eligibility. In some instances, athletic eligibility requirements are based on a grade point index which is low enough so that even if an athlete finishes in four years, he may not have a sufficient grade point average to graduate.

Why does this affect the Black athlete so strongly? The Black athlete frequently comes to the school situation with a poor academic background (a fact that is definitely not his fault but rather is the fault of the social system which creates and operates poor schools in our inner cities) and must have extra academic help in order to do college work. The suggestion that Black youth are not as intelligent as white youth is a rationalization that has been disproved years ago. There is no rationalization that can account for the fact that half as many Black athletes graduate as white athletes. The "jock-trap" in education for the Black athlete is not only a function of the limited number of points that athletes are allowed to take, but is also a function of the low expectations of the Black athlete by coaching staffs, by other students, by their professors and even, by some of their fellow Black athletes. Two or three studies have been completed which have shown that the Black athlete often internalize some of the low expectations of his coaches and his teachers. These low expectations must be purged from the minds of the Black athletes, purged from the minds of the coaches and purged from the minds of his fellow students. The way to do this of course is to set expectations that are high, achievable yes — but high nonetheless. This requires tutoring and counseling; it also requires giving the athlete the time to do the extra studying and the extra work that is necessary for him to get through school. To make all-American is laudible, but does not insure success in life. However, to make *all-American* and *to graduate* is to more or less insure an athlete's success in the future. We should remember that only 132 out of the one thousand odd football players that were drafted last year made it to the pros (and the one thousand that were drafted represents only the cream of all of those who played). The athlete's quest for the million dollar bonus contract does not justify the poor education that the average athlete receives. The main reason for the existence for a college athletic program is the development of the intellectual, social and emotional potential of the athlete of the team members of the social system in which he lives. The athlete is *not* a *"gladiator"* and should be treated as such.

What is my remedy for the "jock-trap?" The remedy which I propose is said by some to be too radical and too infeasible. Recognizing that there might be some legitimate criticisms to the remedy, I still would like to propose it again. Major college athletics, namely basketball, football, track, baseball or whatever the major sport which creates the pressures described above, should become professional. By professional I mean that the college athlete should be paid a salary commensurate with his work as a professional athlete, just as a student who is a secretary or a librarian is paid. I am not prepared at this point to give the exact amount the athlete should be paid, but it should be substantial; a salary that will enable him to support a family and to live in a reasonably adequate style during the four years as a paid college athlete. I would limit his professional status to the usual four years of college eligibility. He may, if he desires, attend college and get an education (with the tuition paid by the institution for which he is participating). I would not require that he attend college because it is the requirement that the athlete be a student that leads to athletes taking easy courses and limiting their programs to twelve points. The four years during which the athlete participates at the college level would be viewed as a kind of minor league, pre-professional training. It's true that some may leave the college before their four years are completed but this happens now when athletes sign contracts while they're still called "amateurs." My proposed remedy would have two effects: (1) it would eliminate the hypocrisy that presently surrounds modern day college athletics, and (2) it would probably bring to the athlete's attention the real value of the schooling that he is supposed to get when he is on an athletic scholarship, but tends to take somewhat lightly because of the "iron-hand" control of the athletic department. Under this proposal he can select the courses that he really wants to take. It might be suggested that his schedule as an athlete might be so arduous that he would never get a chance to study, but contracts could be written so that there is a limitation on the amount of time that the athlete spends in practice for the team. This program might actually be cheaper than the present cost of college athletic programs because some athletes in some of our large colleges are reputed to be taking a cut in salary when they finally go to the pro ranks, at $50,000 a year. I believe that this system would enhance the value of education in the mind of the athlete and give him the motivation and also the bargaining power, the flexibility to seek education as he desires it. The athlete will probably need counseling and would need special help, but this is true with many Black and other minority and poor youth in today's colleges. The suggestion to make college athletics professional will expose the rank injustice of many of the things that happen to the Black athlete. It will say to the Black youth, "caveat emptor" (buyer beware) before you fall into the "jock-trap."

The jock-trap is seductive and has had many deleterious affects on both the Black and white athlete. It is our task as educators, as physical educators, as coaches, to look at the "jock-trap" and determine various ways of avoiding it. Athletics must do more to fulfill the objective of making a healthier, happier, more vigorous and more creative society for those who participate and for those who enjoy being associated with them.

Psychological Health
of the Athlete

The psychopathology of the athlete is largely an unexplored area of sport psychology. Except for the work of Arnold Beisser, Dorcas Susan Butt, and Bruce Ogilvie and Thomas Tutko, attention has not been given to this important topic. There is, however, an abundance of popular literature and mass media coverage of the psychological problems encountered by athletes. Crippling injuries, symptoms of aging, and failure to perform well sometimes increases anxiety beyond manageable levels and leads to a wide variety of emotional problems.

The lack of attention to the emotional health of the athlete is particularly absent during the early years of competition and at career end when high levels of stress imposed by coaches, the press, family and peers may result in permanent psychological scars.

Psychological problems at the end of a career can be just as debilitating as those encountered during the early years of competition. This problem is particularly traumatic for those players who have not prepared well for work in other fields. Possessing the skills to do something else is critical to good adjustment after one's playing days are over. The work experience is often an antidote for psychological problems. Getting one's mind off a particular issue is often accomplished through work and/or recreation.

In the first article, Edmund Burke and Douglas Kleiber talk about the physiological and psychological implications of highly competitive sports for children. After reviewing the physical and psychological attributes of children – 12 years of age, they explore some of the 'myths' about the little league experience. Following their analysis, they make 12 important recommendations for the conduct of youth sport programs.

In the final paper, Bryant Cratty proposes 'models' for the maintenance of psychological health in athletics. Cratty is of the opinion that there exists marked emotional problems among athletes at all levels of competition. His models, the team Psychologist – Psychiatrist, Athlete-Counselors, Institution Sport Council for Sport Sciences, and Community Sports Council are designed to protect the mental health of sport participants. The scope of the problem becomes clearly apparent when Cratty reports that 1 – 2 players on a 40 – 46 member high school football team are usually on the verge of a nervous breakdown and at least 12 – 15 others could benefit from some kind of psychiatric or psychological counseling.

Personally, I was moved by Ryne Duren's and Robert Drury's behind-the-scenes look at baseball and booze in their book: *The Comeback*. By his own admission, Duren was an 'alcoholic junkie' after being the hero of the 1958 World Series for the New York Yankees.

Equally depressing is Lance Rentzel's own account of his psychological problems. *When All the Laughter Died in Sorrow* depicts Rentzel's exhibitionism and his search for an answer to his psychopathology.

In brief, there is no shortage of literature on the kinds of psychological problems that athletes may encounter during or after their careers are over.

Psychological and Physical Implications of Highly Competitive Sports for Children*

Edmund J. Burke, Ph.D.
Ithaca College

Douglas Kleiber, Ph.D.
University of Illinois

In post World War II American, there has been a growing movement towards ever increasing participation in highly structured, competitive sports for boys in the age group 7-12. Since this is a rather drastic departure from our earlier heritage of game playing and since in this respect we differ from most other cultures, the phenomenon deserves serious consideration.

Competition and Children's Sports

A 1956 Report on School Health[20] characterized highly competitive sports for children as follows: "The chief stress is placed on winning, with excessive emotional pressures applied by teachers, parents and others, and with parental interest going to the point of expressing undue concern over winning." Scott[24] has indicated that the Lombardian ethic has so permeated the American sport culture that it extends even to the little leagues. The statement: "Winning isn't everything, it's the only thing," leads to a product oriented system in which "the opponent is viewed at best as an obstacle, at worst as an enemy that must be overcome in order to achieve victory."

There has been little tendency on the part of most parents to question the value of such an ethic to the health and well-being of their children because competitiveness is a cultural value held by most Americans. It is seen by most to be basic and even biological in its relationships to human nature. While the prevailing opinions of psychologists are varied with respect to the origins of competitive behavior, the ubiquity of competition in our culture is at least suggestive of factors that are biologically inherent to human nature. Competition in sport is most likely a combination of the need to achieve and the natural desire to compare oneself to others.

In contrast with those who promote competition as normal and healthy,

*From an article published in *The Physical Educator,* May, 1976. Reprinted with permission of the publisher.

200

some authorities feel that it is dehumanizing and socially destructive. In a review of the sociological literature, Sadler[22] has called for a change in lifestyle:

> As I have attempted to suggest, some of the most horrendous problems encountered not only in sports but throughout our society are in part due to the unprincipled expansion and virtual domination of our life-styles by the spirit of competition. That has set the standard. Competition has become a primary value which operates in many personalities as a major drive. I have not charged that sports have caused this condition; in fact, the institution of sports have become a victim of it. Ironically, like much organized religion in our society, it mindlessly expresses, endorses, and revitalizes the very spirit of competition which is becoming a significant factor in its (and our) own undoing.

There is a growing body of evidence indicating that competition increases antisocial behavior and reduces prosocial behavior.[7] In a series of classic experiments Sherif[23] demonstrated that competition among normal 11 year old boys results in mistrust and interpersonal hostility. Bryan[7] has shown that children who compete, especially those who lose, are less willing to help or share with others.

Regardless of this evidence there are at present over three million 7-12 year old boys playing organized baseball (more than half playing Little League). Over one million play organized football while organized basketball and ice hockey are growing rapidly, as are age-group swimming, tennis, golf and gymnastics.[19]

The practical question is how to redesign these organized sports to take into consideration the well being of the children involved. Initially we will examine the child psychologically and physically and then react to some of the common arguments of those who promote highly competitive sports for children.

The Psychological Condition at Age 7-12

From a developmental perspective, the child at this age is emerging from a state of his life in which parents were the dominant others into one in which his peer group is increasingly significant. Social play and games provide situations which are crucially important to socialization and to identify formation.[27]

In psychoanalytic terms, this is the latency stage or post-oedipal period. The crises and conflicts of family relations have been at least temporarily resolved with the formation of the conscience or "super ego". This is essentially an internalized set of rules which, by acknowledging certain limits and prohibitions, enables the child to be sure of love and approval. This period may be a crucial time in moral development.

With these new tools of human relations, the child is eager to test their validity in other social situations. Games are particularly effective in providing a protected, time-limited simulation of principles of social interaction and "fair play." As such they are a primary socializing agent. Team games in particular provide for "power sharing" thus enabling the individual to experience collective achievement. Similarly, "failures" in groups games are reduced in importance because losses are also shared and because they are otherwise inconsequential; part of the security and appeal of a child-organized game lies in the fact that there is no fear or loss of love due to performance. That adult-organized sports threaten this security will be considered shortly.

Erikson[13], who discusses eight progressive stages in the development of the ego, describes this particular period as "socially a most decisive stage" during which inferiority is a dominant fear. This concern is most often expressed in group play and games where a child has the opportunity to "test himself" in relation to others. Others' attitudes toward both himself and toward common experiences contribute to the development of a child's self-concept and provide a mirror image of himself.

In a game with other children, "getting along" and "making the game work" are important to the individual, for this setting is rich with information about himself and his abilities. Unlike the parent who accepts the child on the basis of love, the peer will relate to the child on the basis of what he offers the group. Thus, mutuality and interpersonal dependence are also developed quite naturally in this setting. Children readily accept rules from each other and make their own agreements for "the greater good" and they rarely require standards imposed by adults.

It appears then that much of the psychological development and socialization that occurs during this stage is a result of the child's entrance into the culture of his peer group. It is unlikely that adult intervention into the realm of children's games will do much to improve on its contribution to the growth of children, but there is a distinct possibility that if there is inter-ference in these activities, damage may be done to the natural process of growing up.

The Physical Condition at Age 7-12

Perhaps the most important concept which must be understood by the adult who supervises the activity of children is that they are not miniature adults. Activities which may be appropriate for the adult are simply too strenuous for the normal development of many children.

Success in motor skill performance is related to the body type of the child. Body type or bone structure is inherited and cannot be altered by training. Physically the child's height and weight are increasing at a fairly constant rate with a large growth spurt around the age of twelve. While boys are usually stronger, girls are often taller and heavier than boys. Boys are twice as strong at age 11 as at age 6. While their bones are harder, they are easier to break. During the growth years, bone growth is more rapid than muscle growth. Temporarily the bones and joints lack the normal protection of covering muscles and supporting tendons thus increasing the tendency for dislocations of joints and permanent injury to bone. Frequently, injury to the growth region of the bone, the epiphysis, goes undetected until later in life. Within any age range there is a wide individual variation in maturation levels. Chronological age is by no means an accurate indicator of physiological age. Thus when children 10-12 compete, the older child could be literally twice as strong due to body type, age differences, the growth spurts at adolescence and relative maturation rates.

Analyzing the Rhetoric of Advocates of Childhood Sports

Taking into consideration the psychological and physical characteristics of children 7-12 years old, let us examine some of the typical arguments offered in support of highly competitive sports for children:

1. *Sports provide additional play opportunities for children:* Devereux[8] has pointed to the lack of play in our culture as compared with cultures in other parts of the world. Eiferman[10, 11] and the Opies[17] have described the rich culture of spontaneous games in other cultures while Sutton-Smith and Rosenberg[27] note a gradual decline in the number of games being played in America. Devereux[8] has speculated that T.V. and the enormous importance placed on big time sports may have led children in their play time away from free and spontaneous games towards a more rigid system of structured sport. Skubic[25] reported that of 96 little leaguers interviewed, 91 indicated that over half of their leisure time was spent playing baseball. Thus, organized sports for children may actually reduce play opportunities.

It is well known to psychologists and teachers that success is the best vehicle for promoting continued learning. Crucial attitudes are being developed toward physical activity. The child who continually fails in motor skills may lower his level of aspiration, relative to physical development. Level of aspiration, body image and self-image or self-concept are related concepts, each contingent in this time period on peer evaluation. The child who is exposed to an environment in which he cannot be successful (such as happens frequently in little league), is quite likely to respond defensively and express hatred for all physical activity. Clearly, one of the most condemning features of "little leagueism" is the fact that the child who needs physical activity the most is often shunted away from exercise by the competitive nature of the sport. Coaches in highly structured sport often are not sensitive to the needs of the little obese boy or the frail child who may have had virtually no experience in the motor skills needed for success.

2. *More highly skilled athletes result from these types of programs.* The defense that more highly skilled players are a result of highly competitive sports for children must be examined carefully. The following statements should be prefaced by the fact that little literature is available to support or contradict the authors' opinions.

In certain sports such as swimming, gymnastics, golf and tennis, participation at an early age does appear to pay large dividends. The world records and general improvements in play in these areas are testament to the above statement; but in team sports such as baseball and football one is hard pressed to find a relationship between competition at an early age and future success. Why the difference? First, children have always played baseball and football in the local playground as opposed to the more specific environment needed to play tennis, swim, etc. Second, it is a mathematical fact that there simply are not enough qualified coaches to adequately instruct three million boys playing organized baseball. Furthermore, in contrast to age-group programs which are often quite lucrative to the coach, there is no economic incentive to get the truly qualified coach to participate in little league baseball. Even if he does, only the boys on his own team will be likely to benefit which is in contrast to the aforementioned age-group programs where a talented coach can reach hundreds of children in a summer.

Still another common criticism from high school and other coaches of adolescents is that "by the time they get to me they're burned out." The young man who has been exposed to rigid authoritarian training since the age of three or four may have reached a saturation point especially when he sees the benefits of the social interaction available to his age group. Thus, for a large number of such athletes, early training often results in later hostility to the skills which they have acquired.

Finally, it should be noted that there are studies which support the hypothesis that significant physiological benefits result from endurance training at an early age[12, 16]. Thus, sport participation requiring great levels of working capacity such as swimming and running may indeed result in greater performance levels at maturity (if the individual hasn't already given up because of the psychological and social problems attending such vigorous training). Since sports such as baseball and football do not call for great levels of aerobic capacity no such benefits could be attributed to these sports[5].

3. *Organized sports are safer and healthier than the sandlot variety.* There is considerable evidence to support the conclusion that highly competitive sports are often harmful to both physiological and psychological growth and development. With respect to physical damage, the most widely researched sport is that of baseball. Adams[1,2,3] has shown that the excessive repetitive strain to the elbow in pitching by children of little league-age can produce severe bone and joint abnormalities. In a study of 162 boys ages 8-14[3], he was able to demonstrate such damage in all of the 80 pitchers and in only a small percentage of the non-pitching baseball players or a control group. Slocum and Larsen[26], have isolated a common epiphyseal injury which occurs in children 9-15, in the knee area as a result of landing from a jump such as in basketball. Rose et al.[21] have warned of the danger of cardiac contusions resulting from spearing in football. Brogden et al.[6] and Dotter[9] have coined the terms "little leaguer elbow" and "little leaguer shoulder" to describe common injuries found in baseball players. Torg et al.[28] recently completed a study in which "the incidence of injuries in a league characterized by a lack of high pressure were fewer and less serious than those occurring to boys subjected to the vigorous competition of traditional Little League." They summarized this issue when they concluded:

> What then is the difference between pitching in the Little League as compared to the Lighthouse program (non-competitive)? Having considered all factors, we believe that the major difference is the circumstances under which the two groups participate. Specifically, Little Leaguers must compete to make the team, must compete to play in each game, and are subjected to intense pressures to win by adult coaches and spectators. On the other hand, the Lighthouse Boys Club members are automatically assigned to a team and must play at least three and one half innings of each game by Club regulations. The general attitude is one of participation for the sake of recreation rather than competition[28].

Psychological damage is far more difficult to measure; but several authorities[8] have noted that while normal game playing allows the child to experiment with his body and with his environment within a "safe", non-judgemental environment, the child who "strikes-out" in front of the whole town may be subjected to the type of ridicule he simply is not emotionally equipped to handle.

Piaget[18] has actually made a case that through free game playing the child may be making moral judgements which contribute to the development of the superego. An example might be the case of pitching more slowly to one who has little skill; a striking contrast to the "win, at any cost" behavior so pervasive in competitive sports.

"The Coronary Heart Disease prone personality studied by Dr. Meyer Friedman is characterized by an excessive sense of time urgency, drive and competitiveness called Type A behavior pattern. In childhood it begins in school with relenting pressure from parents and teachers for high scholastic standing and grade points. Time urgency, competitive striving and a demanding schedule of after school activities can make growing up a grim and joyless time of life. Up-tight children are being raised by up-tight parents who even direct the children's reactional activities into organized, highly structured settings such as Little League Baseball and Pop Warner Football. At best these are poor fitness activities and contribute nothing to cardiovascular or muscular endurance. They may be excessively stress-producing because of the demand by parents to see their child win at any cost. Experiencing the emotionally charged atmosphere at many Little League games explains how many children find physical activity neither relaxing or enjoyable. These highly competitive, adult-controlled sports programs for children may actually discourage the continuation of physical fitness and healthful physical pursuits later in life. It is unreasonable to believe that we can raise our children to be highly competitive in a stressful environment and expect them to reach maturity calm, serene and at peace with themselves."[5]

Joe Paterno, the highly successful head football coach at Penn State[14] was quoted recently as follows:

Whatever happened to the good old days when if you felt like playing baseball you would round up your buddies, get a bat and ball and would go out and play. What do we do now? We dress up our kids in uniforms, give them professional equipment, tell them where to play, when to play, organize their games for them, give them officials and put them in the hands of a coach who doesn't know the first thing about the sport or what's good for an 8-year old.

4. *Children are going to have to learn how to compete; it is better to learn it early than later on in life.* This is perhaps the most common of all arguments used to promote "children's sports." It conjures up thoughts of teaching a 2-year old to swim by throwing him into an olympic pool or teaching him to read by presenting him with *War and Peace*; thus, it is probably not the experience of competition alone, but rather the intensity of that experience that may be dangerous. In other words, there is little acknowledgement of principles of learning (shaping and reinforcement), of intellectual development (gradual assimilation); and of emotional development (the gradual experience of stress to develop coping mechanisms), all of which are well established. And it should be remembered that when adults direct the competition, children are not exercising control of the experience. In fact, they will

have more control of those competitive challenges that they choose to take on in later life.

This is a crucial time for normal development. To the extent that a child is thrown into an environment which he finds impossible to handle emotionally, the results may be devastating. As he grows and matures he can more fully cope with his physical limitations. Furthermore, he may simply be a slow maturer, but if he is exposed to failure at an early age the damage is already done by the time he has "caught up." Finally, to the extent that he is taking his free time to compete he may be robbed of the developmental advantages referred to earlier which may arise from free play.

SUMMARY AND RECOMMENDATIONS

It would seem to be a more constructive view of cultural socialization to promote cooperation — a value that children learn quite naturally through social interaction in forming and maintaining their own games. Perhaps we should change the argument to: Children are going to have to *cooperate;* it is better to learn it early than later on in life.

If there was an opportunity to make drastic social changes, perhaps the abolishment of childhood sports would be recommended. Speaking pragmatically, however, it appears that childhood sports are culturally ingrained at present and will remain with us for some time. Therefore, we should strive to at least minimize the damage being done.

In keeping with the research and thoughts presented in this paper we wish to make the following recommendations which should be followed in an attempt to more fully safeguard the physical and psychological welfare of our children.

1. Every league should have a physician who makes policy concerning medical checkups, health hazards, physical and emotional development of players, etc. He should be familiar with the psychological development of children and be able to advise coaches on such matters.

2. Coaches should be encouraged to develop skill and competencies which will be of assistance in dealing with children to include: concepts in child development, athletic training, first aid, exercise physiology, motor learning and skills in the particular sport.

3. Our colleges should undertake to offer courses appropriate to teach the aforementioned principles to individuals of varying educational backgrounds.

4. Physical examinations should be mandatory.

5. Sports associated with heavy exercise should be preceded by a graduated 3-4 week conditioning program to be supervised by a qualified individual.

6. Programs should be wide and comprehensive to include:
    a. both sexes
    b. a wide variety of individual and team sports
    c. many teams
    d. no exclusion (e.g. cutting) of eligible players
    e. participation by everyone in a given percentage of every game
    f. random assignment of players to teams

7. Coaches should encourage players to report pain and injury.

8. Cooperation ("teamwork") between players should be reinforced and acknowledged as a primary purpose of the activity.

9. To the extent possible, children should be employed in the decision making process (assigning positions, forming strategy, etc.)

10. Coaches should attempt to reduce the stress of evaluation by communicating affection for their young athletes regardless of performance.

Perhaps the most important recommendation from this paper may be that to the greatest extent possible, organized sport should be structured with the goal of allowing children to *play*.

REFERENCES

1. Adams, J. E. "Bone injuries in very young athletes." *Clinical Orthopedics,* 58, 129, 1968.
2. --------------- "Injury to the throwing arm: A study of traumatic changes in the elbow joint of boy baseball players." *California* Medicine, 102:2, 127-132, 1965.
3. ----------------. "Little league shoulder osteochondrosis of the proximal humeral epiphysis in boy baseball pitchers." *California* Medicine, 102-22, 1956.
4. Baldwin, Alfred L. *Theories of Child Development.* New York: Wiley and Sons, 1967.
5. Boyer, John. "Heart attack prevention starts with children." *Journal of Physical Education,* 103-105, March-April, 1972.
6. Brogden, B. G. and Crow, N. E. "Little leaguer's elbow." *American Journal of Roentgenology,* 83, 671, 1960.
7. Bryan, James. "Prosocial Behavior." In Psychological Processes in Early Education. New York: Academic Press, 1977.
8. Devereux, E. "Some observations on sports, play and games for childhood." Paper presented at the Eastern Association for Physical Education of College Women, October, 1972.
9. Dotter, W. E. "Little leaguer's shoulder." *Guthrie Clinic Bulletin,* 23, 68, 1958.
10. Eifermann, Rivka. *Determinants of children's game styles.* Jerusalem: The Israel Academy of Sciences and Humanities, 1971.
11. --------------- "Social play in childhood." In R. E. Heron and B. S. Sutton-Smith, eds., *Child's Play,* New York: John Wiley and Sons, 1971.
12. Ekblom, Bjorn. "Effects of physical training on adolescent boys." *Journal of Applied Physiology,* 27: 3, 350-353, 1969.
13. Erikson, Erik. *Childhood and Society.* New York: Norton and Company, 1950.
14. Harris, Dorothy. "Physical activities for children: effects and affects." Presented at AAHPER National Convention, Minneapolis, April, 1973.
15. Larsen, Robert and McMahan. "The epiphysis and the childhood athlete." JAMA, 196, 99-104, 1966.
16. Magel, John and H. Lange Anderson. "Pulmonary diffusing capacity and cardiac output in young trained Norwegian swimmers and untrained subjects." *Medicine and Science in Sports,* 1:3, 131-139, 1969.
17. Opie, I. and Opie, P. *Children's Games on Street and Playground.* Oxford: Clarendon Press, 1969.
18. Piaget, J. *The Moral Judgment of the Child.* New York: Harcourt, 1932.
19. Rarick, G. L. (ed.) *Physical Activity, Human Growth and Development.* New York: Academic Press, 1973.
20. Report of Committee on School Health. "Competitive athletics." *Pediatrics,* 18, 672-676, 1956.
21. Rose, K. D., Stone, F., Fuenning, S. I., and Williams, J. "Cardiac contusion resulting from "spearing" in football." *Archives of Internal Medicine,* 118, 129-131, 1966.
22. Sadler, W. A. "Competition out of bounds." Presented at AAHPER National Convention, Houston, April, 1972.
23. Sherif, M. "Experiments in group conflict." *Scientific American,* 2-6, November, 1956.
24. Scott, Jack. "Sport and the radical ethic." In G. McGlynn, ed., *Issues for Physical Education and Sports,* San Francisco: National Press, 1974.
25. Skubic, E. "Studies of little league and middle league baseball." *Research Quarterly,* 27, 97-100, 1956.

26. Slocum, D. B. and Larson, R. L. "Indirect injuries of the extensor mechanism of the knee in athletics." *American Journal of Orthopedics*, 6: 248-253, 1964.

27. Sutton-Smith, B. "Play, games and controls." In J. P. Scott and S. F. Scott, eds. *Social Control and Social Change*, Chicago: University of Chicago Press, 1971.

28. Sutton-Smith, B. and Rosenberg, R. G. "Sixty years of historical change in the game preferences of American children." In R. E. Heron and B. Sutton-Smith, eds. *Child's Play*, New York: Wiley and Sons, 1971.

29. Torg, J. S., Pollack, H. and Sweterlitach, P. "The effect of competitive pitching on the shoulder and elbows of preadolescent baseball pitchers." Pediatrics, 19:2, 1972.

Psychological Health in Athletics: Models for Maintenance

Bryant J. Cratty, Ed.D.
University of California -
Los Angeles

Seldom a week passes without an item in the sports pages of our newspapers being devoted to some aspect or outcome of an emotional problem evidenced by a professional athlete. Indeed one could gain the impression that our cadres of professional competitors are overrun with psychological cripples. And while the incidence is not as high as might be gained from a perusal of the headlines, professional athletes, performing under the glare of publicity in situations in which success and failure are easily measurable, do have their problems. For example, a professional athlete recently told me that from 5-7 young athletes on a 40 man team are likely to evidence symptoms of stomach ulcers during a single season, while symptoms of minor and major emotional disturbances may be seen in from a third to a half of all competitors during a sport season, depending upon the sport and its length.

Emotional problems among athletic groups are not only found in the professional ranks. It has been estimated that within a 40-60 member roster of a high school football team, from 1-2 are on the verge of a nervous breakdown during a season, while at least 12-15 others could benefit from some kind of psychiatric or psychological counseling, due to the stresses imposed by their sport. The high school athlete is often too immature to bear the whole brunt of competition, impacts often unaccompanied by support from an adult figure close to him. Indeed the youngster may be derided daily by his coach, periodically by the press, and may even be rejected by members of his family, if the team is not having a successful season. This combination of forces can prove overwhelming, and even culminate in suicide as occurred recently in the northwestern part of the United States. Athletics for the maturing boy is often a wholesome method of self-expression, an uplifting part of his life, and one which provides him with important evidence of self-realization. At the same time athletic success, and team membership, is often the "glue" which is holding a youngster together — a boy or girl whose family and other psycho-social conditions may be less than supportive, or stable. If this glue evaporates when the boy is denied team membership or achieves less than expected success, his entire personality may evidence a concomitant disintegration with accompanying symptoms of unrest, despair or even inappropriate aggression and asocial behaviors.

Even the apparently stable productive athlete, in the high school, in pre-adolescent sport, or professional ranks may undergo emotional changes as he competes for several years or more which will result in psychological trauma. Arnold Beisser has described well some of the problems encountered by athletes at career's end. The loss of a way of expressing one's aggressions as the season or career terminates may result in severe adjustment problems; the loss of status and self-respect felt by high school and college athletes, as their talents do not permit them to ascend to the next higher levels of competition may similarly cause them to need professional help in the re-alignment of values, energies and general outlook upon life in general. Career's end may come following the finish of a "little league" career when the boy or girl finds they cannot "make" the high school team, when the high school "star" finds that his talents are not desired by college or university coaches, when the professional athlete finds himself with a crippling injury, or when the symptoms of aging prove debilitating.

Emotional upset has also been superficially studied in the "little league" type of competition. Vera Skubic, for example, found via questionnaires that about one-third of all the young (pre-high school) competitors in baseball competition evidenced various kinds of signs indicating undue emotional unrest. These included difficulty in eating, unrest at night and similar symptoms. It is interesting to note that in this study it was found that these symptoms appeared more often among children who were winning, than among losers.

It is fair to point out that other investigators have suggested that in general the college and grad school athlete is rated as more emotionally healthy than non-competitors. At the same time the data forming the bases of these speculations are generally inferential rather than the result of careful research, in which athletes and non-athletes are carefully compared, keeping constant such factors as I.Q., academic achievement, age and sex.

Despite the evidence that there tend to be rather marked emotional problems among athletic groups at all levels, there have been few organized attempts by athletic organizations and individuals in this country pointed toward the illumination and correction of these conditions. In contrast, there is, at the time of this writing, an effort underway to provide a central research and service effort directed toward the study and remediation of physical injuries in athletes, organized primarily by those interested in sports medicine.

However, as most agree, athletic endeavor is an emotional as well as a physical undertaking; it is inconceivable to this writer why large and expensive professional franchises do not place more emphasis upon pre-season and continuing psychological and psychiatric testing, interviewing and counseling. While from a humanitarian viewpoint, it is also incomprehensible why communities and school districts do not provide similar services for the young men and women they similarly expose to the stress of emotionally taxing athletic competition.

It is with this general background and orientation in mind that the following models were formulated. These plans, to my knowledge at this point in time, have not been attempted in *any* community or league in any part of the country. At the same time it is believed that their formulation and implementation will exert a positive effect upon the "face" of athletics turned toward the public, as well as upon the emotional health and performance of the participants.

The Team Psychologist-psychiatrist

It is obvious that the most desirable method of dealing with emotional health of athletes is to employ a full or part-time psychological or psychiatric consultant. This individual should be familiar with the sport, and be thoroughly trained in all aspects of clinical counseling. At the present time programs for the Ph.D. in sports psychology are beginning to appear within several university curriculums in the U.S. (including UCLA). Hopefully, highly qualified people will be emerging from those.

This team consultant should be available during some of the team practices as is customary with regard to the team physician. He or she should also be on hand during games and be available for pre- and/or post-game counseling. His duties might also extend to psychological testing, counseling of coaches and of associated personnel as well as of team members.

At the same time, the institution of a team psychologist-psychiatrist at the professional level is fraught with problems. As has been pointed out by Scott, among other writers, players will probably have a difficult time trusting such an individual. They will ask themselves as to "whose man he is?" (Ours, or managements?) They will probably carefully test him to ascertain the confidentiality of the material he will obtain, and how he might use it for their well being or "against them" by exposing their psychic weaknesses to management at contract time. At the same time management is likely to be similarly suspicious of his presence, motives and operations. Is he likely to undermine the authority of the owners or coaches?" they will ask themselves. Indeed the management of one professional team to whom the plan of a team psychological counselor was suggested refused to permit its institution because the psychologist would take the airplane seat of one of the many sportswriters who usually accompanied the team!

Such an individual may be impossible to find, for he must be interested in athletics but not too interested. He should be concerned about the mental health of the players, but not with his personal exposure in the press. Players want his help, not to read in the newspapers the day after a game how he is a primary source of their support and an integral part of their winning. The psychologist who goes on an "ego trip" is likely to render himself quickly ineffectual.

Athlete-counselors

Professional teams invariably contain formal and informal counselors and leaders to whom players confide and go to in time of indecision and stress. At times these individuals acquire formal titles, "team representative" and the like. This player-counselor usually enjoys good rapport with fellow players, is respected and enjoys the confidence of a large number of peers.

One suggestion for imparting good psychological advice to members of athletic teams is to employ this team leader in a more formal counseling capacity. This team "rep" may be exposed to workshops lasting from 2-3 days, once a year, in which the tools of the clinical counselor are explained and in which he learns how to deal with less serious problems, while acquiring the insights necessary to identify more pronounced signs of emotional disturbance symptoms which indicate the necessity for counseling and treatment on the part of a "back-up pool" of professionals. This back-up team, composed of clinical psychologists and/or psychiatrists, might be located in a central part of the country and called upon (flown in) when their services are obviously needed.

This type of model has been espoused by Arnold Beisser and others for use within contexts other than the athletic team. I believe, however, that it represents one of the most viable plans for use within professional athletic teams as they are now constituted in the United States.

The workshops would, of course, be conducted by the core of professionals alluded to previously. These could be conducted yearly and run concurrently or adjacent to regular meetings of the team representatives. The difficulty with this plan, as with the previously presented one, is the fact that various sports seasons run for different durations of time during the year. While problems needing attention may occur throughout the entire calendar year. Thus, part of the year the player might turn to the team representative, while the remainder of the year he might avail himself of the services of the professional "core" described previously.

Institution Sports Council for Sport Sciences

Most colleges and universities presently contain various kinds of athletic policy boards, composed of interested professors, the athletic director, a coach or two, and members of the administration. The primary function, however, if one is to believe the minutes from their meetings, is to formulate athletic policies relative to finances, facilities and the procurement of athletes. Less often do their conversations turn to the physical and emotional protection of athletes once acquired.

It would seem helpful, and even moral, if universities and colleges also constitute a sports council composed of professionals on the campus (the school physician, psychologists, sociologists, etc., might be appropriate members) whose main concerns center upon the well being of the athlete. These counsels might not only recommend policies which would implement the mental health of athletes, in the form of preventative psychiatry, but would also help in the improvement of performance standards. At the present time relationships between the athletic departments and professional schools and departments containing professionals who might aid athletes in rather direct ways are often informal and superficial. A council of the nature described could assist a productive wedding of sport, science, medicine and psychology in rather direct ways and promote practices helpful to all concerned.

212

Community Sports Council

If community leaders, even within moderate size cities, were to total up the number of people, children and adults, within their confines who participate in organized sport each year, they might be surprised at the number complied. It would seem helpful if communities of from 6,000 and up were to form what might be termed "sports councils". This council could be made up of interested and capable professional and lay individuals; people who are not only interested in sport, but who place the interests of participants paramount. Such a council should contain at least one representative from the mental health professions, but need not be confined to this type of professional. Included also should be physicians, (orthopaedists, pediatricians, cardiologists and psychiatrists would seem most appropriate), educators, child development experts, psychiatric social workers, etc.

Such a group, meeting regularly, could formulate and implement policies which would not only include provisions for the protection of the mental-emotional health of sports participants within the community, but could also exert influence over: the nature of insurance protection available; the formulation of standards for adequate facilities, training of officials, and the certification of coaches at all levels; and the constitution of regular workshops available to parents, coaches, trainers and interested workers which would cover such subjects as the prevention, care and treatment of athletic injuries, coaching techniques, mental health aspects of sports participation, skill acquisition, developmental aspects of sports participation, the influence of sports upon adults and upon the aged. This type of council could of course coordinate the efforts of the city government, local school districts, recreation programs, private and public athletic programs for youth, adults and the aged, and amateur athletic and officials organizations. As one of their duties they could appoint personnel and arrange programs which would provide for adequate emotional-health services for the sports participants within the boundaries of the city in which they are constituted.

The School Psychologist

There is hardly a school district of even moderate size in the United States that does not employ at least one school psychologist. This individual or group (numbering from 70-80 in several of the larger cities in the Nation) generally possess at least Master's level training in clinical psychology, and include as duties the counseling of parents and children with educational and/or emotional problems, the administration and interpretation of standard tests covering school achievement, intelligence, vocational aptitude and personality, as well as general consultation in curriculum and related matters.

As a group they form an available and reasonably well trained staff within a school district, which has at least an ancillary relationship to the school athletic program. I believe that one or several of these individuals should be permitted some time in their schedule each week, and during each school year, to aid in the maintenance of good mental health among the athletes participating within the school's jurisdiction.[1] For a school district to confine their attention only to the physical needs of their athletes by providing training room facilities, a consulting physician, without concomitant mental health services, is as short-sighted as similar practices among the large professional organizations who periodically lose the services of extremely high-priced athletes because of various kinds of mental-emotional breakdowns.

The local board of education, I believe, is morally responsible for the mental health of a youngster within their purview if at least part of his or her problems have stemmed from the accompanying stresses inherent in a program of interscholastic athletics. I believe that this responsibility might well be met through the use of the school psychologist(s) who might be engaged in several activities during a typical sports season, including the following: (a) Pre-season counseling of coaches and a meeting of the potential athletes describing the role of the psychologist and associated services; (b) The administration of sensitive and valid psychological instruments; (c) Availability for personal counseling on the part of youngsters who might avail themselves of their services, attendance at a number of team practices and games; (d) Follow-up and referral functions for youngsters who leave the district and who may need further work with a private psychiatrist or psychologist; (e) Parent counseling, outlining the nature of emotional stresses to be placed on their youngsters, how the parent might assist in preventative mental health practices and how the parents' behavior and attitudes may add or detract from the youngster's emotional health during a sports season.

Summary

It has been suggested that several types of models might aid in the maintenance of the mental health of athletes. These models are relatively specific to the various levels of athletics discussed, i.e. professional athletics, inter-school competition and pre-high school competition. These models are as follows.

Level	Suggested Model
Professional Athletics	Team Psychiatrist-psychologist; or the use of team consultants trained to deal with immediate problems and to properly refer the more seriously disturbed teammate to a "backup" professional core.
Inter-Scholastic Athletics	The use of the school psychologist to perform traditional counseling functions, testing, referral during and following a sports season.
Collegiate-University Sports	Institution Sports Council responsible for mental health protection and functions within the confines of the college or University.

| "Little League" type of organization | Community Sports Counsel whose membership should include professional(s) conversant with mental health practices and who would implement helpful operations directly impinging upon coaches and their young athletes. |

There are principles and questions ignored within the proceeding paragraphs, including the nature of mental health counseling and services for female participants who are increasingly placed within stresful competitive situations. Likewise the thorny question of "whose man is he?" with regard to payment and responsibility within the professional organization was skirted. At the same time the procedures and principles when modified to suit specific situations, school districts, and communities should have a positive effect upon athletics, athletes, their coaches and their concerned parents.

REFERENCE NOTES

1. It should be emphasized that I am suggesting paid time as part of their regular duties, not an unpaid extra.

REFERENCES

BEISSER, A. *The madness in sport.* New York: Appleton-Century-Crofts, 1967.

CRATTY, B. J. *Psychology in contemporary sport.* Englewood Cliffs, New Jersey: Prentice-Hall, 1973.

CRATTY, B. J. *Children and youth in competitive sport: guidelines for parents and coaches.* Freeport, New York: Educational Activities, Inc., 1974.

FROST, R. *Psychological concepts applied to physical education and coaching.* Reading, Mass.: Addison-Wesley, 1975.

ORLICK, T. D. Children sport: a revolution is coming. *Journal of the Canadian Association for Health, Physical Education and Recreation, 1972.*

SCOTT, J. *Athletics for athletes.* Hayward, California: Other Ways Book, Co., 1968.

SKUBIC, E. Studies of little league and middle league baseball. *Research Quarterly,* 1956, *27,* 97-110.

Personality of the Athlete

The study of the personality of the athlete is one of the most interesting areas of sport psychology. It is, however, a difficult topic — one that has challenged past and contemporary researchers. Agreeing on a definition of personality, for example, is not an easy matter. At last count, there were more than 50 such definitions. There are also problems associated with the measurement of personality. It is understandable why there seems to be so little research done in sport personology at the present time.

Despite the problems, there is still a great deal of interest in the personality of the athlete. Coaches, for example, would like to be able to relate to players more effectively so that individual and team performances may be improved. Researchers would like to collect facts, formulate laws, and build theories. And, the athletes themselves desire to know more about their own personalities so that they may be more effective in their personal and professional lives. In brief, the need for further work in personality is clearly evident.

The basic question, of course, is: what direction should sport personality research take? At the present time, three approaches are being considered. They are: (1) personologism or trait psychology, (2) situationism and (3) interactionism. Proponents of the trait approach believe that behavior is a result of factors which reside within the person. Situationists contend that behavior is largely due to variables which occur within the environment. Interactionists postulate that behavior results from person by situation interactions. Although the interactionist position makes sense intuitively, problems occur when attempts are made to measure the person by situation interface. For example, since people are integral parts of situations, how do you separate the behavioral variance due to the person from the variance contributed by the situation?

In the first article, William Morgan, U.S. Olympic team psychologist, cogently presents the credulous-skeptical argument that is currently taking place in sport personology. This issue is a spin-off of the larger problem in personality psychology. The critical nature of this controversy led to an international symposium on person by situation interaction in Stockholm in 1975.

In explaining the credulous-skeptical viewpoints, Dr. Morgan states that proponents of the credulous position believe that psychological data, e.g., personality test results, are extremely useful in predicting success. The skeptics, on the other hand, argue that psychological data are of little or no value whatsoever. Dr. Morgan's position is that neither position is acceptable. He argues for a "middle of the road" approach. In sum, Morgan says that the credulous — skeptical debate is a pseudo issue — a problem unworthy of scientific inquiry.

John Kane, British Sport Psychologist, addresses the sport personality controversy in the second article and draws implications for sport studies. Dr. Kane's position is basically in agreement with Morgan's views that trait personology should not be abandoned. Instead, Kane proposes some modification in traditional trait approaches and suggests that Eysenck's extroversion — introversion, stability — neuroticism paradigm might be useful in teasing — out the behavioral variance in sport personality studies. In a word, Kane says that the interaction model is a reemphasis rather than a new mode of thinking about personality. According to Kane, performance ultimately rests on psychological dispositions which athletes bring to competition.

Switching away from the controversy, Walter Kroll, Sport Personologist and Motor Integration Theorist, writes about the psychological aspects of wrestling. Although Dr. Kroll's article addresses such important topics as aggression and anxiety, as well as personality, it is placed in this section because of its practical and heuristic values. The practical nature of Kroll's approach is illustrated in his coverage of the "psyching-up, psyching-out" phenomenon. In brief, Kroll contends that high anxiety players need to be calmed down rather than aroused. In other words, the "rah, rah" coach may be guilty of over-motivating some athletes and inducing poorer, rather than better, performances.

In the final paper, Jean Williams, University of Arizona Sport Psychologist, presents an overview of the personality characteristics of the successful female athlete. Critiquing the research that has been done, Dr. Williams vividly points out some of the problems in assessment, particularly methodological and/or interpretational errors. She contends that.the successful female competitor tends to be assertive, dominant, self-sufficient, independent, aggressive, reserved, achievement oriented, and possess average to low emotionality. In brief, she is an androgenous person, possessing some of the best traits of both sexes.

Sport Personology: The Credulous-Skeptical Argument in Perspective*

William P. Morgan, Ed.D.
University of Wisconsin -
Madison

There are basically two personology camps in contemporary sport psychology, and the members of these two camps espouse either a *credulous* or a *skeptical* viewpoint concerning the prediction of athletic success from psychological data. The credulous psychologist would lead us to believe that psychological data are extremely useful in predicting success, whereas the skeptical would argue that psychological data are of little or no value whatsoever. In my talk today I shall attempt to demonstrate that neither position is acceptable. It will be argued that success in athletics is dependent in part on selected psychological states and traits, but the relationship between various psychological measures and success is far from perfect.

Such a position may not seem very provocative, but it should be kept in mind that it is advanced at a point in time when sport psychologists such as Rushall (1968), Kroll (1976), Martens (1975), and Singer *et al.* (1977) have argued that trait psychology should be abandoned and new inventories developed along with alternative research paradigms while other psychologists such as Ogilvie and Tutko (1966) appear to have adopted an equally extreme position in support of trait theory. Other sport psychologists such as Kane (1970), Miller (1976), and Morgan (1972) appear to have adopted a position between these extremes. These latter investigators working independently in England, Australia, and the United States respectively, have all relied primarily on Eysenckian Theory in their research, whereas the skeptics have chosen to employ Cattellian Theory in their early work. It may well be that their decision to abandon trait psychology may reflect an initial error in judgment relating to adoption of a particular theoretical framework. At any rate, it is reasonably clear that considerable controversy exists in this field and the major purpose of the present paper shall be to resolve this apparent controversy.

On the occasion of the Second International Congress of Sport Psychology, Rushall (1970) concluded his paper dealing with the relationship

*From a paper published in *Proceedings* of the Third Symposium on Integrated Development: Psycho-Social Behavior of Sport and Play, (ed.) Ismail, A. A. Indianapolis: Indiana State Board of Health, 1978. Reprinted with permission of the publisher.

of personality and physical performance by stating,

"...personality is not a significant factor in sport performance (p. 164)." This particular investigation has been frequently cited in support of the skeptical viewpoint alluded to earlier.

It seems reasonable in retrospect to regard Rushall's position as an honest error resulting from various methodological problems which characterized his earlier work. A major problem with his work revolved around the failure to control for response distortion; limitation of his analyses to first order factors; a general lack of precision in operationalization of his independent variables; and a questionable inferential leap from his initial data dealing with a homogeneous, Big-10 Conference, Rose Bowl Football Team, to "sport performance" *per se*. Furthermore, Kane's (1970) results, using the same psychometric inventory (16PF), were in general agreement with Rushall's findings when Kane limited his analysis to the first order factors. It was only when Kane analyzed the second order that a relationship between physical ability and personality was observed. Incidentally, the most important and consistent second order factor in Kane's study was extroversion which, of course, explains why some sport personologists have found Eysenckian Theory to be useful in their research. Kane (1970) made the important point that,

"Previous studies have often argued the personality/physical relationship on the basis of first order correlations between simple unit measures of personality and physical ability, whereas these results demonstrate that the relationship has stability and meaning only when a number of unit measures are ideally combined as in extraversion (which combines five traits)...(p. 135)."

The studies by Rushall (1970) and Kane (1970) are in complete agreement where the relationship between personality and physical ability is concerned if one chooses to only evaluate the first order factors. In other words, abandoning trait psychology as proposed by Singer *et al.* (1977) would not seem warranted. However, the results of Rushall (1970) and Kane (1970) are at odds where Kane evaluates the second order factors of the 16PF. Therefore, Kane's results could be used to support either the skeptical or credulous arguments by simply limiting the interpretation to first order as opposed to second order factors. It is quite possible that Rushall's (1970) skeptical position would be modified were he to (1) eliminate test Ss with faked profiles, (2) extend his analysis to include second order factors such as extroversion and neuroticism, and (3) refine his independent measure of performance. It is doubtful, however, whether first and second string football players from an outstanding Big 10 Football Team would differ appreciably on physical performance much less on personality (Johnson and Morgan, In preparation). Also, it is not at all clear why Rushall (1970) felt that the "sport performance" of a second string halfback or wide receiver, for example, would necessarily be inferior to the "sport performance" of a first string tackle. In other words, the apparent discrepancy between the results of the studies by Kane (1970) and Rushall (1970) are probably due to differences in (1) the dependent variables (e.g., first vs second order factors) and/or (2) the independent variables, and under no circumstances should one abandon trait psychology based upon the results of research such as Rushall's (1970).

It seems reasonable to classify Rushall as one of the major skeptics, but his position has also been supported by other prominent sport psychologists. Kroll (1976) for example, has argued that,

"...the methodological problems associated with such athletic personality research have led to the suggestion that progress may not be made until (a) the use of available standardized psychological inventories be minimized in favor of the development of specific athletic inventories, and (b) that the trait psychology approach be abandoned in favor of an interactional paradigm (p. 35)."

It has also been emphasized by Martens (1975) that,

"Unfortunately, after years of study we know very little about personality as related to sport (p. 14)."

In concluding his lucid commentary dealing with the paradigmatic crisis in American Sport Personology, Martens (1975) went on to emphasize,

"Thus the first step toward improving the quality of research in sport personology is not the correction of methodological or interpretive errors, although these too must be corrected, but is the adoption of a viable experimental paradigm for studying personality (Martens, 1975, p. 22)."

It might be argued, however, that "adopting a viable experimental paradigm for studying personality" actually represents, in fact, correction of one of the most fundamental methodological errors in this field of inquiry. It was proposed earlier (Morgan, 1972), for example, that psychological states and traits should be employed in concert with one another in attempts to predict behavior. Such a proposal represents both a methodological and paradigmatic issue. Furthermore, the efficacy of this proposal has been substantiated empirically (Morgan and Johnson, in press), and the recent paper by Hogan *et al.* (1977) offers additional theoretical rationale. These authors have convincingly demonstrated that states and traits taken in concert will always account for more of the variance than either employed alone. Hence, abandoning trait psychology is again seen as an error in judgment. At any rate, the point of view expressed by Martens (1975) has been echoed in the recent papers by Fisher (1977) and Singer *et al.* (1977).

In the recent paper by Singer *et al.* (1977) it has been proposed that "...the trait approach be abandoned (p. 30)" and these authors go on to recommend "...that sport personologists adopt the interactional paradigm (p. 30)" which, of course, results in a renewed emphasis on the individual and the situation. The research of Morgan (1974) and Morgan and Johnson (in press) offers empirical support for the view that psychological states *and* traits are far better predictors of behavior than either taken alone. In this respect it is difficult to understand why Rushall (1970), Kroll (1977), Martens (1975), Fisher (1977) and Singer *et al.* (1977) feel that a "neurotic, anxious, introverted, depressed, schizoid athlete would perform just as well as an athlete with the converse of such a profile." It should be understood, of course, that abandoning trait psychology leaves one in the difficult position of supporting such a view.

Much of the confusion which presently prevails in sport psychology with respect to trait psychology, situationism, and interactionism is placed in historical perspective in the recent paper by Hogan *et al.* (1977). These authors correctly acknowledge that the major source of contemporary skepticism regarding the value of personality assessment stems from criticisms of the trait approach. They go on to point out that,

"Skepticism regarding the usefulness of personality assessment seems to have become part of the conventional wisdom of contemporary psychology (p. 262)."

These authors develop a position which seriously challenges such "conventional wisdom" and they also offer a number of reasoned arguments in support of employing rather than abandoning trait theory. The recent papers by Singer *et al.* (1977) and Fisher (1977) *selectively adopt* Mischel's (1977) point of view, and rather than *reject* the views of authors such as Hogan *et al.* (1977), they simply choose to *selectively ignore* them. In other words, despite what we have been told by sport psychologists, personality assessment is alive and well!

The recommendation by Kroll (1977) that specific athletic inventories be developed for use in sport psychology; Rushall's (1975) view that use of trait approaches is outdated; Fisher's (1977) specificity argument; and the suggestion by Martens (1975) and Singer *et al.* (1977) that trait approaches be abandoned, all seem, from the standpoint of personality assessment, to represent what Hogan *et al.* (1977) have classified as "...the conventional wisdom of contemporary psychology (p. 262)." The lucid commentary of Hogan *et al.* (1977) dealing with the skepticism surrounding the utility of personality tests, along with their systematic rejection of the skeptical position, places the paradigmatic arguments and pleas for the rejection of trait personology which have emerged in sport psychology in question.

Rather than discard trait theory, or develop new situation-specific inventories, it seems imperative that sport psychologists first demonstrate that existing theory and instrumentation is, in fact, inadequate. Most existing personality theories (e.g., Cattellian or Eysenckian) and their operational extensions (e.g., 16PF and EPI) have been *misused* to a greater extent than they have been *used*. That is to say, these particular instruments have often been used inappropriately, and in many cases sport psychologists have ignored the theoretical underpinnings of the inventories. In other words, the inventories represent extensions of the theories, but investigators have chosen to employ the 16PF and EPI atheoretically rather than using the inventories within the context of Cattellian or Eysenckian theory respectively.

The decision to pursue personality research in an atheoretical versus a theoretical fashion, of course, represents nothing more than personal preference; that is, one approach is not *necessarily* better. There are many other problems, however, which have characterized sport personology research, and these shortcomings cannot be pursued in depth here. One major problem characterizing most of the research in this field can be subsumed under the rubric of *response distortion,* and this one issue will be examined in some detail here since sport personologists have traditionally not dealt with this matter. Indeed, Martens (1977) is apparently the only sport psychologist to even discuss the matter, and his viewpoint does not appear to be in agreement with the position of most contemporary psychometrists. In explaining, for example, why the SCAT does not contain a social desirability or lie scale Martens states "...these scales suffer from the same weakness that they supposedly detect (p. 37)." The test, of course, is whether or not description, explanation, or prediction of behavior is altered as a consequence of inclusion or exclusion of Ss who score high on response distortion scales. This matter will now be reviewed in some detail, and the reader will find a discussion of additional methodological problems in the chapter by Morgan (1972).

The Sixteen Personality Factor Inventory (16PF) represents one of the most frequently employed personality inventories in the field of sport psychology. Sport psychologists who have used this instrument have made the tacit assumption that people in general seldom distort their responses (i.e., lie), and athletes never lie! Such a view, however, reflects psychometric naivete, and the fallacy of this assumption will now be explored.

Forms C and D of the 16PF, which have seldom been used in sport psychology research, contain a Motivation Distortion (MD) scale, and this scale is scored along with the other scales. Forms A and B have been employed most frequently in sport psychology, and these forms do not contain MD scales. Karson and O'Dell (1976), for this very reason, found it necessary to develop specific scales for the measurement of (1) motivation distortion (faking good), (2) faking bad, and (3) random answering. These scales have been designed for use in connection with Forms A and B of the 16PF, and the scales along with scoring instructions are described in Karson and O'Dell's (1976) *Guide to the Clinical Use of the 16 PF*. Also, related background materials will be found in the earlier articles by Irvine and Gendreau (1974), O'Dell (1974), and Winder *et al.* (1976). This research demonstrates that the 16PF is easily faked, and investigators simply must consider this methodological problem.

It is quite conceivable that groups of Ss differing in physical ability may not differ on selected psychological traits simply because of response distortion. The transparent nature of questions contained on most inventories makes this a clear possibility, and this *may* represent the primary basis for the skeptical position. Both Kroll (1976) and Rushall (1970, 1975), two of the leading skeptics, employed the 16PF but failed to utilize motivation distortion scores. Also, other sport psychologists, who have not actually conducted original research on this topic, have used Kroll (1976) and Rushall's (1970) work to serve as the basis for advancing similar skeptical views.

It now seems quite likely that Rushall's (1970) conclusion that "...personality is not a significant factor in sport performance (p. 164)" may simply reflect an honest error based upon invalid data. At any rate, Rushall's (1970) work has been characterized by other equally serious limitations, and it is not appropriate to explain his null findings at a response distortion level alone. It is of some interest, however, that the credulous and scientifically defensible positions of overseas investigators such as Kane (1970) and Miller (1976) have consistently avoided the various methodological problems referred to above. Perhaps that is why they tend to be more credulous!

With respect to the matter of whether or not trait psychology is of any value to workers in the field of sport psychology, the author wishes to make one additional comment concerning members of the skeptical camp who have chosen to play the role of "knowledge broker." In most fields of study one is able to locate evidence in support or refutation of a given hypothesis. An earlier review by Morgan (1972) summarizes studies, for example, which have found that personality traits are related to athletic ability, as well as investigations which have not found such a relationship to exist. Again, this is a fairly common finding in most fields of study. It is, therefore, of considerable interest that skeptics who have proposed that trait psychology be abandoned (Fisher, 1977; Kroll, 1976; Martens, 1975; Rushall, 1975; and Singer *et al.*, 1977) have only been able to locate the negative studies! At the risk of making a personal indictment the author offers the following admonition: "Beware of the *knowledge broker*"!

Psychometricians are well aware of the problems associated with response distortion, and it is widely recognized that most self-report inventories are easily faked. One of the most frequently used measures of state anxiety in the sport psychology literature has been the State-Trait Anxiety Inventory (STAI) developed by Spielberger *et al.* In order to evaluate the extent to which this inventory could be faked the 20-item state scale (X-1) was administered to twenty college Ss with standard instructions. These Ss next completed the inventory with instructions to "fake good" or "fake bad" in a counterbalanced order; that is, ten Ss were tested in the good-bad direction while the other ten were tested in the bad-good direction. The results of this experimental manipulation are illustrated in Figure 1.

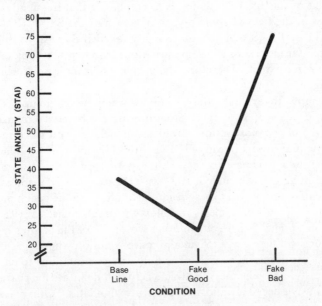

Figure 1. *Response distortion with a 20-item scale.*

Spielberger *et al.* (1970) have also devised a 4-item state scale for use in situations where the longer scale would not be appropriate. A second experiment was carried out with 20 different Ss in which the identical procedure described above was carried out except that the modified 4-item scale (Range = 4-16) was employed. The results of this experimental manipulation are illustrated in Figure 2.

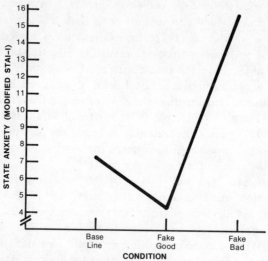

Figure 2. *Response distortion with a 4-item scale.*

While the results will not be presented here, the same experiment was replicated a third time using 20 additional Ss, and the results were identical. In all three experiments the instructions to "fake good" and "fake bad" resulted in significantly ($P < .01$) lower and higher state anxiety scores respectively. The point of this brief discussion is to emphasize that frequently employed measures in the field of sport psychology such as the STAI, SCAT, 16PF, EPI, ATPA, PEAS and so on are easily faked if Ss wish to do so. The problem is far more severe in some situations than in others, but it invariably exists to some extent. Therefore, the problem of response distortion should not be ignored.

Attempts to evaluate the extent to which psychological states and traits influence success in sport situations are characterized by many problems. One of the most serious problems associated with work in this area is the potential for operation of the "self-fulfilling prophecy." That is, there is frequently a tendency for psychologists to specify the *desirable* profile at an intuitive or "armchair level," test athletes, classify them as high- or low potential, and present these recommendations to the coach or selection committee. If the coach elects to follow the psychologist's advice, then the prediction "model" is perfect! In other words, *all* of the predicted successes and failure will be *correct*. Such a practice is not only unscientific, but it is unethical and immoral as well. The only way one can hope to characterize the successful and unsuccessful athlete is to first delineate the characteristics of previously successful and unsuccessful candidates. Otherwise there is a good chance that the self-fulfilling prophecy will be permitted to operate.

It is emphasized that prediction and selection processes should be performed in a blind setting.

The recent research of Morgan and Johnson (in press) dealing with success in crew has demonstrated that selected psychological states and traits can be used in predicting success and failure for both college oarsmen and Olympic Team candidates. However, the accuracy of prediction within the range reported in their study was not acceptable for predictive purposes where one might attempt to identify finalists. It is emphasized in this report that prediction of athletic success should not be attempted within the context of a single domain whether it be anatomic, physiologic, or psychologic. The results of this recent research would challenge the views of both the credulous and skeptical personology camps. That is, psychological states and traits were useful in predicting success, but the precision associated with this prediction was not acceptable for selection purposes.

The above results are supported in part in a forthcoming paper (Johnson and Morgan, in preparation) in which the MMPI was administered to 800 athletes and 500 non-athletes representing five successive freshman classes. The MMPI was administered during the first week of school, and the athletes were characterized four years later as successful or unsuccessful based on the number of varsity letters they earned. While the successful and unsuccessful athletes differed very little, the observed differences always favored the successful group. It should be emphasized, however, that psychometric distortion scales were employed in both of these investigations (Morgan and Johnson, in press; Johnson and Morgan, in preparation). This is an important consideration since those investigators who have consistently observed relationships to exist between personality and physical or sport ability also represent the select few who have opted to consider response distortion in the analysis of their data.

SUMMARY

Two personology camps, the *credulous* and the *skeptical,* have emerged in contemporary sport psychology. A possible third camp represents a small group of individuals such as Kane (1970), Miller (1976), and Morgan (1972) who have not supported either of these extreme views. The credulous sport psychologist would lead us to believe that trait psychology is capable of accurately predicting success in athletics, whereas the skeptic argues that trait psychology cannot do this, and further, members of the skeptical camp have proposed that trait psychology be abandoned.

Both the credulous and skeptical camps, for widely differing reasons, fail to present convincing arguments in support of their positions. Also, a theoretical paper by Hogan *et al.* (1977), and recent empirical evidence presented by Morgan and Johnson (in press), demonstrates that neither the credulous nor the skeptical arguments are scientifically defensible. That is, evidence does exist which supports the view that trait psychology is useful in the description, explanation and prediction of behavior, but the level of prediction is far from perfect. Conversely, the opponents of trait psychology who argue that it should be abandoned fail to consider that a significant portion of the variance can be accounted for where adequate methodological controls are used in connection with trait measures. Hence, it is quite easy to refute the credulous and the skeptical arguments.

There is a great deal of evidence from the fields of both clinical and experimental psychology which supports the view that individuals who possess certain traits will not perform as well as "normal" individuals under stressful situations. For example, one would predict that anxiety neurotics would not perform as well as "normals" under stressful situations. Certain forms of athletic competition, and in particular national selection camps, provide a naturalistic testing ground for such views. It has been observed that athletes possessing selected traits (e.g., neuroticism, introversion and anxiety) are far less likely of gaining a berth on a national team than are athletes who do not possess such traits (Morgan and Johnson, in Press). The magnitude of this effect is not great enough to permit systematic selection based on such data, however. It has also been demonstrated that prediction of success is clearly facilitated when selected traits are used in concert with state measures. Therefore, a state-trait model would theoretically be the most efficacious.

The credulous-skeptical argument relative to trait psychology is not limited to the field of sport psychology. The same debate exists in professional psychology as well (Hogan, *et al.,* 1977; Mischel, 1977). An important consideration, of course, is attempting to understand why the controversy exists. In the present paper it is proposed that the credulous-skeptical argument in sport psychology stems from a variety of factors. Some of the more important being (1) a general failure to adequately operationalize the dependent and independent variables, (2) atheoretical as opposed to theoretical inquiry, (3) use of first order factors alone in some investigations and higher order factors in others, (4) utilization of either state or trait measures as opposed to state-trait models, and (5) a total disregard for consideration of response distortion.

The following recommendations are presented for consideration:

1. The credulous-skeptical argument can best be regarded as a pseudo argument. It is time to set the argument aside and proceed with the task at hand — attempting to understand the psychological aspects of sport and physical activity.

2. The plea to abandon trait psychology represents a serious mistake. Trait psychology is alive and well, and sport psychologists should not discard such models. Psychological traits are quite important when used in concert with selected state measures.

3. It may be necessary to construct sport-specific inventories for use in sport psychology at some time in the future. However, it is recommended that existing instrumentation and theory be first used as intended by test constructors and theoreticians. It is ludicrous to *misuse* theories, and the inventories which represent extensions of theories, and then conclude that the theories and tests are not useful — that is, that trait theory be abandoned and new inventories developed.

4. A tacit assumption in the field of sport psychology has been that response distortion is not a methodological problem, and therefore, need not be dealth with. It is recommended that response distortion, irrespective

of the paradigm or theory employed, be addressed in future research.

5. A final recommendation, and one that is elaborated upon in more detail in a forthcoming paper, is that aspiring sport psychologists be trained in both a selected field of academic psychology as well as a sub-discipline (e.g., sport psychology or exercise physiology) within the exercise and sport sciences.

REFERENCE NOTES

1. Johnson, R. W. and W. P. Morgan. *The Wisconsin MMPI Study of Successful and Unsuccessful Athletes.* Manuscript submitted for publication, 1977.
2. Miller, J. Personality and motor performance: Some necessary future research considerations. Paper presented at the H. Harrison Clarke Symposium, University of Oregon, June 14-18, 1976.
3. Morgan, W. P. and R. W. Johnson. Personality characteristics of successful and unsuccessful oarsmen. *International Journal of Sport Psychology.* (in press).

REFERENCES

FISHER, A. C. Sport personality assessment: Adversary proceedings. In C. O. Dotson, V. L. Katch, and J. Shick (Eds.), *Research and practice in physical education.* Champaign: Human Kinetics Publisher, 1977.

HOGAN, R., C. B. DE SOTO, and C. SOLANO. Traits, tests, and personality research. *American Psychologist,* 1977, *32,* 225-264.

IRVINE, M. J. and P. GENDREAU. Detection of the fake "good" and "bad" response on the sixteen personality factor inventory in prisoners and college students. *Journal of Consulting and Clinical Psychology,* 1974, *42,* 465-466.

KANE, J. E. Personality and physical abilities. In G. S. Kenyon (Ed.), Contemporary Psychology of Sport. Chicago: Athletic Institute, 1970.

KARSON, S. and J. W. O'DELL. *A guide to the clinical use of the 16PF.* Champaign: Institute for Personality and Ability Testing, 1976.

KROLL, W. Reaction to Morgan's paper: Psychological consequences of vigorous physical activity and sport. In M. G. Scott (Ed.), *The Academy Papers.* Iowa City: American Academy of Physical Education, 1976.

MARTENS, R. The paradigmatic crisis in American sport personology. *Sportwissenschaft,* 1975, *5,* 9-24.

MARTENS, R. *Sport competition anxiety test.* Champaign: Human Kinetics Publishers, 1977.

MISCHEL, W. On the future of personality measurement. *American Psychologist,* 1977, *32,* 246-254.

MORGAN, W. P. Sport psychology. In R. N. Singer (Ed.), *The psychomotor domain: Movement behaviors.* Philadelphia: Lea & Febiger, 1972.

MORGAN, W. P. Selected psychological considerations in sport. *Research Quarterly,* 1974, *45,* 374-390.

O'DELL, J. W. Methods for detecting random answers on personality questionnaires. *Journal of Applied Psychology,* 1972, *55,* 380-383.

OGILVIE, B. C. and T. A. TUTKO. *Problem athletes and how to handle them.* London: Pelham, 1966.

RUSHALL, B. S. An evaluation of the relationship between personality and physical performance categories. In G. S. Kenyon (Ed.), Contemporary Psychology of *Sport.* Chicago: Athletic Institute, 1970.

RUSHALL, B. S. Alternative dependent variables for the study of behavior in sport. In D. M. Landers (Ed.), *Psychology of Sport and Motor Behavior II.* College Park: Pennsylvania State University, 1975.

SINGER, R. N., D. HARRIS, W. KROLL, R. MARTENS, and L. SECHREST. Psychological testing of athletes. *Journal of Physical Education and Recreation.* 1977, *48,* 30-32.

SPIELBERGER, C. D., R. L. GORSUCH, and R. E. LUSHENE. *Manual for the state-trait anxiety inventory.* Palo Alto: Consulting Psychologists Press, 1970.

STRAUB, W. F. Approaches to personality assessment of athletes: Personologism, situationism, and interactionism. In C. O. Dotson, V. L. Katch, and J. Shick (Eds.), *Research and practice in physical education.* Champaign: Human Kinetics Publishers, 1977.

WINDER, P., J. W. O'DELL, and S. KARSON. New motivational distortion scales for the 16PF. *Journal of Personality Assessment,* 1975, *39,* 532-537.

Personality Research: The Current Controversy and Implications for Sports Studies

John E. Kane, Ph.D.
West London Institute of
Higher Education

Not withstanding the growth of knowledge and understanding about aptitude, abilities and skills, the explanation of performance differences is acknowledged as depending to a crucial extent on the individual's unique personal and behavioural dispositions. Such dispositions as an individual brings to a performance situation, while clearly important with respect to the outcome, are not yet well understood, neither as to their nature and source, their quantification nor their predictive value. This is not surprising, since this area of psychology — essentially personality psychology — is necessarily complex and currently imprecise embracing such issues as, for example, the relative permanence/impermanence of personality states, the effects of cognitive and perceptual styles, the nature of intrinsic motivation, the person's modes of construing and the effects of learning and experience. Nevertheless the study of the person in the context of behaving and performing is not without a sound pedigree in psychology, and there are current signs of a new and healthy increase of interest in this area which promises to establish stronger theoretical bases for sounder experimental work.

No group of professional workers will be more sensitive to new explanations and findings which make operational sense than those involved in teaching and advising in physical education and sport, where it has long been held that performance, especially in competitive situations, ultimately rests on the psychological dispositions which the individual brings to the event, and that in turn the nature of the event may affect subsequent dispositions. The bases for these assumptions are not hard to find. The physical education literature is, for example, heavy with implied and stated links between personality development and involvement in appropriately conducted programmes of planned physical activities, games, dance and sport. Most recently and interestingly the argument for the existence of these links has focused attention on the possible effects of physical activity on body image and self concept (Kane 1972). Additionally, some recent literature of a psychological nature has tended to strengthen the hopes and expectations of coaches and advisers that the selection, training and performance of talented athletes could benefit from psychological insights (e.g. Cofer and Johnson 1960; Ogilvie and Tutko 1966; Vanek and Cratty 1969; Rushall and Siedentop 1975; Ponsonby and Yaffe 1976).

The research undertaken (mostly by physical educationists) to investigate the validity of these assumptions has not been inconsiderable since about 1960, but on the whole it has not produced coherent and unequivocal findings on which to rely for predictive purposes. It has, however, produced a great deal of useful descriptive information about the nature and extent of the relationship between personality and physical (athletics) ability and performance on which more sophisticated research may be based. The main criticisms levelled at much of this body of research have focused atention on methodological inadequacies (e.g. Cooper 1969 and Rushall 1973), and more recently on the virtual absence of any sound theoretical reference base (e.g. Kroll 1970 and Kane 1976). However, the real cause of the slow progress since 1960 or thereabouts from descriptive to analytical and experimental approaches lies in the conflict and confusion which has characterized the mainstream of research and theory in personality psychology. As a result, the research aimed at accounting for the personality variables in motor and sports performance has had to rely on inappropriate and insensitive tools and models and it is therefore not surprising that the search for enlightenment has been slow. In the last few years, however, a new urgent awakening in the field of personality psychology is apparent, focusing to a great extent on the search for alternatives or extensions of trait theory. Trait 'theory' is under attack not so much because it is an unsound *theory* but because ipso facto personality traits emphasize only the personal dispositions in explaining behaviour and minimize the role of situational factors. The result is that a number of alternative models and approaches have been proposed in an effort to explain a more vital and dynamic concept of personality sensitive to situational factors in behaviour. In these recent developments there appear to be the kinds of explanations, theories and models that may be particularly attractive and appropriate for research in physical education and sport. In particular the current efforts to develop an *interactional* model of personality emphasizing the cognitive interpretations of the person in a given situation deserve special attention, if only to make clearer the nature of the current objections to the traditional *trait* model. It is not quite clear, incidentally, what writers mean by the 'traditional trait model' nor precisely what there is about traits that make them unsuitable or defective (Alston 1976). It depends to a large extent what you mean by 'traits' and certainly the current psychological literature is anything but clear on this point. What is reasonably clear from the present controversy is a serious questioning of the *emphasis* of person factors as the main determinants of human behaviour. My first task must, therefore, be to give a brief and admittedly personalized account of the present state of knowledge to which the trait approach has brought us in the personality/performance area. I shall then consider the theoretical possibilities of the interaction approach before adding a final suggestion about alternative perspectives.

1. *The trait approach.* A number of very useful reviews are available (e.g. Hendry 1970, Harris 1972, Hardman 1976, Kane 1976) which, while not

totally in agreement, give a useful indication of the present understanding of the link between personality and physical abilities and also point up many of the possibilities for clarifying the nature of this link. The studies included in these reviews tend to fall into two categories; those attempting a relatively simple personality (via Cattell or Eysenck) description and/or comparison of selected groups of athletes and a few correlational studies demonstrating the relationship between personality and physical ability variables. While reviewers have found difficulty in coming to unequivocal or generalized conclusions there is a tendency for the male athlete to be described in terms of extraverted and stable dispositions (such as high dominance, social aggression, leadership, tough-mindedness and emotional control) and for women athletes to be shown as relatively anxious extraverts. If, for example, we were to find that certain personality variables are related to outstanding goalkeeping ability in soccer, it would be surprising to find that all the same variables are linked with high level performance in javelin throwing, cross-country running or rifle shooting. A few illustrations and examples may serve best to summarize the kinds of analyses that have been undertaken.

DESCRIPTIVE PROFILES AND COMPARISONS

Figure 1 typifies the profile description. This early and classic account

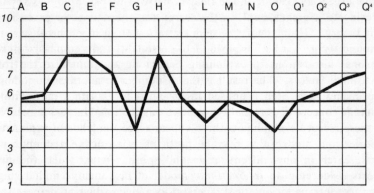

A. Sociability; B. General Ability; C. Ego Strength; E. Dominance; F. Surgency; G. Conscientiousness; H. Adventurousness; I. Sensitiveness; L. Protension; M. Bohemianism; N. Shrewdness; O. Insecurity; Q¹. Radicalism; Q². Self-Sufficiency; Q³. Will-Power and Q⁴. Tenseness.

Figure 1. *Champion athletes.*

by Heusner describes champion athletes as stable (C, L, O traits) and extraverted (A, E, F traits). It is worth noting that subsequent studies have never demonstrated such a definite description of champion athletes. Although this kind of profile analysis has been used mainly to establish fundamental descriptive data of a variety of athletes and activity groups a number of researchers have found that when the activity and level of participation are held constant, interesting similarities of personality type have been recorded for groups of, for example, racing drivers (Ogilvie 1968), wrestlers (Kroll 1967), soccer players and (see figure 2) women athletes (Kane 1966).

Comparison of profile data has often been reduced to focus on similarities and differences based on the two major Eysenckian dimensions of Extraversion and Neuroticism. In most of these studies, even when sig-

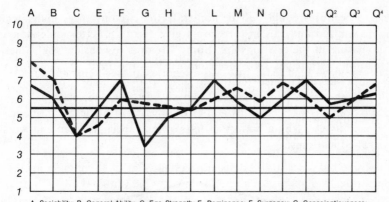

A. Sociability; B. General Ability; C. Ego Strength; E. Dominance; F. Surgency; G. Conscientiousness; H. Adventurousness; I. Sensitiveness; L. Protension; M. Bohemianism; N. Shrewdness; O. Insecurity; Q¹. Radicalism; Q². Self-Sufficiency; Q³. Will-Power and Q⁴. Tenseness.

Figure 2. *Women swimmers and track.*

nificant differences (from the population norms or from other criterian groups) have been established, the problem has been to interpret the real meaning of such group differences. Moreover, group means hide individual differences and in any case the operational implications, for an individual or group, of being, for example, more or less extraverted, tough-minded or emotionally stable has seldom been touched on. This may well have resulted from researchers being more concerned with the personality tests and their popular descriptive meaning than with the theoretical framework which underpins the whole personality assessment procedure being used.

Eysenck (1972) has constantly referred to this point and in particular to the way in which careful attention to the niceties of both personality theory and parameter values are needed in order to interpret experimental findings. As an illustration he refers to the proposed link between extraversion and conditionability and explains the contradictory findings of researches in this area as being a direct reflection of the parameter values used; e.g. weak unconditioned stimulus values favouring quick conditioning of introverts relative to extraverts, while strong unconditioned stimulus values have the opposite effect. It would seem that in the kind of investigation so far described attempting to relate personality to performance, little or no account has been taken of such theoretical subtleties, so that results have tended to be left badly interpreted and unexplained. Lack of reference to a sound theoretical framework has, moreover, caused confusion in trying to explain apparent inconsistencies in findings by different investigators. Nevertheless the better ones of these descriptive studies based on the measurement of traits have been useful in opening up the possibilities for further advanced study. Practically none of them pretended to offer a predictive platform for sports performance.

CORRELATIONAL ANALYSES

Surprisingly few correlational studies have been reported attempting to tease out the nature of the personality/physical performance relationship. If and where a relationship exists it would seem that appropriate correlational procedures could best demonstrate the circumstances under which it is maximized and this in turn could give rise to a better understanding of the nature of the relationship. Some attempts to consider the values of correlational strategies have been reported (Kane 1970, 1972, 1976) and these have included intercorrelation to factor analysis, higher order factoring, multiple regression and canonical analysis. In these correlational studies the two domains — personality and gross physical (athletic) performance — were each assessed by a battery of tests among specialist men and women physical educationists.

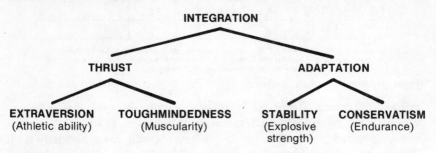

Figure 3. *Personality — athletic ability — hierarchical factor structure.*

Figure 3 summarizes the higher order general factor structure and emphasizes that the largest second order factor links extraversion with general athletic ability (i.e. speed, strength and power). A series of multivariate analyses demonstrated, as expected, the increasing value of the correlation coefficients from simple bivariate techniques (i.e. one personality variable with one physical performance variable) through multiple correlation to canonical correlation. A number of these analyses with multivariate vectors have produced significant coefficients averaging about 0.7 and in many cases permitting a clear interpretation of tough-minded, stable extraversion going with general athletic ability. Notwithstanding the known instability of factor and vector structure these correlational studies have clearly taken the study of the personality physical performance relationship to a serious and useful level. Here again, however, the purpose of the studies using trait measures was not to seek predictive indices of sports performance but rather to search for an understanding of the relationship between the two domains.

THEORETICAL CONSIDERATIONS

Descriptive and correlational studies of the kind so far described are highly valuable if designed and interpreted within the context of a sound theoretical framework and if well standardized measures (with or without trait theory implications) and reasonably sophisticated analyses are used. Few studies so far reported would seem to satisfy these criteria, but as a contribution to seeking an appropriate framework three observations are offered:

      A. Is it not unreasonable to expect personality (however measured) to constitute an equally important explanatory or causative dimension in different types of athletic performance being highly important for success in some, of small importance in others, and of no importance at all in the remainder?

B. Eysenck's theoretical and empiric evidence on the nature and antecedents of behaviour appears to represent an attractive general framework to guide investigation of the personality aspects of performance, especially in activities where the perceptual processes (e.g. vigilance, selective attention, kinaesthetic awareness and recall) are of importance. Such a perceptual framework may be elaborated by reference to the work of Witkin (1962) on perceptual styles, and Whiting (1972) on personality and perceptual sampling.

C. If for simplicity we limit our consideration of personality to the two major dimensions Extraversion and Anxiety, and wish to investigate the performance via arousal paradigm, then again we might well consider the Eysenckian version of the causative neurological substrates of behaviour summated in the excitory-inhibitory balance.

2. *The interactional approach.* It is not clear in the recent and generalized attack on the trait approach to personality what precisely is being attacked. Trait theory and trait theorists are referred to regularly though neither is defined or identified. Mischel (1973), who is one of the leading contemporary opponents of traits, refers to 'traditional trait approaches' and to what he assumes to be the implicit assumption in such approaches that "personality comprises broad underlying dispositions which pervasively influence the individual's behaviour across many situations and lead to consistency of behaviour". But even Mischel does not refer specifically to a trait *theory* nor does he name those who are supposed to uphold such a theory. Firstly then, in trying to understand the focus of current concern about traits, it is difficult to see how the concern can be centered on trait *theory* since it is difficult to identify such a theory in the history of personality psychology. Indeed reliance on traits were probably anti-theory originally in the sense that researchers unconvinced about contemporary theoretical postulates decided to content themselves with simply describing behaviour according to derived categories of traits, dispositions, types, etc. Secondly, the attack cannot surely be directed against individual researchers like Cattell, Eysenck and others for having assiduously developed to a thoroughly rigorous level the *measurement* of meaningful personality traits. Mischel at least seems to be objecting to traits as implying broad dispositions predicating behaviour in different situations but nowhere does he appear to deny the existence of traits but only their usefulness in explaining particular behaviour. Again it is not clear what or who is the focus of the attack. Neither Cattell nor Eysenck, for instance, would deny the impossibility of fully and accurately predicting an individual's behaviour in all circumstances on the basis of measurement on broad personality characteristics, such as extraversion and anxiety, or on simpler ones like those incorporated in the 16 PF. Indeed reference has already been made in the earlier part of this paper to Eysenck's constant insistence on the need for researchers to be sensitive to changes in situational parameter values when interpreting their finding in behavioural experiment. Moreover,

Cattell (1950, 1957, 1965) whose research and development in the area of personality traits is unmatched has distinguished clearly between 'source traits' (the relatively stable underlying causal entities that determine behaviour) and 'surface traits' (the relatively varying and superficial elements that reflect behaviour in special circumstances), and has suggested the use of 'specifications equations' such as —

$$R(esponse) = S_1T_1 + S_2T_2 + \cdots Sn\ Tn$$

where $T_1\ T_2$ etc. are traits and $S_1\ S_2$ etc. the weights relevant to each trait for a given situation.

The notion of personality traits does not require a commitment to completely explaining behaviour in widely differing situations on the basis of broad dispositions.

An interactionist model of behaviour appears to be very much a matter of re-emphasis rather than one incorporating a new mode of thinking. As such, one wonders at the crisis proportions given to the current debate. Indeed the laymen might be forgiven for assuming that to consider both the person and the situation in attempting to explain behaviour was commonsense. Moreover, interactionist explanations of behaviour go back quite a way in the psychology literature. Lewin (1935) it will be remembered, suggested the formula —

$$B = f(P,S)$$

where B refers to the behaviour resulting from a choice of possibilities or a performance measurement on a scale; where P refers to structural dimensions (physiological and psychological) represented in personality measures; where S refers to variable aspects of the situation and f refers to the functional relationship (or interaction between P and S in explaining B.)

There has been a consistant flow of research since Lewin following his general interaction theory of behaviour, emphasizing from time to time different aspects of it. Present day interactionists like Mischel (1976) and Endler and Magnusson (1976) apparently wish to attribute overriding importance in behaviour to the $P \times S$ interaction and support their case in two ways — by theoretical postulates concerning the way a person construes a situation and by demonstrating the relatively large size of the $P \times S$ variance in selected studies. The analysis of variance is the favoured tool to support the interactionist viewpoint and on the face of it the review of chosen studies by, for example, Bowers (1973) and Argyle (1976) are reasonably convincing demonstrating that person variance tends to fall into the 15 - 30 per cent range, situation variance into the 20 - 45 per cent range and $P \times S$ variance into the 30 - 50 per cent range. However, there are a number of unresolved design problems in these studies and Cartwright (1975) has suggested that many of them have been biased against discovering appreciable person variance, while Golding (1975) throws doubt on the appropriateness of variance analysis for seeking out person consistency across situations commending instead the use of Cronbach's coefficient of generalizability!

Nevertheless, the interactionist approach is of undoubted significance to sports psychologists. There had admittedly been a strong campaign over recent years by researchers in this field for the development of sport specific measures of behaviour and there has been a long standing recognition of the variable effects on performance of different sporting situations, particularly where competitiveness and stress are involved. Increasingly researchers have also referred to the importance of the athlete's perception and interpretation of the situation and the way in which such perceptions may be idiosyncratic interactions of relatively stable personal dispositions with experimental factors such as previous experience of such situations, conditioning, and expectation. The attractiveness of interactionist explanations of behaviour seems therefore reasonably assured if only to compliment trait descriptions. Some attempts to follow this line of thinking in sports research are in fact becoming increasingly evident, though Langer (1966) had earlier planned a model design for investigating behaviour and performance in different situations of sporting stress. The study monitored anxiety, as measured by the IPAT scale, of varsity footballers during the off-season (no stress), during the pre-game period (high stress) and immediately after the games (reduced stress) throughout a season and in concluding that anxiety level was a most important determinant of football performance Langer demonstrated the sensitivity of the IPAT anxiety scale for recording changes linked with levels of sporting stress and performance.

Another and more recent attempt to assess a person (trait) x situation model for anxiety in a realistic competitive athletic environment has been reported by Flood and Endler (1976). The measurement of anxiety was based on Speilberger's (1972) state-trait procedures adapted by Endler and Okada (1975) to account for their version of the multidimensional nature of trait anxiety. Although some significant interactions between anxiety state and trait in the anticipation of competition were reported, the results in general were equivocal leaving some doubt as to whether or not the interaction model of anxiety was supportable. In general one is left with some concern in this kind of 'interactionist' study about the methods used for the assessment of personality dimensions. It is almost as if those seeking support for the interaction model too easily and prejudicially discard well-standardized and reliable measures of personal dispositions in favour of superficial and less rigorously developed tests in their reaction against the former trait emphasis. This is a danger that those in sport psychology must avoid in calling for the development of sports specific measures of personality. The futility of employing hastily assembled adjective and observational check lists, questionnaires, self reports and the like should be all too obvious. It is gratifying to note in his connection a few examples of sports specific measures which are being developed systematically with sensitivity to the niceties and scientific rigours of test construction, (e.g. Martens 1976). The problems in allocating the correct amount of importance to the Person, the Situation and the Interaction in sports performance will not be resolved easily or quickly, and certainly not by substituting sound and well-standardized measures of well-rooted personality dimensions for others less carefully developed and more superficial. Neither will fuller understanding of behaviour in sport be achieved by the facile shifting of theoretical perspectives to accommodate all the contemporary moods and 'mini-theories' in psychology.

There is no doubt that behaviour in competitive sport may be properly viewed as a continuous process of multidirectional interaction between the athlete and the situational conditions which prevail and that in this process cognitive factors are critically involved. To this extent the interactionist model is in accord with what must be a commonsense interpretation of the competitive environment and is, therefore, attractive. But to establish the superordinate importance of the interaction as opposed to the person or the situation in sport will need a great deal more subtle and supportive evidence than that which is currently available. The current emphasis on interactionism has nevertheless already had undoubtedly beneficial effects on research directions, not least of which has been an orientation to the actual behaviour in situ, a move, as it were, from the laboratory to the field. In the search for the behavioural antecedents of sports performance such a move is essential.

3. *Alternative perspectives.* The study of involvement of the person in the sporting situation has recently become the focus of another psychological approach, one that is much less concerned with the prediction of successful performance than with personal satisfaction, meaning, fulfillment, levels of consciousness, self-actualization, and, above all, joy. This approach owes much to both cognitive and humanistic schools of psychology where man is seen to be in control of his behavioural choices and decisions, and derives personal meaning and interpretation from his experience. The roots of these kind of psychological speculations are in existential philosophy and phenomenology and in such notions as, for example, 'personal knowledge' (Polanyi 1958) and 'needs of the mind' (Maddi 1970), which lay emphasis on unique knowledge derived by the individual from his perceptions in the course of satisfying his needs to understand himself, to symbolize, to imagine and to judge. Maslow (1970) perhaps goes nearest to setting out a comprehensive, if speculative, theory to encompass the main elements of this psychological thrust which has sometimes been referred to as third-force psychology.

Maslow categorized human needs into five sets which are placed in a hierarchical arrangement of importance and development, ranging from the lower level of physiological needs through those of security, safety, belonging and respect, to the final capping monarchical need for 'self-actualization'. The self-actualizing person, according to Maslow, would have clear perceptions, be self-accepting, spontaneous, autonomous and natural, appreciate the basic qualities of life, have a deep affection and sympathy for all humans, enjoy peak experiences (i.e. mystical or transpersonal experiences) and know himself in order to maximize his potentialities. For Maslow self-actualization is regarded as the highest and most fulfilled state of human existence.

In somewhat more conventional psychological terms Deci (1975) touches on the processes involved in self-actualizing behaviour in his treatise on intrinsic motivation. Deci, basing his interpretations on the work of Robert White (1959) develops the model of intrinsically motivated behaviours as ones chosen by the person in the pursuit of 'feeling competent' and 'self determining' in relation to his environment. He assumes that in these pursuits the person has access to his own internal states (understanding, orientations, attitudes, etc.) in a way which others cannot, and he effectively argues the importance of cognitions and experiences in changing the individual's internal states.

The psychology of self-actualization and intrinsic motivation, especially when linked with the psychology of the body sensation and perception, would seem to be most attractive to researchers concerned with the experience and personality effects of involvement in physical activity and sport. One interesting analysis of the individual's perception of himself links together these notions in proposing that self-through-body awareness has three dimensions, sensori-spatial, existential and valuative. The sensori-spatial dimension refers to the aspects of body conformation shape and spatial position; the existential dimension is suggested to represent the perceptions related to substantiveness, realness and vulnerability; the valuative dimension is proposed to account for the perceived value, worth and satisfaction of the body's appearance and function. Czikszentmihalyi (1975) investigating the inner experiences concerned with joy and pleasure in play games and life styles described a common form of experience enjoyed by the intrinsically motivated. He called this experience *flow* which incorporated feelings of exhilaration, of creative accomplishment and of heightened functioning. He writes, "they concentrate their attention on a limited stimulus field, forget personal problems, lose their sense of time and of themselves, feel competent and in control, and have a sense of harmony and union with their surroundings. To the extent that these elements of experience are present, a person enjoys what he or she is doing and ceases to worry about whether the activity will be productive or whether it will be rewarded."

One of the most common approaches today towards re-establishing the body as a sensitive vehicle for the recognition and enjoyment of feelings is running or jogging. The experience of runners of all kinds are being increasingly recorded and analyzed, and in the process accounts ranging from mystical and ecstatic interpretations to physiologically sensuous occurrences are to be found. On the back of a general revolution which has 'rediscovered' the body as the source of awareness and vital sensation, running seems to be successfully competing with more elaborate practices involving biofeedback mechanisms, various body therapies and even the martial arts as a means of generating and controlling inner states.

Running, is of course, a very personal activity which over time gives rise to a full spectrum of inner feelings from pain to delight. It represents, therefore, a very special body-mind control system and gives rise to heightened perceptions and appreciation of body-into-mind experiences. For some elite athletes and for unaccountable reasons individuals have experienced a fusing of the body-mind link that has given rise to a gigantic release of bodily energy, a sort of unleashing or disinhibiting mechanism, resulting in an outstanding performance almost impossible to analyze and replicate. Less talented runners have also experiences such occasional releases of energy, but have most often gained 'peak experiences' described variously as 'flow', 'smoothness', 'floating', 'exhilaration' and 'pure joy'. Occasionally the experience has described a projection of self, a separatedness, and extension out of the body to another level of existing and operating. This must be what George Sheeham, the articulate middle-aged doctor/runner meant when he wrote, "We begin in the body and end in a Vision".

For the psychologist, the measurement and assessment of such 'peak experiences' touching on the imagination, the transcendental and the intrinsic states of being, constitute an almost insuperable problem. Joy, delight, fulfillment and ecstacy are indeed hard to record, but their existence is undoubted. They are part of the complex but important system of intrinsic motivation and deserve the serious attention of psychologists. For those involved in physical activities and sports at all levels the intrinsic rewards and personal satisfactions are clear and unmistakably the product of sensitized body experience.

REFERENCES

ALSTON, W. Traits, Consistency and Conceptual Alternatives for Personality Theory in R Harre (ed) *Personality*. Oxford; Blackwell, 1976.

ARGYLE, M. Personality and Social Behaviour in *Personality* (ed. R Harre). Oxford; Blackwell, 1976.

BOWERS, K. Situationism in Psychology: an analysis and critique. *Psychological Review* 1973, 30.

CARTWRIGHT, D. Trait and other sources of variance in the S-R inventory of anxiousness. *J. Pers. Soc. Psychol*, 1975, 32.

CATTELL, R. B. *Personality: A Systematic, Theoretical and Factual Study*. New York: McGraw-Hill, 1950.

CATTELL, R. B. *Personality and Motivation Structure and Measurement*. Yonkers: World Books, 1957.

CATTELL, R. B. Some Psychological Correlates of Physical Fitness and Physique in Cureton J (ed) *Exercise and Fitness*. University of Illinois, 1960.

CATTELL, R. B. *The Scientific Analysis of Behaviour*. Baltimore: Penguin, 1965.

CLARIDGE, G. *Personality and Arousal*. London: Pergamon, 1967.

COFER, C. and JOHNSON, W. Personality Dynamics in relation to Exercise and Sport in (ed. Johnson, W.) *Science and Medicine of Exercise and Sport*. New York: Harper, 1960.

COOPER, L. Athletics, Activity and Personality: A review of the literature *Research Quarterly* 1969, 40.

CORCORAN, D. W. J. Studies of Individual Differences at the Applied Psychology Unit in Nebylitsyn and Gray (eds) *Biological Bases of Individual Behaviour*. London: Academic Press, 1972.

CZIKSZENTMIHALY, M. *Beyond Boredom and Anxiety*. San Francisco: Jossey-Bass, 1975.

DECI, E. L. *Intrinsic Motivation*. New York: Plenum, 1975.

DUFFY, E. *Activation and Behaviour*. New York: Wiley, 1962.

ENDLER, N. S. and MAGNUSSON, D. Personality and person by situation interactions in Endler and Magnusson (eds) *Interactional Psychology and Personality*. Washington: Wiley, 1976.

ENDLER, N. S. and OKADA, M. A multidimensional measure of trait anxiety: The S-R Inventory of General Trait Anxiety. *Journ. of Consult. and Clinical Psychol.*, 1975.

EYNSENCK, H. J. Human Typology, Higher Nervous Activity and Factor Analysis in Nebylitsyn and Gray (eds) *Biological Bases of Individual Behaviour*. London: Academic Press, 1972.

FISHER, S. *Body Consciousness*, New Jersey: Prentice-Hall, 1973.

FLEISHMAN, E. *The Structure and Measurement of Physical Fitness*. New Jersey: Prentice-Hall, 1964.

FLOOD, M. AND ENDLER, N. S. The Interaction Model of Anxiety: An empirical test in an athletic competition situation. *York University Dept. of Psychology Report No. 28*, 1976.

GOLDING, S. L. Flies in the Ointment: Methodological problems in the analysis of the percentage of variance due to person and situation. *Psychol. Bull.,* 1975, 82.

GRAY, J. A. The Psychophysiological nature of Introversion-Extraversion: a modification of Eysenck's theory in Nebylitsyn and Gray (eds) *Biological Bases of Individual Behaviour.* London: Academic Press, 1972.

GROVES, R. Assessing the Characteristics of Top-Level and Recreational Players. *Proceedings of BSSP Conference,* Exeter, 1976.

HARDMAN, K. A dual approach to the study of personality and performances in sport in Whiting et al (eds) *Personality and Performance in Physical Education and Sport.* London: Kimpton, 1973.

HARRIS, D. V. *Involvement in Sport.* Philadelphia: Lea and Febiger, 1973.

HENDRY, L. Assessment of personality traits in the coach — swimmer relationship, *Research Quarterly* 39, 1968.

HENDRY, L. Some notions on personality and sporting ability: certain comparisons with scholastic achievement. *Quest* 13, 1970.

HEUSNER, W. Personality traits of champion and former champion athletes. *MA thesis.* Illinois, 1952.

JOURARD, S. and SECORD, P. Body size and body cathexis. *Jounr. Consult Psychol.* 18, 1954.

KANE, J. E. Personality Description of Soccer Ability. *Res. in Phys. Educ.* No. 1, 1966.

KANE, J. E. Personality and Physical Abilities in Kenyon (ed) *Contemporary Psychology in Sports.* Chicago: Athletic Institute, 1970.

KANE, J. E. *Psychological Aspects of Physical Education and Sport.* London: Routledge and Kegan Paul, 1972.

KANE, J. E. Personality and Performance in Sport in Williams J. and Sperryn P. (eds) *Sports Medicine.* London: Arnold, 1976.

KLEINMAN, S. The significance of human movement: a phenomenological approach in Gerber E. (ed) *Sport and the Body.* Philadelphia: Lea and Febiger, 1972.

KROLL, W. Sixteen Personality Factor Profiles of Collegiate Wrestlers. *Research Quarterly,* 38, 1967.

KROLL, W. Current strategies and problems in personality assessment of athletes in Smith L. (ed) *Proceedings of the Symposium on Motor Learning.* Chicago: Athletic Institute, 1970.

KROLL, W. Athletic Stress Inventory. University of Massachusetts. (in press) 1977.

LACEY, J. I. Psychophysiological approaches to the evaluation of psychotherapeutic process and outcome in Rubenstein (ed) *Research in Psychotherapy.* Washington: Nat. Pub. Co., 1959.

LANGER, P. Varsity Football Performance. *Perceptual and Motor Skills,* 23, 1966.

LEONARD, G. *The Ultimate Athlete.* New York: Viking, 1975.

LEWIN, K. A Dynamic Theory of Personality. New York: McGraw-Hill, 1935.

MADDI, S. R. The search for meaning. *Nebraska Symposium on Motivation,* 18, 1970.

MARTENS, R. *The sport competition anxiety test.* Champaign, Illinois: Human Kinetic Pub. 1976.

MASLOW, A. H. *Motivation and Personality.* New York: Harper and Row, 1970.

MISCHEL, W. Towards a cognitive social learning reconceptualization of personality. *Psychol. Rev.* 80, 1973.

MISCHEL, W. *Introduction to Personality.* New York: Holt, Rinehart, 1976.

OGILVIE, B. Psychological consistencies within the personalities of high level competitors. *Journ. Am. Med. Assoc.* 28, 1968.

OGILVIE, B. and TUTKO T. *Problem Athletes and How to Handle Them.* London: Pelham, 1966.

OGILVIE, B. and TUTKO T. *The Athletic Motivation Inventory.* San Jose: Instit. for Study of Athletic Motivation, 1969.

PETRIE, A. Some psychological aspects of Pain and Relief of Suffering. *Ann. of N.Y. Acad. of Science,* 87, 1960.

PHARES, E. and LAMIELL, J. Personality in *Ann. Review of Psych.* 1977, Vol. 28.

POLANYI, M. *Personal Knowledge.* Chicago: University of Chicago Press, 1958.

PONSONBY, D. and YAFFEE, M. Psychology takes the soccer field. *FIFA News,* July 1976.

POULTON, E. On prediction in skilled movement. *Psychol. Bull.,* 54, 1957.

RUSHALL, B. The status of personality research and application in sports and physical education. *Journ. Sports Med. and Physical Fitness,* 13, 1973.

RUSHALL, B. and SIEDENTROP, D. *The Development and Control of Behaviour in Sport and Physical Education.* Philadelphia: Lea and Febiger, 1972.

SINCLAIR, E. Personality of rugby football players. *Thesis* Univ. of Leeds, 1968.

SPEILBERGER, G. D. *Theory and Research on Anxiety.* New York: Academic Press, 1969.

SPEILBERGER, C. Anxiety as an emotional state in Speilberger (ed) Anxiety: *Current trends in theory and research (Vol 1).* New York: Academic Press, 1972.

VANEK, M. and CRATTY, B. J. *Psychology and the Superior Athlete.* London: Macmillan, 1970.

VINCENT W. and DORSEY, D. Body image phenomena and measures of physiological performance. *Research Quarterly, 39,* 1968.

WHITE, R. W. Motivation reconsidered: the concept of competence. *Psychol. Rev.,* 66, 1959.

WHITING, H. T. A. and HUTT, J. The effects of personality and ability on speed of decision regarding the directional aspects of ball flight. *Journal of Motor Behaviour,* 4, 1972.

WILLIAMS, J. Personality traits of Champion Female Fencers. *Research Quarterly, 37,* 1970.

WITKIN, H. A. *Psychological Differentiation.* New York: Wiley, 1962.

WITKIN, H. A. Development of the Body concept and Psychological Differentiation in Werner, H. and Wapner, S. (eds) *The Body Percept.* New York: Random House, 1965.

Psychological Aspects of Wrestling*

Walter Kroll, P.E.D.
University of Massachusetts

A commonly held belief among coaches, athletes, and sport fans is that psychological factors are an essential ingredient for success in athletics. Many coaches avow that desire, the will to win, self-confidence, and mental toughness are essential prerequisites for success in wrestling. Because of the fact that wrestling is a combative sport where the masculine ego is tested, it is not unusual to hear the argument that wrestling makes greater psychological demands upon the competitor than any other sport. Psychological researchers are somewhat in agreement with such experience based insights as Oxendine[26] has postulated that both a high level of motivation as well as emotional arousal are necessary for optimum performance in wrestling.

Unless subjectively derived insights can be matched with objective data and theoretical constructs, the validity of experience based principles remains in doubt. Toward this end, this paper will briefly consider representative research literature dealing with three aspects of psychological factors in wrestling: personality, aggression, and anxiety. Following this, some personal comments will be risked. It should be recognized that this paper does not claim to be a comprehensive review of the research literature or that subsequent personal comments can be adequately defended with scientific evidence.

Personality

Many of the studies dealing with the personality characteristics of wrestlers have suffered from the same problem inherent in all personality research; i.e., confusing and conflicting theories, a scarcity of validated and reliable test instruments, and inadequate analysis techniques. Other studies seem to lack an acceptable sample size or accept any individual on an athletic team as a suitable representative of that sport without giving any attention to the quality of athletic talent such samples represent.

The bulk of the studies assessing personality characteristics of wrestlers have shown few, if any, systematic differences on personality variables between wrestlers and normative samples, other sport groups, or between varsity and junior varsity wrestlers (e.g., [4,17,28,29,32,35]). A few studies, such as those of Brown[2] and Hughes[8], have demonstrated differences between wrestlers and other athletes or non-athletes on the Edwards Personal Preference Schedule. The difference shown by these two studies, however, were not on

*From a paper presented at the American College of Sports Medicine Symposium on Wrestling, Philadelphia, Pennsylvania, May, 1972.

the same variables and the results were not logically consistent with any theoretical orientation.

In 1964 Slusher[31] studied 400 athletes and a random sample of 100 nonathletes from nine high schools with the Minnesota Multiphasic Personality Inventory (the MMPI) and available Lorge-Thorndike Intelligence Test scores. Slusher concluded that football and wrestling groups displayed the most neurotic profiles of the five athletic groups and norm sample studied. Wrestlers had the lowest intelligence scores of all athletic groups, were characterized by a "dominate neurotic profile," and demonstrated the only significantly higher than normal score on the psychasthenia scale suggesting "a tendency toward abnormal fears, worry, difficulties in concentration (obsessive-compulsive syndrome)." An evaluation of these interpretations and conclusions as well as conflicting results appeared several years later[14].

Only a few studies have provided evidence of the quality performance level of the wrestlers being studied. In Morgan's study[24], 23 English speaking wrestlers competing in the 1966 Amateur Wrestling World Championships were studied with the Eysenck Personality Inventory. Twelve of the wrestlers were from the United States, four from Canada, and seven from South Africa. Excluding the South Africans who demonstrated an unusually high neuroticism score, the remaining Canadian and American wrestlers had a neuroticism score well below normative standards for college students, and Morgan concluded these outstanding wrestlers tended to be quite stable as measured by the EPI Neuroticism-Stability scale.

In a more comprehensive study[14] as far as sample size, 94 amateur and collegiate wrestlers were administered the Cattell 16 Personality Factor Questionnaire (the 16 PF). Groups measured included (a) a superior group of 28 wrestlers from the U.S. Olympic Team, NCAA or NAIA champions and place winners, (b) an excellent group of 33 collegiate wrestlers who were varsity representatives, rated excellent wrestlers by their coaches, and who had won at least 60 per cent of their matches during the season, and (c) an average to below average group of the 33 wrestlers remaining on four college teams secured for the study. No profile differences between criterion groups were found using discriminant function analysis techniques. Compared to norms, wrestlers demonstrated a departure from average on factor I, indicating tough mindedness, self-reliance, and masculinity. No support was found for the suggestion that wrestlers may possess a neurotic profile or that they were below average on factor B (intelligence) as suggested earlier by Slusher.[31]

Subsequent analysis of the wrestler data was made comparing the 94 wrestlers against 81 football players, 141 gymnasts, and 71 karate participants selected with due consideration to the quality of participants in terms of level of athletic skill and achievement, with regional or national representation rather than a particular situation[16]. Significant profile differences between the four athletic groups resulted with football players and wrestlers being alike but different from both the gymnasts and karate participants. Support was given to the common belief among coaches of football and wrestling that the two sports share several similar characteristics.

Such apparent success at "matching" 16 PF profiles of wrestlers and football players, however, must be weighed against the negative results from a comprehensive study on Czech athletes[15]. The 16 PF was administered to 320 male athletes representing 23 different sports and 113 female athletes representing 10 different sports. All these Czech athletes were either members of nationally ranked sport teams or had reached the final trials for the 1968 Olympic Games in Czechoslovakia. Using a numerical taxonomy matching technique, the wrestlers' personality profile was found to be matched closest to that of the male volleyball players. The second and third most similar personality profiles to the wrestlers belonged to the male channel canoeists and male motor cyclists. The fourth best match to the wrestlers' profile belonged to female track athletes. It would seem reasonable to say that distinctive personality characteristics for wrestlers, capable of differentiating wrestlers from other athletes or from nonathletes, have not yet been reliably identified with existing measurement techniques.[1]

Aggression

Consideration of the psychodynamics of aggression in competitive sports and motor performance has recently been discussed in two excellent papers[19, 30]. Since aggression involves an initiation of an attack or "fighting" behavior[19], it is obvious that aggression may be of considerable importance in a combative sport such as wrestling. Only a handful of studies on aggression in wrestling are available, however, and their results are equivocal.

Husman[9] concluded that wrestlers exhibited (a) greater overall aggression than did boxers, and (b) a tendency to aggress toward the environment rather than to blame themselves. Using a similar test instrument, the Rosenzweig Picture-Frustration Test, Martin[21] found wrestlers to be less intrapunitive than non-participants or intramural basketball players. Both varsity and freshman wrestlers exhibited less extrapunitive aggression after winning a match while varsity wrestlers were less intrapunitive than freshmen wrestlers. Brown[2] using the Edwards Personal Preference Schedule also concluded that better high school wrestlers were more aggressive than low rated wrestlers, and that both groups of wrestlers were more aggressive than nonathletes.

Conflicting results against the argument that wrestlers exhibit higher aggression generally and particularly in relation to competition have been reported by Johnson and Hutton[12], Horowitz[7], and Hughes[8]. Johnson and Hutton reported an increase in inward aggression during the precontest period with a diminished level of aggressive feelings without direction after competition. Winning or losing a match seemed to have no effect on the results. Horowitz found wrestlers exhibited lessened extrapunitiveness and elevated impunitiveness (aggression evaded or glossed over) following weight losses of over 4 percent. Morgan[23] found a reduction in anxiety in 11 college wrestlers who had lost 4 percent of bodyweight over a one-week period. Hughes studied 10 different freshmen teams at Springfield College and did not find wrestlers differing from the other athletes on the aggression variable.

Anxiety

Anxiety is considered to be an outcome of stress which is capable of influencing behavior. Modern authors elect to define two major kinds of anxiety: (a) *trait* anxiety which is assumed to be a relatively stable and permanent personality characteristic, and (b) *state* anxiety which is assumed to be a specific time and situation locked reaction. Stress is associated conceptually with state anxiety while fear is linked to trait anxiety (see Martens[20] for an excellent review). The obvious nature of wrestling as a combative sport and its purported elicitation of stress and fear makes consideration of anxiety in wrestlers most relevant.

One of the earliest attempts at measuring the emotional impact of impending athletic competition was conducted by Johnson[11] who used a subjective questionnaire and the physiological tests of pulse rate, blood pressure, and blood sugar level in studying 15 football players and five wrestlers a few days before, a few hours before, just prior to, and immediately after competition. Johnson concluded that wrestlers were more affected emotionally than were the football players. In a later study involving swimmers, wrestlers, basketball and hockey players measured one hour before a contest, Johnson[10] found basketball lpayers were more reactive on psychogalvonometer responses to psychosexual and sports word association tests than wrestlers.

Later studies employing standardized paper and pencil tests for anxiety assessment have also reported conflicting results on wrestlers. Newman[25] studied 24 high school wrestlers prior to home matches with the IPAT 8 Parallel Form Anxiety Battery and found no relationship between prematch anxiety and wrestling performance as evaluated by three competent wrestling judges. Morgan[22], however, using the same test on seven college wrestlers in preseason and prematch conditions found prematch anxiety levels before both easy and difficult dual meets was significantly less than anxiety levels in the preseason condition. In a study of 103 college age subjects (40 freshmen football players, 21 freshmen and varsity wrestlers, and 42 nonathletes), Hammer[5] found no differences between the nonathletes and athletes in football and wrestling on the Taylor Manifest Anxiety Scale. High achieving wrestlers, designated as those in the upper quartile based on won and loss records, had higher MAS scores than nonathletes or the low achieving wrestlers. Low achieving wrestlers were defined as those in the lowest quartile based upon won and loss records.

Some help in understanding the conflicting results of anxiety studies on wrestlers may be present in the excellent study conducted by Sullivan[33] with freshmen and varsity wrestlers at the University of Massachusetts. Measures of pulse rate, blood pressure, grip strength, and a self-rating scale to assess approach-avoidance feelings were collected. In agreement with two other studies on college wrestlers[1,6], grip strength was highest prior to actual competition than at any other time. Pulse rate and blood pressure also increased significantly as match time approached with no significant differences between novice and experienced wrestlers. Results from the approach-avoidance scale, however, demonstrated important differences between novice and experienced wrestlers.

The night before competition experienced wrestlers demonstrated their *lowest* approach scores while novice wrestlers scored their *highest*. From the time of weigh-in to warm up prior to competition the experienced wrestlers showed a *rise* in approach feelings (anticipation and desire to compete). The novice wrestlers showed a *decrease* in approach feelings while the experienced wrestlers scored their *highest* approach feelings at the time of shaking hands with the opponent on the mat.

Thus, while both novice and experienced wrestlers demonstrated homogeneous physiological responses with similar increases in systolic blood pressure, pulse rate, and grip strength, the approach-avoidance scale ratings were opposite in direction. The result is in agreement with approach-avoidance patterns from novice and experienced parachutists in the Epstein and Fenz study[3]. Using various measures (word association tests, Galvanic Skin Response, and reaction time latency to word association tests), Epstein and Fenz showed inexperienced jumpers demonstrated a continuous increase in reactivity while experienced jumpers showed a drop prior to jumping. Such a result was taken to indicate that ". . .with experience and mastery of conflict there is an inhibition of anxiety producing responses."

When anxiety is viewed from the vantage point of Sullivan's study and Epstein's approach-avoidance schema it is possible to understand the apparent conflict in results from anxiety studies on wrestlers. Pre-match anxiety in wrestlers can be *either* high or low depending upon the experience and talent level of the individual wrestler. Beginning and lesser talented wrestlers may demonstrate higher anxiety levels than exhibited in pre-season or normal conditions. Experienced and higher talented wrestlers, on the other hand, may demonstrate a reduction in anxiety level prior to a match because of the concurrent increase in approach attitudes.

Consistent with such a speculation is the study reported by Yensen[36] on 61 wrestlers who were NCAA champions between 1947 and 1962. The champion wrestlers listed determination, desire, aggressiveness, and confidence as contributing factors to their success. Feelings before an important match were described as determined, confident, eager, and relaxed 127 times as compared to scared 17 times. Wrestler attitudes were characterized before a match as "no one could beat me" and "best wrestler in the U.S.A." One might predict, of course, that attitudes the night before these important matches would be different. Indeed, from approach-avoidance theory one would predict that the beginning wrestlers would be exhibiting relaxed, confident attitudes while the experienced and better wrestlers would be characterized as nervous, irritable, edgy, and lacking confidence.

COMMENTS[2]

Coaches have an almost mystical belief in the value of motivation and in the "psyching up" of athletes for successful athletic performance. It may be true that for some athletic events and/or for some athletes in any sport that "psyching up" is both necessary and important. It may also be possible in wrestling, however, that some coaches do more "psyching out" of their wrestlers than they do "psyching up." As Langer[18] has pointed out for football players, high anxiety players need to be calmed down rather than further aroused. Langer also demonstrated that better football players tended *not* to be responsive to stress comments made by the coaches and to exhibit a consistent mild-to-moderate rise in anxiety prior to football games.

In direct contrast to "common knowledge" about the value of the coach in motivating and preparing the athlete prior to competition is the notion that coaches may be guilty of over-motivating some athletes and inducing poorer, rather than better, performances. It would almost appear that some coaches perform their "psyche up" routines for their own benefit more than for the benefit of the athlete. The coach, in effect, plays out the stereotyped role of a shrewd practical psychologist who, a la Knute Rockne or Vince Lombardi, brings out the legendary 110 percent effort from his athletes via individual and personalized psychic tricks.

The impending wrestling match, however, is a high stress situation. Stepping out on a mat and facing your opponent in a one-to-one situation can be an alarming experience. There are no time outs for consultation with the coaching staff about changes in strategy. Unlike most other sports, one mistake can result in a fall and complete defeat without any chance for a comeback victory. The ego and masculine adequacy of the competitor are fully involved. The wrestling match, in effect, is in and of itself a pretty damn good motivator without any outside help.

When the coach delivers his inspirational "psyche up" message he probably, as evidenced by Langer's[18] work, does *not* greatly affect the anxiety level of the good wrestlers. The poor wrestler, however, is likely to react to the stress comments provided by the coach and experience higher and perhaps debilitating levels of anxiety. The actual performance of a wrestler troubled by high anxiety, furthermore, is likely to be interpreted by the coach as a poor performance because of a lack of motivation requiring more attention. Assuming no physiological causes, such poor performance might well be traced to too successful a motivational talk by the coach, to too many stress comments during the preceding week of practice.

Rather than increased efforts at motivating the poorer performer the coach might well consider the opposite strategy: demotivate the wrestler to more reasonable and optimum levels of anxiety. Such considerations of optimum activation levels during the prestart period (a day or two prior to competition) and start tension (minutes and hours prior to competition) are adequately discussed in Vanek and Cratty's[34] chapter on psychological preparation of the athlete. Reference is also made to the spreading practice of autogenic training in Europe and Asia in which athletes are prepared for competition by relaxation techniques.

It is also of importance that coaches consider the post-performance period as well. Although very little research literature exists on wrestling per se, it is my opinion that the wrestling coach needs to understand and attempt to cope with aggression and guilt feelings. *Reactive* aggression involves an aggressive act in which injury or damage to the opponent is involved. *Instrumental* aggression is an aggressive act in which injury of the opponent is not primary but the attainment of some goal is. Although certainly debatable,[3] it is possible that wrestlers who are prone to reactive aggression (rather than instrumental) will experience difficulties with guilt feelings leading to impaired performance. If aggression is needed in successful wrestling, reactive aggression would seem to be unsportsmanlike, antagonistic to educational goals, and a threat to the emotional health of the wrestler. Coupled with knowledge about anxiety levels and approach-avoidance feelings, the nature of the wrestler's aggressive feelings (reactive or instrumental) could well identify candidates for exclusion from the sport of wrestling and counseling into less ego involved and aggression demanding sports.[4]

In a similar speculative vein, it may not be too unrealistic to ask if the self-denial necessitated by weight reduction practices helps to allay guilt feelings about reactive aggression. Of the studies available, the findings of reduced anxiety levels after weight reduction by wrestlers reported by Morgan[23] and the elevated impunitiveness by Horowitz[7] would seem to fit such a speculation. Such a possibility would need to be considered as an emotional construct when evaluating weight reduction practices rather than using only physiological measures as a criterion for decision making.

The psychological aspects of wrestling considered, both research based and opinion based, do point to the need for the coach to understand the psychological consequences of athletic competition. More solid evidence is required, of course, before any definitive statements can be made concerning such psychological consequences of athletic competition. The coach, however, by at least being aware of such psychological considerations may be able to help athletes perform better which is, after all, a goal shared by both the coach and the athlete. The coach may also come to understand the psychological consequences of his own actions on both the athlete and on himself. But more importantly, the coach as a professional educator may be able to make the athletic participation a more meaningful and beneficial educational experience to the participant.

[1]For a treatment of the assessment problems in work dealing with personality studies of athletes see reference 13 in the bibliography.

[2]My comments are based upon personal observations and poorly supported extrapolations from research findings.

[3]This depends, in part, upon whether one subscribes to the cathartic or the circular theory of aggression. In one case an aggressive act helps relieve aggressive feelings and in the other an aggressive act reinforces aggressive feelings.

[4]Information about motivation, particularly fear-of-failure motivation, would also be helpful in identifying individuals poorly suited for athletic competition.

REFERENCES

1. Barehan, Ernest F. A study of the grip strength of varsity and freshmen wrestlers during a competitive season. Unpublished master's thesis, Springfield College, 1952.

2. Brown, Edward A. Personality characteristics of wrestlers. Unpublished master's thesis, University of Minnesota, 1958.

3. Epstein, Seymour and Fenz, Walter D. Theory and experiment on the measurement of approach-avoidance conflict. *Journal of Abnormal and Social Psychology* 64: 97-112; 1962.

4. Fowler, William H. A comparative study of evaluative attitudes of outstanding varsity athletes and junior varsity athletes. Unpublished master's thesis, Springfield College, 1961.

5. Hammer, W. M. A comparison of differences in manifest anxiety in university athletes and non-athletes. *Journal of Sports Medicine and Physical Fitness* 7: 31-34; 1967.

6. Hopkins, John S. The relationship between grip strength and wrestling success. Unpublished master's thesis, University of Massachusetts (Amherst), 1967.

7. Horowitz, L. D. Psychological effects of weight loss as measured by the Rosenzweig P-F Study. Unpublished master's thesis, University of Maryland, 1956.

8. Hughes, Thomas. A study of personality characteristics of a selected group of Springfield College freshmen. Unpublished master's thesis, Springfield College, 1963.

9. Husman, Burris F. Aggression in boxers and wrestlers as measured by projective techniques. *Research Quarterly* 26: 421-425; 1955.

10. Johnson, Warren R. Psychogalvanic and word association studies of athletes. *Research Quarterly* 22: 427-433; 1951.

11. Johnson, Warren R. A study of emotion in two types of athletic sports contests. *Research Quarterly* 20: 72-79; 1949.

12. Johnson, Warren R. and Hutton, Daniel C. Effects of combative sports upon personality dynamics as measured by a projective test. *Research Quarterly* 26: 49-53; 1955.

13. Kroll, Walter. Current strategies and problems in personality assessment of athletes. In Leon E. Smith (Ed.), *Psychology of Motor Learning.* Chicago: Athletic Institute, 1970. Pp. 349-367.

14. Kroll, Walter. Sixteen personality factor profiles of collegiate wrestlers. *Research Quarterly* 38: 49-57; 1967.

15. Kroll, Walter; Loy, John; Hosek, Vaclav; and Vanek, Miroslav. Multivariate analysis of the personality profiles of championship Czechoslovakian athletes. Paper presented at Third Canadian Psycho-Motor Learning and Sport Psychology Symposium.

16. Kroll, Walter and Crenshaw, William. Multivariate personality profile analysis of four athletic groups. In Gerald S. Kenyon (Ed.), *Contemporary Psychology of Sport.* Chicago: Athletic Institute, 1970. Pp. 97-106.

17. Lakie, William L. Personality characteristics of certain groups of intercollegiate athletes. *Research Quarterly* 33: 566-573; 1962.

18. Langer, Philip. Varsity football performance. *Perceptual and Motor Skills* 23: 1191-1199; 1966.

19. Layman, Emma McCloy. Theories and research on aggression in relation to motor learning and sports performance. In Leon E. Smith (Ed.), *Psychology of Motor Learning.* Chicago: Athletic Institute, 1970. Pp. 327-343.

20. Martens, Rainer. Anxiety and motor behavior: a review. *Journal of Motor Behavior* 3: 151-179; 1971.

21. Martin, Lawrence A. The effects of competition upon the aggressive responses of basketball players and wrestlers. Unpublished doctoral dissertation, Springfield College, 1969.

22. Morgan, William P. Pre-match anxiety in a group of college wrestlers. *International Journal of Sport Psychology* 1: 7-13; 1970.

23. Morgan, William P. Psychological effect of weight reduction in the college wrestler. *Medicine and Science in Sports* 2: 24-27; 1970.

24. Morgan, William P. Personality characteristics of wrestlers participating in the world championships. *Journal of Sports Medicine and Physical Fitness* 8:212-216; 1968.

25. Newman, Richard E. A comparison of anxiety measures and match performance evaluations of high school wrestlers. Unpublished master's thesis, South Dakota State University (Brookings), 1967.

26. Oxendine, Joseph B. Emotional arousal and motor performance. *Quest* 12: 23-32; January, 1970.

27. Rasch, Philip J. and Kroll, Walter. *What Research Tells the Coach About Wrestling.* Washington, D.C.: AAHPER, 1968.

28. Rasch, Philip J. and others. Neuroticism and extraversion in United States intercollegiate wrestlers. *Association Physical and Mental Rehabilitation Journal* 16: 153-154; 1962.

29. Rasch, Philip J. and Hunt, M. Briggs. Some personality attributes of champion amateur wrestlers. *Association Physical and Mental Rehabilitation Journal* 14: 163-164; 1960.

30. Scott, J. P. Sport and Aggression. In Gerald S. Kenyon (Ed.), *Contemporary Psychology of Sport.* Chicago: Athletic Institute, 1970. Pp. 11-24.

31. Slusher, Howard S. Personality and intelligence characteristics of selected high school athletes and nonathletes. *Research Quarterly* 35: 539-545; 1964.

32. Sperling, Abraham P. The relationship between personality adjustment and achievement in physical education. *Research Quarterly* 13: 351-363; 1942.

33. Sullivan, Edward. Emotional reactions and grip strength in college wrestlers as a function of time to competition. Unpublished master's thesis, University of Massachusetts (Amherst), 1964.

34. Vanek, Miroslav and Bryant J. Cratty. *Psychology and the Superior Athlete.* Toronto: Collier-Macmillan, 1970.

35. Werner, Alfred C. Physical education and the development of leadership characteristics at the United States Military Academy. Unpublished doctoral dissertation, Springfield College, 1960.

36. Yensen, William A. An investigation of factors that contributed to the success of NCAA wrestling champions. Unpublished master's thesis, San Diego State College, 1963.

Personality Characteristics of the Successful Female Athlete

Jean M. Williams, Ph.D.
University of Arizona

There have been extensive investigations of the characteristics of the superior athlete. Typically these studies have researched various physiological, biomechanical, and psychological parameters. Once an athlete becomes proficient in a particular sport, the various physiological and biomechanical assessments have yielded little success in predicting or helping explain the higher echelons of athletic success. Many psychologists contend that personality ultimately makes the difference in performance potential. Also, many coaches and physical educators intuitively believe certain personality variables are essential for athletic participation and athletic success. The benefits to coaches and athletes alike would be substantial if personality characteristics could be identified which would help predict success in athletics and for which sports individuals are more psychologically suited. It is not surprising, therefore, that there have been numerous research studies designed to measure whether certain personality dimensions are associated with athletic participation, athletic success, and participation in specific sports. In addition, there have been a few studies which have investigated the role of athletic participation on personality development.

A closer review of the literature, however, reveals that the overwhelming majority of the research has been on the male athlete. When questions referring to the female competitor are posed, there are relatively few answers available. We cannot generalize the findings on the male athlete to the female athlete unless we believe there are no sex differences in personality, females have the same needs and motivations as males, and females will respond the same way to sport and coaching as males. Such assumptions remain to be proven. It is equally important that the athletic coach and physical educator of the female competitor be aware of her personality characteristics and how they might interrelate to produce maximum performance, particularly today with the growing acceptance and promotion of well-organized, high-skilled athletics for women. The intention of this paper is to examine the few empirical studies which primarily have dealt with the personality characteristics of the high-level female athlete and to draw implications from them regarding the relationship between these factors and sport participation and success.

The majority of the research in the personality domain has been descriptive in nature and has typically employed a trait approach to measuring personality. Trait personality theorists believe behavior can be factor analyzed to identify underlying psychological traits which represent the characteristic tendency a person has for acting or behaving in a certain way. Thus, traits would initiate and guide consistent forms of behavior. They are also bi-polar, that is we all possess the same traits but in varying amounts along a continuum from low to high.

Another important assumption of trait personality theorists is the belief that behavior is quite consistent and predictable across situations. This translates to mean that questions can be asked in a nonsport setting and we can generalize the answers to behavioral responses in a sport situation. They challenge therefore the viability of using trait tools for assessing personality (Fisher, 1977; Kroll, 1976; Martens, 1975; Mischel, 1977; Rushall, 1975; Singer, Harris, Kroll, Martens, & Sechrest, 1977; Straub, 1977). Other sport and general psychologists, however, believe useful information has been gained from a trait personality approach and that trait assessment may ultimately help predict athletic success (Hogan, Desoto, & Solano, 1977; Morgan, 1977).

The purpose of this paper is not to debate the efficacy of trait vs. a situational or interactional approach to understanding personality, but to point out that most sport personality research of the past, as well as the research presented in this paper, has used a trait approach in measuring personality. These investigators therefore, knowingly or unknowingly, accepted the assumptions which underly trait psychology.

Much of the sport personality research done on the male athlete appears to be contradictory, misleading, and unproductive. The difficulty in reaching any general conclusions is partly due to the many methodological problems and shortcomings that have plagued this area of study. Some of these are the inconsistencies in defining terms, the variety of tests used to measure personality, the inability to consider response distortion, the questionable sampling methods, the inappropriateness of data analysis, and the failure of investigators to pursue the study of personality within a theoretical framework (Martens, 1975; Morgan, 1972). In addition to the preceding methodological problems, the difficulty of reaching any decisive conclusions on the personality characteristics of the female sport competitor is made even more difficult due to the limited number of studies on the female athlete. Fortunately research interest is increasing with the recent change in attitude toward competition for women and the resulting increases in competitive opportunities for women. Difficulty in interpreting the literature on the female athlete is also compounded by the fact that personality norms reflect distinctions between masculine and feminine attitudes which existed fifteen or more years ago, and which may now be blurred.

It would be difficult, if not impossible, to reach valid insights into the psychological functioning of the female athlete without first gaining a perspective of the temperament or traits which are considered appropriate and representative of the female in our society. "We know that the female athlete is first and foremost a girl or a woman. From this basis grows her concept of herself as a person and as a performer and from it she develops her direction in life. We know that she certainly differs from her male counterpart (Malumphy, p. 15, 1971)."

Studies by anthropologists such as Margaret Mead have shown that feminine and masculine roles and their associated personality characteristics are more a product of one's culture than of a universal biological cause. Masculinity and femininity, as culturally defined, have been extremely resistant to modification. Early in the life of the North American female, culture begins to extinguish high motor activity where aggression and competitiveness are important factors for success. We see males measuring significant increments in physical skill with age, while females measure significant decrements. *In the past* our culture has been much more inclined therefore to reward the motor activity of the male, while at the same time extinguishing that of the female.

American culture has traditionally advocated that the female should be non-aggressive and passive (Broom & Selznick, 1968), submissive and less able (Ulrich, 1968), dependent rather than independent (Kagan & Moss, 1962), and socially rather than achievement oriented (Edwards, 1959). Whereas passiveness, dependence, conservativeness, and higher emotionality and sociability are found to be characteristic personality traits of the female; the typical male is dominant, self-sufficient, experimenting, tough minded, and aggressive (Cattell, 1965). The preceding sex differences were supported by Garai (1970) when he investigated the needs of each sex. While he found male needs included vigorous physical exertion, motor activity, aggression, achievement, independence, and dominance; the female needs were conversely sedentary, defensive, safety-oriented, passive and submissive.

It is obvious that such sex-role steretypification strongly influences women's participation or non-participation in sports (Mackenzie, 1973). Correspondingly, some of the sociological literature on women in sport stems from a belief that women athletes experience a social conflict between the desire to participate and achieve in sport and the desire to fulfill appropriate feminine roles. However, what little social data there are show that women athletes do not differ from other women in terms of how they view their feminine role (Hall, 1977).

In relation to specific personality dimensions, it is difficult to envision a successful female athlete as someone who is nonambitious, non-competitive, safety-oriented, passive, and sedentary. Hopefully, the studies which have investigated the female athlete will shed some light on the apparent contradiction between the characteristics of the normative female and those personality characteristics which intuitively seem important for athletic performance. The following review will only include research which has dealt with the more proficient female athlete and which has suffered from the fewest design weaknesses. Also, all the reported studies measured personality with the Cattell 16 Personality Factor test (16 PF) and/or the Edwards Personal Preference Schedule test (EPPS). Again it should be noted that any generalizations are seriously limited by the methodological and interpretational difficulties discussed earlier plus the restricted skill level of the athletes.

Low personality variation within a particular activity is reported in the studies on fencers (Williams, Hoepner, Moody, & Ogilvie, 1970), ice hockey players (Bird, 1968), track athletes (Kane, 1966), swimmers (Kane, 1966), lacrosse players (Mushier, 1972) and race car drivers (Tutko, 1969). The preceding studies offer good support for the notion of specific "sport types". Using the 16 PF and the EPPS, Williams et al. (1970) found champion level competitive fencers to be very reserved, self-sufficient, aggressive, dominant, independent individuals with a below-average desire for affiliation and nurturance. They had a strong need to be the very best and were intelligent, creative, experimenting, and imaginative. Almost identical personality profiles were found for Bird's Canadian collegiate ice hockey players (1968) and Tutko's champion female race car drivers (1969).

One of the best studies on the personality characteristics of the female athlete is Mushier's (1972) cross-sectional study in which she randomly selected girls and women from junior high school competition through adult national level competition. Overall, lacrosse players at all levels were characterized as more reserved, intelligent, independent, aggressive and experimenting than the normative population. While these characteristics are consistent with the fencers, ice hockey players, and race car drivers, the lacrosse players were also more happy-go-lucky and tough minded. According to Mushier, the similarity between the lacrosse sample regardless of their age or experience level "suggests that self-selection into sports competition on the basis of existing personality factors may be the prime reason for the personality structure of competitors and not the effect of the experience of sports competition (p. 29)". These findings suggest the validity of Morgan's (1972) proposed gravitational theory. No definite conclusion can be reached, however, until longitudinal studies are conducted.

Intercollegiate competitors in tennis and golf (Malumphy, 1970, 1971) appeared to be more intelligent, reserved, assertive, stable, and happy-go-lucky than their college peers. In addition, they may be more suspicious, casual, placid, and self-sufficient. The psychology of team sport participation may be different in many ways from the psychology of individual sport participation. This assumption has led several researchers to investigate the personality dimensions of team sport athletes compared to individual sport athletes. Malumphy (1968) found differences between Ohio team and individual sport athletes who had participated for two or more seasons. Team sport participants scored higher in group-dependence and anxiety and lower in leadership interest and extraversion than did their peers in individual sports.

Another study by Peterson, Weber, and Trousdale (1967) showed that women who engaged in individual sports were more dominant and aggressive, radical and experimenting, adventurous, sensitive, imaginative, independent, self-sufficient, and introverted than women who engaged in team sports. Peterson et al. concluded that the individual competitor thus likes to make her own decisions and may express dissatisfaction with group situations and their high premium on procedural rules. When compared

252

to norms of similar age and education background, both individual and team sport athletes were more reserved, intelligent, and more stable while the individual sport athletes were also more independent, aggressive, adventuresome and experimenting. Since the Peterson et al. athletes primarily were drawn from the 1964 United States Olympic Team, their personality profile is probably more indicative of highly skilled individual and team sport athletes than are the athletes in Malumphy's study.

Kane (1966) found a marked similarity between British track athletes and swimmers. Both scored high on sociability and surgency and low on emotional maturity and confidence. When he compared his findings to studies undertaken on Amerian subjects, he proposed a possible cultural difference between British and American women with the British being more extraverted and anxious (Kane, 1972).

Cultural differences were not found in a cross-cultural comparison on the EPPS test of 48 American and Hungarian female athletes who participated in the Olympics. In fact, Balazs (1977) found remarkable similarities in the personality make-up of the two countries' subjects. The athletes were drawn from American and Hungarian swimmers, gymnasts, and track and field participants and from the American skiers and Hungarian fencers. Athletes from both countries scored highest on achievement, autonomy, and aggression and lowest on affiliation. In addition to the similarities in personality profile, there were several identical patterns in the developmental dynamics of the two groups. All of the girls talked about themselves as energetic and very active children and as having a strong drive to excel, to be the best. Another recurring theme was the desire to move and the love of movement. Similarities in family dynamics were also found. Families were remembered as very supportive and playing a crucial role in the setting of values and ideals.

Of the other studies using the EPPS test on U.S. athletes, data has been obtained which both supports and conflicts with the Balazs' findings. The fencers in the Williams et al. study scored in the same direction and even higher on achievement (85%), autonomy (75%), and aggression (71%) and lower on affiliation (32%). However, Neal's (1968) study of the U.S. athletes who participated in the 1959 Pan American games only supports the high achievement and autonomy scores. The Pan American athletes did not score significantly higher on aggression or lower on affiliation. In fact, their affiliation scores were very high.

Although one should be suspect of generalizations formed from such a limited number of studies, particularly in light of the acknowledged methodological and interpretational limitations, certain personality dispositions appear to be frequently associated with the skilled and champion-level female athlete. Whereas passiveness, submissiveness, dependence, higher emotionality and sociability, and lower achievement and aggressive needs are characteristic of the normative female; the successful female competitor generally tends to be more assertive, dominant, self-sufficient, independent, aggressive, intelligent, reserved, achievement oriented, and to have average to low emotionality. Longitudinal studies must be completed before any direct cause and effect relationships can be accepted or rejected between these personality dispositions and sports competition. However, the enduring and stable nature of traits would suggest that females have gravitated toward sport as a result of these personality traits rather than sport participation having altered the personality of the athlete.

The ability of the aforementioned traits to predict athletic success in the female competitor remains to be seen. Since the only way one can hope to characterize the successful athlete is to first delineate the characteristics of previously successful and unsuccessful athletes, more studies of personality are needed, particularly longitudinal studies. Based upon the research reviewed in this paper, it appears that trait psychology should not be abandoned when attempting to understand the psychologic aspects of sport and physical activity in the female athlete. Future researchers and coaches may wish to consider that, according to Morgan (1977), prediction of success is clearly facilitated when selected traits are used in concert with state measures.

Morgan therefore recommends that a state-trait model is theoretically the most efficacious. He also recommends that researchers deal with the methodological problem of response distortion since control of this seriously affects success prediction models. Because the 16 PF is easily faked, future use of the inventory should also include the motivation distortion scales recently developed by Karson and O'Dell (1976). These scales were designed for use in connection with Forms A and B of the 16 PF and measure faking good, faking bad, and random answering. The scales along with the scoring instructions are described in Karson and O'Dell's (1976) *Guide to the Clinical Use of the 16 PF.*

Finally, it should be mentioned that since sport selection and athletic success are dependent upon a number of factors, it seems logical to support a multi-disciplinary model for studying sport selection and success. Such models should consist of personality theory as well as biological, sociological, and skill parameters in their theoretic framework.

REFERENCE NOTES

Morgan, W.P. Sport personology: The credulous-skeptical argument in perspective. Paper presented at the Third Symposium on Integrated Development: Psycho-Social Behavior of Sport and Play, Purdue University, West Lafayette, Indiana, April, 1977.

Tutko, T. Personal Communication, Spring, 1969.

REFERENCES

BALAZS, E. A cross-cultural comparison of some outstanding sportswomen. In M. Adrian & J. Brame (Eds.) *NAGWS research reports.* Washington, D.C.: American Association for Health, Physical Education and Recreation, 1977, 105-116.

BIRD, E.I. Personality structure of Canadian intercollegiate ice hockey players. In G. Kenyon (Ed.), *Contemporary Psychology of Sport: Proceedings of the Second International Congress of Sport Psychology,* Washington, D.C., 1968, 149-156.

BROOM, L. & SELZNICK, P. *Sociology.* New York: Harper & Row, 1968.

CATTELL, B. *The scientific basis of personality,* London: Penguin, 1965.

EDWARDS, A. *Edwards personal preference schedule* (manual). New York: Psychological Corporation, 1959.

FISHER, A.C. Sport personality assessment: Adversary proceedings. In C.O. Dotson, V.L. Katch & J.E. Schick (Eds.), *Research and practice in physical education.* Champaign: Human Kinetics Publisher, 1977.

GARAI, J.E., & SCHEINFELD, A. Sex differences in mental and behavioral traits. *Genetic Psychological Monographs,* 1970, *81,* 123-142.

HALL, M.A. The sociological perspective of females in sport. In M. Adrian & J. Brame (Eds.), *NAGWS research reports,* Washington, D.C.: American Association for Health, Physical Education and Recreation, 1977, 37-50.

HOGAN, R., DESOTO, C.B., & SOLANO, C. Traits, tests, and personality research. *American Psychologist,* 1977, *32,* 255-264.

KAGAN, J., & MOSS, H.A. *Birth to maturity* New York: John Wiley & Sons, 1962.

KANE, J.E. Psychology of sport with special reference to the female athlete. In D. Harris (Ed.) *Women and Sport: A National Research Conference.* Penn State HPER Series No. 2 Pennsylvania, 1972, 19-34.

KANE, J.E. Personality and physical ability. In Kato (Ed.), *Proceedings, Sports Science Conference, Tokyo, 1966.*

KARSON, S. & O'Dell, J.W. *A guide to the clinical use of the 16 PF.* Champaign: Institute for Personality and Ability Testing, 1976.

KROLL, W. Reaction to Morgan's paper: Psychological consequences of vigorous physical activity and sport. In M.G. Scott (Ed.), *The Academy Papers.* Iowa City: American Academy of Physical Education, 1976.

MACKENZIE, M. Women and sport: A psychological interpretation. In M. Wade & R. Martens (Eds.) *Psychology of motor behavior and sport,* May, 1973, 14-16.

MALUMPHY, T.M. Athletics and competition for girls and women. In D.V. Harris (Ed.) *DGWS research reports: Women in sports.* Washington, D.C.: American Association for Health, Physical Education and Recreation, 1971, 15-19.

MALUMPHY, T.M. Personality of women athletes in intercollegiate competition. *Research Quarterly,* 1968, *30,* 610-620.

MALUMPHY, T.M. The college woman athlete — questions and tentative answers. *Quest,* 1970, *XIV,* 18-27.

MARTENS, R. *Social psychology and physical activity.* New York: Harper & Row, 1975.

MISCHEL, W. On the future of personality measurement. *American Psychologist,* 1977, *32,* 246-254.

MORGAN, W.P. Sport psychology. In R.N. Singer (Ed.), *The psychomotor domain: Movement behaviors.* Philadelphia: Lea & Febiger, 1972.

MUSHIER, C.L. Personality and selected women athletes. *International Journal of Sport Psychology,* 1972, *3,* 25-31.

NEAL, P. *Personality traits of United States women athletes who participated in the 1959 Pan-American games, as measured by the Edwards Personal Preference Schedule.* Unpublished Master's thesis, University of Utah, 1963.

PETERSON, S.L., WEBER, J.C., & TROUSDALE, W.W. Personality traits of women in team sports vs. women in individual sports. *Research Quarterly,* 1967, *38,* 686-689.

RUSHALL, B.S. Alternative dependent variables for the study of behavior in sport. In D.M. Landers (Ed.) *Psychology of sport and motor behavior II.* College Park: Pennsylvania State University, 1975.

SINGER, R.N., HARRIS, D., KROLL, W., MARTENS, R., & SECHREST, L. Psychological testing of athletes. *Journal of Physical Education and Recreation,* 1977, *48* 30-32.

STRAUB, W.F. Approaches to personality assessment of athletes: Personologism, situationism, and interactionism. In C.O. Dotson, V.L. Katch, & J.E. Schick (Eds.) *Research and practice in physical education.* Champaign: Human Kinetics, 1977.

ULRICH, C. *The social matrix of physical education.* Englewood Cliffs, New Jersey: Prentice-Hall, 1968.

WILLIAMS, J.M., HOEPNER, B.J., MOODY, D.L., & OGILVIE, B.C. Personality traits of champion level female fencers. *Research Quarterly,* 1970, *41,* 446-453.

Leadership in Sport

During the modern era, sport psychologists have studied the role of the coach as motivator, personologist, teacher of motor skills and strategist but have largely ignored the important topic of leadership. At the present time, leadership is often talked about but seldom researched and it remains a vague, little understood term. Since providing effective leadership is one of the coach's most important functions, there is need for research.

Like personality, aggression, team cohesion and motivation, leadership style has received much media coverage. The leadership traits of Woody Hayes, Billy Martin, John Wooden, George Allen or the late Vince Lombardi are well known. And, hardly an article is written about the firing of a coach without some reference being made to the coach's leadership of its absence. In the first article, I cite the Forrest Gregg case as a vivid example of how a coach can become the Associated Press' NFL Coach of the Year and in less than twelve months be fired. Although Gregg's situation may be unprecedented, it dramatically illustrates that leadership style is a critical variable underlying team success.

Most of the work that has been done on leadership has taken place in industrial settings. Fiedler's contingency theory, for example, specifies that leadership effectiveness is a function of leader-member relations, task structure, and leader position power. According to Fiedler, the type of leadership that should be used depends on the interaction of these variables. Gregg's case is explained within this model.

In the second article, Ann Marie Bird shows the relationship between social cohesion, motivation, and leadership style. According to Dr. Bird, different sport groups appear to require different types of leadership. The style on interacting teams, for example, may be quite different from the style employed on co-acting teams where each player performs tasks largely independent of each other. Bird advances an "Expectancy X Affect" model to account for these differences. She also believes that group motivation may be augmented through realistic goal setting and the application of team-contingent reinforcement methods.

In the final paper, Victor Mancini and Michele Agnew report on the analysis of teaching and coaching behaviors obtained with descriptive-analytic techniques. A modification of Flanders' Interaction Analysis System (FIAS) has been largely used for making these important observations. Drawing on their own work and the research of others, Mancini and Agnew conclude that teachers/coaches need to become more aware of not only what they are communicating but also how they are communicating. They believe that communication is one of the important variables underlying leadership success.

How To Be
An Effective Leader

William F. Straub, Ph.D.
Ithaca College

ABSTRACT

One of the most important functions that the coach performs is to provide effective leadership for his/her teams. Although there are a wide variety of leadership styles, leadership in this paper was defined as the influence the coach has on his/her players. Therefore, it was the purpose of this paper to explore some of the facets of leadership effectiveness and attempt to point out their significance to the coaching of athletic teams. The Forrest Gregg Case was used to illustrate the interaction of personal and situational variables which often determine coaching success. Following the presentation of coaching types and research findings, the evolution of leadership theory was presented. Basically, there were five distinct stages of development. They were: leadership by tradition, trait approaches, formal leadership functions, human relations theories and situational leadership. Three well-known models of leadership were covered and illustrated. They were: McGregor's Theory X and Y, Tannenbaum and Schmidt's model, and Fiedler's Theory. Forrest Gregg's Case was used to illustrate Fiedler's validated theory that effective leadership is a function of leader-member relations, task structure, and leader position power.

One of the most neglected topics in sport psychology is leadership. Only a few researchers have carefully examined the underlying dimensions of this important ingredient of coaching and teaching success. The search for the 'ideal' leader continues.

Power sport journalism places a great deal of attention on leadership qualities, or their absence, of coaches. They give it alot on ink so to speak. All one has to do to verify this statement is to pick up the latest edition of most any newspaper or sport magazine. Usually some mention will be made of the leadership traits of Woody Hayes, John Wooden, Bobby Knight, Don Shula, George Allen or the late Vince Lombardi. And, when coaches are fired, as so often happens, some mention is usually made of their leadership style.

Forrest Gregg, former Green Bay Packer great and until recently head coach of the Cleveland Browns, was dismissed because of what Art Modell, principal owner of the Browns, said: "We felt it was in the best interest of the

Browns and Forrest Gregg." Inside sources speculated that Gregg's emotional style of coaching may have sapped the young Brown's spirit. Other informed sources said that Gregg's long series of outbursts and biting remarks, particularly after heartbreaking defeats, turned off some of the older, established players.

Gregg's case is of interest and importance to students of sport psychology because it dramatically illustrates how a coach can become The Associated Press NFL Coach of the Year in 1976 and be just another unemployed person in less than 12 months. Ironically, Gregg's case is not atypical. When things go wrong, as they sometimes do, there has to be a scapegoat and often it is the coach. Later on, I will discuss Gregg's case in terms of Fred E. Fiedler's (1967) model of leadership effectiveness. Fiedler has validated a theory which shows that there are three important dimensions of leadership effectiveness. They are: (1) leader-member relations, (2) task structure, and (3) power position. Leadership style, according to Fiedler, should depend on the interrelationship of these three components. In brief, Fiedler contends that good leaders are flexible and they adopt their coaching behaviors to situational factors.

The purpose of this paper is to explore some of the facets of leadership effectiveness and point out their significance to the coaching of athletic teams. Hopefully, as a result of this analysis coaches will become better informed about the many and diverse facets of leadership and become more aware of their leadership style as they attempt to mold winning teams.

Leadership is a vague, often misunderstood term. Although most everyone has an idea of the global meaning of the word, the specifics usually remain unclear. And, depending on who you talk with, leadership is defined in a multiplicity of ways. To my knowledge, however, no one has spelled-out definitively what leadership means in sport terminology. Let us try and do so.

In the mid 1940's leadership was often defined as a form of dominance in which followers more or less willingly accepted direction and control by another person (Young, 1946). Many people would probably agree that this definition holds true today in sport environments.

In the 1960's leadership was defined as an influence process, the dynamics of which were a function of the personal characteristics of the leader, his/her followers, and the nature of the specific situation (Richards and Greenlaw, 1966). This definition is more in keeping with the humanistic movement in psychology and also suggests that leaders should be flexible. Personally, I believe that leadership in sport settings should stress this approach. Therefore, leadership in sport is defined as the influence the coach has on his/her players. The coach should take into consideration the personal characteristics of himself/herself, the players and the nature of the specific situation.

Coaching Types

The thing that has always amazed me about coaches is how differently they go about getting the job done. I have found a wide variety of leadership styles among coaches even in the same sport. A couple of years ago I had the opportunity to spend a couple of weeks at the training camp of the Washington Redskins at Carlisle, Pennsylvania. George Allen, then head coach of the Skins, provided an interesting contrast to the stereotype of football coaches presented by the media. I found Allen to be mild mannered, somewhat shy and reserved, and extremely dedicated in his approach to his work. He was not, in my opinion, the two-fisted, arrogant, win-at-all-costs personality displayed by the sportswriters.

Basically, leadership style may be categorized into three broad types. Whether in business or in sport, the *'hard driver'* views his/her functions as keeping order. To this coach, discipline is the first ingredient of success. After all, once you have the horses, you must be able to handle them!

Assignments are parceled-out to assistant coaches and action is expected. Practices are well-organized, uniforms are worn properly and even a hair stylist may be hired to groom the team. In brief, this coach believes that athletes should come to play. The coach's task is to function as 'boss'.

The *'thoughtful persuader'* manipulates the team to accept his/her approach to the sport. He/she has little faith in the ability of the players to function on their own. A blueprint or game plan is prepared by the coach in advance and the players are persuaded or manipulated to accept it. This coach often pictures himself/herself as being more democratic than the 'hard driver'. After all, under this system players usually have a chance to voice their opinions before they are persuaded to accept the coach's game plan. Allowing the players to experience catharsis or tension reduction is an integral part of the coach's strategy.

The *'friendly helper'* takes a laissez-faire approach to coaching, that is to say, he/she avoids taking a stand for fear of being called authoritarian. As a result, there are too many 'chiefs' and not enough 'Indians' and the team often flounders because of a lack of direction and clearly formulated goals. According to Williams and Wassenaar (1975), this approach is a cover for persons who have no ability to lead.

Research Findings

In a study designed to assess leadership style, Swartz (1973) compared four types of leadership: laissez-faire, democratic-cooperative, autocratic-submissive, and autocratic-aggressive. The subjects were 72 collegiate coaches in five mid-western states. He classified the coaches into 'successful' (won-lost record over 50 percent) or 'unsuccessful' (won-lost record under 50 percent). Swartz (1973) concluded that successful and unsuccessful coaches employ basically the same leadership style.

In 1965 Mudra (1965) completed a doctoral dissertation in which he attempted to determine the leadership behaviors of collegiate football coaches. To do so, he assessed the coaches' application of learning principles. Learning principles were conceptualized as gestalt-field or stimulus-response (S-R). Leaders who used a gestalt-field approach, Mudra indicated, view man as purposive and interacting with his environment. In brief, they see learning as an acquisition of cognitive structures.

Coaches who used the stimulus-response (S-R) approach, Mudra said, see man as passive and the victim of his environment. Learning is seen as the acquisition of habits brought about by trial and error.

Mudra found small college coaches, on the average, were gestalt-field oriented. Major university coaches, on the average, were S-R oriented.

Coaches Are Born, Made, and Called Upon

What are the components of successful leadership? Quite obviously, heredity, environment, and situational factors play a major role in determining coaching success. Heredity determines capacity. Physical, intellectual and emotional characteristics are due to a person's genetic makeup. Environment molds or shapes personality, particularly during the early years and indirectly determines the limits of social perception and behavior (Williams and Wassenaar, 1975). Having significant others to emulate, particularly during adolescence, may have a profound effect on adult behavior.

The behaviors of coaches are also shaped by situational variables. As one travels from town to town and from one part of the country to another, it becomes obvious that school and college administrators, parents and the athletes themselves have different expectancies about leadership. This fact is why it is often possible for a coach to be fired in one school or college and become coach of the year in another institution.

LEADERS ARE BORN, MADE, AND CALLED UPON

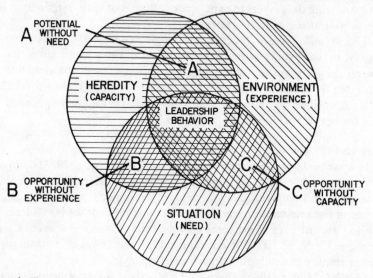

Figure 1. *The interaction of heredity, environmental and situational variables to produce maximum leadership effectiveness. From: Leadership by Williams, P.M. and Wassenaar, D. J. San Jose, California: Lansford Publishing Company, 1975. Reprinted with permission of the publisher.*

Figure 1 shows the interaction of heredity, environmental and situational variables. As shown, capacity plus experience leads to potential without need. Likewise, opportunity without capacity is also defeating. It is only when heredity, environmental and situational factors blend that maximum leadership effectiveness results.

Successful Leadership: The Traditional View

The traditional view of successful coaches is that they are dominant,

260

authoritarian, hardworking, artless, toughminded and manipulative. They are also thought to be task-oriented rather than player-centered. The leadership styles of coaches came under a barrage of criticism during the turbulent 1960's. Jack Scott (1969, 1971), Bruce Ogilvie and Thomas Tutko (1971), Tutko and Jack Richards (1971) all suggest that, as leaders, most coaches believe in strong discipline, rigid rules, extrinsic motivation and impersonal approaches toward their players. In brief, the coach is viewed as being hard-nosed and authoritarian.

George Sage (1975), after making an exhaustive review of the literature on this topic, concluded that "each coach has a unique leadership style of his own and generalizations concerning coaches' leadership behaviors to not capture the individual patterns which exist" (p. 416). Sage goes on to say that if coaching practices follow trends in industrial management, we may expect to see leadership in sport become more player-centered and more emphasis given to player input in the decision making process.

Table 1 presents some of the traditional ways of looking at leadership.

Successful Leadership Is Based On:	The Successful Leader Will:
• Making the most of personal abilities • Bringing out the best characteristics in other people • Ability to cooperate • Mental alertness • Decisiveness • Accomplishing the assigned or desired tasks	• Take an interest in players • Awaken enthusiasm • Keep morale high • Communicate clearly • Praise in public, reprimand in private

Table 1. *The traditional view of leadership (adapted from Williams and Wassenaar, 1975,*

Although the statements make sense intuitively, they do not hold true in certain situations.

The Evolution of Leadership Theory

The historical mile-stones in the evolution of leadership theory may be divided into five distinct stages. Figure 2 shows the development of leadership theory. The stages are as follows:

Leadership by Tradition

This is the oldest source of leadership and is still used in many countries, particularly those nations like England who have kings and queens. In ancient times, the tribal chief's oldest son automatically became the head of the tribe when his father died. This type of control is called inherited leadership and it is practiced because it is said to bring stability, order, reverence, and dignity to countries who practice it.

There is evidence of leadership by tradition in sport. It is interesting to note how many sons and daughters of coaches and teachers of physical education follow in the footsteps of their parents. The history of town team baseball reveals that many of the sons of managers succeeded their fathers. In a word, the fathers trained their sons for this transition to take place.

EVOLUTION OF LEADERSHIP THEORY

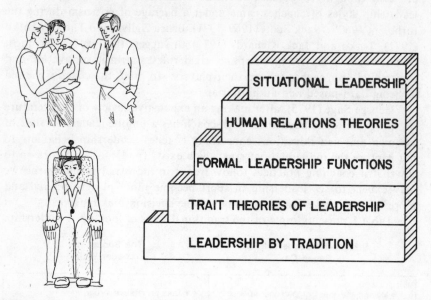

Figure 2. *Evolution of leadership theory. Adapted from: Leadership by Williams, P. M. and Wassenaar, D. J. San Jose, California: Lansford Publishing Company, 1975. Reprinted with permission of the publisher.*

Trait Theories of Leadership

The second stage in the development of leadership theory evolved because of the early research on leadership. For many years it was assumed that leaders are born — that they possessed certain innate characteristics that made them "born leaders". For many years, heads of states and armies looked for potential leaders in terms of physical stature, presumed energy levels, forceful voice, and similar characteristics. Later on, personality traits such as, aggressiveness, integrity, intelligence, and dependability were stressed. The emphasis was on what man/woman is, rather than on what he/she does. The most fallacious assumption was that all groups of followers and all situations required the same traits in a leader. According to Fiedler (1967), this practice proved to be unproductive. Nevertheless, the thought that leaders possess unique personality traits continues.

Formal Leadership Functions

Organizing, controlling and coordinating, known as formal leadership functions, become the focus of classical management theorists. The shift was to what effective leaders do, rather than what they are or are not. The assumption was that good leadership can be learned by paying attention to sound management principles. Studies by psychologists at Ohio State University produced a leadership concept called 'initiating structure'. Effective leaders, the studies found, spent more of their time and talents on *'structuring'* the work of others. That is, they did a better job of organizing, controlling, staffing and coordinating than the less effective leaders. Some authorities called this approach instrumental leadership.

Human Relations Theories

Due to the well-known Hawthorne studies, the decade of the 1950's saw a dramatic upsurge in the human relations school. Basically, this approach stressed that a good leader sympathizes with the personal problems of his/her subordinates. He/she supports them emotionally, lets them participate in decision making, listens to them, etc. In brief, the leader is a ball player's ball player.

Situational Leadership Theories

The most recent trend in leadership theory is the attention given to situational variables. The basic premise is that leadership style which is effective in one situation may not work in another. This school also postulates that a good leader is flexible — that he/she can behave in different ways. The personality of the leader, the personality of players, the organizational climate and other factors determine the best leadership style.

With the evolution of leadership in mind, let us focus attention on theories of leadership. We will begin with McGregor's Theory X and Y.

McGregor's Theory X and Y

According to McGregor (1967), a manager or supervisor may formulate two sets of basic assumptions about human behavior. Table 2 shows an adaptation of McGregor's well-known 'Theory X and Y' applied to leadership in sport.

Theory X	Theory Y
• Athletes inherently dislike work and will avoid it if they can.	• The expenditure of physical and mental effort in work is as natural as play or rest.
• Players must be coerced, controlled, directed, and threatened in order to make them work.	• Players can exercise self-direction and self-control in the service of objectives to which they are committed.
• On the average, players prefer to be directed, wish to avoid responsibility and have relatively little ambition.	• On the average, players learn under proper conditions; not only to accept but to seek responsibility.

Table 2. *McGregor's Theory X and Y applied to leadership in sport.*

If a coach accepts Theory Y as a more accurate reflection of true human nature, he/she will place heavy emphasis on the human relations aspects of leadership. 'Player oriented' coaches are concerned about the morale of their athletes. In doing so, however, the humanistically oriented coach may not focus enough attention on the task at hand. High morale does not necessarily mean high productivity (Davis, 1972). As shown in Figure 3, coaches should keep a balance between concern for players and concern for winning, situational factors such as the philosophy of administrators, parents and players may balance the arm toward one side of the scale. Perhaps Forrest Gregg's problem in Cleveland was that he became too involved with winning and as a result lost the respect and admiration of his players.

Tannenbaum and Schmidt's Model

A classic article on leadership was written by Tannenbaum and Schmidt (1958) entitled: 'How to choose a leadership pattern'. Figure 4 shows the

BALANCING CONCERN FOR PLAYERS AND CONCERN FOR WINNING

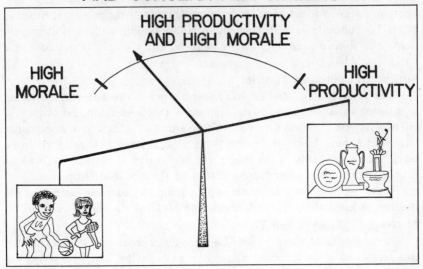

HIGH PRODUCTIVITY AND HIGH MORALE

HIGH MORALE

HIGH PRODUCTIVITY

Figure 3. *Balancing concern for players and concern for winning. Adapted from: Leadership by Williams, P. M. and Wassenaar, D. J. San Jose, California: Lansford Publishing Company, 1975. Reprinted with permission of the publisher.*

continuum of styles from coach-centered to player-centered leadership. Agreeing with Fiedler, Tannenbaum and Schmidt contend that effective leadership is a function of the leader, the followers and situational variables.

TANNENBAUM and SCHMIDT'S MODEL of LEADERSHIP BEHAVIOR

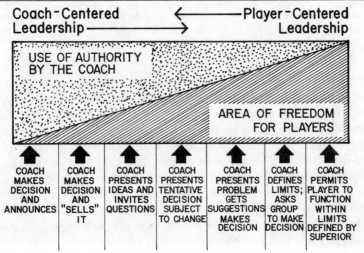

Coach-Centered Leadership ⟶

⟵ Player-Centered Leadership

USE OF AUTHORITY BY THE COACH

AREA OF FREEDOM FOR PLAYERS

COACH MAKES DECISION AND ANNOUNCES

COACH MAKES DECISION AND "SELLS" IT

COACH PRESENTS IDEAS AND INVITES QUESTIONS

COACH PRESENTS TENTATIVE DECISION SUBJECT TO CHANGE

COACH PRESENTS PROBLEM GETS SUGGESTIONS MAKES DECISION

COACH DEFINES LIMITS; ASKS GROUP TO MAKE DECISION

COACH PERMITS PLAYER TO FUNCTION WITHIN LIMITS DEFINED BY SUPERIOR

Figure 4. *Tannenbaum and Schmidt's model of leadership behavior. From: Robert Tannenbaum and Warren H. Schmidt, "How to Choose a Leadership Pattern," **Harvard Business Review,** May-June, 1973, copyright© 1973 by the President and Fellows of Harvard College; all rights reserved.*

The leadership style of some of our most successful coaches suggest that neither a strongly authoritarian approach nor a fully participative one should be used. Effective coaches, like successful managers in industry, seem to be able to vary their style with the needs of the situation.

Fiedler's Leadership Model

Fred E. Fiedler, (1967, 1971) has developed and validated a theory which shows the situational nature of effective leadership. As shown in Figure 5, there are three important leadership dimensions. They are: leader-

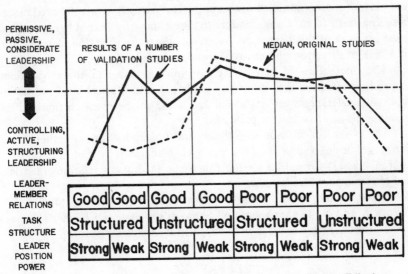

Figure 5. *Fiedler's leadership model. From:* **A Theory of Leadership Effectiveness** *by Fiedler, F. E.*

member relations, task structure and power position.

Leader-member relations refer to the leader's feeling of being accepted by subordinates, i.e., in sport — the players. Task structure refers to the degree to which the follower's jobs are routine versus being unstructured and undefined. Power position refers to the power inherent in the leadership position, including support from higher management or the front office.

Returning to the Forrest Gregg Case, after the Brown's began to lose after getting off to a great start, according to the press, Gregg's credibility with the players and particularly with Art Modell, principal owner, began to decline. Therefore, leader-member relations were moderately poor. The task, playing football, was highly structured, i.e., players, for the most part, performed routine assignments. For example, the center snapped the ball to begin every offensive play. Therefore, according to Fiedler's model (Figure 5), when leader-member relations are moderately poor, the task is structured, and the leader's power position is weak, the most effective style to use is permissive.

Instead of loosening-up a little, Gregg apparently became very forceful and autocratic in his approach. The results were disastrous.

SUMMARY

It was the purpose of this paper to explore some of the facets of leadership effectiveness. Leadership was defined as the influence the coach has on his/her players. In arriving at the most effective leadership style, the coach should consider his/her own personal characteristics, the personal characteristics of the players and the nature of the specific situation.

Basically, there are three broad types of leaders found in sport. The *'hard driver'* views his/her task as keeping order. To this coach, discipline is the first ingredient of success. The *'thoughtful persuader'* manipulates the team to accept his/her approach. This coach has little faith in the ability of the players to function on their own. A blueprint or game plan is prepared and players are manipulated to accept it. The *'friendly helper'* takes a laissez-faire approach to coaching. Failure to take a stand for fear of being rejected is the earmark of this approach. As a result, the team often flounders because of a lack of direction and clearly formulated goals.

The interaction of heredity, environmental and situational variables to produce effective leadership was explained and illustrated. Traditional views of leadership were explained and some of the research findings regarding this approach were presented.

The evolution of leadership theory was covered. Basically, there were five stages of development. They were: (1) leadership by tradition, (2) trait approaches, (3) formal leadership functions, (4) human relations theories, and (5) situational leadership.

Three models of leadership were presented. They were: McGregor's Theory X and Y, Tannenbaum and Schmidt's model, and Fiedler's theory. The Forrest Gregg Case was used to illustrate Fiedler's position.

REFERENCES

DAVIS, K. *Human behavior at work: human relations and organizational behavior* (4th ed.). New York: McGraw-Hill, 1972.

FIEDLER, F. E. *A theory of leadership effectiveness.* New York: McGraw-Hill, 1967.

FIEDLER, F. E. *Leadership.* Morristown, New Jersey: General Learning Press, 1971.

MC GREGOR, D. *The professional manager.* New York: McGraw-Hill, 1967.

MUDRA, D. E. *A critical analysis of football coaching practices in light of a selected group of learning principles.* Unpublished doctoral dissertation, University of Northern Colorado, 1965.

OGILVIE, B., & TUTKO, T. *Problem athletes and how to handle them.* London: Pelham, 1966.

RICHARDS, M. D., & GREENLAW, P. S. *Management decision making.* Homewood, Illinois: Richard D. Irwin, 1966.

SAGE, G. An Occupational analysis of the college coach. In D. W. Ball & J. W. Loy (Eds.), *Sport and social order.* Reading, Massachusetts: Addison-Wesley, 1975.

SCOTT, J. *Athletics for athletes.* Oakland, California: Other Ways Book, 1969.

SCOTT, J. *The athletic revolution.* New York: Free Press, 1971.

SWARTZ, J. L. *Analysis of leadership styles of college level head football coaches from five midwestern states.* Unpublished doctoral dissertation, University of Northern Colorado, 1973.

TANNENBAUM, R., and SCHMIDT, W. H. How to choose a leadership pattern. *Harvard Business Review,* 1958, *36,* 95-101.

TUTKO, T., & RICHARDS, J. *Psychology of Coaching.* Boston: Allyn and Bacon, 1971.

WILLIAMS, P. M., & WASSENAAR, D. J. *Leadership.* San Jose, California: Lansford, 1975.

YOUNG, K. *Handbook for social psychology.* London: Routledge and Kegan Paul, 1946.

A Group Dynamics Approach to Effective Coaching of Team Sports*

Anne Marie Bird, Ph.D.
California State
University - Fullerton

Abstract

Evidence from group dynamics research is used in order to present rationale for enhancing coaching effectiveness. Specific reference is made to the social cohesion and causal attribution perspectives. It is argued that group motivation can be augmented through a systematic program of realistic goal setting and team-contingent reinforcement.

Undoubtedly, no question is of greater interest to coaches than what can be done to facilitate sport team success. Yet, little research has been completed in an effort to provide answers to that inquiry. As a result, potential and practicing coaches have traditionally been forced to rely solely on their own or their former coaches' strategies. This is neither an efficient nor an economic method of learning. This paper is an attempt to present and summarize a large portion of the available research evidence which relates to sport team success and effective coaching behaviors.

In order to understand the final group product, that is, successful or unsuccessful performance, three variables are of interest: group structure, group process, and leadership or coaching behaviors. Davis (1969) defines group structure in terms of the recurring patterns of interpersonal relations which occur between group members. These patterns are considered to be somewhat consistent and are actually determined by the nature of the task at hand. For instance, if a group has a task such as "tug-of-war," obviously the group which wins the battle will be the one whose members work together effectively and in unison. If, on the other hand, the group goal calls for the identification of the person who is to be the leader, then different interpersonal interactions will occur among team members. Group process pertains to the relations or intermember dynamics which take place along

*An article published in *Motor Skills: Theory Into Practice* 2:92–101, 1978. Reprinted with permission of the publisher.

the structural paths. As we shall see shortly, group processes are affected by both structure and the quality of the output of the group. The final variable of interest, leadership, again relates quite directly to the nature of the group itself and to the task at hand. Different groups appear to require different types of leadership style. Thus, if a coach is to be successful, he must first gain an understanding of the nature and functioning of his particular sport group. We will attempt to clarify this by addressing each of the three variables, structure, process, and leadership, separately. Subsequently, an attempt will be made to integrate the research findings in order to provide a unified picture of effective coaching behavior, specifically in terms of team sports.

Sport Group Structure and Classification

Based upon the nature of the relations which occur between members as a function of the group task, two major classifications have generally been employed (Fiedler, 1967). *Interacting* teams are organized such that members must work together in a coordinated effort in order to achieve success. Members are interdependent upon one another. If one player moves toward the goal, all members benefit. For example, on a basketball team, if one player makes a field goal, the resultant two points are awarded to the team as a whole. Thomas (1957) called this means-controlling facilitation. By this he meant that when a group is formed or structured for the purpose of obtaining a specific goal, and when attainment of that goal necessitates that members work together in a coordinated effort, then members are interdependent in the sense that failure on the part of one member hinders the progress of all. Other sport teams which are classified as interacting are: volleyball, football, soccer, and hockey.

Coacting teams are structured in a manner which allows members to remain independent from one another during pursuit of a common goal. Furthermore, as Steiner (1972) has pointed out, such groups ordinarily require that all members perform a similar skill, with the final goal attainment or loss being determined by the sum or average of their individual performances. This classification becomes clear when one thinks of teams such as bowling or riflery.

As the reader has most likely already noted, not all sport teams can be accurately classified as being exclusively interacting or coacting. For instance, when track and field teams compete we see mixed elements. The relay teams could be viewed as coacting, while the field events are actually individual performances. Yet, the team wins or loses on the basis of all members' contributions. Until conflicting evidence is produced, it is probably quite defensible to treat members of teams such as track and field or swimming on the basis of individual psychology rather than what we know about group dynamics and group behavior. For our purposes here, we will restrict our attention to the latter.

Group Processes

Historically, the group process which has received the most research notice has been that of social cohesion. Recently, however, sport researchers have investigated a second process called causal attribution. Very simply, causal attributions are the explanations which people give regarding the causes underlying either successful or unsuccessful performance.

Cohesion

The earliest definition of cohesion was that offered by Festinger, Schachter and Back (1950) which said that cohesion was the sum of all forces which act upon members so that they remain in the group. It is difficult to argue with the reasoning underlying their definition, however, it is also almost impossible to test its veracity. How would one go about identifying, much less measuring, all those unknown forces? Hagstrom and Selvin (1965) did much to remediate this problem. Using a statistical analysis called factor analysis, they identified and measured 19 separate dimensions of cohesion. The results of their analysis revealed that two distinct dimensions contributed to overall group cohesion: social satisfaction and sociometric cohesion.

Social satisfaction involves satisfaction with the group in terms of its ability to allow the individual to obtain the instrumental goals for which he joined the group in the first place. More simply, if a player joined a particular sport team with the objective in mind that the team would have a highly successful season and if the team was indeed successful, then his membership on the team allowed him to achieve his objective. Given that set of circumstances, the player should then perceive a high degree of social satisfaction. *Sociometric cohesion* pertains to the amount of positive affect or good emotional feelings which team membership brings. This dimension is highly related to other sociometric measures such as the proportion of best friends on the team, the amount of time spent in group-related activities, and the degree of group influence on significant behavior.

Social Cohesion and Group Structure

At first when researchers attempted to ascertain the relationship between sport team success and degree of cohesion, the findings appeared to yield contradictory results. Then in 1974, Landers and Lueschen clarified these supposed conflicts. They accomplished this by relating structural dimensions to degree of cohesion. Briefly, what they found was that when sport groups were characterized by a coacting structure, more successful teams evidenced less cohesion. Obversely, more successful interacting teams have been found to have higher degree of cohesion (Bird, 1977; Klein & Christiansen, 1969; Martens & Peterson, 1971; Trincia, 1976).

Two important points need to be emphasized here. First, simply because cohesion appears to be related positively to interacting team success, does not mean that a causal relationship exists. We cannot say that cohesion causes success or that success must absolutely result in increased cohesion. All that can be said is that these two variables appear to be highly related. Second, given that cohesion and interacting team success are related positively, it would seem prudent for coaches to attempt to facilitate the development of a highly cohesive team. Recall, Hagstrom and Selvin's two dimensions of cohesion, social satisfaction and sociometric cohesion. Social satisfaction pertained to instrumental goal attainment and sociometric cohesion referred to positive feelings or affect associated with team membership. Viewed in another way these factors can be incorporated into what is commonly called an Expectancy X Affect model. Expectancy is defined as the anticipations which one has regarding the outcomes of a performance. That is, expectancy of success relative to instrumental goal attainment. Affect, as defined previously, incorporates the sociometric cohesion dimension. Taken as a whole, the higher the degree of expectancy and affect, the greater the degree of cohesion. Subsequently, we will explore ways in which the coach can attempt to augment both of these variables. For now, however, let us look at another process which is also thought to fit the Expectancy X Affect model.

Causal Attribution

Attribution theory concerns itself with the explanations which are made regarding the outcome of an event or performance. Generally, four causal elements are employed: ability, effort, luck, and task difficulty (Weiner, 1974; Weiner, Freize, Kukla, Reed, Rest, & Rosenbaum, 1971). These four causal elements can be viewed along two dimensions: locus of control and stability. Locus of control refers to the location, either internal or external, of the cause relative to the performer. Stability refers to the variability of a causal element. Conceived in this way, ability is stable and internal, effort is unstable and internal, luck is unstable and external, and task difficulty is stable and external.

Now let us see how these elements and dimensions are thought to relate to the Expectancy X Affect model. In regard to expectancy, it has been shown rather convincingly (Weiner, Nierenberg & Goldstein, 1976) that when a performance is attributed to a stable cause, then the individual's expectancy concerning future performances at the same task should remain about the same. Therefore, success or failure which is ascribed to either ability or task difficulty should generate the perception that the same outcome will be produced on the next attempt at that task. Performance outcomes which are attributed to unstable factors should, on the other hand, yield greater shifts or changes in expectancy. Thus, if an outcome is ascribed to effort or luck, then the present outcome could be expected to differ in the future. In a team sport situation then, outcomes which are attributed to unstable elements should be perceived of as being changeable or modifiable in the future.

With respect to the affect dimension of the Expectancy X Affect model, it is proposed that the dimension of locus of control is connected with feelings of either pride or shame associated with performance outcome. If a positive or successful outcome is attributed to a causal element which is internal, then the individual should experience pride or positive affect. A negative or unsuccessful outcome which is ascribed internally would then generate feelings of shame or negative affect. Outcomes which are attributed internally indicate that the performer is taking personal responsibility for the consequences of task performance. As could be predicted, outcomes which are attributed to external elements such as luck or task difficulty should elicit little or no positive affect. By attributing externally, the performer is diffusing responsibility for the outcome away from himself and onto the environment.

Causal Attributions and Sport Team Performance

Very few studies have investigated the question of attributions for self versus attributions for the team. However, some limited data are available. Roberts (1975) studied Little League players and found a significant interaction between individual and team ascriptions for effort in relation to team outcome. When successful, players saw team effort to be higher than when unsuccessful. However, relative to themselves, as individuals, effort did not vary as a function of team outcome. Iso-Ahola (in press-a) also studied Little League players and found results similar to those of Roberts.

In a separate study, Roberts (Note 1) found conflicting results. Using a two-person relay team, he found that failure subjects tended to employ team attributions for task difficulty and self attributions for luck more than successful subjects. Iso-Ahola (in press-b), interestingly, found that internal factors provided the greatest amount of discriminatory power in terms of ascriptions for team outcome.

No definite pattern appears to emerge from the findings cited. However, it should be pointed out that factors such as the structure of the team (Little League) or the nature of the task (two-person relay) have not been taken into account. To date, only one study has been completed using an interacting team. Bird and Brame (Note 2) studied collegiate, women's basketball teams in California. They found that members of losing teams perceived that they, as individuals, had exerted more effort that did their team. In regard to ability, no such discrepancy was evidenced. Of perhaps greater interest was their finding which indicated that winners, overall, tended to be more positive about both their own and their team's internal qualities when compared to losers. In fact, winners demonstrated enhanced positive perceptions of their team's ability as compared to their own. It is of importance to note that the internal factors of ability and effort have been said to have the greatest amount of influence on both the modification of achievement behavior and the quality of affect accompanying performance outcomes.

Let us now turn to the question of stability. Previously, we said that effort was variable, while ability was ordinarily thought to be stable. Contrary to this, Bird and Brame have argued that when basketball players view the element of team ability they do not perceive it as being a stable factor. Why would this be so? The ability of an interacting team is, by definition, a consequence of the quality of the interactions which occur among players. This does not exclude the variable of individual player ability, it says instead that on interacting teams, success results from more than simply the sum or average of the individual player motor skills. Some support for this position comes from a study done by Jones (1974). He assessed the individual abilities of two separate athletic groups, a baseball and a basketball team. He found that in the case of baseball, prediction of team outcome was 90% correct based merely on the physical abilities of the individual players. In the case of basketball, however, prediction accuracy fell to 35%. Basketball is an interacting sport, baseball is not.

Therefore, in the case of interacting teams, some process or variable must operate above and beyond simply the combined physical skill of the individual players. Play executions in sports such as basketball require member interdependency and cooperation. It may be that players on interacting teams see team ability as a changeable element which is dependent upon the quality of those intermember relations or efforts. If this position has merit, then two implications can be drawn. First, the ability of interacting teams can be viewed as being greater than merely the sum of the separate member abilities. Second, it appears that team ability may operate in conjunction with the other internal factor, effort. Therefore, increased team effort in terms of enhancing the effectiveness of player interactions should result in augmented team ability. We see then that group process appears to play a significant role in the product produced by interacting teams. Furthermore, apparently the two internal elements of effort and ability are directly related to group-oriented social processes. Thus, we will now incorporate the findings concerning the internal elements of team effort and team ability into what we know about the predictions generated from the Expectancy X Affect model.

Expectancy X Affect and Sport Group Performance

If team ability and effort can be considered as internal, unstable elements, then failure attributed to these factors should have certain predictable consequences in terms of expectancy and affect. An attribution which is made to an unstable element should cause the performer to believe that a similar outcome may not necessarily occur in the future. Instead, future performance outcomes can differ as a result of increased effort or enhanced team ability. Failure ascribed internally should result in shame. From what we know of cohesion then, what do the findings from attribution theory and the Expectancy X Affect model suggest? If social satisfaction is associated with instrumental goal attainment, then failure should decrease the social satisfaction dimension of cohesion. Further, feelings of negative affect which are connected with team failure should reduce sociometric cohesion. In summary, it would appear that the causal attributions made by players regarding their sport team's performance may also reflect the presence or degree of the social process called cohesion.

If we accept the analysis presented above, of what use is it to the coach of interacting team sports? First, we will look briefly at what the research evidence appears to tell us about effective coaching behavior as it relates to interacting sport teams. Then, an attempt will be made to synthesize that evidence with that which we now appear to know about social processes as they operate in team sports.

Effective Coaching Behaviors

Zander (1975) illuminated three common approaches to the building of individual achievement motivation. Subsequently, he suggested how such approaches might be used to enhance group motivation. *The Supportive Approach* is founded on the logic that a well-satisfied person, more than a less-satisfied one, puts out more effort on an assigned task. For example, in athletics it is not uncommon to provide grants-in-aid or even room and board to incoming athletes. These benefits are provided in the hopes that the individual will perform to his optimum in the future. Thus, they are given regardless of the player's actual performance. One of the most common truisms in psychology is that rewards are capable of maintaining a desired behavior. When a desirable behavior occurs and a reward is administered contingent upon that response, then the likelihood that that same response will recur is increased. The key word in the preceding sentence is contingent. When rewards are administered noncontingently, *i.e.,* regardless of the response emitted, then no relationship should be evidenced between the reward and the emission of the desired response. The point being made is that the supportive approach violates the principle of contingency. Rewards are given prior to and not contingent upon a desired response. In the supportive approach high and low producers are treated similarly. Few would disagree with the conclusion that the supportive approach is probably not the most effective for motivating individual behavior. There is certainly no reason to suspect that a similar approach would be any more effective with groups.

The Reinforcement Approach calls for the application of rewards contingent upon the observation of a desired response. For example, a standard of excellence is set and upon achievement of that standard the performer is rewarded. Such occurrences are very common in sport settings. For example, the rewarding of stars on football helmets or athletic letters. Although the reinforcement approach has much to say for itself, it too has some problems. For instance, the coach only has so many rewards that are available to him. After awhile, the rewards lose their potency. The price keeps going up and, therefore, the desired behavior-reward contingencies tend to weaken. Within interacting team sports, another problem emerges. If rewards are administered contingent upon responses made by individuals, then inequalities are likely to occur. Rivalries among players may take place. As a consequence, social processes such as cohesion may be affected adversely.

Zander refers to the third approach as the *Pride-in-Performance Approach.* Very simply, this approach attempts to facilitate pride (positive affect) by the setting of reasonable, challenging goals. Upon the achievement of the specified goal, the person feels pride and should have increased expectancy regarding future performance. The work of the coach is to identify appropriate goals, to evaluate goal-directed behavior, and to reward positive outcomes. The pride-in-performance approach can be applied to either individual or group-oriented goals. We will turn our attention to the latter.

Group Motivation

As we have seen above, a combination of the reinforcement and pride-in-performance approaches appears to be most effective for increasing individual achievement motivation. The question then becomes that of group achievement motivation. Can a member of a sport group simultaneously maintain both an individual-oriented and a group-oriented motive to achieve? Previous research (Forward, 1968; Zander, 1968) has indicated that these two motives are both independent and additive. Therefore, one motive such as the individual-oriented motive, is not necessarily the cause of the other. Both, however, could be affected by the consequences of team sport performance in terms of success or failure.

From what we know concerning attributions for self and team, it is easy to see that a sport team member's post-competitive evaluation of himself and his group may be very different, even though both evaluations were based on the same criterion, team outcome. In the case of the Little League baseball studies (Iso-Ahola, in press-a; Roberts, 1975), a team failure outcome had no adverse effect on players' internal ascriptions for themselves. On the contrary, the results of the basketball investigation (Bird & Brame, Note 2) indicated that members of winning teams had more positive self-evaluations as compared to losers. Differences in patterns of team attributions between baseball and basketball players were also evidenced. Decreased evaluations of the team's internal qualities were made by members of unsuccessful Little League teams. That is, members of those losing teams tended to deny personal responsibility for team failure by diffusing the entire blame onto the team as-a-whole. This procedure would then allow for maintenance of consistently high self-evaluations. In the case of basketball, however, the major difference in regard to players' evaluations of winning and losing teams was that of team ability. More specifically, losers saw no difference between their own and their team's ability, while winners demonstrated enhanced positive perceptions of their team's ability as compared to their own. For interacting teams then, we see two important attribution trends occurring as a consequence of team outcome. First, the self-attributions for the internal elements appear to be tied directly to team outcome. Second, a successful team outcome appears to be explained by reference to higher team ability as compared to individual player ability. The last trend supports the notion that interacting team ability is indeed more than merely the sum of the individual abilities of the team members.

Recall that in the case of interacting teams, group structural demands require that members coordinate their efforts interdependently. Without such intermember coordination, success is not possible. No individual can achieve success unless his team does also. It seems reasonable then that teammates become quite involved in the team's outcome, as well as their own individual contribution. Further, team goal attainment is mandatory in order for a team-oriented motive to achieve to occur. The effective coach of an interacting team sport must establish group-contingent goals. After consultation with all players, realistic, challenging group goals should be identified. The expected standard of excellence must be communicated and must be accepted by the group. That is, the criterion by which or against which performance is to be evaluated must be made clear. Group attempts at goal achievement must then be evaluated. After evaluation, group achievement should be rewarded. If achievement of the goal has been found to be too difficult or unrealistic, the goal must be redefined.

Group goals should be more specific than general. Setting an objective such as winning the game leaves too much to chance. Goals should be identified which can be achieved through inter-member effort. When the team fails to achieve a goal, and if the goal is still thought to be sound, then the coach should stress that goal attainment is possible through increased effort. Effort is changeable and internal. Goals which are obtained through coordinated, member efforts should elicit both positive affect and increased expectancy regarding the future performance of the team. Thus, a systematic program designed to facilitate group goal achievement should result in some observable consequences. Social cohesion should be increased. Players should also perceive that the ability of the team is more than simply the sum of the individual abilities of the players. Since the group goal achievement program was formulated and implemented on the basis of intermember dependencies, success could not have been accomplished without player cooperation and mutual effort. Therefore, the group-contingent plan should foster the adoption of the group-oriented achievement motive and player concern for the group outcome should be at least equal to, if not greater than, that for self.

Group goals should be more specific than general. Setting an objective such as winning the game leaves too much to chance. Goals should be identified which can be achieved through inter-member effort. When the team fails to achieve a goal, and if the goal is still thought to be sound, then the coach should stress that goal attainment is possible through increased effort. Effort is changeable and internal. Goals which are obtained through coordinated, member efforts should elicit both positive affect and increased expectancy regarding the future performance of the team. Thus, a systematic program designed to facilitate group goal achievement should result in some observable consequences. Social cohesion should be increased. Players should also perceive that the ability of the team is more than simply the sum of the individual abilities of the players. Since the group goal achievement program was formulated and implemented on the basis of intermember dependencies, success could not have been accomplished without player cooperation and mutual effort. Therefore, the group-contingent plan should foster the adoption of the group-oriented achievement motive and player concern for the group outcome should be at least equal to, if not greater than, that for self.

REFERENCE NOTES

[1]Roberts, G. C. *Children's assignment of responsibility for winning and losing.* Paper presented at the University of Washington Symposium, Contemporary Research on Youth Sports, March 1977.
[2]Bird, A. M., & Brame, J. M. *Self versus team attributions: A test of the "I'm O.K., but the team's so-so" phenomenon.* Manuscript submitted for publication, 1977.

REFERENCES

BIRD, A. M. Development of a model for predicting team performance. *Research Quarterly,* 1977, *48,* 24-32.

DAVIS, J. H. *Group performance.* Reading, Mass.: Addison-Wesley, 1969.

FESTINGER, L., SCHACHTER, S., & BACK, K. *Social pressures in informal groups: a study of a housing project.* New York: Harper, 1950.

FIEDLER, F. E. *A theory of leadership effectiveness.* New York: McGraw-Hill, 1967.

FORWARD, J. Group achievement motivation and individual motive to achieve success and to avoid failure. *Journal of Personality,* 1969, *37,* 297-309.

HAGSTROM, W. O., & SELVIN, H. C. The dimensions of cohesiveness in small groups. *Sociometry,* 1965, *28,* 30-43.

ISO-AHOLA, S. Effects of team outcome on children's self-perception: Little League baseball. *Scandinavian Journal of Psychology,* in press (a).

ISO-AHOLA, S. Immediate attributional effects of success and failure in the field: testing some laboratory hypotheses. *European Journal of Social Psychology,* in press (b).

JONES, M. B. Regressing group on individual effectiveness. *Organizational Behavior and Human Performance,* 1974, *11,* 426-451.

KLEIN, M., & CHRISTIANSEN, G. Group composition, group structure and group effectiveness of basketball teams. In J. Loy, Jr. & G. S. Kenyon (Eds.), *Sport, culture and society.* London: Macmillan, 1969.

LANDERS, D. M., & LUESCHEN, G. Team performance outcome and the cohesiveness of competitive coacting groups. *International Review of Sport Sociology,* 1974, *9,* 57-71.

MARTENS, R., & PETERSON, J. A. Group cohesiveness as a determinant of success and member satisfaction in team performance. *International Review of Sport Sociology,* 1971, *6,* 49-61.

ROBERTS, G. C. Win-loss causal attributions of Little League players. *Mouvement: Act du 7 symposium en apprentissage psycho-moteur et psychologie du sport,* 1975.

STEINER, I. D. Models for inferring relationship between group size and potential group productivity. *Behavioral Science,* 1966, *11,* 273-283.

THOMAS, E. J. Effects of facilitative role interdependence on group functioning. *Human Relations,* 1957, *10,* 347-356.

TRINCIA, L. S. R. *Cohesion and leadership within high school girls' varsity basketball teams.* Unpublished master's thesis, University of Southern California, 1976.

WEINER, B. *Achievement motivation and attribution theory.* Morristown, N. J.: General Learning Press, 1974.

WEINER, B., FRIEZE, I., KUKLA, A., REED, L., & ROSENBAUM, R. M. *Perceiving the causes of success and failure.* Morristown, N. J.: General Learning Press, 1971.

WEINER, B., NIERENBERG, R., & GOLDSTEIN, M. Social learning (locus of control) versus attributional (causal stability) interpretations of expectancy of success. *Journal of Personality,* 1976, *44,* 52-68.

ZANDER, A. Group aspirations. In D. Cartwright & A. Zander (Eds.) *Group dynamics.* New York: Harper & Row, 1969.

ZANDER, A. Motivation and performance of sport groups. In D. M. Landers (Ed.) *Psychology of sport and motor behavior II,* University Park, Pa.: Pennsylvania State University Press, 1975.

An Analysis of Teaching and Coaching Behaviors

Victor H. Mancini, Ed.D.
Ithaca College

Michelle Agnew, M.S.
University of Scranton

The success of many athletic teams is contingent on the talent available, but even the most talented of clubs often attribute much of their success to the leader or coach. Is there a key to sucess in leadership? Can we predict who will be successful and who will not? For years we have tried through tests and interviews to select people who will succeed. This approach has met with little success. Perhaps some of our shortcomings come from the theories behind our search or the methods that we employed in studying the leadership styles of coaches.

Cratty (1973) stated that most of the information concerning coaching was based upon research that was more exploratory than definitive. The analysis of coaching methods has been based mainly on tradition and opinions, instead of being based on knowledge of scientific coaching theories (Percival, 1974). Psychologists have classified the success-failure of a coach according to certain personality qualities (Lawther, 1972; Ogilvie & Tutko, 1966; Tutko & Richards, 1971; Penman, Hastad & Cords, 1974); the media has stereotyped the coach as dominant, aggressive, and authoritative (Hendry, 1972); educators have postulated that the successful and better prepared coaches were determined by the schooling they received (Gaylord, 1967).

Athletic coaches often teach physical education, and physical educators often coach athletics (Gillen, 1972; Holden, 1971). Gallon (1974), Lawther (1972), and Bucher (1975) stated that coaching athletics was like teaching. Tutko and Richards (1971) believe the role assumed by the coach will incorporate a certain style or manner of behavior. Hendry (1974) also stated that behaviors found in coaching and teaching are dissimilar, concluding that he had found defined personality clusters unique for coaches and teachers. It was Edwards (1973) and Governali (1974) who wrote that the methods and the interactional behaviors involved in teaching and coaching were unrelated. Coaching was different because of "the strains resulting from value incongruencies centering upon relations between the institutional functions of sport and demands created by our society"

(Edwards, 1973, p. 41). Edwards (1973) and Governali (1974) believe that the autocratic behavior of coaches is more typically the norm than is a pattern of interaction characterized by compromise and democratic interchange. Teaching styles found in physical education have been predominantly patterned after styles of coaching found in athletics (Stevenson, 1974).

Due to these inconsistent findings and beliefs, the need for objective information is clearly apparent. If the interaction between coach and player is taken directly from its environment, true behavior can be identified (Anderson, 1971). Yet very little attention has been given to the study of interaction analysis of the coach (Vanek & Cratty, 1970; Kasson, 1974). Tutko (1971) talked of communication as essential to coaching efficiency, the difference between winning and losing. He divided communication into information giving and information getting, believing the "good" coach seeks feedback from the players. The interpersonal relationship a leader has with the group is probably the most important single variable in determining one's power and influence (Fiedler & Chemers, 1974). Because it is a leader's actions that affect the group, they should be the predominant characteristic studied.

Although the behaviors of physical education teachers and coaches are presumed to be different, little research has been done to specify the nature of such differences (Bain, 1978). Perhaps the coach should be evaluated in terms of his/her behavior in a teaching role (La Grand, 1970).

Descriptive-Analytic Techniques

One can determine the types of teaching and coaching styles through the identification of teaching/coaching behaviors that are evident in actual classes and practice sessions through the use of descriptive-analytic investigative techniques. Descriptive-analytic techniques have been utilized in the physical education classroom for about 10 years. When disagreement developed over the educational worth of physical education in the schools, highly descriptive analyses were done of physical education and athletic settings to determine what was actually happening in the physical education environment and whether it contributed to the education of the students. The development and use of descriptive analytic techniques have made it possible for the researcher to collect specific objective data of the teacher and pupil behaviors as they are manifested in educational settings.

One objective observation technique is called interaction analysis. Each interaction is appropriately categorized and recorded by a trained observer, the purpose of which is to provide objective feedback of the actual behaviors occurring in the teaching-learning process. Interaction analysis (IA) is used to discriminate between patterns of teaching, and the indirect and direct influence of the teacher. Researchers have acquired large samples of descriptive data through IA systems. As a result, they are able to examine, explain, and experiment.

Flanders (1970) developed the most widely known interaction analysis system. Flanders' Interaction Analysis System (FIAS) is a method for observing and coding the verbal interaction between a teacher and a pupil. Interaction analysis has been used to study the direct and indirect influence of the teacher, spontaneous teacher behavior, to help teachers modify their behavior, and to discriminate between patterns of teaching. Flanders (1970) referred to "direct" teacher behaviors as those that discouraged student initiative and freedom of action and involved much teacher lecturing and direction giving. Openness to ideas and suggestions, asking questions, and encouraging student freedom of action and initiative behavior have been characteristics with "indirect" teachers.

Teaching Behaviors of Physical Educators

Using FIAS, 40 physical education teachers and their students on the elementary, secondary, and college levels were analyzed by Nygaard (1971; 1975). He found that the male teachers used lecture significantly more than did the female teachers. The female teachers used praise and encouragement, directions or command, criticism or justification of authority, and student talk — initiation, significantly more than did the male teachers. It was revealed that both male and female physical education teachers: 1) used verbal behaviors which had a "direct" influence on students (use of lecturing, giving directions, and criticizing or justifying authority behaviors); 2) did most of the talking; 3) placed a great deal of emphasis on content; and 4) viewed themselves as authority figures in the classroom. These data indicated that physical education teachers are characterized by direct, authoritarian forms of interaction behavior.

Behneman (1971) made comparisons between sex and the verbal behaviors of 42 physical education teachers (21 male and 21 female) by using an IAS. His study revealed that female teachers used significantly less criticism of their students than males and initiated more talk in the classroom. However, direct behavior was the dominant style of both sexes in this study. The use of less criticism in the classroom was contrary to Nygaard's (1971) findings.

Although Flanders' efforts were appropriate to analyze the verbal behavior and interactions between teacher and student, considerable ground rules were needed before FIAS could be used effectively in physical activity settings. Since much of the activity in physical education classes is nonverbal as well, there was a need to develop an observer system that could measure both verbal and nonverbal behavior. Cheffers (1972) undertook one of the most extensive expansions of FIAS to include categories for nonverbal behaviors to be used in physical activity settings. His expansion is called the Cheffers' Adaptation to the Flanders' Interaction System (CAFIAS).[1]

Using CAFIAS, Batchelder (1975), compared 25 elementary teachers and their interactions which she observed in physical education, math, and English classes. Elementary teachers were found to be more direct in their behaviors during physical education classes, more indirect in their behaviors in math classes, and more varied (use of direct and indirect) in their behaviors during English classes. Extended teacher lecture or information giving was the most frequently observed behavior pattern. An interesting finding was that nonverbal communication was used 50 percent of

[1](For a more complete description of CAFIAS see Cheffers, Amidon & Rodgers, 1974).

the time in the physical education class, while approximately one-third of all behaviors in elementary math and English classes were nonverbal.

In a recent study, Cheffers and Mancini (1978) compared 40 elementary and 43 secondary physical education teachers of the Videotape Data Bank Project directed by Anderson (1975) and his associates at Teachers College, Columbia University. The tapes were coded using CAFIAS. The results revealed:

1. Minimal differences existed in category usage, interaction parameters and in interaction patterns between male and female teachers and between elementary and secondary teachers.

2. Teachers used lecture and direction giving as their overwhelmingly predominant mode of teaching.

3. By comparison with total recorded teacher behaviors, virtually no acceptance of students' feelings, and ideas, praise or questioning behaviors were recorded.

4. Punishment and correction of student behaviors were minimal.

5. Virtually no genuine student initiated activity was recorded.

6. Out of the total behaviors which took place in the physical education classes, the students' contribution was more than is seen in academic classes. Student contribution was predominantly nonverbal.

The only study which described and compared teacher sex, leadership style, leader behavior, and their effort on teacher-student interaction was conducted by Keane (1976). CAFIAS was used to study the teacher-student interaction patterns. The teachers' leadership style was measured by Fiedler's (1967) Least Preferred Co-worker Scale (LPC), and the students' perception of the teacher leadership behavior was recorded by the use of the Leader Behavior Description Questionnaire XII (Stogdill, 1963). The description of the observed classroom interaction patterns revealed differences in only one CAFIAS parameter, that of pupil initiation. Female teachers scored significantly higher than male teachers. This finding lead to the conclusion that students may be willing to take more risks with female teachers or that female teachers encourage more student initiation. Keane (1976) also found that leadership style was significantly related to CAFIAS variables describing total teacher effort and teacher emphasis on content. It was concluded that leadership style could be predicted from selected CAFIAS parameters. Sex of the teacher was also investigated in terms of leadership style and found not to be a factor. This finding is supported by Chapman's (1974) results which suggested that there were no significant differences between male and female leadership style in business and in the military. Chapman encouraged more research into this area in physical education and athletics (Keane, 1976). Differences in leadership style appear to be greater within groups rather than between groups; that is, the greater differences in leadership style were within the males in their group and within the females in their group, rather than between the male and female groups.

Coaching Behaviors

There has been little research devoted to the study of coaches' behaviors, especially the female during the process of teaching and coaching. Until recent years, studies of coaches have used various techniques, such as questionnaires and personality trait inventories. The studies conducted by Danielson, Zelhart, and Drake (1975), Hendry (1974), and La Grand (1970) are examples of these types of investigations.

Using 304 athletes, La Grand (1970) studied behavioral characteristics of coaches. A rating form describing the behavioral characteristics, such as amount of enthusiasm, willingness to give individual help, ability to inspire, and the use of discipline, was used to evaluate the coaches. La Grand (1970) found basketball players and wrestlers rated their coaches' "methods of teaching" and "use of discipline" higher than did the soccer or tennis players. Wrestlers rated their coaches' "ability to inspire" as sharper, stronger, more important, and more valuable than the team players rated their coaches. La Grand concluded that there was no hierarchy of behavioral characteristics discernible among athletic coaches.

Danielson, Zelhart, and Drake (1975) found, through their study of male ice hockey coaches, communicative behavior was emphasized in the coaching environment. The Coach Behavior Description Questionnaire was administered to 160 players in order to rate their coaches. The behavior most frequently attributed to hockey coaching ws the integrative behavior of encouraging members to work as a team. Other commonly perceived coaching behaviors were organized communication, recognition through feedback and reinforcement to the players, general excitement, and interpersonal team operation. As recognized by Danielson, et al., the majority of behaviors observed by the athletes appeared to be related to the passing of information to and from the coach. Positive communication between the athlete and coach in ice hockey was evident in this study.

In comparing the teacher and coach, Hendry (1974) examined the two leaders in relation to their personalities and social orientation through the use of a questionnaire. The main differences shown were: teachers had qualities of overt sociability, high aspiration, and drive; whereas, the coaches were more controlled individuals with restricted ideas but with high organizational abilities.

Kasson (1974) was the first researcher to report the use of interaction analysis to evaluate the interactions patterns of three male physical educators while teaching and coaching. He recommended that more attention be directed to the analysis of teacher/coach behaviors. Three hours of teaching and three hours of coaching were utilized as the basis for the analyses of their behaviors in this study. There was a significant difference in the amount of verbal and nonverbal behavior displayed by the male physical educator in teaching and coaching sessions. In physical education classes, 39% of teacher behavior was categorized as nonverbal and 36% as verbal behavior. In coaching sessions, 37% of the total behaviors was verbal and 25% was nonverbal. The results also showed that coaches were not any more direct in their behavior than teachers, but more direct behavior than indirect behavior was used in both environments. The behaviors shown most in teaching were lecturing or demonstrating, performing a physical skill, giving directions nonverbally, and silence. The coaching behaviors repeatedly used were lecturing or demonstrating, and silence.

Using CAFIAS, Mancini and Agnew (1978) conducted an investigation to determine if there were significant differences in the behavior patterns of 20 female secondary physical education instructors when teaching and coaching. This investigation gave the writers the opportunity to observe many classroom and coaching situations (40 PE classes and 40 practices) and to study the behaviors which were actually being used while teaching and coaching through the use of IA. Each female physical educator was videotaped during the winter and spring programs in 1977 on two different days. A 30-minute session of teaching and a 30-minute session of coaching was videotaped on each day. Schedules of the coaches were secured and a week's notice was given to each instructor. They were asked to maintain a normal lesson and practice plan that was scheduled for that week in order to observe as natural a setting as possible. The investigation revealed the following: 1) interaction between the pupil and the teacher/coach was more evident in the coaching setting; 2) more pupil initiated behavior, as a result of the teacher's suggestion, was observed in the coaching environment; 3) female instructors used more praise and acceptance, verbal and nonverbal, during the coaching setting as opposed to the teaching setting; and 4) the interaction exhibited between female coaches and their athletes was more varied and flexible than the interaction used in the classroom. Positive communication between the female secondary school coaches and their athletes was evident as was found with the ice hockey coaches and their athletes in the study by Danielson, Zelhart, and Drake (1975). In opposition to Kasson's study (1974) the investigators found the prevalent behaviors used in coaching to be more indirect than direct. We found more interaction in the coaching environment as opposed to both the teaching and coaching sessions studied by Kasson (1974).

When studying teaching and coaching behaviors of 15 male college physical educators, Mason (1978) found similar findings to those of Mancini and Agnew (1978). The one different CAFIAS behavior exhibited by Mason's male college physical educators was the use of questioning. This behavior appeared more frequently in coaching than was observed in the physical education class and also by the female secondary physical educator in coaching.

Summary

All of the teaching behavior observed and studied by Bahneman (1971), Batchelder (1975), Cheffers and Mancini (1978), Keane (1976), and Nygaard (1971) was found to be direct, lacked flexibility, and involved little student input. Communication, both information giving and information getting, is essential to teaching and coaching efficiency. The review of these studies revealed that coaches exhibit a greater variety of behaviors in the coaching sessions but less variety of teacher-pupil interaction in the physical education classroom. The physical education classes are more teacher-centered. Students in the physical education class need praise and encouragement, questioning, and a chance for involvement in the class. Physical educators, with all the varied interaction pattern existent in their coaching environments, seem to exhibit more enthusiasm while coaching than while teaching.

As of this writing, research using descriptive-analytic techniques to study the leadership styles of the physical education teacher and athletic coach has been scant. However, a few other systems have been developed to assess the behaviors of the physical educator/coach (Bain, 1978; Smith, Small, & Hunt, 1977; Tharp & Gillimore, 1976). Studies by Mancini and Agnew (1978) and Mason (1978) were the initial investigations conducted at Ithaca College to assess the coach's behavior. Seven more studies of the teacher and coach's behaviors (leadership style) are presently under investigation.

When teachers are initially introduced to descriptive techniques, they usually express strong reservations. Once they become familiar with these techniques and realize that data presented through interaction analysis can be helpful, exciting, and challenging, their attitudes change. They begin to become involved in a process of self-change which brings deep satisfaction to their teaching effort.

If we are to explain the moment to moment events during the teacher learning process, we must employ the use of some form of systematic observation to produce the feedback about one's teaching style. The use of systematic observation is moving the teaching process away from the realm of unexplainable, hit-or-miss interaction toward a process that can be objectively planned, observed, assessed, modified, and carried out.

The basic phenomenon in the teaching/coaching settings is a pattern of interaction among human beings. If teachers are to become more effective in their teaching/coaching, they need to become attentive not only to what they are communicating but also to how they are communicating. Communication is the key to success in leadership.

REFERENCES

ANDERSON, W. G. Descriptive-analytic research on teaching. *Quest,* 1971, *15,*.1-8.

ANDERSON, W. G. Videotape databank. *Journal of Physical Education and Recreation,* 1975, *46:*31-34.

BAHNEMAN, C. P. *An analysis of the relationship between selected personality characteristics and the verbal behavior of physical education teachers.* Unpublished doctoral dissertation, University of Pittsburgh, 1971.

BAIN, L. L. Differences in values implicit in teaching and coaching behaviors. *Research Quarterly,* 1978, *49,* 5-11.

BATCHELDER, A. S. *Process objectives, observed behaviors, and teaching patterns in elementary math, English, and physical education classes.* Unpublished doctoral dissertation, Boston University, 1975.

BUCHER, C. A. *Administration of health and physical education programs, including athletics.* St. Louis: The C. V. Mosby Co., 1975.

CHAPMAN, J. *A comparative analysis of male and female leadership styles in similar work environments.* Unpublished doctoral dissertation, University of Nebraska, 1974.

CHEFFERS, J. T. F. *The validation of an instrument designed to expand the Flanders System of Interaction Analysis to describe non-verbal interaction, different varieties of teacher behavior and pupil responses.* Unpublished doctoral dissertation, Temple University, 1972.

CHEFFERS, J. T. F., AMIDON, E. J., & RODGERS, K. D. *Interaction analysis: An application to nonverbal activity.* Minneapolis: Association for Productive Teaching, 1974.

CHEFFERS, J. T. F. & MANCINI, V. H. Teacher-student interaction. In W. G. Anderson & G. T. Barrette (Eds.), *What's going on in gym: Descriptive studies of physical education classes.* Monograph 1 *Motor Skills: Theory Into Practice,* 1978.

CRATTY, B. *Psychology in contemporary sport: Guidelines for coaches and athletes.* Englewood Cliffs, New Jersey: Prentice-Hall, Inc., 1973.

EDWARDS, H. *Sociology of sport.* Homewood, Illinois: The Dorsey Press, 1973.

FIEDLER, F. E. *A theory of leadership effectiveness.* New York: McGraw-Hill, 1967.

FIEDLER, F. E. & CHEMERS, M. *Leadership and effective management.* Glenview, Illinois: Scott, Foresman and Co., 1974.

FLANDERS, N. *Analyzing teaching behavior.* Reading, Massachusetts: Addison Wesley Publishing Company, 1970.

GALLON, A. *Coaching: Ideas and ideals.* Boston: Houghton Mifflin Co., 1974.

GAYLORD, C. *Modern coaching psychology.* Dubuque, Iowa: Brown Book Co., 1967.

GILLEN, F. G. The principal looks at coaches and their qualifications. In M. Maetozo (Ed.), *Certification of high school coaches.* Washington, D.C.: American Association of Health, Physical Education and Recreation, 1971.

GOVERNALI, P. The physical educator as coach, *Quest,* 1974, *7,* 30-33.

HENDRY, L. B. The coaching stereotype. In H. T. A. Whiting (Ed.), *Readings in sport psychology.* London: Kimpton Press, 1972.

HENDRY, L. B. Coaches and teachers of physical education: A comparison of the personality dimensions underlying their social orientation, *International Journal of Sport Psychology,* 1974, *5,* 40-53.

HOLDEN, E. Improving the preparation of high school coaches. In M. Maetozo (Ed.), *Certification of high school coaches.* Washington, D.C.: American Association of Health, Physical Education and Recreation, 1971.

KASSON, P. L. *Teaching and coaching behaviors of university physical educators.* Unpublished doctoral dissertation, University of Wisconsin, 1974.

KEANE, F. J. *The relationship of sex, teacher leadership style, and teacher leader behavior in teacher-student interaction.* Unpublished doctoral dissertation, Boston University, 1976.

LA GRAND, L. *A semantic differential analysis of the behavioral characteristics of athletic coaches as reported by athletes.* Unpublished doctoral dissertation, Florida State University, 1970.

LAWTHER, J. *Sports psychology.* Englewood Cliffs, New Jersey: Prentice-Hall, Inc., 1972.

MANCINI, V. H. & AGNEW, M. M. *Comparisons of female teaching and coaching behaviors in secondary schools.* Paper presented at AAHPER Eastern District Convention, Baltimore, Maryland, March 1978.

MASON, A. J. *Comparisons of male teaching and coaching behaviors in colleges and universities.* Unpublished masters project, Ithaca College, 1978.

NYGAARD, G. Interaction analysis of physical education classes, *Research Quarterly,* 1975, *46,* 351-357.

PENMAN, K. A., HASTAD, D. N., & CORDS, W. L. Success of the authoritarian coach. *Journal of Social Psychology,* 1974, *92,* 155-156.

PERCIVAL, L. Coaching — art and science? In J. W. Taylor (Ed.), *Proceedings of the Symposium on the Art and Science of Coaching.* Vol. 2, Toronto: Fitness Institute, 1974.

SMITH, R. E., SMALL, F. L., & HUNT, E. A system for the behavioral assessment of athletic coaches. *Research Quarterly,* 1977, *48,* 401-407.

STEVENSON, C. Concept curricula, experimental learning, and teacher education. In G. H. McGlynn (Ed.), *Issues in physical education and sports.* Palo Alto, California: National Press Books, 1974.

STOGDILL, R. M. Manual for the leader behavior description questionnaire XII, Columbus: Ohio State University Bureau of Business Research, 1963.

THARP, R. G. & GALLIMORE, R. What a coach can teach a teacher. *Psychology Today,* 1976, *9,* 75-78.

TUTKO, T. A. Communication and coaching efficiency. In J. W. Taylor (Ed.), *Proceedings of the Symposium on the Art and Science of Coaching.* Vol. 2, Toronto: Fitness Institute, 1974.

TUTKO, T. A. & RICHARD, J. *Psychology of coaching.* Boston: Allyn and Bacon, Inc., 1971.

VANEK, M. & CRATTY, B. *Psychology and the superior athlete.* London: the MacMillan Co., 1970.

Team Cohesiveness

In a recent penetrating review of the cohesiveness and performance literature, Diane Gill, University of Waterloo sport psychologist, concluded that sport cohesiveness research is marked by its equivocality. That is to say, the notion that cohesive teams win more games is intuitively appealing. Gill contends, however, that the empirical evidence is lacking to support such a broad generalization. Dr. Gill found studies supporting both the positive and negative performance – cohesiveness relationship.

Despite the research evidence to the contrary, coaches almost unilaterally support the virtues of "togetherness". Baseball coaches, for example, frequently room pitchers and catchers and shortstops and second basemen together to promote better rapport among the players so that their on-field performances will improve. And, wasn't it Bill Walton who said: "We enjoy playing well together as a team" after the Portland Trail Blazers won the 1977 NBA Championship. Other players, including 'Whitey and Mickey', talk about the cohesion of those great Yankee teams of the 1950's. Even the colorful Casey Stengel thought it was important.

In the first article, I discuss team cohesiveness within Cartwright's conceptual model. The sport specific hypothesis is also examined and research evidence is presented to support the premise that cohesiveness may be a prerequisite for success in certain sports.

Professor D. Stanley Eitzen, in the second article, argues that to understand the variables that account for team success, one must study more than the physical properties of the athletes. Psychological and sociological properties must also be considered. Dr. Eitzen discusses such important factors as racial heterogeneity, managerial and player turnover, and other factors which influence group structure and group performance.

Team Cohesion in Athletics*

William F. Straub, Ph.D.
Ithaca College

Team cohesiveness was studied within the context of Cartwright's conceptual model of group cohesiveness. According to this model, a person's attraction to a group is determined by (1) his motive base for attraction; (2) the incentive properties of the group; (3) his expectancy of rewards; and (4) the quality of outcomes he believes he deserves. Research evidence was examined and practical suggestions for the development of team cohesiveness were presented. The sports specific hypothesis of team cohesion was carefully examined, and the evidence to suggest that cohesiveness may be a prerequisite to athletic success was presented.

The study of small groups comprises one of the major areas of sociology and social psychology. According to Clovis Shepherd (1964, p. 1), more than 1385 articles and books have been written on this topic, most since the mid 1950's. This finding illustrates the increased interest which sociologists and social psychologists have attached to small groups research.

Until most recently however, social researchers have not studied small groups within a sports setting. As Harry Edwards (1973, p. 6) points out: "disciplines outside physical education have traditionally ignored sport as a realm of human behavior worthy of serious scholarly investigation." Edwards goes on to say that nowhere in academe has the neglect of sports as a legitimate scientific concern been so conspicuous as in sociology. However, sociologists and psychologists are not alone in their lack of concern about sports. Only one philosopher of note, Paul Weiss, has written a book about sport. Unfortunately, Weiss' book, *Sport — A Philosophic Inquiry,* is not well known among physical educators.

There is evidence today that the lack of scholarly interest in the study of sport by sociologists, psychologists, et al., is changing. Recently, a psychology department at a prestigious Ivy League university approved a course in psychology of sport; and although it is still thought to be somewhat degrading, students of human behavior are beginning to study sport in the United States and abroad.

The central focus of this paper considers the importance of team cohesion to success in athletics. To do justice to this topic, within the space

*An article published in the *International Journal of Sport Psychology,* 6:125–133, 1975. Reprinted with permission of the publisher.

allocated, consideration will be given to: (1) a definition of cohesiveness, (2) the findings of research investigations, and (3) suggestions for further research. However, consideration will not be given to the means by which team cohesiveness is developed. It is interesting and probably productive to speculate about this topic, but sufficient research evidence is lacking to answer it definitely.

Cohesiveness Defined

Although various theorists define the term differently, most students of small groups consider group cohesiveness to be "the degree to which the members of a group desire to remain in the group" (Cartwright, 1968, p. 91). In applying this definition to sport, one could generalize that members of a highly cohesive team are more concerned with their membership than members of a team with a low level of cohesiveness. In addition, highly cohesive team members are more strongly motivated to contribute to the team's welfare, to advance its goals and to participate in its activities. Documentation for this theory may be found by studying the number of drop-outs on winning and losing teams. Experience shows that not many players leave teams while they are winning. A losing team, on the other hand, frequently experience a loss of personnel. Winning teams therefore seem to have much higher cohesiveness than losing teams. However, the type of sport may have something to do with the importance of cohesiveness to team success. Research findings, by and large, support the premise that winning makes teams more cohesive; losing destroys cohesiveness (Arnold, 1972; Petley, 1973).

Cartwright's conceptual model of group cohesiveness (Fig. 1) helps to explain what Festinger (1968) calls the resultants of all forces acting on members to remain in the group. The diagram shows that team cohesiveness is the resultant of two sets of component forces acting on members to remain on the team. First, there are those forces which arise from the attractiveness of the group, and second, those forces which are derived from the attractiveness of alternative memberships.

A person's attraction to a team is determined by (1) his motive base for attraction; (2) the incentive properties of the group; (3) his expectancy that membership will result in beneficial, or detrimental consequences for him; and (4) the quality of outcomes he believes he deserves.

The final principal consequences of team cohesiveness are shown on the right side of Fig. 1. They are: (1) the ability of the team to retain its members; (2) the power of the team to influence its members; (3) the degree of participation and loyalty of members; (4) the feeling of security on the part of team members; and (5) the self evaluation which each player makes of his performance. When team cohesiveness is high these components will be clearly evident. However, losing will tend to destroy or lessen these characteristics.

Research Evidence

Perhaps we should begin our review of the conceptual and research literature with a penetrating analysis of such well known classics as: William Foote Whyte's (1943) *Street Corner Society;* or Harold Hodge's (1963) *Peninsula People* or better still William Golding's *Lord of the Flies*. But, space does not permit us to cover these excellent sources.

Instead, research will be cited of studies of cohesiveness which have taken place in sports settings. For example, John Loy and Gerald Kenyon (1969) focus attention in their book: *Sport, Culture and Society,* on small groups research from two perspectives. First, they cite investigations in which small groups in sport are studied as a special type of social system; and second, they treat small groups as subcultures or what they later refer to as microcosms of larger societies.

A classic study of team cohesiveness was completed by Hans Lenk (1968) on West German Olympic rowing crews. Lenk found that despite sharp subgroup and leadership conflicts, these crews won the European Championship and received a silver medal in the 1964 Olympic Competitions. According to Lenk, the development of conflict paralleled increments in performance. On the basis of this four-year long investigation, Lenk concluded: the premises that only small groups which are low in conflict can produce highly integrated performances is untenable. In fact, the results of Lenk's study suggest that high conflict groups can achieve high levels of performance.

The 1973 edition of Completed Research in *Health, Physical Education and Recreation* lists two investigations on team cohesiveness. The first study was by Grant Long (1972) of Southern Illinois University, the second by Jeffrey Seagrave of Washington State University. Long (1972) studied the cohesiveness of three high school baseball teams (N=47). Oddly enough, he found through linear regression analysis that cohesion was a better predictor of team success, measured by games won, than skill. In a comparison of Club and Varsity athletic teams for men, Seagrave (1972) found that a greater degree of group cohesiveness was present in sport clubs (soccer and rugby) than in varsity baseball and track and field teams. He concluded that the sports club organization appears to be more effective than the varsity organization in achieving group cohesiveness. However, further research is needed to determine if the above finding holds true when the same club and varsity sports are studied systematically.

Guy Arnold (1972) and John Petley, students of mine, studied the cohesiveness of high school basketball and wrestling teams, respectively. Arnold's investigation of high school basketball teams showed that winning teams at postseason were significantly more cohesive than losing teams. In addition, Arnold found that members of successful teams were more closely knit, more task motivated and exhibited more leadership or power than members of less successful teams. Arnold concluded that cohesiveness appeared to be a prerequisite for success in varsity high school basketball competition.

Essentially, Petley found the same thing to be true for high school varsity wrestling teams. The members of winning teams were significantly more cohesive than the members of losing teams. Arnold and Petley's findings were supported by the results of Peterson and Martens' (1972) investigation of intramural basketball teams at the University of Illinois. They found that cohesiveness was an important determinant of team success. Landers and Crum (1971) concluded, following their study of high school baseball teams, that team cohesiveness was a necessary factor for team success.

The inter-racial problems which occurred with increasing regularity during the 60's in society at large were reflected among members of athletic teams. More than one team was ruined by these interpersonal conflicts. Tom McIntyre's study of the cohesiveness of integrated junior high school boys intramural flag football teams showed that winning teams were more cohesive than losing teams. However, there was no evidence that highly cohesive teams produced more favorable attitude changes toward race than less cohesive teams.

Other studies of team cohesiveness could be cited, however, the results by and large suggest that cohesiveness is a prerequisite for success in team sports such as football, basketball, wrestling and baseball.

Interpretation of Research Findings

How does one interpret these results? What implications do they have for coaches and teachers of physical education? How may the coach implement these findings so that his team's performances may be improved? Admittedly, these are difficult questions and at the present time data are not available to adequately answer them. However, it is interesting and probably productive to speculate about the "state of the art".

One of the most common generalizations about team cohesiveness is that it is sports specific. That is, cohesiveness is important to team success in some sports but not in others. This generalization seems like a valid conclusion, but research evidence is lacking to support strongly the sports specific hypothesis.

Tutko and Richards (1971) offer the coach practical suggestions for the development of team cohesion. Unfortunately, there is little hard data to support their assertions. They also qualify their approach by stating: "The development of team cohesion is one of the most difficult tasks facing a coach" (Tutko and Richards, 1971, p. 97).

Before a team becomes a cohesive unit, according to Tutko and Richards, the players must place the welfare of the team ahead of their own personal goals. In other words, there must be (1) mutual respect among players and coaches, (2) effective communication; (3) the feeling of importance, (4) common goals; and (5) fair treatment.

Coaches who desire to develop a particular image for their teams should study the self-fulfilling prophesy. That is, players will have a tendency to do those things they already believe about themselves. For example, if a team believes it can come from behind and win games, it probably will do so; if the players picture themselves as aggressive or in physical condition, they will usually emit this type of behavior. Building confidence is undoubtedly one of our most important responsibilities as coaches. The coach may manipulate this variable through the scheduling of appropriate opponents.

More specifically, Tutko and Richards (1971), recommend that consideration be given to the following suggestions for developing team cohesion:

— Have the players become acquainted with the responsibilities of other players.

— Have the players observe and record the efforts of other athletes at their position.

— Coaches should know something personal about each player.

— Develop pride within the sub-units of the team and recognize players for their special contributions.

— Allow representative from each sub-group to meet regularly with the coach.

— Set goals and take pride in their accomplishment.

— Allow players to know their status on the team and provide a justification for that status.

— Emphasize the value of discipline.

Final Statement

The development of team cohesion is one of the most difficult aspects of coaching. At this time, research evidence is not available to definitely answer the question: How is team cohesiveness developed? All that is available are hunches, half-truths and the results of a number of conflicting research investigations. However, the results of these studies seem to indicate that cohesiveness is a prerequisite for success in team sports such as baseball, basketball and wrestling.

In order to provide more definitive evidence, experimental studies must be undertaken in which such variables as type of leadership, team size and interpersonal relationships outside the team are controlled. Unfortunately, coaches are reluctant to allow researchers to conduct such studies. Until we do so, however, this important facet of team success will remain largely a mystery.

REFERENCES

ARNOLD, G.: *Team Cohesiveness, personality traits, and final league standing of high school varsity basketball teams.* Master's degree thesis, Ithaca College, Ithaca, N.Y., 1972.

CARTWRIGHT, DORWIN: *The nature of group cohesiveness.* In Cartwright, D., Zander, A. (Eds.) *Group Dynamics.* New York: Harper & Row, 1968.

EDWARDS, H.: *Sociology of Sport.* Homewood, Illinois: Dorsey, 1973.

FESTINGER, L.: *Informal Social Communication.* In Cartwright, D., Zander, A.: *Group Dynamics.* New York: Harper & Row, pp. 182-191, 1968.

FIEDLER, F.E.: *Assumed similarity measures as predictors of team effectiveness.* Journal of Abnormal and Social Psychology, 49:381-388, 1954.

GOLDING, W.: *Lord of the Flies.* New York: Capricorn, 1959.

HODGES, H. M.: *Peninsula People: Social Stratification in a Metropolitan Complex.* In Kallenbach, W. W., Hodges, H. M.: *Education and Society.* Columbus, Ohio: Charles E. Merrill, 1963.

HOMANS, G.: *The Human Group.* New York: Harcourt Brace, 1950.

KLEIN, M., CHRISTIANSEN, G.: *Group composition, group structures and group effectiveness of basketball teams.* Loy, J., Kenyon, G. (eds.). In *Sport, Culture and Society.* London: Macmillan, pp. 397-408, 1969.

LANDERS, D. M., CRUM, T. F.: *The effect of team success and formal structure on interpersonal relations and cohesiveness of baseball teams.* International Journal of Sport Psychology, 2:88-96, 1971.

MC INTYRE, T. D.: *A field experimental study of cohesiveness status and attitude change in four biracial small sport groups.* Ph.D. in Physical Education, 1970, 202P. Pennsylvania State University, College Park, Pa.

PETERSON, J. A., MARTENS, R.: *Success and residential affiliation as determinants of team cohesiveness*. Research Quarterly, 43:62-76.

PETLEY, J.: *The Cohesiveness of Successful and Less Successful Wrestling Teams*. Research Project, Ithaca College, Ithaca, N.Y., 1973.

SEAGRAVE, J. O.: *Comparison of group cohesiveness in club and varsity athletic teams for men*. M.S. in Physical Education, Washington State University, Pullman, Washington, 1972, 65 p.

SHEPHERD, C.: *Small groups. Some Sociological Perspectives*. Scranton, Pa.: Chandler, 1964.

SHERIF, M., SHERIF, C.: *Groups in harmony and tension*. New York: Harper, 1953.

SINGER, R. N., WEISS, R. A. (eds.): *Completed Research in Health, Physical Education and Recreation*. Washington, D.C.: American Association for Health, Physical Education and Recreation, 1973.

TUTKO, T. A., RICHARDS, J. W.: *Psychology of Coaching*. Boston: Allyn & Bacon, 1971.

WEISS, P.: *Sport — A Philosophic Inquiry*. Carbondale, Illinois: Southern Illinois University Press, 1969.

WHYTE, W. F.: *Street Corner Society*. Chicago: University of Chicago Press, 1943.

Group Structure and Group Performance*

D. Stanley Eitzen, Ph.D.
Colorado State University

Under what conditions is group-oriented motivation maximized? No one would argue with the importance of team spirit in attaining team success. Although there are notable exceptions such as the current Oakland Athletics, winning teams appear to have players with a strong identification with the team.

I want to approach this problem of group performance from a different perspective. Instead of focusing on the role of motivation among team members in team success, I want to examine those structural conditions of the team that maximize the probability of team success. In other words, I want to provide a sociological look at some of the properties of groups and how these have been found to affect team performance.

I will limit this review of the literature to those studies of interacting teams. Sports such as basketball, baseball, softball, and soccer rely on each team members' contribution for the completion of the task. "To be effective, members of [these teams] must combine their different specialized skills through interdependent action, to achieve the performance output of the team — a process commonly referred to in sport as team work" (Landers and Lueschen, 1974, p. 59). The analysis will omit those studies, then, that use sport teams where the group outcome result is derivable from the individual efforts by simple summation (e.g., bowling and rifle teams).

Homogeneity of Team Members

There is a widespread finding in sociological research that the more alike the members of a group, the more positive the bonds among the members (Berelson, Coleman, 1957; Durkhiem, 1974; Homans, 1950, 1961; Lazarsfeld & McPhee, 1954; and Lazarsfeld & Merton, 1954). This is usually explained by the assumption that internal differentiation on some salient characteristics such as religion, race and socioeconomic status leads to the greater likelihood of clique formation (Davis, 1966, p. 86).

Three studies of basketball teams support these findings. The first was conducted by Klein and Christiansen (1969). These researchers found that in game situations players mutually paired on sociometric tests tended to pass the ball to each other more frequently than to others unless the opposing

---

*An article published in *Psychology of Sport and Motor Behavior II.* Edited by Landers, D. M. College of Health, Physical Education and Recreation, The Pennsylvania State University, University Park, Pennsylvania, 1975. Reprinted with permission of the publisher.

team was especially strong. They also found, supporting Professor Zander's work, that the higher the average achievement motivation of the team (compiled by averaging the players' scores on an achievement motivation scale), the greater the team performance. The study of 144 intramural basketball teams at the University of Illinois by Martens and Peterson (1971) also found that team cohesiveness was positively related to team success. They note that the relationship is circular in that cohesiveness leads to greater team success which, in turn, leads to greater satisfaction which positively affects cohesiveness.

I have also conducted a study of the affect of member homogeneity on the success of basketball teams (Eitzen, 1973). Data were gathered on the member composition of 288 Kansas high school basketball teams and the degree of team success. Using the characteristics of father's occupation, family prestige in the community, religion, and place of residence,[1] I found that the greater the homogeneity of a team, the smaller the probability of cliques being present and hence, the greater the probability of goal attainment by the team.

Racial Heterogeniety

An extremely important variable affecting the possible formation of cliques among the team members is a race. Of all social variables, race has proved to be the most divisive. Of great importance, then, for both theoretical and practical reasons is the determination of the conditions under which racially mixed teams are most effective in goal attainment. McClendon and I have made such a study (1975). Using the insights of Allport (1954) and Sherif (1958, 1961), we examined the various interracial contact situations that might reduce tension and increase the chances of team success on college basketball teams. We found, using Sherif's theory of superordinate goals, that white players on teams that win because of the significant contribution of both races were less anti-black and more pro-integration in their attitudes than were whites on integrated teams that were less successful. The data from the black players, however, did not support the superordinate goal theory. These findings, I might add, are tentative because of a number of methodological problems with our study. Carefully designed longitudinal studies are necessary to demonstrate convincingly whether super-ordinate goal achievement is associated with favorable changes in racial attitudes by whites and blacks.

Managerial Turnover

Sociologists specializing in formal organizations have had an enduring interest in the effect of leadership turnover on organizational effectiveness (cf., Gouldner, 1954). The traditional study of organizations, however, has been limited by three factors: (1) the difficulty of studying more than a few organizations at a time; (2) the controlling of extraneous variables; and (3) the problem of accurately measuring goal attainment (cf., Clark, 1956; Scott, 1964, p. 493). Oscar Grusky's pioneering study of major league baseball teams showed how these difficulties could be overcome rather easily by the use of athletic teams (1963). Grusky found that the lower the turnover rate of managers, the higher the organizational effectiveness. He explained that managerial changes contribute to declining morale and expectations of failure, leading to a deterioration of team performance. In a critique of Grusky, Gamson, and Scotch (1964) analyzed only midseason changes in baseball managers and found that a change had little effect on team performance.

Norman Yetman and I (1975) investigated coaching changes on college basketball teams to determine whether Grusky or his critics were correct. We chose basketball because the turnover rate of coaches is relatively high and we could easily exceed the small N of major league baseball. We examined the effects of 656 coaching changes at 129 schools from 1930 to 1970. Initially, we found the same relationship as Grusky — the higher the turnover, the poorer the winning percentage. But when we controlled for the record of the team prior to the coaching change, we found a regression to the mean. In other words, new coaches taking over a team with a poor record improved their teams' records while coaches replacing successful coaches tended to be relative failures. Our data, then, lead to the conclusion that *managerial turnover and team performance are inversely related, but that this relationship depends upon the team's performance prior to the change.*

Longevity of coaching tenure was found to be a significant aspect of group structure affecting team performance. We found that the longer coaches remain at a school the more successful they tend to be — up to a point. Coaches leaving after 8 or 9 years tended, when compared to their early years at the school, to leave as winners. Coaches whose tenure lasted 10, 11, or 12 years were evenly split between winners and losers. For those coaches, however, whose longevity at one post exceeded 12 years, their final years tended to be less successful than their initial years.

Player Turnover

Player turnover occurs in two ways and both have been found to affect team performance negatively. The first type occurs when the starting lineup is disturbed by player substitutions. Essing (1968) in a study of 18 German soccer teams found a strong relationship between a stable team line-up and team success. He argues that the exchange of starting players with reserve players disturbs the team structure and the smooth coordination of performance by the team.

A second type of player turnover is when players join and leave teams. In professional sports this is typically done involuntarily through trades accomplished by management. John Loy (1970) investigated this type of personnel turnover in major league baseball. He found an inverse relationship between the number of new players and the won-lost percentage of the team. In other words, *the higher the player turnover, the lower the league standing.*

Conclusion

This review of literature has suggested the impact of some group priorities on team performance. There are others that are part of the structure and culture of athletic teams and may have important consequences for team effectiveness in goal attainments: the sociometric structure of the friendship relationships, team consensus on the informal team leaders, coaching style, unity of the supporters, tradition, and rigidity of group boundary maintenance. Clearly, further research is needed to understand the possible impact of these variables on team performance.

To summarize, I would argue that to understand the variables that account for team success, one must look beyond the physical properties of the athletes to psychological and sociological variables. These include the psychological characteristics of the team members (i.e., motivation to succeed as an individual and as a team, fear of failure, ego strength, control of emotions) and the structural properties of the teams themselves (i.e., homogeneity on social characteristics, and turnover of player and management personnel). Only when the psychologists and sociologists of sport provide the research data linked to theory, will we finally understand the mysteries of why some teams consistently fail while others succeed.

REFERENCES

ALLPORT, G. *The nature of prejudice.* New York: Anchor Books, 1954.

BERELSON, B. R., LAZARSFELD, P. E. & MC PHEE, W. N. *Voting: A study of opinion formation in a presidential campaign.* Chicago: University of Chicago Press, 1954.

CLARK, B. R. Organizational adaptation and precarious values. *American Sociological Review,* 1956, *21,* 327-336.

COLEMAN, J. S. *Community conflict.* Glencoe: Free Press, 1957.

DAVIS, J. A. Structural balance, mechanical solidarity, and interpersonal relations. Berger, J., Zelditch, M. & Anderson, B. (eds.), *Sociological theories in progress I.* Boston: Houghton Mifflin, 1966.

DURKHEIM, E. *The division of labor in society.* Simpson, G. (trans.), Glencoe: Free Press, 1947.

EITZEN, D. S. The effect of group structure on the success of athletic teams. *International Review of Sport Sociology* 1973, *8,* 7-17.

EITZEN, D. S. & YETMAN, N. R. Managerial change, longevity, and organizational effectiveness. *Administrative Science Quarterly,* 1972, *17,* 110-116.

EASING, W. Team line-up and team achievement in European football. Kenyon, G. (ed.), *Contemporary Psychology of Sport.* Chicago: Athletic Institute, 1968.

GAMSON, W. A. & SCOTCH, N. A. Scapegoating in baseball. *American Journal of Sociology* 1964, *70,* 69-72.

GOULDNER, A. W. *Patterns of industrial bureaucracy.* Glenoe: Free Press, 1954.

GRUSKY, O. Managerial succession and organizational effectiveness. *American Journal of Sociology,* 1963, *69, 21-31.*

HOMANS, G. C. *The human group.* New York: Harcourt & Bauce, 1950.

HOMANS, G. C. *Social behavior: Its elementary forms.* New York: Harcourt & Brace, 1961.

KLEIN, M. & CHRISTIANSEN, G. Group composition, group structure and group effectiveness of basketball teams. Loy, J. W. & Kenyon, G. S. (ed.), *Sport, culture, and society: A reader on the sociology of sport.* New York: Macmillan, 1969.

LANDERS, D. M. & LUESCHEN, G. Team performance outcome and the cohesiveness of competitive coacting groups. *International Review of Sport Sociology,* 1974, *9,* 57-71.

LAZARSFELD, P. F. & MERTON, R. K. Friendship as a social process: A substance and methodological analysis. Berger, M., Abel, T. & Page, C. H. (eds.), *Freedom and control in modern society.* Princeton: D. Van Nostrand, 1954.

LOY, J. W. *Where the action is: A consideration of centrality in sport situations.* Paper presented at the meeting of the second Canadian Psycho-Motor Learning and Sport Psychology Symposium, Windsor, Ontario, 1970.

MARTENS, R. & PETERSON, J. A. Group cohesiveness as a determinant of success and member satisfaction in team performance. *International Review of Sport Sociology,* 1971, *6,* 49-61.

MC CLENDON, M. J. & EITZEN, D. S. Interracial contact on collegiate basketball teams: A test of Sherif's theory of superordinate goals. *Social Science Quarterly,* 1975, *55,* 926-938.

SCOTT, W. R. Theory of organizations. Faris, R. E. L. (ed.), *Handbook of modern sociology.* Chicago: Rand McNally, 1964.

SHERIF, M. *Intergroup conflict and cooperation: The Robber's Cave Experiment.* Norman, Oklahoma: The University of Oklahoma Book Exchange, 1961.